Body and World

Samuel Todes

with introductions by Hubert L. Dreyfus and Piotr Hoffman

The MIT Press, Cambridge, Massachusetts, and London, England

© 2001 Massachusetts Institute of Technology

All rights reserved. No part of this book may be reproduced in any form by any electronic or mechanical means (including photocopying, recording, or information storage and retrieval) without permission in writing from the publisher.

Library of Congress Cataloging-in-Publication Data

Todes, Samuel.
　Body and world / Samuel Todes ; with introductions by Hubert L. Dreyfus and Piotr Hoffman.
　　p.　cm.
　Rev. ed. of: The human body as material subject of the world. New York : Garland Pub., 1990.
　Includes bibliographical references and index.
　ISBN 978-0-262-20135-3 (hc.: alk. paper) — ISBN 978-0-262-70082-5 (pbk.: alk. paper)
　1. Body, Human (Philosophy)　2. Subject (Philosophy)　3. Perception (Philosophy)　4. Kant, Immanuel, 1724–1804—Contributions in philosophy of perception.　I. Todes, Samuel. Human body as material subject of the world. II. Title.

B105.B64 T63 2001
128'.6—dc21   00-053385

The MIT Press is pleased to keep this title available in print by manufacturing single copies, on demand, via digital printing technology.

Printed and bound by CPI Group (UK) Ltd, Croydon, CR0 4YY

Contents

Foreword — xi
Hubert L. Dreyfus

Introduction I: Todes's Account of Nonconceptual Perceptual Knowledge and Its Relation to Thought — xv
Hubert L. Dreyfus

Introduction II: How Todes Rescues Phenomenology from the Threat of Idealism — xxviii
Piotr Hoffman

Author's Introduction — 1

1 The Classic View of the Way the Human Subject Has His Body, and Descartes's Rejection of It — 10

1.1 The Classic View — 10
1.2 Descartes's Rejection of the Classic View — 13
    1.2.1 The discovery of human necessity, and its first consequences for the philosophy of the body — 13
    1.2.2 The ambiguity of Descartes's version of the human subject — 14
    1.2.3 Summary of Descartes's view — 21

2 Critique of the Resulting World-Subject of Leibniz and Hume, with an Introductory Exposition of the Thesis That the Human Body Is the Material Subject of the World — 23

2.1 The Mitosis of Cartesian Philosophy — 23

2.2 A New Consensus: The Human Subject as
Explicating the Unity of the World   23
2.3 The Change in the Sense of the
"Representational" Character of Experience   27
2.4 The Human Body Veiled   29
   2.4.1 Leibniz's veiling of the human body   30
   2.4.2 Hume's veiling of the human body   40
2.5 Phenomenological Interlude   44
   2.5.1 Body feelings as objects   44
   2.5.2 The three functions of the body of the
   active subject   46
   2.5.3 The body as an object   47
   2.5.4 Space and time as correlates of the active
   subject's body   48
   2.5.5 A note on method   52
   2.5.6 Types of spatiotemporal emptiness   57
   2.5.7 Satisfaction   58
   2.5.8 Pain   59
   2.5.9 Disappearance   60
   2.5.10 Antifacts   61
   2.5.11 Responsiveness   62
2.6 Re-consideration of Hume   71
   2.6.1 The nonvariability of the human body
   unnoticed by Hume   71
   2.6.2 Observation, perceptual inference, and
   poise: Hume's view criticized   71
   2.6.3 Critique of Hume on pleasure and pain   72
   2.6.4 Critique of Hume on the uniformity of
   nature   73
   2.6.5 Critique of Hume on the foundation of
   probability   83
   2.6.6 Clarification of Hume's view of belief   84
   2.6.7 The problem of the continued existence of
   unobserved objects   85
   2.6.8 Hume's admission of an inadequate
   account of the active life   86

2.7 Conclusion	87
2.8 Transition to Chapter 3	88

3 Introductory Discussion of Kant's View That the Human Subject Makes the World of His Experience   90

3.1 The Development of Kant's Thought	90
3.2 Summary of My Kant Criticism: That Kant Imaginizes Perception	95
3.3 Phenomenological Studies To Be Used in Support of My Kant Criticism	100

4 Development of the Phenomenology of Practical Perception, as a Prelude to the Criticism That Kant Imaginizes Perception   102

4.0 General Statement of Problems Considered in This Chapter, and of the Conclusions To Be Demonstrated	102
4.1 Defense against Aristotle's Thesis That a Self-Moved Mover Is Impossible	107
4.2 The Perceptual Sense of the Passage of Time: A Correlate of the Self-Activity of the Percipient	110
4.3 The Perceptual World as a Field of Fields-within-Fields: The General Significance of This Fact, and the Significance of the Particular Order of Field-Inclusion	114
4.4 Why the Percipient Is Satisfied with the Perception of an Object; How It Fulfills His Active Body	117
4.4.1 The bodily basis of the irreversibility of perceptual time	118
4.4.2 How passing an object enables the percipient to determine it as a concrete unity	119
4.4.3 The vertical field	122
4.4.4 Perceptual fulfillment as practical self-composure	128

5 The Phenomenology of Imagination, as a Final Prelude to the Criticism that Kant Imaginizes Perception — 130

5.0 Introduction: Restriction of the Topic — 130
   5.0.1 Restriction of the topic in respect to the mediation of perception and imagination by inactive spectation — 133
   5.0.2 Restriction of the topic in respect to the fusion of perception and imagination in imaginative perception — 135
   5.0.3 Restriction of the topic to the single modality of conceptual imagination — 137

5.1 The Imaginative Transformation of Our Relation to the World — 138
   5.1.1 Our imaginative capacity is its own initial field of productivity — 139
   5.1.2 The imaginative transformation of balance and poise — 140

5.2 The New Kind of Series Possible in the World of Imagination — 143

5.3 The World of Imagination as a Field of Explicatable Images instead of Determinable Objects — 145

5.4 The Imaginative Transformation of the Extent to Which the World Can Be Filled — 149

5.5 The Imaginative Transformation of Our Role in Contributing Significance to Our Experience — 153

5.6 Summary of the Main Contrasts between Imagination and Perception — 154

6 Development of the Thesis That the Human Body Is the Material Subject of the World, as a Critique of Kant's View That the Human Subject Makes the World of His Experience — 155

6.0 The *Critique of Pure Reason* in the Light of a Phenomenology of Impure Experience — 155

6.1 Kant's False Dilemma of A Priori Knowledge: How It Arises from Imaginizing the World	156
6.2 The Ego, According to Kant: Its Three Stages of Self-Evidence	161
6.3 Phenomenological Criticism: Kant Imaginizes the Ego	173
6.4 Kant's View of Spatial Objects: Spatialization as Conceptualization	181
6.5 The Missing Perceptual Stage: How Is a Local Object Determinable?	189
6.6 The "Common, but to Us Unknown, Root"	199
6.7 Kantian Categories as Imaginative Idealizations of Perceptual Categories	202
6.7.1 Deduction of perceptual categories from the felt unity of the active body, as Kant deduces imaginative categories from the transcendental unity of apperception	202
6.7.2 The concept of nothing (= 0) versus the perceptual sense of nothing (= –x)	220
6.8 Kant's Dialectic: Perception Takes Revenge	229
6.8.1 The antinomies of the Paralogisms: the suppressed perceptual thesis vs. the imaginative antithesis	239
6.8.2 The perceptual thesis vs. the imaginative antithesis of Kant's Antinomies; or, the fruitless question: Which form of objectivity is the right one?	243
6.8.3 The antinomies of the Ideal of pure reason: the suppressed perceptual thesis versus the imaginative antithesis	256
6.9 Summary, and Concluding Remarks	259
General Conclusion	262
Appendix I: The Subject Body in Perception and Conception: A Brief Sketch	263

**Appendix II: Sensuous Abstraction and the
Abstract Sense of Reality** 269

Appendix III: Anticipatory Postscript 277

Notes 293
Index 319

Foreword

Hubert L. Dreyfus

For a work that offers a detailed account of situated knowledge, this book seems strangely desituated. There is no clue that it was conceived almost half a century ago in Cambridge, Massachusetts, when analytic philosophers were discussing the confrontation between Russell and Wittgenstein and continental philosophers were poring over Heidegger's *Being and Time*. Samuel Todes, rather, seems to be engaged in a timeless dialogue with Hume and Kant that could have been written in the eighteenth century. Yet his text also enters the current philosophical debates concerning realism/antirealism and the nature of nonconceptual perceptual content and its relation to thought. The latter has come increasingly to occupy the attention of Anglo-American philosophers since Charles Taylor exposed Gareth Evans to Maurice Merleau-Ponty's account of the role of the body in perception and action. While in the 1950s practically no one in the United States was thinking along these lines, now there is a converging interest in embodiment not only in philosophy but also in psychology, linguistics, cognitive science, anthropology, artificial intelligence, and neuroscience.

In the 1950s, the one exception to the tradition of disembodied philosophy was the work of Merleau-Ponty. So, in his 1963 doctoral dissertation, *The Human Body as Material Subject of the World*, Todes starts with Merleau-Ponty's account of the lived body and goes on to develop a description of the structure of the active body, and of the role that structure plays in producing the spatiotemporal field of experience. He then examines how the spatiotemporal field makes possible objective knowledge of the objects that show up in it. Todes's goal was to show that perception involves nonconceptual but nonetheless objective forms of judgment. Thus, one can think of *Body and World* as fleshing out Merleau-Ponty's project while presciently relating it to the current scene.

Although there was practically no one thinking along these lines in the United States when Todes was doing his graduate work at Harvard and teaching philosophy at MIT, his interest in the issues raised by Merleau-Ponty did not come out of the blue. He stands in two connected intellectual movements brought to the United States in the 1940s by German refugees: Gestalt Psychology and Phenomenology. The connection between them was first pointed out in the 1920s by Aron Gurwitsch. Gurwitsch worked closely with Husserl in Freiburg until the Nazis came to power in 1933. He then spent seven years in Paris lecturing on the confluence of Gestalt Psychology and Transcendental Phenomenology, where his lectures were attended by Merleau-Ponty. Merleau-Ponty subsequently transposed Gurwitsch's Husserlian phenomenology of perception into his own existential account of the role of the lived body in experience.

Gurwitsch fled France in 1940, and by 1948 he was teaching at Brandeis University and living in Cambridge, Massachusetts. There, in 1955, he met Todes, who had worked with Wolfgang Köhler as an undergraduate psychology major at Swarthmore. Gurwitsch and Todes had weekly discussions centered on their mutual interest in the Gestalt theory of perception and its relevance for phenomenology.

Todes carries forward existential phenomenology by elaborating the Gestalt description of the field of consciousness proposed by Gurwitsch, while giving an account of the role of the lived body in perception and action that goes beyond the work of Merleau-Ponty. Thus, Todes's dissertation can be seen as the latest development in the philosophical movement that leads from Köhler and Husserl to Gurwitsch and then to Merleau-Ponty.

Given its lineage and ambition, the dissertation was an anomaly at Harvard. Todes worked with no one. The peculiarity of this situation is reflected in Willard V. Quine's involvement as one of the three thesis readers. Perhaps Quine took on the job because he already knew and respected Todes. In fact, in the second edition of *Methods of Logic*, Quine thanks Todes for calling his attention to the need for "more substantial emendations" than the correction of mere typos. It takes less stretching to make some sense of the choice of the other two readers. Dagfinn Føllesdal was an expert on the transcendental phenomenology Merleau-Ponty and Todes opposed, and D. C. Williams taught the eighteenth-century rationalists, especially Leibniz, whose disembodied account of knowledge Todes thinks of himself as correcting. None of the readers, however, favored the existential phenomenology Todes was advancing. Despite this, Todes's dissertation was published in 1990 by Garland Press in a series of distinguished Harvard dissertations edited by Robert Nozick—a collection that includes, among others, the dissertations of Goodman, Davidson, Putnam, and Quine.

Todes died in 1994, before he could complete his project. He did, however, leave a summary of his work so far and his plan for the completion of his work (Appendix 1V).

Body and World is an edited version of Todes's dissertation, supplemented with relevant published and unpublished material. In *Body and World*, Todes implicitly criticizes his immediate predecessors for not doing justice to the complex structure of the human body and consequently missing the correlative structure of perceptual experience. According to Todes, speaking of *the* field of consciousness, as Gurwitsch did, does not do justice to our embodied experience of the perceptual field as a nested set of fields within fields that accounts not only for the unity but for the situatedness of perceptual objects. Moreover, describing the body merely as *a unified capacity for action*, as Merleau-Ponty did, leaves out the fact that the body has specific needs, a front/back asymmetry, and that, in moving so as to get a grip on the world, it has to balance in a gravitational field. These characteristics of the lived body account for the motivation of action, the structure of the spatiotemporal field, and the determinateness of perceptual objects, and thus for the objectivity of perceptual knowledge.

In offering an original account of the role of the body in making knowledge possible, Todes opens new ways of thinking about such problems as the relation of perception to thought and the possibility of knowing an independent reality. These problems have occupied philosophers since Kant and still actively concern analytic and continental philosophy. The two introductions that follow take up these two ways in which Todes's thought is relevant to current philosophical debate. Todes's work is so fresh and powerful, however, that even a series of introductions cannot do justice to the light it casts on the philosophical tradition and on the current philosophical scene.

***

A number of people helped to produce this edition. In particular, I would like to acknowledge the contributions of Dagfinn Føllesdal, Danah Hays, Daryl Hine, Piotr Hoffman, Sean Kelly, Lenny Moss, Charles Parsons, and Charles Spinosa.

Introduction I
Todes's Account of Nonconceptual Perceptual Knowledge and Its Relation to Thought

Hubert L. Dreyfus

Are there two fundamentally different ways we make sense of the world, or does all understanding consist in using concepts to think about things? The philosophical tradition has generally assumed—or, in the case of Kant, argued persuasively—that there is only one kind of intelligibility, the unified understanding we have of things when we make judgments that objectify our experience by bringing it under concepts. But there have always been others—painters, writers, historians, linguists, philosophers in the romantic tradition, Wittgensteinians, and existential phenomenologists—who have felt that there is another kind of intelligibility that gets us in touch with reality besides the conceptual kind elaborated by Kant.

Samuel Todes enters this debate by opposing the intelligibility of conception and perception. He sums up his project as follows:

Kant [does justice] neither to the claims of conceptual imagination nor to the claims of perception. My solution is to show that there are two levels of objective experience: the ground floor of perceptually objective experience; and the upper storey of imaginatively objective experience.... I attempt to show *that* the imaginative objectivity of theoretical knowledge presupposes a pre-imaginative, perceptual form of objectivity, by showing just *how* this is so. (100)

Todes proposes to show further that, just as Kant summed up his argument for the unity and comprehensiveness of our theoretical understanding by systematizing the forms of detached, conceptual judgment in his Table of Categories, one can systematize the forms of practical perceptual judgment in a parallel Table of *Perceptual* Categories.

In attempting to help Kant out by supplying the categories of perceptual judgment he sought in vain, Todes's work seems *timeless*. But it turns out to be *timely* too. Donald Davidson holds that the only philosophical relevance of perception is that it causes us to have beliefs and other attitudes that are directed toward the world. John McDowell, in *Mind and World*, answers that we can say at least this much: that, for perception to enter into the space of reasons, it must have conceptual content "all the way out":

> To avoid making it unintelligible how the deliverances of sensibility can stand in grounding relations to paradigmatic exercises of the understanding such as judgments and beliefs,... we must insist that the understanding is already inextricably implicated in the deliverances of sensibility themselves. Experiences are impressions made by the world on our senses, products of receptivity; but those impressions themselves already have conceptual content.[1]

Neither Davidson nor McDowell tries to describe perceptual objects as they are in themselves and how they become the objects of thought. By calling attention to the structure of nonconceptual, practical perception and showing how its judgments can be transformed into the judgments of detached thought, Todes is able to provide a framework in which to explain how the content of perception, while not itself conceptual, can provide the basis for conception. Thus, Todes's *Body and World* can be read as a significant anticipatory response to McDowell's *Mind and World*.

Todes's account of the nature of nonconceptual content builds on the work of Maurice Merleau-Ponty. Merleau-Ponty claims that, in perceiving things, I sense that they could be more clearly perceived and my body is drawn to get a firmer grip on them:

> My body is geared to the world when my perception offers me a spectacle as varied and as clearly articulated as possible, and when my motor intentions, as they unfold, receive from the world the responses they anticipate. This maximum distinctness in perception and action defines a perceptual ground, a basis of my life, a general milieu for the coexistence of my body and the world.[2]

In Todes's terms, our perception of the things around us is a response to our dissatisfaction with our lostness in the world. We make ourselves at home in the world by moving so as to organize a stable spatiotemporal field in which we use our skills to make determin*ate* the determin*able* objects that appear in that field. The skills we acquire then feed back into the perceptual world, which becomes more and more determinate as we learn to make more refined discriminations and have more reliable anticipations. Merleau-Ponty calls this feedback phenomenon the *intentional arc.*

To explain how perception hides its essential indeterminacy, Todes introduces a phenomenological account of need. A *need*, whether for getting a maximal grip or for something more specific, is at first experienced as an indeterminate deprivation, not a simple absence. This distinction, according to Todes, is the difference between *perceptual negation* as a positive lack that calls for a response, and *logical negation* as the absence of something specific that might have been present. In moving to meet a need, the perceiver makes both the need and the object that satisfies that need sufficiently determinate so that the need is satisfied. The perceiver then understands the object as the determinate object that was needed all along. As Todes puts it:

The retroactive determination of needs by their being met covers up the fact that they first become determinate by being met. The meeting of a need first fixes it; but it is fixed retroactively as having been that determinate need all along. (178)

Thus, although perception is temporal, moving from lack to satisfaction and from indeterminacy to relative determination, after the act is completed, the dissatisfaction and the objects of perception that satisfied it are experienced as having all along been determinate.

A similar tendency to read back into everyday coping the result of a transformation of that coping takes place in our experience of acting. When Todes describes our absorbed, skillful coping, he is clear that in coping we are not *trying* to achieve a goal that can be described apart from our activity, as John Searle, for example, claims.[3] Absorbed coping does not require that the agent's movements be governed by a representation of the action's success conditions. Todes agrees with Merleau-Ponty that, in absorbed coping, the agent's body is led to move so as to reduce a sense of deviation from a satisfactory gestalt without the agent being able to represent what that satisfactory gestalt will be like in advance of achieving it.

Merleau-Ponty calls the embodied coping that is directed toward objects but that has no propositional success conditions *motor intentionality*. Todes calls this nonconceptual, ongoing coping *poise*.[4] He notes that "the primary form of directed action is an intention of the *body*.... This intention of the active body is *poise* in dealing with the things and persons around us"(65). Todes, however, goes further than Merleau-Ponty in that he not only, like Merleau-Ponty, distinguishes the *expected success conditions* of willful trying from the ongoing *satisfaction of the anticipations* of poised perception; he adds that the continuing activity of ongoing coping gives us *perceptual knowledge* of the things with which we are coping.

My response to an anticipated object reveals to me directly, merely by virtue of its existence, not merely the self-produced movements of my own body by which I make that response, but also, and equally immediately, that thing in respect to which I have been able to make the response. This is not true if I construe the primary form of directed action on the model of an act of will, . . . so that I must await the effect of actions to see whether they coincide with my previously definite intentions. . . . Poise does not, when successful, "coincide" or "agree" with its later "effects," as does will with its achievement. . . . The success of poise is not in its *execution*, but in its very *existence*, by which the body is, to begin with, knowingly in touch with the objects around it. As soon as I am poised in my circumstances, I know . . . something about those objects to which I am doing something with my body. (65–66)

For example, I can't be skillfully coping, say dribbling a basketball, unless I am responding to the actual object. Successful ongoing coping is thus itself a kind of knowledge.[5]

Trying to achieve *conditions of satisfaction* only occurs when the flow of ongoing coping is somehow disturbed.

When I act in an effective, poised way, it is not merely that what I was trying to do is in *agreement* with what I (distinguishably) did do. Rather, . . . there were no two things to compare, but only the *perfect fit* of me-in-my circumstances. . . . It is only in failure of response, and loss of poise, that a distinction appears between what I was trying to do and what I did. (70)

What happens in the conversion of absorbed coping to willful trying will be a helpful guide in understanding what happens in perception when the nonconceptual is converted into the conceptual. When my nonconceptual coping skill fails, and I have to make an effort to bring about what my skill should have effortlessly accomplished, it seems that, since I am trying to achieve the same end toward which my skill was directed, I must have been trying to achieve that goal all along. But, on careful reflection, it should be clear that trying does not simply make explicit *a willful effort* to achieve a *goal*—both of which were already there but unnoticed. If a doorknob sticks and I have to make an effort to turn it, that does not show that I had been *trying* to turn it all along—that my movements have been caused by my entertaining those success conditions—anymore than it shows that I *believed* that turning the doorknob would enable me to open the door or that I *expected* the door to open, even though I did, indeed, *anticipate* its opening in that my body was set to walk though it. The transformation from nonconceptual, absorbed coping to attentive action introduces a new element: the conceptual representation of my goal.[6]

A further, more fundamental, dependence of the conceptual on the nonconceptual arises from the way both absorbed coping and attentive trying are dependent on the spatiotemporal field produced by the body. That field is produced by the way the body's specific structure constrains and enables its coping skills. To make his case that, in structuring the spatiotemporal field the body plays a fundamental unifying role in *all* human experience, Todes goes beyond Merleau-Ponty's account of the body as a pure "I can" that responds to the world's solicitations. He describes in detail how the structure of the active body produces our unified experience of space and time. Since the body moves forward more effectively than backwards, it opens a *horizontal field* that organizes experience into what can be coped with directly, what can be reached with effort, and what is over the perceptual horizon. Furthermore, the front/back asymmetry of the active body—the fact that it can cope well only with what is in front of it—organizes the temporal field. In everyday coping, what has yet to be faced is experienced as in the future, what is currently being faced and dealt with makes up the pragmatic present, and what already has been faced and is behind us is experienced as both spatially and temporally passed. Todes concludes: "Thus through movement we do not merely notice but produce the spatiotemporal field around us, our circumstantial field, the field in which things appear to us" (49).[7]

Because perceptual objects can be experienced only in a spatiotemporal field, they can never be given as fully determinate. Rather, a perceptual object has a front and a back and an inside and an outside, so that any particular experience of such an object "perceptually implies"[8] hidden aspects soliciting further exploration and determination. For example, what I take to be a house seen from the front *looks* like a *house* not a *façade*. It is not as if I see what looks like a house front and I then *infer* that it has a back and inside. In confronting what I take to be a house, my body is solicited to go around it, while, if I take it that I am seeing a façade, I embody no such readiness. In the second case, the façade consequently looks thin and seems to hide empty terrain behind it, whereas a house looks thick and as if it conceals rooms to be discovered upon further exploration. Thus one has nonconceptual perceptual "beliefs" about perceptual objects; for example, one of my "beliefs," in seeing a *house*, is my being set to walk through the front door. The intentional content of such a perceptual belief is in the motor intentionality of my bodily set, that is, in the way I am prepared to act and do act if nothing intervenes.[9]

According to Todes, we also make perceptual *inferences* and form perceptual *judgments*. To take another example, on the basis of past experience with similar boxes, one might mistakenly see a belted box as heavy, with the "perceptual implication" that lifting it would require an effort. A "perceptual inference" would then normally lead me to be set to use more force than necessary to pick it up. My readiness to use such force would be a mistaken "perceptual judgment." Philosophers generally agree with Aristotle and Kant that, in making a judgment, we subsume a particular under a general concept. In a *perceptual* judgment, however, although our set to lift the object is similar to our set for lifting other heavy objects, we bring to bear a *specific* body-set—in the example, a set to lift this particular heavy object in this particular situation. Indeed, one cannot specify the perceiver's practical knowledge of an object independent of the perceiver's actual disposition to cope with it.[10]

Introduction I

McDowell proposes as a test for *conceptual* content that its objects must be reidentifiable.[11] To determine whether the content of *perceptual* attitudes is an alternative and irreducible kind of content, we must therefore ask: Does the content of motor intentionality pass the reidentification test? It is crucial, in answering this question, to realize that, as Todes points out, when objects are made determinate by skillful coping, it is our whole, unified body that gets a grip on the whole unified object in a specific unified context:

In the last analysis, . . . we can have an object in perception only by our whole perceptual field and all its contents being sensed as centered in the felt unity of our active body. (206)

We can now anticipate that Todes will seek to show that, just as practical perception involves its own sort of implications, beliefs, judgments and knowledge, it has its own nonconceptual form of reidentification. In thought, I can reidentify an object as the same object in a wide variety of possible contexts. So, for example, I recognize a chair by subsuming it under the general concept chair and can then reidentify it in any context as long as I retain that concept. In practical perception, on the contrary, my "reidentification" does not depend on the intellectual act of *recognizing* that this is the same object I have encountered in other situations; it consists simply in my coping with the object in a way that is *in fact* similar to the way I have coped with it on other occasions.

I may, for example, have a body-set to deal with a particular chair in my office, and, while that particular body set is in fact similar to my set for dealing with other chairs, and with this chair on other occasions, I don't experience this chair *as* similar to other chairs or *as* identical with the one I sat on yesterday. I am simply disposed to sit on this chair, in this situation, in this stiff or relaxed or seductive way. I perceptually *identify* the chair I am about to sit on as my office chair simply by being set to sit on it in the way I usually sit on my office chair. I don't *reidentify* it as a chair that I could encounter in other possible contexts. Indeed, while I can *conceptually reidentify* the chair in my office as an instance of a type of chair and as having certain characteristics that would enable me to recognize it even on the street, my *perceptual identification* of the chair in my office is so concrete, contextual, and tied to my current disposition to cope with it that it does not follow that I could reidentify it in other possible contexts.

Just as the body-set involved in the practical perception of an object is too responsive to the specific external context to assure reidentification in other contexts, the body set for coping with the whole object makes it impossible to isolate the various characteristics of the object from their internal context as characteristics of that specific object. The characteristics of a perceptual object are, therefore, not experienced as *isolable features* that could be features of other possible objects, but, rather, as the *aspects* of that particular object. Todes points out that we always perceive aspects *of an object*.

Merleau-Ponty makes the same point when he says: "It is impossible to understand perception as the imputation of a certain significance to certain sensible signs, since the most immediate sensible texture of these signs cannot be described without referring to the object they signify." In this connection he speaks of seeing the woolly-blueness of a carpet.[12] That is, given the perceiver's current coping capacities (which are based on skills formed in prior experiences with this carpet or similar ones), the carpet looks to be a blue rich with perceptual implications, as one's body is set to feel the carpet's particular flexibility, weight, warmth, fuzziness, etc. On the basis of other past experiences and their correlated body-set, a block of ice would presumably look slick-hard-cold-blue. In general, the experience of any characteristic of an object of practical perception is tied to the perceiver's holistic body-set. Thus, the aspects of the objects of practical perception, such as the wooly-warm-flexible-blueness of this carpet are so contextually determined that they cannot be seen as the features of other possible objects and so could not be reidentified in a different object. Yet the perceiver's anticipations are determinate enough to have conditions of satisfaction. That is, the perceiver anticipates the experience of this warm-flexible-blue carpet. It follows that the intentional content by means of which the aspects of perceptual objects are perceived must be nonconceptual.

But, that leaves us with a troubling question: If perception is, indeed, holistic and nonconceptual all the way in, how are we able to entertain propositional beliefs about isolable perceptual objects and their isolable properties, and, more generally, how are we able to make judgments on the basis of perceptual experience?

The objects of thought must be context-free, as must be the perceived properties of such objects, but it is important to see that, just as in absorbed coping there is neither an act of trying nor a representation of a goal, so in practical perception, when I am transparently coping, I do not encounter context-independent objects or reidentifiable *properties* or *features* of the object I am perceiving. But if the context-free and thus reidentifiable objects and properties that thought takes up are neither perceptual objects nor aspects of perceptual objects, how do the objects of practical perception become the objects of abstract thought?

According to Todes, the transformation of *contextually determined perceptual* objects with *integrated aspects* into *decontextualized conceptual* objects with *isolable features* takes place in two stages. To begin with, the spectatorial attitude, by deactivating one's bodily set to cope, transforms the integrated *aspects* of the perceptual object into a set of isolable *qualities*. In this book, Todes explicitly excludes a treatment of this transformation of the embodied, involved attitude into the disembodied, spectatorial attitude, but he does describe the genesis of the spectatorial attitude and the transformation it brings about in an article included as appendix II.[13] There, Todes points out that practical perception takes place in three stages:

(1) In the first stage we prepare ourselves to perceive an object by getting into a proper position or attitude in respect to it.

(2) Having prepared ourselves to perceive it, we next ready the object to be perceived. This is done by "getting at" the object in some essentially preliminary, tentative, and easily reversible way that allows us to test, with comparatively light consequences, the desirability of going on to perceive the object fully.

(3) In the third stage we finally perceive the object.

Todes then claims that, when we inhibit stage three, we transform practical perception so as to produce sensuous abstractions. "In . . . cases of skillfully inhibited perception . . . one becomes aware of *qualities* rather than things" (274).

Thus, the contemplative subject no longer experiences perceptual objects through their integrated aspects, but rather experiences collections of qualities. However, since they still experience themselves as in the world, spectators still experience objects in a shared context with other objects, and so as *stable* collections of *stable* qualities.[14] Such objects and qualities are precisely the reidentifiable elements required by thought.

In the spectatorial attitude, if I come across the same quality in several objects, I can reidentify it as the one I saw before. It is as if one held a painter's color chart up to Merleau-Ponty's wooly-blue carpet and found that the carpet's color matched color chip #29, which was not woolly at all, and, indeed, also matched the tangy-blue of blue berries and the icy-blue of ice. But such conceptual content is still not in the space of reasons.

Thinking about objects requires more than simply being able to reidentify their properties. Much of our thinking concerns *possible* objects in *possible* situations that need never in fact occur. So Todes next explains how our imagination enables us to understand the products of spectatorial decomposition as *possible* objects with *possible* properties. Once we contemplate an object so that our unified and unifying body is no longer involved, our imagination enables us to conjure up the object in various possible contexts, and to imagine the qualities we have disengaged as the qualities of other possible objects. That is, we can imagine the object we are contemplating as a *type* of object that could be encountered and reidentified on other occasions, and we can conceive of it as having a set of reidentifiable features each of which could be a feature of other objects.

Such imaginative representations nonetheless depend on our embodied involvement. For

only by reference to a character-of-this-world, as distinct from objects-in-this-world, can we have any ground for holding such imaginative verbal beliefs about, or undertaking such imaginative purposive action in respect to, objects not in our perceptual field. For such long-range suppositions and purposes pre-suppose that the concrete as well as formal kinds of order self-evidently manifest to us within our perceptual field (in virtue of our centrally habit-forming active body), generally hold also in the apparently placeless regions beyond our perceptual horizon—merely in virtue of the fact that these regions are also regions in the same world as the perceptually present region.[15] (135)

Introduction I

   Thanks to our disengagement and our imagination, the object of perception is transformed from an *actually existing* object into a *possible* object about which we can form hypotheses and on the basis of which we can make inferences; that is, we have turned the perceptual object into an object of thought. And just as when we abandon absorbed coping and act attentively, it seems that we have been trying to achieve a goal all along, and when we make our needs determinate by satisfying them, we seem to have had those determinate needs all along, so when we abandon practical perception for the detached, imaginative attitude in which we think and do philosophy, it seems that the objects of practical perception must have been objects of thought all along.
   Once the stages by which the body turns the objects of practical perception into objects of thought have been covered up by detached philosophical reflection, McDowell, like Kant, can conceive of only two alternatives: either perception is so radically nonconceptual as to be totally outside the space of reasons and therefore blind, or, if it is to enable us to form beliefs and make inferences, it must be as conceptual as thought itself. McDowell, therefore, can understand perception as the result of a causal, mechanical interaction of the physical body and the world, but he holds that what one receives in perception must be directly available for forming judgments and so must be permeated by conceptual content. There is no place in such a view for the body's motor intentionality and for the perceptual objects that it reveals. But, as we have now seen, Todes shows how, thanks to our bodily dispositions, perceptual objects are articulated without being *conceptually* articulated. Conceptual articulation is then accomplished by means of a detached, spectatorial perception that can transform perceptual articulations into decontextualized qualities, so that these qualities, in turn, can be represented as possible features of possible objects by the imagination, and thus serve as material for conceptual thought.
   Todes concludes:

Phenomenological analyses have shown that perception and imagination are radically different. We have two irreducibly *different* ways of experiencing things: by anticipating them, and by immediate production of them. Neither capacity is derivable from the other. Yet we are *not* bound to understand one in terms of the other. We can pass back and forth between them as modes of understanding. Together with our two radically different ways of experiencing things, we have two basic modes of worldly understanding: we have . . . *two sets of categories* of matters of fact. (201)

We have seen that the embodied subject is able to meet its factual needs by developing more and more refined skills for coping with the various determinable objects that show up in its spatiotemporal field. We have also seen that the perceiver's nonconceptual readiness to cope with the world and the things in it exhibits the perceptual equivalents of belief, inference, and judgment. Finally we have see that, for ongoing coping to take place at all, it must be continually succeeding in getting a grip on its object. Todes, therefore, claims that the perceiver has *practical objective knowledge* of the world and the objects in it. He sums up this crucial claim as follows:

We perceive always *that* something is so. "I see a chair," implies "I see that there is a chair." . . . Perceptual determinations make sense only in the context of a judgment. (217)

This may sounds at first like a concession to McDowell's claim that in order to enter the space of reasons perception must be conceptual, but we must remember that, for Todes, perceptual knowledge is the result of a movement from need to satisfaction. Successfully coping with an object "justifies" the "judgment that" there is, in fact, an object that satisfies and retroactively makes determinate the need that motivated the coping. For example, as I enter my office, I "judge" that coping with this as yet indeterminate object as a chair will give me a grip on my circumstances. That is, I am set to exercise my specific skill for sitting on this chair in these circumstances. "I see that there is a chair" means, where practical perception is concerned, that I successfully sit on it.

Todes assumes, with McDowell, that Kant has worked out the kind of intelligibility characteristic of thought. Todes wants to show that perception, like thought, reveals the world as it is and, as a mode of intelligibility, has a parallel structure to the structure that Kant worked out for thought. So Todes sets out to "deduce" a Table of the Twelve Categories of *Perceptual* Knowledge. He reasons as follows:

Introduction I

A perceptual judgment is an argument. . . . We have, in addition, found the primary form of this argument. It is a three-stage motivational argument: from our ineluctable unity of need that prompts all our activity, through our consequent finding of some unity of object, to a concluding unity of satisfaction derived from this object. All perceptual sense makes sense in the context of this argument. To determine the fundamental quantities, qualities, relation to an object, and modalities that characterize perception, we need merely to ask these four questions about each of the three stages of perceptual knowledge, in what we now see to be their phenomeno-*logical* order. (217–218)

Given current interest in the body in philosophy and in so many other domains both in the English-speaking world and on the Continent, we now have a context for appreciating Todes's achievement. Indeed, Todes's original account of the role of the body in disclosing a spatiotemporal field in which practical perception is directed by need and reaches satisfaction by means of nonconceptual skillful coping, as well as his account of how our capacity for disembodied observation and our conceptual imagination make possible the compatibility of perception and thought, appear so in step with contemporary concerns that his book reads as if it were a response to the most recent development in both analytic and continental philosophy.

Introduction II

How Todes Rescues Phenomenology from the Threat of Idealism

Piotr Hoffman

The Human Body as Material Subject of the World—the author's doctoral dissertation at Harvard—was written in 1963 and was first published in 1990.[1] The author wrote an "Anticipatory Postscript" for that edition (included here as appendix III). This short but revealing piece situates his thinking on the spectrum of contemporary ways of philosophizing. The reader may note Todes's repudiation of two dogmas that dominate current philosophy: the dogma that interpretations alone (as opposed to various concoctions of dinosaur thinking called "facts," "data," "the given," and so on) constitute the human world, and the closely connected dogma that human individuals are products of socially constituted fields of meaning.

Unfortunately, much of this "Anticipatory Postscript" will remain forever a promissory note. We will never know how Todes would have carried out the research program he delineated there. For *The Human Body as Material Subject of the World*, republished here in an edited version, represents only the first part of what was to be a fullfledged philosophical system addressing the central issues in the major areas of philosophy. Nonetheless, the theory argued for in the present book is developed in enough detail to stand on its own merits. Had it been published at the time it was written, it would have been recognized as one of the most valuable contributions to philosophy in the postwar period and as the most significant contribution in the field of existential phenomenology since the work of Merleau-Ponty. Pursuing his original insights and arguments, Todes does very little, indeed close to nothing, to bring out several advantages his theory offers when compared with the philosophies of such kindred spirits as Heidegger and Merleau-Ponty. This is the gap I hope to fill here.

Let me start with the obvious: the phenomenologies of both Heidegger and Merleau-Ponty were put forward as being, among other things, alternatives to the philosophical idealism that—from Descartes through Kant to Husserl—represented the main current of European philosophy. Both Heidegger and Merleau-Ponty attempted, each in his own way, to work out an account of human being-in-the-world through which the untenable idealistic conclusions would be overcome, and both of them failed at critical junctures. As I will now show, Todes's account is clearly superior to theirs at precisely these crucial points.[2]

The charge of idealism raised against Heidegger has been around for well over half a century, and it has been advanced, and kept alive, by the foremost commentators on his philosophy.[3] The grounds for such a charge can be found in the very introduction to *Being and Time*, where Heidegger lays out the entire general framework within which his philosophical moves will unfold.[4] Temporality is identified—Heidegger's entire *magnum opus* is one long confirmation of his thesis—as the meaning of Dasein's being. But Dasein's temporality will also supply the horizon of the meaning of Being, and since the latter is disclosed in Dasein's understanding of it, no entity can be intelligible in any of its aspects (i.e., not only in its "essence" but in its "existence" as well) outside of Dasein's understanding of the meaning of Being.

Much of what is customarily viewed as (commonsensical and philosophical) "realism" is thereby rejected out of hand. The realist believes that he beholds and acts upon objects that "present" themselves as independent of him. But for Heidegger, this outlook is nothing other than the "metaphysics of presence" (either taken for granted by the man-in-the-street or raised to the status of a sophisticated philosophical system), that is, a form of Dasein's own understanding of what there is (BT, 47). And it is not just that "presence" is an ontological articulation of Dasein. The same must be said of the very "independence" of entities—be they *otherwise* articulated as "present" or in some other way. We are now at the critical juncture of the issue of Heidegger's idealism. Heidegger stresses repeatedly (BT, 255, 272) that only Being (and not the entities themselves) is dependent upon Dasein's understanding of Being. And yet these very same entities cannot even be said to exist "independently" or "in themselves." Explicitly endorsing idealism on *this* particular issue, Heidegger holds that any talk of this or that (or any and every) entity as "independent" or "in-itself" is only Dasein's own conception (BT, 251, 255). Thus, even Kant's talk of a "thing in itself" or "things in themselves" cannot be sustained, for it too represents a human articulation. But then in what sense can we attribute *any* independence to those "entities" Heidegger wanted to save from being absorbed within Dasein's understanding of Being?

In a way, our question itself suggests, if not an answer, then at least a general direction in which we should move in our search for an answer. For if the categories laid out within our understanding of Being cannot put us in touch with a truly independent reality, then the latter would have to consist in, and be accessible as, some "nonhuman" or "alien-to-man" aspect of what there is. And this is precisely Heidegger's solution. In the period of *Being and Time*, Heidegger identifies this aspect of reality as "nature," and he opposes it to the man-made, inhabitable and humanized, "world." The "world ... is ... a characteristic of Dasein" (BT, 92), indeed "the world is, so to speak, Dasein-ish."[5] It is otherwise with nature. "World is only, if, and as a Dasein exists. Nature can also be when no Dasein exists."[6] Nature, then, is precisely the element that must exist, and must be discovered as existing by Dasein, if Dasein is to have a sense of what lies beyond the parameters of the man-made world.

Unfortunately, Heidegger's opening move in *Being and Time* does not bode well for the possibility of Dasein's encounter with such an alien, undomesticated nature. "Only in some definite mode of its own Being-in-the-world can Dasein discover entities as Nature" (BT, 94). This means, in the first place, that typically, and for the most part, nature is encountered as already interpreted by the understanding of Being embedded in our everyday circumspective concern. In this sense, "[t]he wood is a forest of timber, the mountain, a quarry of rock" (BT, 100), etc. Admittedly, this may be said to characterize the everyday attitude only when everydayness is equated with inauthenticity (for Heidegger at times identifies and at times distinguishes these two terms). Perhaps, then, this need not characterize the everyday but still authentic Dasein—the Dasein loyal to its historical roots and tradition. But then "even Nature is historical . . . as a countryside, as an area that has been colonized and exploited, as a battlefield, or as the site of a cult" (BT, 440). Whatever attitude we take vis-à-vis nature, as long as the world as a whole remains intact, nature will not break through in its alien, nonhuman face. Of course, I can always make a strained and artificial effort at apprehending a *particular* object as stripped of its worldly meanings. But I never succeed. If I begin to look at the piece of granite in my neighbor's house foundation merely in order to contemplate the rock's color, fine grain, and so on, I still see it as falling in place within a human world (of building, of hiking in the mountains where such rocks are to be found, etc.)—so much so that "it is *utterly unthinkable* how something, a natural thing, could be encountered in its pure bodily presence, if not on the basis of the *prior presence of world*."[7]

But, it soon turns out, this is only one part of Heidegger's position. For even in the *Being and Time* period—which is the only period in Heidegger's development we are analyzing—he makes an important distinction. Although nature is an "intraworldly" entity, "for all that, intraworldliness does not belong to nature's being."[8] The very same conception is put forward in *Being and Time*'s important paragraph on "Understanding and Interpretation." The "unworldly" nature is said to be "unmeaning" [*unsinniges*]. "Here unmeaning does not signify that we are saying anything about the value of such entities, but it gives expression to an *ontological characteristic* [my emphasis—PH]. *And only that which is unmeaning can be absurd* [*widersinnig*]. The present-at-hand, as Dasein encounters it, can, as it were, assault Dasein's Being; natural events, for instance, can break in upon us and destroy us" (BT, 193). There can be no doubt about Heidegger's intention in these passages: here nature is taken precisely as that nonhuman, truly alien and undomesticated, element threatening to assault and destroy the entire niche of the man-made world. But just *how* are we to "encounter" this nature in all of its alienness to man? Heidegger speaks of it as present-at-hand, but this too is a human conception defining for us what counts as real in perceptual contemplation, or in science, or in traditional metaphysics. Perhaps, then, the expression "present-at-hand" is here used in a unique sense for lack of a better word; and perhaps the entire emphasis ought to be put upon that "assaulting" and "destroying" power of nature to which Heidegger here draws our attention. In this quality nature is said to be "unmeaning" to us.

But now: what is the meaning of this "unmeaning"? It is nothing other, Heidegger here explains, than the assaulting nature's "ontological characteristic." But Dasein alone is responsible for positing the ontological characteristics of entities through its own understanding of the being of these entities. So if, "in commerce with this being, nature in the broadest sense, we understand that this being *is* as something extant, as a being that we come up against, to which we are delivered over, which on its part already always is,"[9] then the very terms Heidegger is here forced to use imply philosophical idealism. If nature is alien in its being, it is so not simply *in* Dasein's understanding of it, but also *due* to Dasein's understanding of it—for (in the "early" Heidegger at least) Dasein and Dasein *alone* determines what counts as the being of entities. To say, as Heidegger here does, that we understand the being of nature as "always already there" only aggravates the threat of idealism, for the man-made "world"—with all of its equipmental complexes, its practices, its traditions, etc.—is itself often described as "always already there," and yet Heidegger *contrasts* its man-made character with the nonhuman—alien and often hostile—nature as such.

We need not go any further in supplying the evidence for the lack, in *Being and Time*, of an adequate conception of nature (adequate to Heidegger's own purposes), for such is the final conclusion of Heidegger himself. In an important footnote in *Vom Wesen des Grundes* (written only a year after the publication of *Being and Time*) Heidegger tells us that the concept of nature in that indispensable "primordial sense" was missing in *Being and Time*; and, he adds, nature as "primordially manifest" is encountered by Dasein only due to Dasein's "situatedness (thrownness)."[10] Apparently, then, he is here implying that these ideas as developed in *Being and Time* were still insufficient to allow for Dasein's encounter with an alien and nonhuman nature.

Has Heidegger underestimated the potential of his *Befindlichkeit* and *Geworfenheit* as developed even in *Being and Time*? This may *seem* to be the case for, after all, the state-of-mind (the Macquarrie-Robinson translation of *Befindlichkeit*) is ontically nothing other than our moods (*Stimmungen*) (BT, 172); and our moods, in turn, make us affected by what there is (BT, 176–177). Now, our moods make us affected by reality, because our moods reveal our thrownness, that is, our ontological vulnerability and powerlessness. For this reason, we cannot be *genuinely* "indifferent" to the conditions of our life; the latter must "get through to us" in one way or another.

But Heidegger also argues that the state-of-mind "always has its understanding" (BT, 182), and we can notice immediately a significant shift in his philosophical vocabulary. In paragraph 29 of *Being and Time*, entitled "Being there as State-of-mind," our thrownness, our pure "that it is and has to be" is "disclosed moodwise" and it thus "shows itself" or even "burst[s] forth" as "naked" (*nacktes*) (BT, 173). But only two paragraphs later, when Heidegger focuses on "Being there as Understanding," our thrownness ceases to merely "show itself," and to show itself as "naked," for "Dasein is such that in every case it has understood (or alternatively, not understood) that it is to be thus and thus" (BT, 184). To say that Dasein has "not understood" does not mean, of course, that Dasein is back to experiencing its "naked" thrownness, but only that it has a deficient or inauthentic mode of understanding. "And only *because* Dasein, in understanding, is its there, *can* it go astray and fail to recognize itself" (ibid). But Understanding in general is projected by Dasein. It follows from this that Dasein's grasp of its thrownness is now shaped and conditioned by Dasein's understanding of its own being and of the being of entities other than Dasein. Thus both how Dasein is "affected" and what is even capable of affecting Dasein depend upon Dasein's own understanding of being. There is no hope, thus far, of encountering (and being affected by) some "alien," other-than-human elemental power of nature.

It could be objected immediately that this conclusion remains valid only for the everyday moods, but not for the privileged mood of anxiety. For, it could be argued, even though the ordinary moods are mediated by our understanding, the latter collapses in the mood of anxiety. Anxiety would then be in a position to make us encounter that "alien," "nonhuman" element of reality.

Now anxiety is a very complex phenomenon and there are at least two senses of it in the early Heidegger, indeed even in *Being and Time* itself. I will call them the "weaker" and the "stronger" senses. The weaker sense is not sufficient to make us encounter some radically alien "other"; the stronger sense, even if sufficient, will force us to allow for a truly mystical experience, with all the contradictions that go with it.

The weak sense of anxiety is rather simple and transparent. It is fleshed out in paragraph 40 of *Being and Time*. There is no need to summarize these well-known descriptions. Let us only note the following: even though the world is now apprehended as "completely lacking significance" (BT, 231), indeed as "insignificant" (ibid.), it is precisely this lack of significance that discloses the "world as world" (BT, 232, 233). The analysis of the "as" structure (BT, 189–193) shows the latter to be derivative from Dasein's ways of understanding and interpreting being. Thus, anxiety's transformation of the public world into "insignificant" means only that the anxious Dasein gets a deeper and more adequate understanding of the "world as world" (by realizing that the entire framework of practices, conventions, meanings, and so on, sustaining the everyday world is merely contingent and "artificial").

Only later in *Being and Time* are the more far-reaching aspects of anxiety brought out. "The nothing with which anxiety brings us face to face, unveils the nullity by which Dasein, in its very basis, is defined; and this itself is as thrownness into death" (BT, 356). Moreover, the thrownness that is thus unveiled in anxiety is now naked (BT, 394). Since (unlike in the ordinary moods) the naked thrownness is seen squarely as thrownness "into death," "[t]he present-at-hand must be encountered in just *such* a way that it does *not* have *any* involvement whatsoever, but can show itself in an empty mercilessness" (BT, 393). And, it seems, at least this "empty mercilessness" of the present-at-hand (if not the conception of the present-at-hand as such) goes beyond everything that can be encountered not only within the everyday domesticated world, but even within the "world as world" disclosed to us by anxiety in the weak sense we have already considered. Using anxiety in this strong sense, Heidegger dots the i in *Was ist Metaphysik* (his 1929 lecture, written in 1928): nihilation "discloses these beings in their full but heretofore concealed strangeness as what is *radically other*.... In the clear night of the nothing of anxiety the original openness of beings as such arises."[11]

This is the much needed move: anxiety makes Dasein encounter the *radical otherness* of the nonhuman, undomesticated being. Have we said "being"? But "in the face of anxiety all utterance of the 'is' falls silent."[12] The entire dilemma created by Heidegger's present view can be gathered from this. If the "is" falls silent in anxiety, then the "radically other" cannot be said to "be" in any sense available to Dasein. This need not imply that the radically other "is not," but this does imply, and it does so in conformity with the overall thrust of Heidegger's own position, that the "radically other" (whether we view it as "nature" or as something else) can only be encountered—if it can be encountered at all—in an experience inexpressible with the aid of the very *category of existence* and exhibiting all the features characteristic of the experience of a mystic.[13]

There is no trace of mysticism in Merleau-Ponty's attempt to come to terms with the issue of philosophical idealism. His is the philosophy of the human *body*, and it seems almost obvious that any such philosophy will be able to steer away from the reefs of idealism. No doubt, we can expect to see an account of the human body's exposure to the presence and impact of a truly independent reality.

Merleau-Ponty "propose[s] to approach *the phenomenon of reality* by studying perceptual constants" (PP, 299, my emphasis). Why such an approach? Because, to begin with, what appears as reality to us must be accessible to our experience, and nothing that is not endowed with a minimum of enduring determinateness *can* be an object of our experience. If this or that object were to be undergoing truly Protean changes at each instant of its career, then we would either fail to recognize such a strange "object" altogether or, at the very best, we would have to achieve such a recognition by relying upon the object's determinate surroundings, with *their* shapes, sizes, colors, and so on. And so Merleau-Ponty moves on to account for our experience of the perceptual constants. In doing so he criticizes, as he does everywhere in his phenomenology, the two prevailing explanatory models: the empiricist and the rationalist. Contrary to these traditional philosophical accounts, we do not recognize the constancy of perceived shapes and sizes (for these are the first targets of Merleau-Ponty's analysis) either as a result of an association of mental images, or by subsuming such images under some rule of the intellect. Prior to and independently of any association or intellection, the perceptual object is understood by us as having *its own* shape and size. We determine them as *the* shape and *the* size the object displays to us when we succeed in seeing it— "like a picture in an art gallery" (PP, 302)—under certain appropriate conditions (of distance, direction, light, etc.) that will allow us to apprehend the object in its "maximum visibility" (ibid.), that is, in the full articulation of its perceptual meaning. Our perceptual exploration relies upon this "maximum" as upon the *norm* (ibid.) guiding our identifications of the object under less favorable perceptual conditions. The constancy of colors receives a parallel account, aided with the same analogy of a "picture in an art gallery" (PP, 313). In perception, at least, colors are not apprehended as free-floating, context-free qualities, but as expressive of their objects. This green is the beautiful and calm meadow-green; and to apprehend it as such I must see the meadow itself with the appropriate bodily set (quite different from the bodily set of a developer ready to unleash upon the meadow his bulldozers and backhoes) and under the appropriate perceptual conditions (say, without the electric light flooding the meadow during the evening football match). Nor is this analysis valid for visual qualities alone. The object's constant weight, for example (Merleau-Ponty speaks also of sounds and temperatures), is also identified with the aid of a similar "norm"—the norm the object's weight achieves for us at the moment when our tactile exploration of it becomes a truly "knowing touch" (PP, 315); and the same goes for the object's smoothness and roughness (ibid.). In general, the intersensorial thing as such becomes determinate for us "when it is in every way at its maximum articulation" (PP, 319), that is, when the thing at issue (the glass, the ashtray that Merleau-Ponty describes here) expresses its significance to the perceiver in all of its sensory qualities.

Even this brief outline of Merleau-Ponty's account of what he calls the "phenomenon of reality" allows us to see the danger of idealism. The determinateness of experience is not a given, for it presupposes a *norm* achieved by the activity of the perceiver. Since no experience is possible without some measure of enduring

Introduction II

determinateness, and since the latter is posited by the perceiver, no "reality" other than the reality-for-the-perceiver can ever be experienced. Is it then to be wondered that Berkeley is praised repeatedly for having argued just that,[14] and is it to be wondered that some of Merleau-Ponty's own formulations approximate those of Berkeley? "The thing is inseparable from a person perceiving it, and can never be actually *in itself* because its articulations are those of our very existence, and because it stands at the other end of our gaze or at the terminus of a sensory exploration which invests it with humanity" (PP, 320). If, as Merleau-Ponty adds immediately, "[t]o *this* extent, every perception is a communication or a communion" (ibid., my emphasis), then the meaning of this last metaphor—and of several other related metaphors[15]—only strengthens our conviction that for Merleau-Ponty too *esse est percipi*. To be sure, throughout the *Phenomenology of Perception* Merleau-Ponty argues consistently that the perceiving body gains its own unity only through coping with the perceived objects. But (to use the Hegelian terminology Merleau-Ponty so often relies upon) the object is only one indispensable term in a relation in which the perceiving body is not simply the other term, but the whole relation as well. If, given the presence of the appropriate bodily set, I cannot think that I perceive a pipe or an ashtray without taking for granted that there really is that perceived pipe or that ashtray (PP, 374), then this may or may not be enough to rule out the threat of my experience being here a perceptual illusion, but this is certainly not enough to show that the perceived reality as such has a component independent of my perception. If "the world itself . . . is . . . the universal style of all possible perceptions,"[16] then in what sense can we still allow the perceiver to encounter a truly independent reality?

Merleau-Ponty must be given the credit for not only acknowledging the issue, but for confronting it head on: "we must understand how, paradoxically, there is *for us* an *in itself*" (PP, 71). A paradox indeed, against which the recurring waves of modern idealism have been breaking again and again. Was it because the understanding of the very terms of the debate was superficial and not thought through to the end? This is precisely what Merleau-Ponty suggests: we must "reexamine" and thereby "escape" the "dilemma of for itself and in itself" (PP, 213, 215); and the escape, if successful, will allow us to remove the danger of philosophical idealism. And so Merleau-Ponty goes on, immediately after having made this programmatic declaration, to offer two arguments meant to remove the threat of idealism. Another argument is to be found later on in the *Phenomenology of Perception*. I shall now consider these arguments one by one.

1. Unlike intellectual consciousness, perceptual consciousness can be "saturated" with an independent object because, to begin with, "perception takes place in an atmosphere of generality and is presented to us anonymously" (PP, 215). This is not a new theme in Merleau-Ponty's philosophy; what is new are its presently drawn anti-idealistic implications. Since perceptual activity is prepersonal and anonymous, any perceiver aspiring to the title of the constituting ego finds himself anchored in an already deployed perceptual field. As a perceiver, I cannot even, properly speaking, claim that I perceive; rather, perception is a process that I ought to describe by saying "that *one* perceives in me" (ibid.). By itself, this does not take us very far. It relativizes the perceived world to a prepersonal, anonymous process of perception—but then Kant himself grounded his experience not in this or that self but in *Bewusstsein überhaupt*—without allowing us to discover any trace of a reality independent of the perceptual process itself. The body is still the maker of the experienced reality, even if the body is here taken merely in its prepersonal and general function.

There are more promising signs posted along the present route. The general and prepersonal power of the body is referred to as the "passivity derived from nature. The body is our general medium for having a world" (PP, 146). But how are we to understand this natural passivity of our body? What could this passivity mean if, as Merleau-Ponty here indicates, the natural passivity of our body allows it to operate as "our general medium for having a world"? Since Merleau-Ponty finds it important to stress that "the relation of having" (*la relation d'avoir*) is even etymologically related to the word "habit" (*habitude*) (PP, 174)—as he tells us this makes it justifiable, against Gabriel Marcel's then fashionable opposition of "*avoir*" and "*être*" (being) to speak of ourselves as "having" our body (ibid.)—we may begin to suspect that the natural passivity we "have" in our body is nothing more than the power of the body's

Introduction II

general and prepersonal "habits" of constituting the world. And this is in fact Merleau-Ponty's final word on the matter: "the natural object is the track left by this generalized existence" (PP, 347).

2. Our sensory exploration of the object is always "incomplete," and there is "a depth (*profondeur*) of the object that no progressive sensory deduction will ever exhaust" (PP, 216). This, we may grant Merleau-Ponty, is a fact of our perceptual experience. But what does it prove? The "depth" of the object is part and parcel of the perceptual *meaning* the object discloses to our body. Merleau-Ponty derives this meaning—predictably and correctly, given his entire theory—from the body's general and prepersonal grip upon the world: "what we in fact have, is consciousness of an inexhaustible object, and we are sucked into it because, between it and us, there is this latent knowledge which our gaze uses" (PP, 238). The much vaunted "depth" of the object is, therefore, the correlate of the body's latent and tacit grasp of the world, the correlate of what Merleau-Ponty, following Husserl, calls "passive synthesis" (PP, 427). If this is the function of passive synthesis, we should not be surprised by Merleau-Ponty's clarification that "[w]hat is called passivity is not the acceptance by us of an alien reality" (ibid.). In point of fact, Husserl's own idealistic solution of the puzzle of the object's unexplored "depth" is here exactly the same, even in its wording.[17]

3. Thus far, we have considered two arguments whose unsatisfactory outcome was a foregone conclusion because of their common focus upon perceptual *meaning*. Given Merleau-Ponty's theory, any such meaning—be it prepersonal or not, be it the meaning of the object's inexhaustible "depth" or of its transparent surface—had to be traced back to the organizing powers of the body. But, it seems, our body has the capacity of suspending its ordinary involvement in the world and of raising to the apprehension of an *un*meaning, other-than-human reality: "the thing holds itself aloof from us and remains self-sufficient. This will become clear if we suspend our ordinary preoccupation and pay a metaphysical and disinterested attention to it. It is then hostile and alien, no longer an interlocutor, but a resolutely silent Other" (PP, 322). This passage is quite unique in the *Phenomenology of Perception*. It is highly metaphorical and—unlike Sartre's description of a metaphysical "nausea" or

even Camus's description of the feeling of the "absurd"—it is not backed up by a systematic theory *allowing* the body to achieve such a sophisticated, "metaphysical" grasp of an unmeaning world. While such or similar "metaphysical" attitudes have always been ascribed to the *personal* self, it is not even clear whether the prepersonal and purely natural current of our perceptual life could ever become their source. Last but not least, even if we were to grant the purely natural body the capacity to become the subject of such metaphysically loaded feelings, the latter could only deliver their message—the message that there does exist that "hostile and alien . . . silent Other"—by destroying the body's everyday coping with the world. No such message would be conveyed within our plain, everyday existence. All of this—as we are about to see—is a far cry from the results achieved by Todes with his theory of the body's constitutive neediness and dependence upon the material environment.

In effect, the specter of idealism will not appear within a philosophy organized around the pivotal idea of the human body as "material subject of the world." It would be pointless to speculate whether, by choosing this formula for the title of his study, Todes wanted to give readers helpful clues for distinguishing his own approach from those of his illustrious predecessors in the field of existential phenomenology. But the title performs precisely such service, and Todes's own explanations of this paradoxical sounding phrase are even more helpful to the reader. "The contention is . . . that the human body is indeed a material thing in the world . . . but that it is so in such unique way that it is thereby the defining subject of the world" (88). Thus, as a material thing among other such things, the human body remains rooted in the material world; as a subject, however, the very same human body is the organizing center of the world. The book's argument shows that the tension between passivity and activity is neither altogether abolished by a simple removal of one of its terms (in Todes's analysis, the philosophy of Hume represents a particularly striking attempt at eliminating the self's organizing activity in favor of the pure circumstantiality of cognition, while the philosophy of Leibniz represents the opposite tendency—the enterprise of dissolving the entire circumstantiality of knowledge within the realm of a self-enclosed monad), nor is it resolved, as in the phenomenologies of Heidegger and Merleau-Ponty, by an external juxtaposition of passivity and activity. For if the knowable world must still have a necessary reference to the actively organized experience of a bodily percipient, that experience itself is "nothing but our quest to meet our needs" (178). Thus, the human body is the active organizer of the experienced world *insofar as* the body responds to its general neediness and passivity. Let as now take a brief look at these two aspects (the active and the passive) of our body's predicament.

Experience presupposes a minimum of determinateness and uniformity (for Todes shows how determinateness implies uniformity), and these two are established by our body's skillful coping with tasks and challenges encountered within the field of circumspective perception. For Todes, perception as such is inherently practical. There does exist, of course, a more contemplative ("spectatorial," as Todes calls it) form of perceptual exploration, but this form is derived from original circumspective perception, and it never loses its bond with the latter. In this respect, perceptual contemplation is very different from imagination, the emergence of which presupposes a creative self-transformation of the subject from a perceiving into an imaginizing contemplator. We need not pursue this issue here. Let us only note that the challenges and the tasks taken up by our body do not appear as scattered and disjoined pieces, but are always encountered within the unifying horizon of the perceptual world. The enduring unity of this world is secured by the enduring unity of the subject viewed as an active self-moving bodily perceiver. We here touch upon what is not only the recurring theme of many of Todes's phenomenological analyses, and the outcome of many of his arguments, but the main point made in his brief "General Conclusion": the unity of the world "is correlative with the felt unity of our active body in it" (262).

Experience, then, is not a given, but an achievement of our body as the latter maintains "poise" in dealing with the perceptual field; indeed, as we just said, the perceptual world itself is the counterpart of our body's constantly renewed activity of a poised response to challenges and tasks of life. Thus far, however, we seem to be moving rather smoothly along the road of philosophical idealism and there seems to be no hope of avoiding the standard idealistic conclusions. For if experience is an active achievement of an embodied self, if even the very minimal conditions of there being any experience at all—the presence of some measure of determinateness and uniformity—are derived from the body's application of its perceptual skills, then, to paraphrase another philosopher, the limits of our body are in danger of becoming the limits of our world. And so they are, it seems. "The knowable world, I seek to show, is the human body's world. To appear, to be anything at all is to be a function of the human body" (42). If this is not a confession of a philosophical idealist, it is difficult to see what could ever count as one. Kant, perhaps even Berkeley, would have been happy to endorse these statements by substituting such words as "ego," "apperception," or "spirit" for Todes's "body." And, as we already saw, the case of Merleau-Ponty shows clearly that even the selection of the body as the ultimate source of experience does not guarantee success in avoiding idealistic conclusions.

But Todes's "body" is not Merleau-Ponty's "body." For Todes, as for Merleau-Ponty, the body's active involvement constitutes the entire experiential reality. But for Todes, unlike for Merleau-Ponty, "our experience *is* nothing but our quest to meet our needs" (178); and the spatiotemporal field (our everyday world) that supplies the framework of all experiences is the "field of our needs" (50), indeed "this field *is* simply the apparent set of our body-needs" (51). In other words, it is not just that our needs motivate us to deploy the perceptual field, but, above all, the very meaning of the latter cannot be understood independently of that functional correlation with our bodily neediness. And this means, in the first place, that the very determinateness and uniformity indispensable to any experience at all would disappear altogether if the world around us failed to exhibit some features favorable to the satisfaction of our needs. Since the experiential world is the field of our needs, "our needs must be to some extent satisfied if there is to be any experience at all" (51). But this is simply another way of saying that the organizer of experience—the human body—finds itself sustained by an independent reality: "the world of human experience is the humanly habitable world, not just because we make it so, *but because the world enables us to make it so*" (176, my emphasis). As for various postmodern clichés ("there are no facts, only interpretations"; "there is no 'there' out there"), they must be rejected out of hand as frivolous. Both our needs and the properties of the world allowing for those needs' satisfactions are not constructed by an (individual or social) agent. They are, Todes argues repeatedly, *discovered* ("creatively" discovered, in the case of needs) as the very conditions of our body's perceptual organization and interpretation of reality. Even the "alienness" of nature need not dawn upon us in some special "metaphysical" experience destructive of our everydayness. Unlike in Heidegger and in Merleau-Ponty, our sense of the "alienness" of nature is present *within* everyday life, since our needs are always endangered—albeit in varying degrees—by the "blind, dark, and worldless forces" (58) of an undomesticated nature (menacing the body with droughts, floods, etc.).

Exercised as a response to our needs, our bodily agency has *itself* a material structure constitutive of our experience: the vertical, erect position of our body that must be constantly maintained in the earth's gravitational field, and the asymmetry between the backward- and the forward-oriented movements of our body. These specific features of the body are, to repeat, *constitutive* of our experience; for us, at least, they are not merely contingent peculiarities without which our experience would remain more or less the same as it is. In some sense, this seems obvious. In Darwin's *The Descent of Man*, as well as in more recent studies of human evolution, our erect posture and bipedalism have been recognized as being of paramount importance in the formation of the specifically human form of life-activity.[18] Yet, strangely enough, such important features of our bodily constitution are almost totally absent from the account of human embodiment given not only by Heidegger (whose interest in the human body is, after all, rather marginal) but even by Merleau-Ponty.[19] To be sure, phenomenologists are under no obligation to incorporate such facts into their account unless they find themselves compelled to do so by the force of evidence supplied by the data disclosed within the lived experience of the world. The material structure of our body cannot be called upon, in phenomenology, to causally explain the formation and the functioning of our everyday agency, for the supplying of such explanations is simply not the task of the phenomenologist. On the other hand, a phenomenological account capable of bringing out the experiential, lived significance of the material structure of our body in the constitution of the everyday world must be viewed as superior, for it allows us to build a bridge between the phenomenological and the causal approach to the human predicament. And this bridge established between phenomenology and naturalism is precisely what is so characteristic of Todes's account.

Let's look at the natural asymmetry of our backward- and forward-oriented motions: far from being relegated to the status of a contingent peculiarity of our bodies or, at best, to the status of an indispensable reference point determining our sense of what is "behind" or "ahead" of us in an already organized spatiotemporal field, this purely natural asymmetry of our movements proves to be constitutive of the spatiotemporal field itself, and especially of its temporal axis. The centrality of the notion of time in philosophy in general, and in phenomenology in particular, needs no sustained argument; and for this if for no other reasons, we can appreciate the significance of Todes's discovery of the very source of perceptual time in the natural, material features of our self-moving body.[20]

Let us first note the obvious. "Our body is built with a front-back asymmetry such that effective activity is directed toward what lies ahead" (118). Our backward-oriented actions are naturally clumsy and rarely effective; and unless we decide to turn around, our exploration of the perceptual field behind us requires artificial, man-made devices (a rearview mirror, a TV camera, etc.). Action and active perception are always forward-oriented: our body sets out to "face" or "confront" the object, to "approach it," to "come close to it," and so on—briefly, to make the object "present" to us in the sense of making it accessible to our use and exploration. Drawing upon this understanding of our forward-oriented movement, we often speak, in specifically temporal terms, of putting this or that experience "behind us" or of still having this or that experience "ahead of us," and so on. Above all, our forward-directed movement underlies our notion of the *passage* of time. Thus, on the level of perception at least, both the static order of time and the dynamic flow of time as well are derived from the asymmetry between our body's backward and forward motions. Natural language itself can lead us to this phenomenological evidence.[21] In addition, since the passage of perceptual time has its

Introduction II

own arrow (its irreversible direction), the latter too is shown to be derived from our bodies' natural motion forward (117–119).

The horizontal field generated by our bodily self-movement is itself grounded in the vertical field of gravitation. While the horizontal field is centered around the active body of the percipient, the vertical field supplies the ultimate condition of the possibility of both the material percipient and the horizontal field itself. Once again, we are offered an analysis in which the purely natural, indeed the purely physical, predicament of our body (its subjection to gravitation) is disclosed in its phenomenological significance. As we have already pointed out, in deploying the horizontal field, our body—both active and needy, active *insofar as* needy—aims at positing the object as endowed with some measure of determinateness and uniformity. That the body succeeds, and enduringly so, in this fundamental venture is testified to by our sheer endurance as a material, inherently needy subject. But there would be no horizontal field at all if the objects the body deals with lacked the stability and the "weight" that they owe to the earth's gravitational field. "Objects thus appear to be encounterable and determinable only in virtue of our appearing to be *thrown* together with them ... in the vertical field of a common world" (123, my emphasis). Todes's "thrownness"—involving as it does the physical subjection to gravitation—goes far beyond the Heideggerian *Geworfenheit* (into moods, social practices, historicality, etc.) and beyond Merleau-Ponty's anchorage of the body in the midst of the perceptual field. At the same time, this purely physical component of "thrownness" as understood by Todes shows immediately its lived, phenomenologically accessible significance. Given our erect posture and our bipedality, we need to balance ourselves constantly within the vertical field. This is why Todes speaks of the priority of "balance" over "poise" (124). Our poise, we have already noted, is nothing other than our body's mastery of its skillful coping with the objects around us; our balance, in contrast, signifies our constantly maintained (and normally taken for granted) effort to preserve our upright posture within the gravitational field.

Having now pointed out the importance, in Todes's philosophy, of the natural features of our body, we must stress again that the body as so understood remains the *subject* of the world. Even our alignment to the gravitational field is our own achievement; and, of course, the entire horizontal field, albeit meant to secure the body's needs, is organized by the body's strictly interdependent activities of self-movement and perception. This means that the disclosure of the world is spontaneous, no less than receptive, and this in turn makes it imperative to bring out and analyze the original layer of perceptual *meaning* without which the spontaneity of our body would remain blind and inarticulate, if indeed it would still merit being viewed as spontaneity. The problem, and even the vocabulary, of "spontaneity" and "receptivity" are Kantian (Todes even speaks of Kant's need for, and failure to find, a perceptual "spontaneous receptivity"), and it is in his long and sustained discussion of Kant that Todes works out his own view on this crucial issue. Kant saw clearly the need for what he called "judgments of perception," different from, and prior to, the properly intellectual "judgments of experience." If, in the end, he was unable to account for the difference between these two types of judgment (most commentators are in complete agreement on this point), it is because, Todes argues, the author of the *Critique of Pure Reason* was oblivious to the body's deployment of a perceptual meaningful world. To be sure, Merleau-Ponty himself, and numerous of his followers, have raised the same objection against Kant. But Todes goes much farther in this direction. In response to Kant's unresolved dilemma, he not only points to the body's own spontaneity—prior to, and given as the precondition of, the "I think" of apperception, with its rule-like concepts, both empirical and pure—but he also goes on to offer a table of the specifically perceptual categories corresponding to the intellectual categories of Kant. The reader will find, in the book's fascinating final chapter, Todes's parallel treatment of Kant's *Transcendental Dialectic*. This part of his work, it is to be hoped, will be read with great interest not only by philosophers in general, but by Kant scholars as well.

Author's Introduction

This is a study in the natural philosophy of the human body. That is to say, it is a study of our body's role in our knowledge of *objects*. All issues in the social philosophy of the human body, all issues concerning our body's role in our knowledge of persons, are carefully avoided. These social issues are more obvious than the natural ones, and of more general interest, but their solution turns out to presuppose a solution to the natural issues, though the converse is not the case. Likewise avoided are all issues in what might be called the theology of the human body, that is, all issues concerning our body's role in our sense of death and our intimations of immortality. These theological issues turn out to presuppose solutions to the natural and social questions, though the converse is not the case.

The reader is thus forewarned that the analyses presented in this study are not of our normal experience in its full complexity. The point of view is sufficiently new that very little of the reader's familiar philosophic knowledge can be taken advantage of to help along and speed up the course of argument. It was therefore necessary, to keep the book to manageable proportions, to limit the scope of its topic—even to the point of leaving the discerning reader with many unanswered questions. Thus, for example, for the purposes of this study of the human body as the *material* subject of the world, our experience is simplified by disregarding our experience of other human beings. Analyzing our experience of circumstantial objects, I conclude that we experience all objects as circumstantially related to our active body in the midst of circumstances. Now at the same time I make the commonsense assumptions that I live in the same world with you, my reader; and that your body plays the same role, philosophically speaking, in your life as mine does in my life. I do this by writing of "our" active body, meaning that common function exercised by my body in my experience and by your body in your experience. The discerning reader will want to know: if, considered as alone in the world, our experience of objects is centered in our *own* body, how, when confronted by other persons, do we gain knowledge of them as, equally, centers of experience in their own right; and how do we know that our knowledge of objects agrees with theirs. Throughout this book I *assume* that this question is answerable, without *giving* the answer or claiming to do so. I hope to whet the reader's appetite for a sequel: The Human Body as the *Social* Subject of the World. From the very way I know circumstantial objects, it follows, I conclude, that I am the center of my material world. Yet I agree with common sense that I am not the center of my social world, but *share* my social world with others. It therefore follows on my view that the way I know *persons* differs from the way I know *objects*.

I cannot take up this difference in any detail, but the reader deserves, perhaps, at least an inkling of what it might be. The body does not, as commonly thought in the philosophic tradition, merely separate individuals from one another. It is, on the contrary, an indispensable condition of one person's sharing his experience with another. So the result that our knowledge of objects is body-centered does not turn out to make the problem of intersubjectivity more difficult; it turns out rather to open the way for a *solution* of this problem. *Traditional* epistemology is perennially plagued with the problem of avoiding solipsism, just as *traditional* epistemology regards our body merely as an object in the world and merely as something separating us from one another insofar as we are identified with it. But when reasonable doubt is cast on this traditional view of the body, the purportedly solipsistic implications of our body-centered sense experience are also called into question.

Pure spectators are isolated from one another and can regard each other solipsistically, as in a tourist cafe. But those who live and

Author's Introduction

work together, those who move and act in respect to one another, cannot regard each other solipsistically while co-operating in this way. Our circumstantial field of objects is, as I show, uni-directional because of the functional asymmetry of our forward-directed body. No apparent object is capable of altering this directedness of our perceptual field, because the very appearing of it is its way of *fitting into* this directed field: the localization and determination of an object is possible only in respect to our forward-directed body, and only through our forward-directed anticipation of and response to that object. But persons, unlike objects, are not merely encountered; they are *con-fronted*. My uni-directional field is evidently countered by another's uni-directional field; a pervasive change is thereby made in the structure of my whole field, not merely in one of its contents. I appear to *share* my experience with another, rather than to have it by myself alone, because the whole field of my experience, whose left-right, front-back order is body-generated, comes to have a character that I cannot give it by myself.

Our body also plays a fundamental role in our impersonal sense of social identification with "fellow-citizens" whom we may never have met. The analysis required to clarify this relation is too long to be hinted at here. But the irrepressible metaphor for society as the "*body* politic" (as in Plato, Aristotle, St. Thomas, Hobbes, Hegel, Spencer) bears some witness that the features of civil society may reflect those of our individual body.

As noted, this study simplifies our experience by disregarding the social, ethical, and religious experience characteristic of our daily lives. In the course of the study I will explain why even some functions of our knowledge of objects (e.g., the way we know them as inactive spectators of them) are not treated at length. The general explanation in all cases is the same: all possible restrictions on our topic have been imposed in order to keep this study down to manageable size while allowing it sufficient scope to express the general sense in which our body functions as a subject in all our knowledge of objects.

This, then, is a study of the role of our body in knowing objects. Its method is historical and phenomenological. I try to understand this function of our body by determining what classic philosophers have thought it to be, and by using phenomenological analyses to interpret and criticize their views. A certain problem proves helpful as a guideline for the general organization of the historical material. I call it the problem of the "unity of the world," and I try to show that its solution lies in understanding the role that the felt unity of our active body plays in our experience. But my goal is to understand our body's contribution to our knowledge of objects. The problem of "the unity of the world" is taken up only as a means to this end. It is nevertheless convenient, for expository purposes, to begin with a clarification of this problem.

We make a commonsense, intuitive, natural language distinction between the *world* and something *in* the world. We have a commonsense conviction, which we cannot easily surrender, that there is one and only one actual world, viz., this world we live in. Furthermore, everything seems related to this world; whatever we can think of (perceive, imagine, conceive, entertain in any way) seems to be in terms of a possibility of this world. In imagining a centaur, I need not imagine it as actually in the world, but it seems that I must be *able* so to imagine it, or I am not imagining anything. There seems to be at least a "possibility in principle" of there being a centaur. Likewise, in conceiving an abstract proposition, I need not conceive it as true of anything in the world, but it seems I must be *able* so to conceive it, or I am not conceiving anything—or else I am conceiving a self-contradiction as a limit of this world's possibilities. I may think of possibly creating or destroying, ruling or misruling, leaving, etc., this world. I can think of Nothing, but only, it seems, as the absence or disappearance of this world.

As a person of common sense, however, I am unable to demonstrate that there is one and only one world, and that everything I can think of is in terms of some possibility of this world. I have no arguments to support my convictions; my convictions are supported only by their natural strength in me. As a philosopher, I cannot rest satisfied with this state of affairs; I seek a justification of these convictions, unless I discover some reason why no justification is possible. Now by "the unity of the world" I mean the evidence demonstrating the truth of these commonsense convictions. To determine for given philosophers what represents the unity of the world in their philosophy, I ask: Assuming that this philosophy were true, what would be the evidence from which it would follow that there is one and only one actual world, and that everything we can think of is in terms of its possibilities? For some philosophers (e.g., Plato), this evidence is some knowable parameter *out of* the world (e.g., the realm of Forms) to which everything I can think of relates, and to which the one actual world (e.g., the Receptacle) also relates. For other philosophers (e.g., Leibniz), this evidence is some knowable parameter *of* the (one and only) actual world (e.g., its horizonality, or "sufficient reason," by which each thing in the world implies each other) to which everything I can think of (e.g., God, and possible worlds) relates.

I will take up an historical study of the philosophy of the human body in terms of the problem of the unity of the world. On the classic (Platonic-Aristotelian) view, the human subject is conceived as hovering between two positions: one of identification with his body in the world; and one of contemplative identification with the unity of the world (the realm of Forms, or the Prime Mover). On this view, the unity of the world is approachable by the human subject, but is not defined in terms of him. It is not dependent upon his existence for its "Being." Descartes's *cogito* is seen to imply that the unity of the world (in Descartes's case, God's mind, which creates it) *is* defined in terms of the human subject who is in turn defined in terms of his own mind. But Descartes retains the classic conception of the human body as merely an object in the world. He is thus forced to reject the classic view that identification of the human subject with his body is even possible. Whereas on the classic view the separation of the subject from his body is possible and partial, on Descartes's view it is necessary and total. But Descartes does not completely master his new insight that man is ineluctably a world-phenomenon. He counters his argument that the certainty of the *cogito* grounds the certainty of the existence of God by the argument that the latter certainty grounds the former. This vacillation in Descartes's position is seen to follow from his view that experience is representational of nonexperiential elements in the world. And it is seen to imply a vacillation between the views that man is identified with the unity of the world, and that man is a fragment of the world.

Leibniz and Hume are seen to carry Descartes's insight to its logical conclusion. They have a clear-cut conception that the unity of the world is defined in terms of the human subject. This consistency is achieved by rejecting Descartes's view that experience is representational of nonexperiential elements, and adopting instead the view that it is representational of other experiences. But this implies that nothing can come "into" our experience. The subject is therefore regarded as merely making explicit an antecedently existent world-unity. The subject *is* the unified activity of manifesting (not being) the unity of the world. This eliminates *any* role for the subject's identification with his body as object, for this identification implies that something can come "into" our experience. The very thoroughness of this elimination of our identification with our body as object opens the way for an implicit philosophic expression of our body as subject, viz., as *active*.

With the rigorous elimination of our identification with our body as object, only two views of our body are possible: (1) our body is pure subject, with which we are identified; (2) our body is pure object, with which we are in no way identified. Leibniz implicitly takes the first view, and Hume explicitly takes the second view. Our familiar situation is that of being in some sense identified with our active subject-body in the midst of circumstances whose givenness implies that our body is also an object. Leibniz's view distorts this familiar situation by, in effect, swelling our active subject-body to incorporate our circumstances. The familiar relation of "being in the midst of" is eliminated from experience. We are conceived to "have" experience, much as we in fact "have" our active body. Our body acts as a whole, and the articulation of this action *is* (not merely meets) the expression of our desire. Leibniz correspondingly holds that we are a windowless Monad, an isolated substance in Aristotle's organic sense. In his doctrine of *"petites perceptions"* he draws the necessary though incredible conclusions that *each* perception implies *all* perceptions, and that the succession of perceptions *is* our activity of appetition. Hume's view, on the other hand, distorts the familiar situation by, in effect, shrinking our active body down to the vanishing point of our visual point of view as a pure spectator with an inactive body. The familiar relation of "having an active body" is eliminated from experience. We are conceived to "have" our body much as we in fact "have" our experience. Our circumstances are comparatively ungovernable and undependable; our body, comparatively governable and dependable. Experience is the outcome of the influence of our dependable active body on our undependable given circumstances. Our experience is therefore likely, though not certain, to have some dependable order. Having rigorously eliminated the contribution of our active body, Hume draws the necessary though incredible conclusion that *no* perception implies *any* other perception; that there is no justification for believing that our experience is even likely to be ordered.

Kant attempts to synthesize these extreme views of Hume and Leibniz. He tries to understand *both* the Humean givenness of our experience *and* the Leibnizian spontaneity of it. In this attempt, he re-introduces the problem of how things come "into" our experience. But he does so in a new way. The problem is no longer how things *enter* into experience, but how they are transformed into experience. Kant thus implicitly tries to understand our situation in all its familiar but baffling complexity. We are somehow self-active in the midst of passively received circumstances. The whole problem is, How can we be autonomous in the midst of circumstances? It seems[1] comparatively easy to understand our autonomy if Leibniz is right that we have no circumstances; that we are "windowless." And it seems comparatively easy to understand our circumstantiality, if Hume is right that we are wholly passive in our experience. But how shall we understand both *together*—one through the other, as complementary functions in a single whole of experience? Does it not seem that our circumstantiality *defeats* our struggle for autonomy? Or, that we can be autonomous only *despite* our circumstances? Kant's answer is, in effect, "yes and no." There cannot be autonomy in the midst of circumstances, but autonomy *is* the overcoming of circumstantiality. Kant at least recognizes the problem as one of understanding autonomy in terms of circumstantiality, and in this he surpasses his predecessors. But like his predecessors, he continues to regard the existence of autonomy as incompatible with the existence of circumstantiality. In his first Critique, he tries to show how, ideally, circumstantiality can be overcome, and autonomy achieved, by *assimilating* our circumstances to our spontaneous self. Our activity of understanding is directed toward overcoming the receptivity of perception by approaching an ideal in which reason legislates its own object. Kant thus agrees with Leibniz about the nature of complete knowledge; he disagrees only in seeing what a radical transformation of sense experience is required to achieve it. In his second Critique, Kant tries to show how, ideally, circumstantiality can be overcome and autonomy achieved by *separating* our self from our circumstances. As understanding seeks, ideally, to assimilate sensibility by legislating its own object, so our will seeks, ideally, to disengage itself from inclination and to approach the condition of being a "holy will." Thus Kant holds in the first two Critiques that man seeks to gain autonomy by overcoming his circumstantiality: by assimilating it through understanding; and by disengaging himself from it through moral action. In the third Critique, however, Kant reverses direction. Autonomy continues to be interpreted as the overcoming of the circumstantiality that implies a discrepancy between man and his circumstances. However, in the first two Critiques this meant *man's* overcoming his circumstantiality. But now in the third Critique it means *Nature* gaining autonomy by becoming harmonious with man. It is no accident that this Critique led to the idealism of Fichte, Schelling, and Hegel.

Modern existentialism begins with a rejection of Hegel by Kierkegaard and Nietzsche. It is most significantly carried forward by Heidegger and Merleau-Ponty, as aided by the work of Husserl. All these philosophers see that it does not make sense to speak of "overcoming" circumstantiality. They do not transform our familiar everyday problem of how to be autonomous *in the midst of circumstances* into the purely imaginative problem of how to gain an ideal autonomy by *overcoming* this condition.

The fundamental aspect of this problem is to understand a *local* situation in the world, as distinct from the *universal* condition of the world's total content. It is the primary thesis of this study that a local situation is understandable only in terms of the *felt unity of our active body* in these circumstances. I will demonstrate this by a series of phenomenological analyses, which are at first loosely organized around historical material but later systematized in their own right. These analyses are finally brought to a head in a *deduction of perceptual categories*. In the course of this deduction, I will work out the *form of a perceptual judgment* by which local knowledge is expressed. In addition, I will outline the general relation between local and universal judgments. This is done on the basis of a comparative phenomenology of perception and imagination. For while local judgment is perceptual, universal judgment is the work of our theoretical imagination.

1
The Classic View of the Way the Human Subject Has His Body, and Descartes's Rejection of It

1.1 The Classic View

According to Plato and Aristotle, the unity of the human subject ("soul") is complete only insofar as he comes to know (contemplate) the source of this world's order—for Plato, the realm of Ideas; and for Aristotle, pure thought thinking itself. They believed that one becomes, in respect to form, what one knows. Thus Plato and Aristotle held that the human subject is unified only insofar as he becomes identified with the ordering unity of the world. But they also believed that the human subject might not—and indeed, except for the rare exception of the true philosopher, does not—achieve very much of this unity. It is further questionable whether they even thought the true philosopher could achieve this unity perfectly, and it seems they thought that, while alive, he could not. For common men with distinctly lesser capacities, the difficulties were thought correspondingly greater. Nevertheless, they held that, despite the general failure of men to gain access to it, the perfectly unified source of the order of the world remains in being, is indeed "Being itself." Thus, for Plato and Aristotle, the unity of the world can be shared by the human subject insofar as he achieves perfection. But it rarely, if ever, is fully shared, so that, though access to the world's unity is the goal of the human subject, as it is of everything in the world, this unity is not *defined* in terms of the human subject, much less considered to derive its existence (or, more precisely, its being) from the human subject.

The Classic View and Descartes's Rejection of It

The actual living human subject is merely something (for Aristotle, a "substance") *in* the world, with the rare and seldom realized capacity to identify himself somewhat imperfectly, through contemplation or *dianoia*, with the world's unity. And this identification, such as it is, is accomplished only by the human subject forsaking his bodily involvement as someone in the world. Thus, for my purposes, the view of Plato and Aristotle, the "classic view," is that the human subject begins, by virtue of his body, as something in the world, as one thing in the midst of others; and that, by virtue of his mind, he has the capacity to raise himself from this status to the status of being identified with the unity of the world itself. But insofar as a man achieves the higher status, he forsakes the lower.

For Plato especially, these two states are in opposition. It is one part, his body, that draws the human subject toward the lower state; and another part, his mind, that draws him (i.e., his soul) toward the upper state, requiring him in general to subdue rather than meet the claims of his body. Plato expounds this view at length, in its most simplified form, in the *Phaedo*; and more cursorily, in the same form, in the *Apology*. It is, in addition, implicit in the *Timaeus*. He gives the view more subtle form in the *Republic*, where he attempts to understand the transition of the human soul from one to the other of its two extreme states, depicted in the *Phaedo* as so sharply separated. A momentary exception to this general view occurs in the *Symposium*, where Diotima, speaking as the voice of inspired truth, tells Socrates that "love is not for the beautiful, as you think.... It is for begetting and birth in the beautiful," and yet, as she later says, "love is for immortality also." Insofar, thus, as Plato believes that the act of begetting the beautiful achieves immortality, he has a notion of how "mortality partakes of immortality, both *in body* [my italics] and in all other respects." But this line of thought is soon dropped in favor of Plato's dominant theme, which is expressed in Diotima's "higher revelation" of "the ladder of love," as it has come to be called in Platonic literature. This "higher revelation" teaches us that,

Whoever shall be guided so far towards the mysteries of love, by *contemplating* [my italics] beautiful things rightly in due order, approaches the last grade where he will suddenly behold a beauty marvelous in its nature, that very Beauty, for the sake of which all the earlier hardships had been borne.... This beauty will not show itself to him like a face or hands or any bodily thing *at all* [my italics] ... but it is by itself with itself always in simplicity.... All the beautiful things elsewhere partake of this beauty in such manner, that when *they* are born and perish *it* [Plato's italics] becomes neither less nor more, and nothing at all happens to it.

In comparison to Plato, Aristotle believes there is less conflict between the demands raised by a man's mind and those raised by his body. Aristotle, unlike Plato, emphasizes a moderate norm of rational life, in which mind and body are mutually adjusted, neither being wholly subjected to the other. But Aristotle's greater acceptance of the importance, for a proper, rational human life, of meeting the claims of the body merely signals his greater acceptance than Plato of the imperfectibility of man, as contrasted, for example, with the perfection of the heavenly bodies. The latter, possessing a higher (more intelligible) grade of matter in their bodies than man, are, accordingly, conceived by Aristotle to have a more perfect norm of "life" or existence. Thus, for Aristotle as for Plato, insofar as the human body (human matter) plays a role in man's life, man is merely one substance among others in the world. Only insofar as some other element (the human intellect, human form) plays a role in his life does man have a measure of access to the ordering unity of the world. This access is in the form of identity. And the measure of identity with the unity of the world achieved by the nonbody element of the human subject is construed by both philosophers as a measure of release from being in the midst of things in the world, in favor of a state of pure thought beyond the world. For Aristotle, this identity with the unity of the world can be achieved only in a more partial and indirect way than for Plato. It is possible only through participation in the mediating active intellect;[1] and through "knowledge" of the merely analogical categories, and of what the Scholastics called "the Transcendentals," such as Being, Unity, Truth, Goodness, Thing, Other. Indirect and partial though it may be, the greatest happiness and the greatest good for man is nevertheless realized, according to Aristotle, in the contemplative life.[2] In this form of life, man is most nearly released from being in the midst of things, and most nearly identified with pure thought thinking itself *beyond* the *primum mobile*.

1.2 Descartes's Rejection of the Classic View

1.2.1 The discovery of human necessity, and its first consequences for the philosophy of the body

The first effective philosophic challenge to this classic view came with the work of Descartes. By the argument of the *cogito* the necessary (indubitable) existence of the human subject was demonstrated by showing that even the human attempt to dispense conceptually with this existence presupposes it. Descartes here introduced into philosophy, albeit merely on the conceptual level, a notion of *human necessity*—a notion colloquially familiar in reference to human life in all its aspects, as expressed by the phrase "the necessities of life." What is "necessary" in this sense is that which the human subject is unable to dispense with, try as he may, because he needs it even to undertake the act of dispensing with anything.

The primary consequence of this philosophic discovery of human necessity was that philosophy ceased to regard the human subject as a thing or substance *in* the world, and began instead to define the human subject in terms of the *world* in which things are. In the philosophy of Descartes himself, these consequences were only partially drawn; they were fully worked out only a century and a half later, by Kant. On the classic view, the human subject had been regarded as moored in the world by his body. As a direct consequence of the *cogito* argument in which he discovered the conceptual form of human necessity, Descartes cut this mooring. His reason, in effect, though he did not understand it this way, was that he had discovered no bodily form of it. Descartes's method had been to discover that about the human subject which is required by the very attempt to reject it, and is thus invulnerable to the subject's attempt to dispense with it intellectually. In short, Descartes sought to discover the human subject's indispensable beliefs.[3] Descartes discovered that what immediately resists a purely intellectual rejection is only the belief in the existence of one's own intellect—a point implicitly repeated in Leibniz's later criticism of Locke, "*Nihil est in intellectu . . . nisi ipse intellectus.*"[4] Descartes never thought of broadening his method in order to discover *all* that the human subject can not dispense with because he has to use it in order to dispense with anything. Instead, he concluded that whatever could be dispensed with in a purely intellectual way was not philosophically necessary to the human subject, that it was not "of the essence" of the human subject.[5] Thus, as the first result of his discovery of human necessity, he came to define the human subject solely as a "thinking substance."

> I concluded that I was a substance whose whole essence or nature was only to think, and which, to exist, has no need of space nor of any material thing. Thus it follows that this ego, this soul, by which I am what I am, is entirely distinct from the body and easier to know than the latter, and that even if the body were not, the soul would not cease to be all that it now is.

True, Descartes elsewhere tries to modify the implausible extremism of this utter separation of mind and body, as in the *Meditations* (p. 64), where he writes, "I do not only reside in my body, as a pilot in his ship, but am intimately connected with it, and the mixture is so blended that something like a single whole is produced." But though Descartes sometimes insists, without satisfactory explication, that the human mind and body are "intimately" connected and "like" a single whole, he never gives up his fundamental position, which was the influential one in the history of philosophy: in "essence," mind and body are entirely distinct, so that one could exist without the other.

1.2.2 The ambiguity of Descartes's version of the human subject

Descartes's version of the human subject as a thinking substance leaves man hovering somewhat ambiguously between the world and things in the world. On the classic view, too, man hovers between these extremes, but in a different way. On the classic view, man hovers clearly between these extremes; he always has some definite position, and his "hovering" connotes merely that he can change his position, falling lower into association with material things in the world or ascending toward participation in the unity of the world itself ("Being as such"). But for Descartes, man's position as a thinking substance somewhere between things (elements of the one, infinite "extended substance") and the world's ordering unity (represented in Descartes's philosophy by God) is not so much variable as indeterminate.

The thinking subject, in existing outside of space and only in time, is conceived by Descartes to be outside the world; existing in time alone is not, for Descartes, existing in the world:

> I could imagine that I had no body, and that there was no world nor any place that I occupied, but I could not imagine for a moment that I did not exist.[6]

For the human subject to be in the world, the human body must be essential to him. But still, though Descartes raises the human subject from his classic status as placed (by his body) in the world, he does not quite raise him to the only definite alternate status of identification with the ordering unity of the world itself. Descartes seems confused about the relation between God and a thinking substance.

In some ways, Descartes treats the human subject in a manner that scholastic philosophy had reserved for God. In general, of course, Descartes replaces the Scholastics' central concern with God by a central concern with man. He concentrates on how *man* knows, on the proper "method" for human inquiry, whereas the Scholastics had concentrated on how *God* orders the world. But more specifically, Descartes's philosophy is built upon the argument of the *cogito*, which, in form, parallels the traditional ontological argument for the existence of God. In both cases, the necessary existence of the subject is held to be demonstrable from the mere conception of it; in both cases, the actuality of the subject is held to follow necessarily from its mere possibility, so that the *cogito* might well be called "the ontological argument for the existence of the human subject." As we will later see in discussing Kant, a new yet recognizable form of this argument is important in the work that at once consolidates the Cartesian venture and makes a fundamental point of refuting the ontological argument in its old form. This is additional evidence that the parallel is not fortuitous or merely verbal, but instead reflects the basic thinking of these philosophers.

In general, however, Descartes vacillates between identifying the human subject with the ordering unity of the world and giving him a lower status as what is perhaps best called "a fragment of the world," a status still above that of something merely in the world. This vacillation is rooted in Descartes's doctrine that the human subject does not experience things in the world but only (sensory) appearances or (conceptual) representations of these things. If things in the world are, however implicitly, *completely* represented (by appearances or representations) in the mind of the "thinking substance," then this substance (the human subject) is equivalent to the world in which things are. And if the representations in the mind follow from the very nature of the mental substance, as they do for Descartes insofar as he regards the representation as complete, then this mental substance is equivalent to the ordering unity of the world. On the other hand, if things in the world are *incompletely* represented in the thinking substance, then this substance is equivalent to a mere fragment of the world; it is neither the world nor something in it, but merely a fragmentary representation of it. On this view, we have fragmentary data from an original that we cannot directly experience, investigate, and know. However consistent a picture we make of our fragments, we can never be *sure* that the coherence is not simply a fortuitous condensation of representations of logically scattered fragments of things in the world; we can never be sure that this condensation is more than momentarily possible, and that it is not soon to be disrupted by new data from things in the world logically intermediate between the fragments already represented. As at a roulette table, if the winning numbers are successively, 1, 2, 3, . . . , 200, there is still no reason to believe the next number will be 201 (provided we know that the machine is not rigged), so, from the regularity of our impressions to date, we have no *reason*, if things in the world are incompletely represented in our mind, to believe that the next impression received will conform to the antecedently established pattern.

    For Descartes, since all events in the world are rational effects of its first principles, and since man is always capable, if sufficiently careful, of indubitably correct inference from indubitably correct premises, it follows that, if man can have absolutely certain knowledge of the first principles of the world, there is in theory no upper limit short of completion to the possible extent of his knowledge of the world; there is no assignable limit of truths about the world beyond which he cannot in principle extend his knowledge. And conversely, since the "knowledge of causes from effects" can never be certain beyond doubt, it follows that, if these first principles are not accessible to man in his representations, there is in theory no lower limit above absolute ignorance to the possible extent of his knowledge of the world; there is no assignable minimum of truths about the world that he can be certain of possessing. Nor can we, using the term in Descartes's sense, hold that we "know" at least certain effects even though we do not know the causes from which they follow. For Descartes, "knowledge," being indubitable, must consist either of a self-evident principle or of a deductive inference from such a principle proceeding either directly to the given effects or indirectly, by an unbroken series of deductive inferences, to effects that can be understood as causes of the given effects. We could never prove to Descartes's satisfaction that simple data (representations merely of effects, but not of their causes) do not offer us illusory representations of the world of things.

Thus on Descartes's view, the extent to which the world of things is represented in the world of appearances, whether the world of appearances is an indefinitely complete or an indefinitely incomplete representation of the world of things, and accordingly, whether the human subject is equivalent to the ordering unity of the world or only to a fragment of the world, depends upon whether or not a perfect representation of the self-evident first principles about matters of fact in the world is possible for the finite thinking substance.

Descartes's answer to this crucial question is vacillating and confusing. In general, Descartes claims certainty but offers only uncertainty. He claims to be in possession of first principles from which all matters of fact about the world are in principle deducible—though the *de facto* capacity of man's finite mind to complete the deduction is in question. But there is a marked discrepancy between the philosophical ideal of certainly that he claims to have achieved and the scientific practice (scientific results) by which he claims to demonstrate that achievement. The scientific first principles that Descartes used in the treatises on optics, geometry, and meteors, to which the *Discourse* serves as an introduction, are explicitly given as only "hypotheses" justified by their explanation of observed "effects."[7] Descartes merely claims, but does not show, that these hypotheses are deducible from self-evident first principles, such as the *cogito*. Furthermore, Descartes's claims for the knowability of matters of fact on the basis of self-evident first principles rest upon the applicability of his four "rules of method" to our information about the world. He begins auspiciously with the statement that "I made a firm and unalterable *resolution* [my italics] not to violate them even in a single instance."[8] However, when he actually comes to "some questions of physics" and "the study of nature," he blandly admits that, descending to the consideration of particulars, he believes it "impossible for the human mind to distinguish the forms of species of objects found on earth from an *infinity* [my italics] of others which might have been there if God had so willed."[9] But, granted this "infinity," how can one possibly apply Descartes's fourth rule in accordance with his "unalterable resolution . . . to make enumerations so complete, and reviews so general, that I would be certain that nothing was omitted?"[10] Descartes's will (resolution) to judge seems here to outreach his capacity to understand, a condition that he elsewhere calls the source of error.

One might argue that these discrepancies between Descartes's claims and his demonstrations are only secondary. One might agree with Descartes's claim that he could have deduced his "hypotheses" from self-evident first principles, but merely chose not to do so in his published work; or that, however difficult to achieve, Descartes had at least outlined the correct *ideal* for knowledge. One might argue that the applicability of Descartes's method to general truths (e.g., about "skies, stars, an earth, and even, on the earth, water, air, fire, minerals"[11]) is sufficiently impressive, even though their applicability to "particulars" (objects on the earth) is questionable. Or one might attempt to save the applicability of the rule of complete enumeration to particulars, by weakening it so as to admit what Kant calls "limiting" predicates, such as "nonmortal." But this does not seem to be what Descartes intended.

The ambiguity of Descartes's version of the human subject, and the argument of the cogito

Descartes vacillates in a more crucial place between holding that the human subject is and is not in complete possession of a representation of the first principles from which, by God's will, the world of things is generated. Descartes vacillates not merely by exhibiting a discrepancy between the kind of investigation of matters of fact he claims is possible and the kind he actually reports.

The Classic View and Descartes's Rejection of It

He also vacillates within his argument about the relation between the human subject and God, before he even broaches the question of man's knowledge of matters of fact, i.e., man's knowledge about things in the world, man's knowledge of extended substance. After having, to his satisfaction, demolished traditional belief, Descartes begins the reconstruction of philosophy by judging that he can "safely accept (the *cogito*) as the first principle"[12] of the philosophy he is seeking. From the *cogito* he derives the validity of the rule that clarity and distinctness are the criteria of truth, on the ground that he "sees" that the indubitability of the *cogito* is marked by these properties. From the *cogito* and these criteria, with the aid of the "evident" principle of "good sense" that nothing more perfect follows from something less perfect, he derives the existence of God.[13] Thus the initial thrust of Descartes's argument is to derive the existence of God from the existence of the human subject.

Descartes's attempt all along is to gain *knowledge*, in the strict sense, of matters of fact in the (extended) world. Granted Descartes's representational view of experience, he cannot derive any knowledge of the world of things merely from knowledge of the self and the contents of its consciousness. He first has to demonstrate the accuracy of experiential representation, by finding a bridge between its first principles and the first principles generating matters of fact in the world. These first principles must be self-evident principles of the purely rational intellect so that the finite thinking substance can share them, but they must also be endowed with the ability to create and order all things in the world. These self-evident principles, considered as endowed with the free capacity to create and order things down to the last detail, are what Descartes mainly means by "God"; God is for Descartes mainly the free rational architect of the world, the rational intellect that freely creates the world from one moment to the next. Thus, in deriving the existence of God from the existence of the human subject, Descartes proves that the ordering first principles of the world are accessible to man, so that man's representational world is indefinitely completable in correspondence to the world of things. It is in the spirit of this view that Descartes is sometimes so optimistic as to suggest that he can actually bring his (purportedly) deductive investigations of the world to substantial completion. Thus he writes, "two or three further victories of equal importance would enable me to reach my goal."[14] Only on the basis of this view, furthermore, can Descartes even speak of the indefinite increase of our knowledge of the world.[15]

But Descartes here proves too much to keep man's world merely representational! By this proof, as we have seen, the human subject becomes equivalent to the creatively ordering unity of the world of things, because he becomes capable of generating a world of representations that corresponds to the world of things completely, or with indefinitely great completeness. But since knowledge of the unity of the world of things (God) has been *derived from* knowledge of the human subject, the human subject threatens to become not merely the originator of a corresponding world, but of the world of fact as well, so that the original is threatened with assimilation to its representation. This is so because of Descartes's "failure"[16] to distinguish between a reason and a cause. On Descartes's view, the logical and the causal sequence of things is the same, so that a proposition "p" implying a proposition "q" is, if true, about an event "e_p," which causes an event "e_q." Thus, if the existence of God is rationally implied by the existence of the human subject, it would seem to be also brought about or caused by the human subject, and, mediately, the world itself would be the product of the human subject.

Descartes cannot accept this, perhaps because he is convinced that "nothing more perfect can come from something less perfect," perhaps because of prudent regard for the power of the Church and a consequent unwillingness to publish his innermost thoughts,[17] or perhaps because his analysis of perceptual illusion and mistaken judgment has convinced him that experience is representational of a world that man might not know, and that he therefore cannot have originated. In any case, Descartes's representational view of human experience is incompatible with this originative view according to which the human subject would have occupied roughly the position of Spinoza's God.

Whatever his reasons, Descartes does not accept this originative view. Having derived knowledge of the existence of God from knowledge of the existence of the human subject and from the derivative criterion of truth, Descartes then writes that the criterion of truth is itself valid, and that all clearly and distinctly conceivable propositions, such as the *cogito*, are known to be true only because we know that they come to us from God.[18] This makes the knowledge, and therewith the existence, of the human subject derivative from that of God. It makes man a *passive* creature of God, receptive to His works in the world. In deriving the existence of man from the existence of God, Descartes, taken strictly, proves that the creative first principles of the world are inaccessible to man. For man is only one of their effects, and "knows" at best only himself. Yet from effects causes can never be judged with certainty. This position fits well with Descartes's views of perception as receptive, fragmentary, and fallible. It accounts well, moreover, for his emphasis on the usefulness of experiments, and for the position he sometimes takes that there are certain things that we cannot know except by experiment. For this position is that man is essentially passive, receiving his existence and all his representations from God, as an effect of God.[19]

This conclusion poses insuperable difficulties for Descartes's theory of knowledge. If man is not in possession of the very first principles of knowledge, then he cannot really know anything. The truth of man's beliefs is now radically in doubt, and man's representational fragment of a world may be indefinitely incomplete in its correspondence to the world of fact. And among all the propositions conceivable by man that are thus thrown in doubt is, of course, the very proposition Descartes has sought to sustain by this reversal, namely, "that all reality and truth within us come from a perfect and infinite Being," for this was proven only by regarding the *cogito* as independently certain. Hence, just as the derivation of the existence of God from that of man proved too much to keep man's world merely representational, the derivation of the existence of man from that of God proves too little to keep man's world faithfully representational. Since we cannot be certain of God's existence, being unable to argue validly from our representations as effects to Him as their cause, we cannot be certain that there is any material world at all of which the contents of the human mind are representations.

1.2.3 Summary of Descartes's view

By separating the human subject from his body, Descartes raises man from his classic status as being placed, by virtue of his body, *in* the world; but he does not quite raise man to the only definite alternate status envisaged by the classic tradition, viz., identification with the ordering unity of the world itself. Instead, Descartes is ambiguous and vacillating on this point. Sometimes he treats the human subject as equivalent to the ordering unity of the world, analyzing him primarily as an active deductive intellect capable of indubitable and unlimited knowledge of matters of fact. But sometimes he treats the human subject as merely a fragment of the world, analyzing him primarily as a passive perceiver capable of being deluded without limit about matters of fact. The uneasy balance, or better, imbalance, between these two sides of Descartes's thought is maintained by his view that the human subject does not experience things in the world but only representations corresponding variably to them. The inconsistency between these two sides of Descartes's thought comes to a head in the contradiction between Descartes's derivation of God's existence from that of the human subject, which assures the validity of our representations but threatens to make them legislative of the world; and his derivation of the existence of the human subject from that of God, which assures the representational character of our representations but threatens to deprive them of any validity as representing another world of fact. Insofar as our representations are shown to be valid, they do not seem to be merely representations, but rather to determine the nature of God. They seem, at least, to be the same as those of God, who is considered to create the world with a will of the same kind as our own;[20] it becomes in any case exceedingly difficult to distinguish the "object of the geometricians"[21] from extended substance itself. And on the other hand, insofar as our representations are shown to be merely representations, there does not seem to be any justification for holding them to be valid of the world of fact that they are supposed to represent; there does not seem to be any way of being sure from them that they are representations of anything else. In the former case, the implication of the world of fact by our experience is too strict to be representational; in the latter case, it is too loose to be so.

2

Critique of the Resulting World-Subject of Leibniz and Hume, with an Introductory Exposition of the Thesis That the Human Body Is the Material Subject of the World

2.1 The Mitosis of Cartesian Philosophy

The two sides of Descartes's thought, held in such uneasy imbalance in his philosophy, split apart in the century following their publication. The two divergent streams of thought that had their common source in the troubled headwaters of Descartes's mind were, of course, Continental Rationalism and British Empiricism, which reached their pure and limiting forms in the philosophies of Leibniz and Hume. In the course of this mitosis and purification of Descartes's thought, his two notions of the general nature of human experience were separately developed into two philosophies that contradicted each other on that score. According to Leibniz, human experience is active and spontaneous, perceptually as well as conceptually, and each representation fully implies all other representations. According to Hume, human experience is passive and occasioned, perceptually as well as conceptually, and no representation implies any other.[1]

2.2 A New Consensus: The Human Subject as Explicating the Unity of the World

In the course of this mitosis and purification of his thought, Descartes's vacillation, between regarding the human subject as a fragment of the world and regarding him as the ordering unity of the world, was resolved by convergence upon a new view of how the human subject is a function of the world as a whole. This final consensus did not represent complete agreement with Descartes's view, insofar as he held it, that the human subject is equivalent to the *ordering* unity of the world, that is, to the unity that first gives order to the world. The function of the world that Leibniz and Hume attributed to man was that of *explicating* the unity of the world. The human subject was identified as the agent making explicit an order that he merely discovers as already in his world of experience as soon as he has this world. Leibniz implies this when he writes that "a Monad can only come into being . . . all at once."[2] And Hume expresses this view when he writes that "memory does not so much *produce* as *discover* personal identity" (Hume's emphasis).[3] For Hume, the unity of the world is the regularity of impressions in our mind, which also produces whatever personal identity there may be, but the mind (the human subject) merely discovers rather than creates this order in itself. There may thus be a unity of the mind (regularity of its impressions) that the mind does not know, of which it happens to have no "idea." For Hume the mind does not give its impressions their order, but is simply capable, with the aid of language, of noticing this order. And for Leibniz all possible order in human experience is already fully implicit in the initial perceptual field that is created not by the human subject but by God, and that the human subject already inhabits as soon as he exists. Thus for Hume as for Leibniz the order of the world is identical with the order or unity of the self, but this order is merely possessed rather than produced by the self, although it may be, but is not always, actively known by the self.

For these philosophers not only is the human subject less than the ordering unity of the world, but there is no such unity, in the strict sense, as had been claimed in the classic philosophies and by Descartes. For Hume there is *no* "source" of the order in the world; there simply is such an order, to some extent. For Leibniz there is a unified order in the world, but its source is *divided* between the logical truths and the logical compossibilities, which God simply knows but did not himself create,[4] on the one hand, and, on the other hand, God's moral will, which, operating in accordance with the principle of sufficient reason, creates this as the best world logically possible. Neither of these philosophers could agree with Descartes, writing in a letter to Père Mersenne, "in God, willing and knowing are one," or in holding elsewhere that God is perfectly free to make it untrue that the three angles of a triangle equal two right angles.

For Plato and Aristotle, the source of the order in the world has no will or desire to give that order to the world; it is self-sufficient and indifferent to the world; it is strictly impersonal. The world has to look out for itself, and it achieves whatever measure of order it does only by looking up to the perfect order in emulative desire or in the vicarious participation of contemplation. Descartes, being "Christian," could no longer take this view, but he still agrees with the classic philosophers that the source of possible order in the world orders matter in the world merely by *being* that source of possible order, and not by doing anything *in addition* so as to actualize this possibility. Descartes goes beyond the classic philosophers only in holding that being a source of possible order in the world means (necessarily) giving that order to the world. Leibniz, however, being more "Christian," preserves the distinction between what God did by granting order to the world, and what He could have done, as perfectly free, by not granting any existence at all to the world, or by granting it a less orderly one; that is, one in which there was less multiplicity in its unity. In this way the personality, specifically the benevolence, of God is stressed whereas on Descartes's view God seems devoid of personality, that is, mainly, of feelings.

That God, one of two ordering poles of the world, has more personality on Leibniz's view than on Descartes's implies Leibniz's reduction of the power of man to that of merely making explicit the unity of the world that God has already produced. Since God's creation is "all at once,"[5] it follows both that the human subject, as a rational Monad, merely exfoliates the unity of the world; and that God's creation of the universe of Monads is a decision, an act of will, distinguishable from His eternal nature, which endures (logically) "after"[6] this creation. Thus Leibniz's God *is presented with* what He has done in creating the universe of Monads, just as He is presented with a variety of logical possibilities before making His decision. Therefore motivation may be attributed to Him. On Descartes's view, however, God has nothing presented to Him; He *is* all He knows and does. God's creation of the world—which is not a *fait accompli* but must be re-accomplished from instant to instant so that even all evidence of the "past" could be eradicated—and His knowledge of this world, *are* simply His *pure willing*, which is *Himself*. He is an *actus purus*. As Aristotle's Being is pure thought thinking itself, so Descartes's God is pure act willing itself. To have personality is to have feelings; to have feelings is to have motivations; to have motivation requires that one come up against something that is presented to him but that he might not want. Thus Descartes's God has no personality.

On Hume's view, as noted, there is no source beyond the world of the order in the world. The main implication this has for Hume is that man ought in all he does to follow the dictates of his feelings, so that his "follies shall at least be natural and agreeable."[7] Thus we see that for Hume as well as for Leibniz, one result of lowering man's power to that of merely explicating the world's unity is to change the conception of the kind of world man lives in, increasing the importance of feeling in its constitution. We will soon see the explanation for this: feeling is a function of the way the human subject "has" his body; and both Hume and Leibniz were forced, in order to purify a side of Descartes's philosophy, to give a better analysis than had yet been given of the way in which the human subject "has" his body. Therefore the importance of *feeling* in the world of experience began—however indirectly—to appear.

On the classic view man has the alternative of being identified either with his body as one material thing among others in the world, or with the unity of the world. Descartes dropped identification with the body as impossible, and vacillated between the old alternative of identifying man with the unity of the world and a new, compromise alternative of identifying him with a fragment of the world. Now in the preliminary, pre-Kantian working out of the Cartesian tradition, a fourth, but this time definite alternation is worked out: the human subject is understood as the unity of explication of the unity of the world.

Why did this consensus on the interpretation of man emerge among the progeny of Cartesian philosophy who were in so many other ways diametrically opposed? This consensus is particularly striking in that it is an agreement on something that Descartes himself did not merely fail to hold, but that his philosophy did not even visualize as possible. For insofar as man is passively receptive in sensation, he lacks the resources to make his experience fully explicit; and insofar as he is deductively active in thought, he does not merely make explicit a pre-existent order but himself creates or re-creates that order after the manner of God.

2.3 The Change in the Sense of the "Representational" Character of Experience

Descartes's double view of man as passively receptive in sensation and actively creative (or re-creative) in conception is held together, however inconsistently, by his representational view of experience as an informative "effect" of a nonexperiential world that can be determined by conception. This view is untenable because Descartes has no way of showing how representations come "into" the mind. On his account, elements are either completely in or completely out of the mind. Sensations are representations completely in the mind; conceptions are representations completely in the mind although not clearly distinguishable from corresponding ones in God's mind, which are in turn difficult to distinguish from the external elements of actual extended space,[8] though Descartes seems to have intended such a distinction.

Descartes has this difficulty in an acute form because he has so sharply divorced the human subject from the human body. Normally the human body is regarded as somehow responsible for introducing representations "into" experience. But on Descartes's view, the human body is clearly outside of the world of experience. It is clearly extended in exactly the sense in which rocks and mountains are extended; it is of the same "essence," and obeys the same laws as they. Despite Descartes's occasional protestations that the "intimate union" of body and mind is responsible for the entrance of representations into the mind, his philosophy does not leave open the possibility of explaining such intimacy, and it was so interpreted by his influential followers.

Since they could not understand how something could possibly come "into" experience, they drew the logical consequence of ceasing to regard representations as having come into the world of experience from outside in the first place. They no longer sought from representation the capacity to know and deal with what was not true of and apparent in our own world of human experience. The result was a change in the view of the way in which experience is "representational." Descartes's followers ceased to hold that experience is representational as an informative effect of, or reference to, a nonexperiential world. They ceased to hold that experiences represent *nonexperiential* elements. Instead, they adopted the view that experiences represent *other experiences*. For Leibniz the representations in the interior horizon of a rational (human) "windowless"[9] Monad represent other Monads only *indirectly* by implicitly representing their *own* complete explicitation, that is, their state as made perfectly clear and distinct, as wholly conceptualized. This is the state they would be in if wholly perfected in the "realm of grace," the realm of "final causes." In this state, their order would be equivalent to the order of the material world of extended Monadical point-forces. The conceivable material world represented by perception is thus for Lebniz not nonexperiential, as for Descartes, but rather the ideal (though unattainable because nonperspectival) fruition of our experience. Men's "minds are also images of the Deity or Author of nature Himself."[10] Our representations are thus fuller than those of simple Monads, since we know something of other Monads. But this does not imply, as for Descartes, that we know something outside our world of experience. It implies only that we know the "final cause" of our world of experience, a cause that is completely implicit in our experience, and for which our experience exists. That Hume too rejects a nonexperiential world is clear. The notion of things in themselves that "give rise" to our impressions, a Lockean "something, I know not what," is for Hume an empty notion. He writes,

It is impossible for us so much as to conceive or form an idea of anything specifically different from ideas and impressions.[11]

Representations, he holds, simply represent for us certain other representations which, by force of habit, we cannot help associating with them.

Thus both Hume and Leibniz gave up the idea of something coming "into" experience from outside because, with Descartes's severing of man's definitive connection with his body, it had become impossible to understand how something could come "into" experience. Hume, then, developing the empirical side of Descartes, develops a notion of experience in which the human subject is passive, but without being receptive of anything coming "from without." And Leibniz, developing the rationalist side of Descartes, develops a notion of experience in which the human subject is active and spontaneous, but without being creative by introducing something "into" the world of experience. For Hume, as for Leibniz, the world of experience has no permeable outside. The human subject, being defined in terms of the world of experience, but not in terms of its making, thus merely "has" the world of experience with whatever degree of interconnection there may *already* be among the things in it. For this reason, his only additional role is to discover that interconnecting: not to make it, but only to make it explicit.

Only with Kant, in the subjective deduction of the categories, was the problem first broached of how objects of experience come into the world of experience, and even there, as we will see, it was not broached radically enough. For Kant only asked how sense experience was objectified. In Kantian terms, Kant posed the question of how the transition from "inner sense" to "outer sense" was made, but he never posed the question of how the matter of sensibility first came into inner sense. Of course, this was not merely an oversight on Kant's part, but stemmed from the fact that he had no way of posing the question meaningfully. It does not follow that the question cannot be posed in a meaningful way. I believe, as will be shown later, that this question can be meaningfully posed in terms of a correct analysis of the way in which a human subject "has" an active body. However, the need for such analysis was implicit in Kant because, as will be shown, it is only by way of such an analysis that a philosophic interpretation such as Kant sought can be found, namely, an interpretation of the obviously necessary middle ground between Hume's account of representations as not implying any other representations, and Leibniz's account of representations as fully implying all other representations.

2.4 The Human Body Veiled

Hume and Leibniz, then, left with an isolated world of experience, had to understand how we live wholly in it without reference to anything outside, and without "having" a body in any different way than we "have" experience in general, e.g., of houses or islands. But we in fact "have" our body in such a central and distinctive way that no plausible analysis of experience can ignore it. These philosophers were thus forced to make an analysis of certain ways we "have" our body, and then to veil it, even from themselves, by attributing these ways we "have" our body to our ways of "having" experience in general.

2.4.1 Leibniz's veiling of the human body

According to Leibniz the human subject is the single, governing "soul" or "entelechy" of its Monad, pressing for the complete, clear, and distinct realization of all the potentialities for order implicit in it to begin with. The human subject is the unified force for the explication of its "internal" order, the order that, "externally" or spatially regarded, is that of a point-force. This Monad is not a fragment of the world. The entire physical (extended, spatial) world is represented in the Monad's own internal (temporal) horizon. Like Descartes, Leibniz regards the order of representations in the mind (Monad) of the human subject as temporal but not spatial, whereas the order of material things in the world is regarded as spatial but not temporal.

Both Leibniz and Descartes regard material things as capable of motion, which would seem to be inconsistent with the view that the temporal order is purely psychic. The temporal dimension of material motion is, however, suppressed by regarding this motion as a merely *logical* succession of different spatial distributions. This tendency is implicit in Descartes, though it is belied by his view that motions in space are those of an actual created substance. It is, however, made fully explicit by Leibniz, who seems to regard the "motion" of "extended" bodies as merely the relation of logical consequence holding between true principles having a certain logical "extension," as particular or universal judgments. This interpretation of motion is possible because all physical motion is conceived to be strictly lawful. Such an interpretation would not be possible in the context of a philosophy like Aristotle's, in which somewhat unordered matter plays a part in all motion. In such a philosophy, physical motion would have to be regarded as taking place in time as well as in space.

Leibniz and Descartes agree in regarding human representations, i.e., what appears to the human subject in experience, as incapable of motion. Motion is regarded as spatial representations are regarded as "in" the human subject, and the human subject is regarded as nonspatial. Strictly speaking, the human subject can have only temporally successive sets of representations such that from the remembered (or projected) variation in membership (or in patterns of clarity and distinctness among the members) in these successive sets of simultaneous representations he can infer, or judge, that certain spatial changes have occurred in the world of material things. He does this by first hypothesizing the spatial changes and then deducing that the given representations would *follow* as a con-*sequence*[12] of the hypothesized spatial change. Thus, the commonsense temporal sequence of material (spatial) things is replaced by their logical sequence.

Strictly speaking, on this view there could be no perceptual space. Thus, spatial variables such as motion, figure, and size, regarded as "primary qualities," are transported from the manifest content of experience to the material world. Only "secondary qualities," that is, qualities regarded as nonspatial, e.g., colors, tastes, sounds, smells, and tactile sensations, are considered perceivable. On this view we can conceive of spatial qualities but we can never directly experience them, i.e., perceive them, as characterizing something actual. For Descartes, this is so because it is not possible for us to experience space directly, although space is actual and has actual perceptual effects. For Leibniz this is so because space is not actual but merely ideal, having no effects in the actual interior temporal horizon of a Monad. Even God merely conceives of, rather than creates space. He created Monads in a *virtual* spatial order, but did not create "a Space" as anything in addition to the created Monads.

Thus, the extension that Descartes cast out of the representational world of the human subject became, partially for Descartes and wholly for Leibniz, a purely abstract, logical construction. It was no longer, as for common sense, an open field for things in order or disorder, but became instead entirely an order of a logically tight plenum of things. Likewise, motion was no longer regarded as taking place in an open field of separate moving things with empty spaces between them, spaces capable of receiving either them or other moving things that might newly appear. Instead, things were thought to fill up their spatial field. The *spatial* field became identical with the *plenum* of ordered things in it. And the *motion* of these things became identical with the *order* of this plenum of things.

The human subject is in fact extended and in motion (movement) only by virtue of his body. When he is conceived to be divorced from his body, as by Descartes, he can no longer be considered to be either extended or in motion. But since he has been identified instead with the world or a fragment of it or the function of explicating it, he cannot even have representations of extension or motion. For now, instead of his being in the world together with his representations (i.e., what appears to him) but distinct from them, his representations are held to be in him (or in his world, with some function of which he is identified). What is not extended cannot "contain" anything extended. As the human subject was once regarded as extended through having an extended body, so he is now regarded as nonextended by virtue of having a nonextended, purely temporal, world of experience. Ordinarily the human subject is regarded as *himself* having the properties that his body has. If his body is tall or short, fat or thin, *he* is regarded as tall or short, fat or thin. For Descartes and Leibniz the human subject is regarded as himself having all the properties that uniformly characterize whatever appears to him. In this formal way, at least, the world of representations of the human subject has taken the place of the body from which he has been "raised." The subject has become the life and ruler and sufferer of his experiential world as a whole, not just of his body in his experiential world. The human subject has come to "have" his experiential world in the general way he ordinarily seems to "have" his body.

With the Leibnizian completion of the rationalistic side of Descartes, however, the human subject is interpreted as "having" his world of experience not merely in the *general* way he is ordinarily interpreted as "having" his body (viz., by himself having all the properties that his body has), but in the *particular* way he "has" his active body. We have just seen that, with the Leibnizian development of Descartes, nothing remains "extended" and "moving" in the old perceptual sense of these terms. One might suppose that since time was regarded as the true domain of direct actual perceptual experience, *its* ordinary characterization would at least be left intact. If men are held to be only indirectly aware of the spatial character of things, it is relatively safe for a philosophy to offer an unusual characterization of such things and to attribute its strangeness to the ignorance of the ordinary man. But if men are held to be directly aware of the temporal character of things in the normal course of their lives, it is relatively dangerous for a philosophy to offer an unusual characterization of the temporal field of things. For, in order to be at all persuasive, a philosophy must somewhere offer an adequate account not merely of how things are, but also of how they normally *appear*, so that one can be led from knowledge of the latter to conviction about the former. This point of contact occurs for Leibniz in his characterization of the temporal field of perceptual experience. A critical analysis of Leibniz's account of temporal, perceptual experience is thus crucial as a test of the general adequacy and particular shortcoming, if any, of his entire philosophy.

Leibniz in fact gives a distorted account of temporal experience as it occurs in perception. The nature of this distortion reveals that the basic error Leibniz made was to interpret the human subject as "having" his world of experience in just the way that he "has" his body when active *in* the world of experience. Ordinary spatial experience is of separable things moving into unoccupied areas of the spatial field. Leibniz, purifying Descartes, radically transformed this notion of spatial functions by making indistinguishable: the spatial field; the ordered totality of objects in this field; and the movement of these objects in this field. The plenum of ordered (extended and moving) points (objects) became equivalent to space (the spatial field). Ordinary temporal experience is also of separable events occurring in previously unoccupied areas of the temporal field. Leibniz, here going far beyond Descartes, filled up the temporal field just as tightly as he filled up the spatial field.[13] Ordinary time, like ordinary space, was transformed into a plenum.

The present is big with the future, the future might be read in the past, the distant is expressed in the near.[14]

Or again,

> [H]e who sees all might read in each what is happening everywhere, and even what has happened or shall happen, observing in the present that which is far off as well in time as in place.[15]

The future becomes fully implied by each apparent moment. This is certainly not the way temporal events ordinarily appear. On such a view, time is not what it appears to be, viz., a medium in which something can apparently just *happen*; in which something can apparently come *into* existence; in which, as an e-vent, something can apparently come out of nowhere. Time is re-interpreted as a state in which things substantially (indeed, literally, as definitive of the same substance) go "on" just as before; all of time is reflected and born in each moment; changes occur only in the patterns of clarity and distinctness with which this enduring whole is revealed.

Leibniz refrains from holding that we are consciously aware of all these connections. Such a view would be too blatantly in contradiction with ordinary experience. Instead, he tries to draw back from the extreme and incredible version of his position by distinguishing from ordinary perceptions a special sort of perceptions that he calls "*petites perceptions.*" *Petites perceptions* are "those perceptions of which we are not consciously aware."[16] If our perceptions are taken as including our *petites perceptions*, then and only then each moment fully implies all moments. Thus we may not be *aware* that we are each moment perceiving a representation of all perceptions that ever were, or will be had, or are really compossible with any perception that ever was or will be had. Nevertheless, and this is the important point, Leibniz is committed to the incredible view that each perceptual appearance *is* so related to all other perceptions. That this is not the way the world is ordinarily taken to appear emphasizes the distance not only between Leibniz's account and the ordinary sense of the way the world *is* (spatially regarded); but also the distance between Leibniz's account and the ordinary sense of the way the world *appears* to be.

Leibniz's account of *petites perceptions* is a valuable advance in perceptual theory insofar as it points out that the perceptual appearance of a thing ordinarily represents *somewhat* more than what actually appears; it represents also, in a virtual way, what we can *expect* to appear. *Petites perceptions* thus give Leibniz an interesting way of accounting for the influence our past experience obviously has on our current expectations, even though we may have long forgotten these past experiences. Leibniz holds, in effect, that representations of them are subliminally present, and that through them we can perceive the regularity of our past experience. The lawfulness of the world is built into the nature of perception by the fact that the regularity or strength of connection between past perceptions of a certain kind is *alone*[17] sufficient to lead to the representation of future perceptions completing the present perception in a similar way. We become aware of these perceptual representations of the future by becoming aware of definite *habits of expectation* of future perceptions, although we may not be aware of the multitude of *petites perceptions* producing these perceptual habits. Thus Leibniz writes,

> Memory furnishes souls with a sort of consecutiveness which imitates reason . . . [Souls] expect, through the representations in memory, that which was associated with [the given representation] in the preceding perception. . . . [In this way] a strong impression often produces all at once the effect of a long-continued *habit*, or of many oft-repeated moderate perceptions.[18]

But Leibniz's view is incredible when he claims unrestrictedly that, in virtue of *petites perceptions*, perceptions represent in detail *everything* else that may possibly appear; in short, when he claims that *all* our perceptions are *fully* determined by pre-existent (though perhaps sub-liminal) perceptual habits.

That this view is "incredible" on the basis of ordinary experience is of course no conclusive argument against it, though it rightly predisposes us to regard this view as suspect, and to seek an effective argument against it. I believe we can find such an argument when we come to understand the logical place this view occupies in Leibniz's philosophy, as the focus of his attempt to elaborate a substitute human body for the human subject who, as a result of Cartesian philosophy, has been deprived of "having" his ordinary body in any special and definite way. If we see that this view is primarily important as producing such a substitute and that such a substitute can not in fact function as a body, as it is meant to do, then we have removed all logical motivation[19] for adopting this view, and belief in it would be no more than arbitrary. Further, this view becomes foolish if it can be shown, as will be attempted in this study, that a contradictory solution of the same problem is credible in terms of ordinary experience—where all *interesting* problems start, and by which all solutions to such problems are eventually *tested*, if they are tested at all.

Let us take a closer look at the "interior horizon" of a Monad, that is, at the temporal perceptual field of experience, as depicted by Leibniz. We have already seen that according to Leibniz real Time, like ideal Space, is a plenum of ordered elements. Space is a plenum (field) of ordered (logically "extended" and "moving") points or Monads (objects). Time is a plenum (field) of ordered (simultaneous and successive) perceptions (objects). For further investigation, three quotations are of particular interest:

The passing condition which involves and represents a multiplicity in the unit or in the simple substance is nothing but what is called *perception*.[20]

The activity of the internal principle which produces change from one perception to another may be called *appetition*.[21]

Or, again,

The perceptions in the Monad spring one from another by the laws of desire (*appétit*).[22]

From these quotations we can understand how Lebiniz conceived the human subject (or any Monad-subject) to "have" its temporal plenum. The internal perceptual "activity" of a Monad consists of the ordered succession of groups of perceptions. It consists of a (temporal) unity of a successive multiplicity (of moments) of unities (in a single moment) of simultaneous multiplicities (of perceptions), such that this succession is brought about *merely by the desire* governing the temporal-perceptual field. Activity and change in the whole perceptual field occur by desire alone, and not through the body as a particular element *in* the field.

This is in fact a correct analysis of the way the human subject moves his *body* in the perceptual field, but it is not a correct analysis of the ways in which things *about* us, that is, things about our bodies, appear to change or move in the perceptual field. It is indeed characteristic of our body that its movements or activities appear immediately responsive to our desires, without the intervention of any third agency by which this is accomplished, and without any resistance by our body to our desires, unless inhibited by our will. Occasionally, it is true, our body does seem to protest against the demands we make upon it, as, for example, when we are fatigued and yet demand continued bodily exertion. But in these cases, desire is gone and the body resists not the call of desire but the summons of the will. On these occasions, moreover, when our body is activated by will but not by desire, we come to "have" our body in a different way.[23] We come to "have" it much more as an object with which we have to deal. We do not identify ourself with our body but (our self) attempt to make *it* (not our self) go and do things, appearing our self to act from and to be localized in the detached and disembodied position of our visual point of view. On the other hand, when things about us in the perceptual field do change in accordance with our desire, it is normally only because we have expressed that desire through some *bodily* movement that has brought about this change, as, for example, when lifting an apple to our mouth makes the apple appear closer to our mouth in accordance with our desire to eat it. Often, however, things about us appear to change quite independently of our desire; apparently, they merely happen to change. And often, even when we move so as to produce the desired change, this change is apparently not produced, either because we have been misled by the initial appearances to expect what is not there, as when we bite an artificial apple we have mis-taken for a real one; or because we fail to *do* what we tried to do, as when we try to reach something on a high shelf. Leibniz is committed by his theory of the pre-established harmony between the spatial and temporal worlds of Nature to holding that in all these cases we have, however subliminally, perceptual habits that completely anticipate all of these, and just these, perceptual eventualities.

Thus, regarded in terms of ordinary experience, Leibniz treats the "interior horizon" of a Monad like the body of an animal, and he treats the entelechy of a Monad like the life of an animal. It is thus quite appropriate that Leibniz's classical model for his "Monad" was an organism. What Leibniz "forgets" from the point of view of ordinary experience, is that *to live as an animal is to live not in one's body, but in one's nonbodily circumstances,* which one has to make habitable as best one can. These circumstances in which we live as animals are given to begin with as precisely *not* fully governed by us, in the way our bodies *are.* That is why our embodiment is our *danger* as well as our opportunity. Command over our circumstances is not initially given but is a life-*task*; indeed, a task never finally accomplished in life, for we may minimize but never wholly eliminate our circumstantial vulnerability. Even command of our body, while eventually completable in a way not possible for command of our circumstances, must be initially won. Thus, since the circumstancedness of life is in effect denied by Leibniz's account, and since it is from our circumstances that mortal danger producing mortal dread (our animal sense of our mortality) normally seems to come, it is very much in conformity with the rest of Leibniz's philosophy to hold as he does that the Monad is indestructible.[24]

For Leibniz, then, to desire *is* to change the temporal, perceptual world. Correspondingly, for Leibniz, to judge rationally and morally[25] *is* to legislate not merely for oneself and one's own activities, but for the whole universe of Monads, and thereby for the whole temporal world we live "in"; or at least to recapitulate God's legislation for it. We are held to legislate in this way not merely what ought to exist, but also what therefore does exist. Human subjects are regarded by Leibniz as "rational souls" who are thereby distinguishable from others in possessing "the knowledge of necessary and eternal truths,"[26] and in being "images of the Deity, capable of knowing the system of the universe, and to some extent of imitating it."[27] In fact, however, again judging Leibniz's philosophy in the light of everyday experience, to judge rationally and morally is to give the laws that are felt to be *binding* upon the activities of human subjects, but in such a way that they may often be *broken.* Awareness that certain laws are moral and rational gives us immediately, and without any further ado or reflection about the consequences, the sense that our activity and the activity of all other persons we live with are judged by these laws, and are found by them to be either wanting or satisfactory. Insofar as our conscience is strong, we therefore will to act accordingly, and we succeed or not depending upon the relative strength and agreement of our will and our desires. But it does not normally appear that what ought to be the case is in any way binding upon what is the case in respect to circumstantial objects in the world about us. They must, apparently, be to some extent lawful but they might, apparently, obey any one of a number of incompatible laws, so far as we can tell. It seems incumbent upon us to discover what laws are in fact obeyed by the objects around us, but it does not seem at all incumbent upon them to obey any particular set of laws.

Thus, in the case of judgment as in the case of desire, Leibniz regards the whole world of experience as determined in the way in which our active bodies are determined when they are optimally active. For the whole world of experience, to desire *is* to act, and the whole world of experience is always full of desire, never fatigued or sick, and thus emptied of desire. For the whole world of experience, to judge rationally and morally *is* to produce, or to recapitulate God's production of, activity in accordance with that judgment. There is, for the whole world, and always, a perfect harmony of conscience, reason, will, desire, and fact. If our bodies were without circumstances, and if we thus lived without danger to life and limb, without resistance, and without objects incompletely subjected to our control; if we were, in short, embodied as worlds unto ourselves, then perhaps, if we were initially in good health, we would be the perfectly indestructible and harmoniously self-regulating creatures (Monads) that Leibniz describes. But the world of our experience is in fact not such a world. It is a circumstantial world that we do not "have" as we have an optimally active body, but *in* which we have a body that may not be optimally active. And our being embodied in the midst of circumstances is furthermore so fundamental a characteristic of the world of our experience that it is not even possible to imagine or conceive of what it would be like to have a "body," "desires," "will," "conscience," or "understanding," or to engage in "activities" of any kind, except in the midst of circumstances. We can assign nothing more than a grammatical sense to this counterfactual conditional.

2.4.2 Hume's veiling of the human body

For Hume too the human subject is the functional identity of explicating the unity of the world, insofar as there is any such unity. But Hume keeps the perceptual sense of a time open to the future, and of an open space in which objects move about separately. For Hume too the human subject loses his body as something by which he is specially identified. As for Leibniz, man's personal identity is conceived to lie with the manifest unity of all his experience; no content of experience is singled out as having a privileged relation to this identity. But there remains a fundamental difference between Leibniz the rationalist and Hume the empiricist. Leibniz, having loosed the human subject from identification with his body, and having identified him instead with the functional unity of explicating the world, proceeded to regard the human subject as having his world much in the sense that he in fact has his active body. From the familiar situation of a person having an active body in the midst of circumstances, the relation of "having" a body was in effect saved, though applied instead to the whole experiential world in which the subject is conceived to be uniformly spread out. But the relation of "being in the midst of" circumstances was entirely lost. Hume also identified the human subject with the functional unity of explicating the world, instead of with his body. But he proceeded to regard the human subject as having his world of experience much as a pure spectator "has" experience by "having" an inactive body. From the familiar situation of a person having an active body in the midst of circumstances, Hume saves the relation of "being in the midst of" circumstances, though he applies this relation to the whole experiential world in which the subject is regarded as uniformly spread out, having everywhere his center or point of view, so that all impressions (objects in the world) are equally "in" his mind. But the relation of "having" an active body is entirely lost.

Leibniz rejects identification of the human subject with his familiar body *in* a circumstantial world, he does so by *swelling* the familiar body to the enormous proportions of the whole circumstantial world, literally incorporating the body's circumstances into the body itself.[28] Hume rejects the same familiar identification, but by *shrinking* the familiar body to the incorporeal proportions of a visual point of view on the world of experience. Regarding the human subject as having no dependably governable body through which to cope with undependable circumstances in the world, Hume views the human subject as entirely passive in the determination of matters of fact. The human subject can notice, remember, and compare his impressions, and thereby, with the aid of words, he can acquaint himself with the regularity or unity of the world of his experience to date. But he cannot then do more than *expect* a continuation of this regularity. Whereas for Leibniz even novel (though prefigured) desire by the subject is sufficient to guarantee a corresponding change in the perceptual field, for Hume the most conservatively based expectation offers not the slightest rational ground for the subject to confidently await its being met. For Hume, impressions are to be awaited without any justification for expectations about them; for Leibniz, perceptions are produced by desire without any possibility of interference by uncontrolled forces. Hume's view is, in effect, that since the human subject has only undependable "circumstances" and no dependable body, his experiences cannot be dependably ordered. Leibniz's view is, in effect, that since the human subject has no undependable circumstances, and only a dependable "body," his experiences cannot be less than optimally ordered. But in practice we cannot help believing that since the human subject has both a dependable body and undependable circumstances, his experiences are moderately ordered. This implies that there is at least a moderately dependable regularity in appearances of things in the world, because the world, as the body's world, must be at least a somewhat habitable world. Any other view is incredible in practice.

In this book I seek to develop the view that we can understand the general but incomplete regularity of our experience only by understanding that it is the experience of a human subject having an entirely governable body that is, however, set in the midst of initially alien and ungovernable circumstances into which he must introduce order so that they may be livable and durably endurable. A regular connection can be established between appearances that may have little or no direct connection with one another by threading them to one another through our single body, which, in action, is responsive as a whole. I try to show how it is by bodily movement that all our different experiences are integrated. The integrated, moving body is the great melting pot of all experiences, throwing them all in together to find a *modus vivendi* with one another in the same single stew of life. However experiences may differ, they have at least this much affinity, that they are all able to be experienced by virtue of the subject's having the *same* body, a whole thoroughly responsive among its various members and functions. The elements in the knowable world, the world of experience, are not a wholly random collection. The knowable world, I seek to show, is the human body's world, and only those elements that have some kind of affinity to the human body can enter it. For others there can be no names; others are inconceivable, imperceivable, undesirable, unimaginable, unapproachable. To appear, or to be anything at all, is to be a function of the human body. For the world itself is such a function and is so made as to allow only such things in it. What is not a function of the human body is outside the world, and hence can neither be nor appear to be anything at all. Whatever is or appears to be anything, must be or appear to be *in* the world, and is thus a function of the human body that stands at the portals of the world and allows entrance only to that which can be domesticated for its uses, so as to make the world of experience livable.

Let us now turn to the text of Hume's *Treatise* in an effort to develop this view in greater detail, though still in a preliminary way, by showing more clearly how it differs from Hume's view. Hume begins his *Treatise* with the crucial statement,

All perceptions of the human mind (impressions and ideas) . . . strike upon the mind, and make their way into our thought or consciousness.[29]

This statement must be understood in the context of Hume's fundamental belief that "it is impossible for us so much as to conceive or form an idea of anything specifically different from ideas and impressions."[30] Hume thus holds that everything in experience "strikes upon" the mind. This is in fact true of what appears *to* us as an object, but it is not true of our active body, *through* which we make objects appear. In action, our body is already "in" our consciousness as soon as we become aware that something has to be done. In beginning to act, the human subject does not first perceive his body, then take it up and use it, as he does an umbrella on a rainy day. Rather, when active, he becomes aware of objects only as they are brought to his attention as relevant to what he (inseparable from his body) is doing. It is not merely his body that he is moving or is prepared to move, that he perceives to come into new relationships with objects; it is *himself* that he perceives to come into these new relationships through his bodily movement. When he is active, therefore, things appear to the human subject through his body, but his body does not itself appear to him as an object. When he is active, objects appear to him-as-having-a-body; his having a body is the way in which objects appear to him. Of course, the active human subject has in some way a sense of his body as well as of objects that appear to him. I will discuss this sense of the active body later,[31] resting content for the moment with pointing out that the active body is not experienced by the human subject as appearing *to* him, as "striking upon" his mind, or as making its way "into" his consciousness, after the manner of objects.

Hume, however, consistently regards the human body as a particular object, accidental like all others, in the field of human experience. He writes,

It is absurd to imagine the senses can ever distinguish between (the content of) ourselves and external objects.[32]

This is so when our sensations are merely those of an inactive observer detached from his body and ensconced in his disembodied visual point of view.[33] It is so, for example, when one "has" his body in the sense that leads Hume to argue that our bodies are as external (or internal)[34] to ourselves as objects around them because, "properly speaking, it is not our body we perceive, when we *regard* (my italics) our limbs and members, but certain impressions, which enter by the senses."[35] Hume is here arguing against the view that there are material substances logically independent of experience, and his view on this matter is not at the moment of interest to us. What is of interest is that, in the course of this argument, he indicates the way he conceives us to characteristically have our bodies, mentioning that we "*regard*" our "limbs and members." Note here, too, that in the course of being "regarded," i.e., experienced in just the same way as an observer experiences an object, Hume's body appears to him as dismembered, i.e., separated limb from limb. I will try to show why all this is characteristic of the way the human subject "has" his body when he is a pure spectator.

2.5 Phenomenological Interlude

In order to understand the experience of a pure spectator, such as Hume's philosophy depicts, e.g., to understand how he regards his body as an object, it will prove helpful to begin with a phenomenological account of what it is to regard body feelings as objects.

2.5.1 Body feelings as objects

To regard body feelings as "objects" is to localize them in respect to our visual point of view, so that a feeling in part of the body below the horizontal plane of the eyes, such as an itch in one's foot while standing, is regarded as "down there." Similarly, for feelings in parts of the body before and behind the vertical lateral midsectional plane of the head. With this attitude a body feeling is regarded as "in" the part of the body that has it. It is, moreover, felt not merely *in* but *by* the body part that has it, though it is felt *from* the visual point of view. With this attitude, I am *an immobile observer of my body*.

I can even maintain this attitude as a *mover of my body*, when I, detachedly ensconced in my visual point of view and thus distinguishable from my body, move parts of my body much as I might move an object, e.g., I raise my arm much as I might lift a stick. When I thus raise my arm, the command for the movement seems to come from my visual point of view, where the disembodied "I" seems to be located, and it seems to terminate in the arm. Likewise, when I move an object (though not when I move an instrument), e.g., when I lift a stick, I sense that I am giving a direction that terminates in the object. From this point of view, the only difference between raising my arm and raising a stick is that the former seems miraculous, because in that case a material thing seems to be moved by an immaterial agent, namely, my visual point of view. But when I raise the stick I am a *user of my body*; that is, I move a part of my body as an instrument. In this case I give direction not *to* a part

Critique of the World-Subject of Leibniz and Hume

of my body, but *through* it to the object moved.[36] In such a case, it is very difficult to regard, e.g. my tactile feelings, as "in" my arm. *I*, not my arm, tend to feel the stick. And the stick tends to be felt not in but *with* my arm.[37] This tendency becomes irresistible if I do something requiring me to move not a part but the whole of my body. I then become a *self-mover of my body*. With this attitude, a body feeling is not regarded by a visually detached self as in the part of the body that has it. Nor is it felt in and by that part of the body. "The feeling" is itself disregarded, or, rather, it is not yet regarded as "something" by itself. Rather, *by* the whole body (from which the self is felt to be inseparable), and *with* some part of the body, we feel not some feeling but the need to *do* something. For example, if I am outside on a cloudy day without raincoat or umbrella and feel the first few drops of rain on my arm, it is not the case that some wet, cool and tactile sensations or feelings are felt to exist down in and by my arm. Rather, *I*, and therewith my *whole body*, feel *with* my arm the *need* to get out of the rain that is coming. That is what my feeling means to me as an active person at the time. Such an attitude may be, and in fact almost always is adopted even when no gross body movement is prompted by the body feeling involved. The point of my previous illustrations was simply to emphasize that while body feelings *may* be, although they normally are not, regarded as objects when we "have" our body as observers or as movers or as users of it, nevertheless body feelings *cannot* be so regarded while gross body movement is being prompted by them. Itching, for example, though it does not normally prompt gross body movement, is usually felt in this way. With this attitude, there does not exist "an itch" felt in or on my palm; an itch felt by my palm, and simply known by me, ensconced in my visual point of view, to be felt down there. Rather, my palm itches and therewith itches my whole body (though my whole body does not itch) in the sense that my whole body is thereby set and tempted to scratch my itchy palm with my other hand. My palm itches, and I (thereby my whole body) have a need to scratch my palm with my other hand. Normally, in the case of itching as in the case of all body feelings, body feelings are felt by the whole person as inseparable from his whole body, and they are felt with some part of his body as a need to do something with that or some other part of his *same* body. Thus body feelings in the active body presuppose a global feeling of the body as a whole, so that needs felt with *one* part of the body may be felt as needs requiring to be met with *another* part of the body.

2.5.2 The three functions of the body of the active subject

When the self, becoming a pure inactive spectator, retreats from the body, detaching itself as a disembodied visual point of view, its body feelings become inert "in" the body. They lose the mobility that is characteristic of body feelings in the active body. First of all they lose their ability to influence and respond to all other body feelings; their ability to feel that a need felt with one part of the body *is* a need for the whole body, to be met with that part of the body most capable of meeting it effectively. This involves loss of the basic sense of vital, corporate *unity* in one's body. One's body, as we saw for Hume, comes to seem to be a set of parts-outside-of-parts; a set of limbs fitted onto one another as for Descartes's body-"automaton": no more than a curiously (inexplicably) animated corpse. Consequent to this loss of a basic feeling of unity in the body, is the loss by body feelings of their capacity actually to mobilize the whole body into action. This involves loss of *coordination*. The person who lacks a feeling of the unity and wholeness of his body can act only by moving parts of his body at a time. He is thus awkward, ridiculous and jerky in his movements, trying to do something with one part of his body while "getting in his own way" with another part of his body. An athlete, on the other hand, who has this organic sense to perfection, seems always to move with ease because, even when he fails to do what he is trying to do, his body movements are at least consistent with one another. Thirdly, consequent to the loss of coordination is a loss by body feelings of external reference (beyond the body) to circumstantial objects. By this reference our body feelings enable us to anticipate and carry our purposeful movements in respect to the objects around us. Loss of the external reference of body feelings involves loss of *skill*. The person who cannot coordinate his actions, and is awkward, spends most of his movements in fighting himself. He cannot turn his attention to "foreign affairs" and to "defense" because he is the ruler of a hopelessly anarchic domestic society that does not carry out his orders. To deal effectively with objects around us, we must be able

Critique of the World-Subject of Leibniz and Hume

to anticipate them before we reach them, or they us, so that we can then be prepared at the actual moment of meeting to respond effectively. If we can act only with parts but not with the whole of our body, then the sets or anticipations of parts of our body are very likely to be blocked at the crucial moment of meeting by the unpreparedness of the rest of our body. This is so because we can prepare effectively only if we know just how we will meet the object concerned. And insofar as the object moves toward us in unanticipated ways the given body part cannot manage by itself. We may, for example, have to move (our whole body) to another spot, or to turn (our whole body) about, or to bend—in order to meet the object effectively with the hand that is prepared for it. For example, if I attempt to catch a fly ball it will not normally be sufficient to act limb by limb. However I prepare with my right hand to catch it, I will normally be unable to catch it (unless it is hit right to me) unless my whole body can help prepare me to catch it with my right hand, by constantly moving toward where the ball seems to be going so as to place me eventually in such a spot and oriented in such a way (facing the ball) that I can catch it with a skillful right hand.

2.5.3 The body as an object

Having presented in a preliminary way the nature and consequences of viewing body feelings as objects, let us now return to a consideration of the nature and consequences of viewing the body itself as an object, a way of viewing the body that seems attributable to Hume. Regarding the body as an object is the result of regarding body feelings as objects. In this state, one "has" his body but without feeling it. One "has" a body in the same sense as one "has" experience of all things, namely, in the sense that one *localizes* (gives location to) these things in the field of one's experience in which they appear. The body appears to differ from other things only descriptively. It does not appear to differ in its relation to the subject, but only in the properties that it has. The subject finds the body distinctive only in that it alone has feelings. The subject has experience of a body that has feelings and, in the same sense, he has experience of numerous other objects that do not have such feelings or indeed any feelings, but may have colors or shapes that the body does not.

2.5.4 Space and time as correlates of the active subject's body

The result of regarding the whole body as an object, by regarding all its feelings as objects, is to dissolve the global unity of experiential space and time, which is the correlative of the global unity of the active, felt and not merely observed body, We may discover this consequence in Hume's philosophy. Hume holds that we are aware of extension through sight and touch,[38] but he never understands that we may become aware of extension through movement. The kind of sight and touch he has in mind is rather that of visual and tactile sensations or "impressions" in which there is nothing on the side of the subject but the empty mind into which these impressions come; in effect, the empty visual point of view in respect to which impressions are localized but of which there are no impressions. Such indeed are the visual and tactile experiences that occur without movement, as, for example, by staring fixedly or by resting our hand inertly on an object. These experiences alone, however, are not sufficient to give us a sense of Space, but only of isolated points in Space. It is therefore not surprising to find that Hume believes apparent space is made up of a series of points and that he has difficulty understanding how this can be so. Hume's difficulty with space is paralleled by his difficulty with time. His conclusion is:

The ideas of space and time are, therefore, no separate or distinct ideas, but merely those of the manner or order in which objects exist.[39]

Now it is precisely in this "order" that Hume is unable to find any necessity. Our expectation of any connection between moments or between points remains for Hume inexplicable. This is so because the explanation of this connection lies in the way the human subject "has" an active body, and Hume's analysis is restricted to the experiential world of a human subject who "has" an inactive body, regarding that body as merely another object in his experience. Through understanding the role of body movement in experience we can understand how there can be a measure of "necessary connection between impressions (appearances of things)." For it is only through body movement that we gain a sense of a *global* space in which various apparent objects can be located. This is so because in movement alone we are not restricted to being passively aware of objects, in the way Hume thinks characteristic of all our experience. Through movement we also actively *make* objects appear, in the way Leibniz thinks characteristic of all our experience; or, more accurately, through movement we are always at least engaged in actively attempting to make objects appear.

Body-direction and the practical spatiotemporal field

Insofar as we actively attempt to make objects appear we generate the spatial and temporal fields in which they first may appear. When we are inert, our front and back appear merely as two different sides of our object-body, much as two sides of a coffin. But when we are active our front and back generate and acquire a temporal significance. Our front apparently brings into appearance what is *coming* to be because of what we are (forwardly) *going* to do; it thereby produces the (future) field of what lies ahead of us. Our back apparently leaves behind what has appeared and thereby produces the apparent field of what is now *passed* (past),[40] so that the front-back body distinction makes possible the *passage* of time.[41] When inert, our left and right also appear to be merely two different sides of our body. But when we are active they generate an apparent spatial field for all objects, and themselves acquire a place in this field. They do this by bearing our capacity to *turn in place*; that is, to turn around without moving or passing, and therefore to turn, in a certain sense, in an instant. Turning in this in-stant (literally, standing-in), or the sense of our ability to do so, apparently gives us at once our simultaneous spatial circum-stance (where what stands around us is), and our own position or place as the in-stance (that which stands inside) of that circum-stance. In one full turn we apparently turn our circumstances instantaneously into one instantaneous, and therefore spatial, field about us. When moving we thus move from one circum-stance to another, so that action take place in circumstan*ces*, and is replete with many instan*ces*.

Thus through movement we do not merely notice but *produce* the spatiotemporal field around us, our circumstantial field, the field in which things appear to us and in which we feel alive. Without our moving in it there would be no apparent spatiotemporal field in which objects might appear. This field has a necessary connection of its parts because it is produced as a whole. It is *one field* in a sense exactly correlative to that in which we feel ourselves to be living *one life* in it through the efforts of our *one active body* in it. No quadrant of this spatiotemporal life-field could exist without the others. We could not be passing something (thereby having an apparent past) unless we were going somewhere (and thereby having an apparent future). Nor could we be going somewhere (thereby having an apparent future) unless we were passing something (and thereby having an apparent past). Nor could we appear to be passing-anything-going-anywhere (thereby having an apparent time) unless we were in the course of changing our circumstances; that is, moving from circumstance to circumstance about us (and thereby being continually in the midst of an apparent simultaneous spatial field in which we felt alive). Nor could we feel alive in any circumstances without feeling it possible to change our circumstances by moving, by going, somewhere else.

Someone can be aware of his circumstances without being aware of much movement as possible, e.g., if he is imprisoned. But then he is always privatively aware of the restriction on his movement, and this restriction diminishes his sense of time. He drags out his days; time tends to seem unreal; he tends to lose track of objective time because he tends to lose the practical subjective sense of time that gives import to the objective measurement of it. But so long as he retains some sense of his ability to move, if only within the confines of his cell, he retains some sense of time.

Thus if any quadrant of this spatiotemporal field exists, it all exists. And if no quadrant exists, nothing can appear to us nor can we feel alive; particular things do appear to us, and we do feel alive only *in* this field. Of course, what appears to us in this field is not produced by movement; objects may surprise us in their appearance. How then does the wholeness of the movement-generated field guarantee any ("necessary") connection, such as Hume sought, and thought impossible, between things appearing in it?

The practical spatiotemporal field as life-field

To understand this, we must understand that the apparent spatiotemporal field is a *life-field*. It is the field of our needs, and as such it can endure only insofar as these needs are met by what appears in this field. *The field of our experience can endure only so long*

Critique of the World-Subject of Leibniz and Hume

as our experience in it is endurable. This implies, as will be shown, that the regularity of our experience is a measure of the satisfaction of our needs, and that our needs must be to some extent satisfied if there is to be any experience at all. In this chapter I will attempt to demonstrate these theses in a preliminary way by phenomenological analyses at once supporting and clarifying them. I will try to show how the regularity of experience stems from the *determination* of objects of experience as objects of a particular sort; how this determination is made possible through our making an active *response* to anticipated objects of experience; how this response is directed toward the satisfaction of a body *need*; how this satisfaction consists of the *filling* of some place in the single, integrated field of experience; how this field *is* simply the apparent set of our body-needs; and how this set of body-needs forms to begin with a single, consistent and integrated *whole*. Stated somewhat differently, I will try to justify the following theses. Through a response, experience becomes determinate as the meeting of some need in the field of our experience. Localization takes place by the development of habits or skills; that is, by the ability to respond effectively to anticipated things even before reaching them. When we "have" a wealth of experience, we "have" a large, well-ordered (i.e., well-placed) inventory of accessible objects of experience, each of which is known to be capable of satisfying certain specific needs we may from time to time have.

This dogmatic analysis may seem at first more plausible, or at least less implausible, as an analysis of our relation to perceivable things in respect to which we act, e.g., our groceries, than as an analysis of our relationship to objects of which we theoretically conceive, e.g., electrons. But we will see that the latter sort of relationship is derivative from the former; that our theoretical knowledge presupposes that we have an active body in the world. Thus, for example, the world we live in is the *partially empty* field of our *needs*; but we conceive of the universe as a *plenum*. The need-field of our experience is thus represented as completely filled up with exhaustively determinate objects as, e.g., by Leibniz. We will see that the abstract thinker's state of being *in*-actively aware, is a *privative* state. It is not an initial state of a person but a highly complicated and subtle *re-action* to being actively aware. As such it presupposes that all the achievements of activity have taken place. It is, when properly understood, merely a way of responding to these achievements, but not a way of replacing them; that is, of starting again from the beginning with an independent way of experiencing things. Inactive awareness is always a motivated withdrawal from conscious activity. It is a way of experiencing things that acknowledges the active foundation of experience by being itself an attempt to solve those problems of experience that only active experience can pose and render formulable.

2.5.5 A note on method

My initial theses and all the ordinary evidence for them are not about the way things *are*, but only about the way they *appear*. In chapter 6, I try to show that our sense of what is so is derivative from our sense of how things appear to be so; hence that this account of how things appear is presupposed as "really" accurate by all objective considerations of how things are. I try to show that even the search for an objective account *makes sense* only on the presupposition that the felt world we actively live in is just as it appears to be.

These points require fuller explanation. Some particular thing that could appear in the world of experience, such as an oasis, may seem to, even if it does not in fact, appear in the world of experience, as in the appearance of a mirage of an oasis. I am not arguing that to appear to be something in particular is really to be that apparent thing. I wish to distinguish sharply between *what* appears and the *way* it appears; between the *appearance* and the *appearing* of things in the world of experience. My analysis does not concern any particular thing of a certain sort that may merely happen to be what appears in the field of experience; it does not concern the appearance of any particular thing. It concerns only how any possible thing must appear in order to appear as "in" the world, or field, of our experience; it concerns the appearing of any particular thing. While some particular thing may seem to but not really, *appear* in the world of experience, there is no way in which things could seem to but not really, *appear as* in-the-world-of-experience. There is a certain sense in which we cannot possibly be mistaken about the *way* things appear, although we may be mistaken about *what* appears.

Critique of the World-Subject of Leibniz and Hume

The contrast between veridical and illusory appearances

The oasis that could appear is distinguishable *in its manner of appearance* from the mirage of an oasis-that-merely-seems-to-appear. The mirage, unlike the oasis and all other really apparent things, merely appears to, but does not, have anything about it that is concealed at first appearance and can then be revealed by subsequent movement. The mirage, like all illusions about particular things, *disappears rather than further appears in the course of movements designed to make it further appear;* in the course of movements designed to reach it and to revise or dis-cover further things about it. One cannot successfully argue that the illusion appears at any rate exactly the same as the real object *so long as* one does not in fact so move as to discover what is illusory about it. For this is to reify the appearance; to identify "it" as divested of its temporal dimension. This temporal dimension is, however, essential to it as taking place in the world of active experience. Every illusion is an illusion by virtue of some difference, discoverable by movement, between itself and what it seems to be. To divest the experience of its temporal aspect is to transform it into a purely passive experience, spectatorially regarded. Once the appearance of a thing is regarded as "a momentary appearance of that thing" rather than as "that apparently still to be further revealed thing momentarily appearing," there is indeed no difference between the appearance of the "actual" and the merely or seemingly apparent thing. But that is because the umbilical cord of body movement, which binds apparent things to the unitary spatiotemporal field of experience, has been cut. What remains is a spectator's "object," but not the "object" of the active man. To be a spectator is to "have" experience of objects differently than when one is active, and this difference involves a difference in the kind of "object" that is experienced. It involves a different sense of what it is to be an "object" of experience. To deny that both kinds of "object" exist, to insist that one is really the other, is foolish. The interesting problem is to explore the relationship between the *two*. My conclusion will be that the actively felt object is primary and the inactively regarded object is phenomenologically derivative.

The momentary appearance of a given thing in the world in which we actively live is *not* dissociable as a separate thing from the entire perceptual fate of that one thing (momentarily appearing in the given way), which is uninterruptedly given to us during the whole spatiotemporal course of our movements with respect to it. *Whatever the apparent object turns out apparently to be, is also what it turns out to have been all along.* Therefore, in terms of active experience it is the *same* apparent thing that we first saw that turns out to be a real oasis; and it is the *same* apparent "thing" that we first saw that turns out to disappear upon our attempting to reach it, and thus turns out apparently not to be (nor to have been) any apparent thing at all, but only an illusory appearance, a mirage of an apparent thing. Therefore, in terms of *active* experience there is an apparent distinction between an apparent thing and an illusion that merely seems to be that apparent thing.

But this is admittedly not so for *inactive* experience. Regarding the body as an object, as we have seen, dissolves the unity of the apparent spatiotemporal field, and transforms appearance in it into things ("impressions," in Hume's language) outside of and next to one another. Illusions in this case are not *apparently* (i.e., in the manner of their appearance) distinguishable from apparent real objects.[42] I will try to illuminate the nature of this transformation by considering the relation between the manner in which appearances appear as a result of it, and the manner in which illusory appearances appear in active experience. I have noted that, in active experience, illusions, unlike apparent real things, disappear rather than further appear in the course of movements designed to make them further appear. Consider the case of the apparently bent stick in water, viewed from successive positions. In this case, unlike the mirage, the illusion changes rather than disappears in the course of movement. This may seem to contradict my general statement. But notice that in this case the movements by which the illusion is finally exposed, e.g., the movements of feeling the stick along the waterline, or of withdrawing the stick from the water, finally reveal that there had been all along *many illusions* about *one thing* (the stick). The illusions do not appear to have been successive complementary appearances of the same thing, progressively revealing more of that thing. Instead, they

Critique of the World-Subject of Leibniz and Hume

appear to have been temporally isolated appearances, appearances merely of a moment, transitory appearances, incapable of being given an enduring location in the field of our enduring, surviving movement. Because the movements by which we finally reach them[43] turn out to make illusions disappear, we cannot give illusions any place in the apparent field of our activity, which is a matrix for those things we *can* reach, possess, or use by movement.[44] Having no place, the various illusory appearances are retroactively broken apart, turning out to have been merely separate appearances parasitically and indeterminately in the "logical" neighborhood of the object that they were illusions "about." We attempt to give all our illusions at least such an indefinite neighborhood-location, signifying not that they are in some definite, though as yet undetermined place around the object they appear to be "about," but only that they are somehow (logically) relevant and attributable to this object, though they apparently belong to it as deceptive rather than revealing appearances of it.

Now the spectatorial view, in effect, illicitly transforms all appearances of things actively felt into appearances like those of exposed illusions about things actively felt. Then it produces a merely logical "real object" in the merely logical "neighborhood" of which even the various, now separated, veridical appearances are construed to appear. These veridical appearances are transformed into logical atoms, connected to one another in merely verbal nonmaterial ways, to form the logical objects they are construed to be appearances "of." This illicit transformation has also taken place in those philosophical interpretations of experience that are based on an analysis of all experience as inactive. Locke's material substance, his "something, I know not what," was the least articulate notion of such a logical object. Hume's associated "object" is an improved version, equivalent not to something unknowable but to the knowable, regular succession of separate impressions "of" it. In modern positivistic and phenomenalist or selectivist theories of various sorts, including primarily those of Carnap and Russell, the Humean version was made more elegant by transforming Hume's basic relation of temporal sequence[45] into one of logical consequence. This logifying of temporal appearances in philosophies based on an analysis of inactive "observations" directly parallels the

Cartesian and Leibnizian logifying of the nonapparent time of material things; that is, of material motion that was also conceived as "inactive" in the sense that conscious body movement was specifically excluded from it.

In any case, for inactively observed experience, the distinction between illusory and veridical appearances is not an apparent distinction but a logical one, to be made with the help of judgment about the consistency, coherence, simplicity, etc., of the family group of appearances that can be formed by including or excluding the given appearance from among them. But for active felt experience, the distinction between illusory and veridical experience is an apparent one.

The impossibility of an illusory way of appearing

Every illusory appearance is an illusion by virtue of some difference, discoverable through movement or through judgment, between itself and what it seems to be. If there were no such discoverable difference, there would not be a case of illusion. There is no distinction, however, between the way something merely seems to appear and the way it really appears as in-the-world-of-experience. For to appear is to appear as in-the-world-of-experience. Whenever something appears, it really appears *as* in-the-world-of-experience. No further experience, however illusory the given "object" may turn out to have been, could show that this "object" never had really appeared as in-the-world-of-experience. Indeed, the appearance of the object can have a "further," hence spatiotemporal, perceptual fate only if the object always did appear as in-the-world-of-experience. And no judgment, however illusory it demonstrates the "ostensible object" to have been, can show that this "object" never had really appeared as in-the-world-of-experience. Thus no sense can be made of that kind of experience of an object that could show that its way of appearing as in-the-world-of-experience was illusory, so that, though it had seemed so to appear, it had really appeared as not in-the-world-of-experience.

Let us now return to a consideration of the "subjective" felt world we actively live in, in an attempt to adduce evidence for the theses dogmatically stated in Section 2.5.4.

2.5.6 Types of spatiotemporal emptiness

My spatiotemporal life field, which I generate about me by moving in it, is replete with emptiness of various degrees. There is the *emptiness of impermanence* in those places in my apparent spatiotemporal field occupied at the moment by apparent objects that are apparently movable. If these objects are moved, the places they occupy would appear to have an *emptiness of inoccupancy*, such as actually appears between all apparent, noncontiguous objects, so that we commonly say that "there appears to be some room between them." Apparent objects that merely occupy, but, unlike landmarks, do not define a place, appear as susceptible to being moved. Thus the emptiness of impermanence anticipates a possible emptiness of inoccupancy. In addition, there is always, beyond the horizon of apparently determinate and localized objects, an indeterminate spatiotemporal field that apparently extends without limit into the past and future. For example, for the country boy who has never gone beyond his own valley, the distant ridges of the surrounding mountain range appear to delimit the known from the unknown circumstantial world of his experience. But they do not appear to be the end of the world itself, only of the known world. What lies beyond "them thar' hills," however, is a markedly different kind of apparent spatial field. It is a field without places in it. It is a wholly indeterminate field with as yet unmarked places, though it is at the same time a wholly indeterminate field *for* places; that is, it appears as a wholly indeterminate field in which places can be marked, and in which the marking of places is solicited. The horizon of determinate places appears to beckon the boy to go beyond it, to give what lies beyond it the determination of place. This placelessness beyond the horizon of determinate places is inexhaustible, though the inner area of determinate places is expandable without limit. This is the *emptiness of placelessness.*

Spatiotemporal emptiness and need

All these emptinesses of the apparent spatiotemporal fields—the emptiness of *im*permanence, of *in*occupancy, and of placelessness—signify our unfilled *needs.* They are the appearance of the very same unfilled body needs that first moved us to create this field by moving in it, thus first making it possible for things to appear to us in this field as satisfying our expectations of them. These emptinesses, these holes representing our unfilled needs, are the hollows of the pipes through which wholly unhumanized brute forces force their way into our human world. These forces make their initial worldly appearance in a way that is not wholly subject to our control, and not such as to give them any specific determination as particular localized things of a certain sort, but only such as to give them the apparent character of something-or-other in need of determination and determinable as a particular localized thing of a certain kind. Through these empty pipes of our unfilled needs our experience is porous to the blind, dark, and worldless forces that we try to domesticate by bringing them into our world so as to make this world habitable and endurable, and that we simultaneously *feel as threatening* our very existence and with it that of our world. These pipes of our needs are thus not merely the way in which our experience is porous to the *entrance* of matter into it, but also the way in which it is porous to the *exit* of matter from it. These pipes of our needs are also the drains down which things may *disappear* from our human world, once again stripping down into the same naked, blind, dark forces that we had once before so carefully clothed by experiencing them in a determinate and reliable way.[46] To adduce evidence for this, I must give brief analyses of satisfaction, as the meeting of needs; of pain and its relation to the disappearance of things; and of responsiveness and its relation to the determination and localization of things in the field of experience.

2.5.7 Satisfaction

The spatiotemporal life-field of apparent circumstances, which we generate about ourselves by moving, is the field of our body needs in which things can appear only insofar as they are relevant to our needs by meeting them or failing to meet them. In satisfactory objects that appear in the field of our experience, we "meet our needs," that is, we close the motivational gap, we eliminate the motivational distance, which separates us from the circumstantial field that we at once generate and find ourselves in the midst of. Satisfaction involves a relation not just between ourselves and the satisfying object, but also between both of these and the world of experience that is to some extent closed and completed in the satisfaction. Thus, for instance, at least momentarily and to some extent, satisfaction, by means of *satiation,* eliminates our sense of an open world-field, of a future still to come, and of circumstances still not fully under our control. To be satisfied is to be content; it is to be full-filled with the given content of the world of our experience, so that our world no longer seems open, empty, still-to-be-satisfactorily-filled.

2.5.8 Pain

Sometimes we have needs that it appears impossible to fill; these needs constitute challenges with which it appears impossible to cope. In case these needs that are now apparently unsatisfiable were previously met by something, that thing now seems to have *disappeared,* and with it its place in the field of our experience seems also to have disappeared. It is nowhere to be found. When apparently unsatisfiable needs are represented by body feelings, these feelings are feelings of physical ache and *pain.* These feelings, about which there is apparently nothing I can do, become, willy-nilly, objectified; that is, they come to appear to me in the same manner as objects around my body. Along with them, the body areas that they affect become objectified, and, consequently, immobilized, incapable of feeling and responding to the needs of my body as a whole, and incapable of participating in the generation of my apparent circumstantial field. I thus come to "have," from my visual point of view, *a* pain down there *in* my foot. I "have" the pain by virtue of giving location to it as a feeling, localizing it in "my" immobilized foot, which I also "have" in the same way. But I do not feel the pain as in *me,* but only as in my *foot. I have* the pain, but I have it *in my foot.* So long as the pain endures, my foot is objectified and disappears from the felt schema of my active body. Of course, it still appears to be *my* foot in a way other objects around me do not appear to be "mine." No part of my body, unless it becomes devoid of *all* feeling, can appear to me *exactly* as an object.

The pain of pain consists rather in the *tension* by which a certain proper part of my body seems to be in the process of withdrawing or disappear*ing* from my felt body, and becoming merely an object to me. If this process is completed, the body part loses all feeling and becomes numb, or, more accurately, ceases even to feel numb, and loses all feeling as, e.g., with the numbness or loss of feeling that succeeds the pain of becoming frostbitten in some extremity. If the process is entirely reversed, health and easy functioning are restored to the body part, and the pain disappears. Pain is the middle state of a body area in the process of being forcefully turned into an object for the subject having that body.

In excruciating pain I do not merely "have" a pain out there in some body area. I am *myself in pain*. In this case, the pain is so overwhelming that it racks and pains my whole body, so that I can scarcely distinguish any more where in my body it is coming from. My *entire* responsive, active felt body schema disappears, so that I lose all mobility by which I can generate a spatiotemporal field around me. I am left only with my single, isolated visual point of view, which is itself enveloped in the pain, the only thing I feel. This *is* my world, and my world has only one location, which is me, my visual point of view, in my world. Or, more accurately, this pain is the disappearance of my world, felt by me, from my visual point of view. I feel this disappearance as simultaneously my losing of my world (my experiential field in which objects can appear to me) and, in this loss, my losing of myself (as living *in* that world). The pain in which *I* am, is my losing of myself in my losing of my world by my losing of my body.

2.5.9 Disappearance

The disappearance of something in my experience involves always the disappearance also of the part of my apparent spatiotemporal field with which the given thing was concerned. The disappearance of an object that once appeared to me in the field of my experience involves also the disappearance of the place in the field of my experience in which it once appeared. The disappearance, in physical pain, of a body area from the felt schema of my active body, involves the disappearance also of the part of the field of my experience that was generated by the given part of my felt body. The disappearance, in excruciating pain, of the whole of the felt schema of my active body, involves the disappearance of the whole of the field of my experience that was generated by my active felt body. If some needs appear incapable of being met, by virtue of the disappearance of the things that once satisfied them, and that were hence affixed to, or localized in them, then these needs disappear; they are no longer felt. However, if too many of our felt needs disappear, as, for example, by virtue of the pain or dis-ease of the body, which in its health is the condition of the possibility of their being met, then the entire field of our experience disappears; our entire apparent circumstantial spatiotemporal field in which objects could appear, disappears. My need, like the apparent field of my experience, can be discerned only so long as it appears possible to fill it.

2.5.10 Antifacts

Only endurable conditions can endure in the world of experience. One can not really conceive of unendurable conditions; unendurable conditions are "inconceivable conditions," "unimaginable conditions." When one attempts, for example, to imagine or conceive of conditions at Auschwitz, one generally "succeeds" only by drawing a false curtain or semblance of reasonableness over them; one soberly reckons up the number of people killed, the sociological causes, etc. But the hellish experience of those who died there is not expressed by such thoughts. Perhaps a great novelist could express the forced human disintegration that, for the most part, was Auschwitz. Still he would succeed only in making us feel the unimaginability and inconceivability of this hole in the world.[47] Auschwitz did not really happen "in" the world, in the full sense of that term. It was an *exit from* the world. This does not mean there was no Auschwitz. To arrive at such a conclusion would be to treat the people who died there less barbarously only than they were treated at Auschwitz itself, for it would be to hold that no special "event" (using the term *merely* in its ordinary sense) occurred near the town of Auschwitz. Something did occur at Auschwitz, but what it was, was not merely an event in the world, but a *break-out-from the world*.

Auschwitz was its grim chimneys, and these did not empty into the heavens we can see but into that brutal night where the delicate web of experience is torn to shreds; where no man can live, and of which no man can know. *Auschwitz was not compatible with the nature of the world.* In it space and time, body and life, heaven and earth were rent. Auschwitz was a negative fact, an *antifact*; not a fact, but a *defect of the world.*

2.5.11 Responsiveness

It is through our responsiveness that objects come to appear in the field of our experience (the field of our needs) as having at once a determinate character as particular things of a certain sort and a determinate location as in a particular place in our apparent field. In movement[48] we usually know what we are doing because we are ourselves usually making it happen. Generally speaking, we do not merely have dubitable, or even indubitable, *evidence of* what is happening. *We know* what is happening because we are aware of ourselves as making it happen, as responsible for its happening; because what we are doing is *self*-evident. Sometimes we do not know what we are doing. These are the times when our movement is uncoordinated and unskilled; when we are clumsy, fumbling, disoriented, ill at ease (dis-eased) in our actively felt bodies; when we are awkward, that is, etymologically, wrongly turned, as though back-ward, in our "movements."[49] In forward movement, we generally know what we are doing. In back-ward "movement" we rarely know what we are doing; we appear not so much to be doing something as to be un-doing things. By this I mean that, doing things right, we skillfully bind them together through the development or exercise of effective habits in respect to them. But doing things wrong, we awk-wardly take them apart by handling them in such a way as to prevent or destroy habitual ways of handling them.

Taking backward "movement" as the paradigm of awk-ward "movement," let us consider why this is so. If I approach things backwards, I first become aware of them only *after* I have already passed them. Therefore, I cannot *come* to have them in any way. Things first appear to me as passing away, without having ever apparently come into my presence. In order to develop a habit of responding to something, however, I must be aware *that* something is coming, before it comes, and even before I know *what* it is. My knowledge of what it is, is largely fixed by my response to it, which is first possible only after some anticipation of it. *To develop a habit in respect to something, I must be able to anticipate its presence,* that is, to face it while it is still before me and before I have reached it, or it me. Then I can pass it by responding to it. Passing something by responding to it, I can fix it as a thing of a certain kind, because in responding to it I know what I am doing. In passing an object by responding to it as an anticipated object, I retroactively give a place and a character to the anticipated as well as the presently apparent object. If I am taken unaware, if something happens too suddenly and unexpectedly, I *cannot* know what is happening because the gap between expectation and occurrence is narrowed within the minimally discernible range. This range may differ somewhat from person to person, and for a given person from time to time, but each person always has some such threshold of expectability, some minimal reaction-time, which sets a limit to his ability to respond. If things first appear, and then become present to someone, within this minimum response-time, he must be taken by sur-prise; that is, taken over by something before he has had a chance, through being able to anticipate it, to respond effectively to it and thus take *it* over. To act awk-wardly is to act without being aware of what you are going to do before you do it. Lacking anticipatory knowledge of your own movements, you are unable to anticipate the motions of objects "coming" toward you, or toward which you are "going." Lacking anticipatory knowledge of your own movements, you can have no idea where you will meet any object, hence you cannot anticipate the "coming" of any object. Being unable to anticipate an object you become unable to respond to its coming, and thus you become unable to fix its nature by self-produced movement in respect to it as passing.

To illustrate, let us return to our baseball, which is still in the air. To catch a ball well, we must be able to anticipate our own movements with respect to it. Seeing the ball coming, we must be able to anticipate our own movements in order to anticipate how it will meet us, become present to us. This done, that is, being set or limber to receive the ball, we may respond to the ball's actual arrival by catching it, holding it fast in our hands as a caught-ball. *We come to know for sure that it is a ball by catching it as a ball.* If I merely wait inertly for the ball to reach me, wait as a pure spectator with an inactive body, then when the ball finally reaches me it will appear to do so all of a sudden, hitting me or whizzing by me, allowing me no opportunity to respond to it by catching it. At best, at the last moment I may make a grotesque, jerking motion,[50] more in startled bewilderment than in a real effort to catch the ball. The "ball" then appears to me mainly as a missile of indeterminate character that is not so much to be responded to as to be avoided. Or the ball may appear to me as a puff of smoke in the air, in which case I would have my belief in virtue of a posture of indifference to this apparently insubstantial and inconsequential thing; or I may have heard that it is a ball, and, if asked, would verbally identify it as a ball. But only the ball-player understands feelingly that it is a ball, i.e., knows at first-(his own)-hand, that it is a ball.

The actual a priori of poised response

I have to "catch onto," or "get," whatever I know by anticipating it, and then somehow confirming this anticipation by an actual (present) response to the thing anticipated. It is the terminal (postanticipatory) response to a thing that enables me to know it; to fix it as certainly having a certain meaning; to put an end to the ambiguity of its merely anticipated, suspected character; finally to de-*termine* it, to give it a de-*termination.* The final (actual, present) response to a (future) anticipated object enables me to *know* that object because the response, as *my self-produced movement,* is directly and evidently known to me in virtue of its mere existence or occurrence. *For effective movement, and only for effective movement, to be is to be known. I know what I am doing just insofar as I am really doing it.*

The activity of our body is required for the world of our experience to exist as the humanly habitable world. This activity of the body, the sense of its ability to be active, is attested to even by the body in its state of inactivity, for in-active experience appears as a merely privative state of the normally active body. The existence of the human body as capable of activity is necessary for the world of human experience. But the human body has not merely the kind of "necessity" that the philosophic tradition from time to time accorded to the existence of various beings, such as God, or the thinking substance; nor does it have the kind of "necessity" that this tradition from time to time accorded to the truth of various principles, such as the principles of sufficient reason, of noncontradiction, and of the schematized Kantian categories. For all these "necessities" were the necessities of something that *could* be known to be necessary. The point of the demonstration of their necessity was to bring the reader to first *learn* of their necessity, and thus the manner of their demonstration itself demonstrated that they might *not* be known to be necessary, though they would not for that reason cease to *be* necessary. *But the existence of the human body as capable of activity* is not merely necessary for there to *be* a world of human experience, it is also *necessarily known, in order for there to be a world of human experience.* This is so because the activity of the human body is necessarily known in the responsive act by which we first know anything in the world; the act by which we first make the world habit-able; the act, in other words, by which we first make the world a world, i.e., a place in which we can live.

My response to an anticipated object reveals to me directly, merely by virtue of its existence, not merely the self-produced movements of my own body by which I make that response, but also, and equally immediately, that thing in respect to which I have been able to make the response. This is not true if I construe the primary form of directed action on the model of an act of will, or other intention of the mind, so that I must await the effect of my actions to see whether they coincide with my previously definite intentions.[51] The primary form of directed action is an intention of the *body*, a body-directedness, which first gives us the global sense of space and time presupposed by all our higher personal forms of directed activity, principally those of will and judgment. This intention of the active body is *poise* in dealing with the things and persons around us. It is sharply to be distinguished from its correlate, the *pose* of the inactive body. Poise is always a way of responding to, of dealing with, objects around one; pose is a way of separating oneself from these objects. Poise does not, when successful, "coincide" or "agree" with its later "effects," as does will with its achievements. Rather, when successful, poise *is* its own effect.

The success of poise is not in its *execution*, but in its very *existence* by which the body is, to begin with, knowingly in touch with the objects around it. In the case of poise, unlike that of will or some other intention of the mind, its goal of knowing what it is doing is achieved *immediately* with the initiation of the activity concerned. As soon as I am poised in my circumstance, I know *what I* am doing. I know not merely what movements *I* am making. I know at once, by doing it, not merely what *I*, with my body, am doing, but also *what* I am doing, i.e., something about those objects to which I am doing something with my body. Poise is not merely a matter of internal bodily coordination, but also of skill in handling things (and persons) about us. Thus, when one fails in what he is attempting to do, one necessarily loses his poise and is, at least momentarily, thrown off balance, however quickly one may recover his balance and poise. To be poised is to be *self*-possessed by being in touch with one's *circumstances*. To lose touch is immediately to lose one's poise. One can, in considerable ignorance of one's circumstances, *pretend* and even *appear to others* to have poise in the given circumstances. But one can never actually be poised, and one can never *appear to oneself* to have poise, in circumstances with which one is presently out of touch. On the other hand, in the case of will, as soon as I make up my mind, I know what *I* am doing. I know where and to what I am *directing* my efforts. But I must await the returns of my activity to discover *what* after all I was doing in the sense of what my activity did to the objects it was directed toward. What I was doing might turn out to be completely different from what I intended to do. In willing, I can clearly distinguish *my own act* from *what it makes of my circumstantial objects*, both from what it makes them out to be, and from what it makes them become. But in poise, no such distinction is possible. My poise is the way I make of my circumstantial objects—merely the circumstantial objects that they originally are, viz., those of felt, active experience.

Response and need

The response to an anticipated object is the meeting-ground of myself and that anticipated object. *In my response I meet my needs*, in two senses: as encountering them; and as satisfying them. I meet the merely anticipated object that appeared first as an ambiguous opportunity for the satisfaction of some-need-or-other. The indeterminate appearance of something distantly before me *is* merely the appearance of something-or-other dangling before the open mouths of the apparent field of all my unslaked needs that together suggest, in clamorous chorus, "perhaps I can be fed by this one." By responding to the anticipated object, when it finally arrives, in a certain way, rather than in some other way, I determine it as food for one of these needs rather than another, and drop it into the corresponding need-mouth by putting it in one place rather than another, which at once types and localizes it. In responding to the anticipated object when it finally arrives, I thus "meet," in the sense of encountering, a specific pre-existent need, finally selected from among all my pre-existent needs, by determining the object in such a way as to "meet," in the sense of satisfying, that particular need.

I need to clarify the relation between our responsive localization and our determination of an object. Insofar as apparent things are of indeterminate nature, we have difficulty localizing them precisely. They bewilder and disorient us. Only when we know what is coming, and therefore what to expect, can we carefully trace the course of its approach. If we do not know what is coming, we do not know what to expect, and we cannot continually prepare or brace our self to meet it. Because we cannot continually re-orient our self so as eventually to meet it, we tend to lose track of it. For we "locate" something by orienting our self in respect to it, by attending to it. If we do not know what something is, it tends continually to escape our at-tending to it, much as we tend to lose track of a fly ball if we do not feelingly know what it is to catch it; that is, if we do not know with our bodies how to catch it; in a word, if we cannot *poise* our self to catch it.

Localization, determination, and need

Localization is knowing *where* to find something; determination, knowing *what* can be found there. Finding is the satisfaction of seeking. Seeking is being moved by a need. Finding is the satisfaction of need-impelled movement. Finding is the "meeting" of one's needs through determining and localizing something as filling the very needs that moved one to seek. By filling one's needs through the finding of some determined thing in some localized place, one first becomes aware of the determinate nature of the need itself. Just as the disappearance of things in the field of experience is attended with a disappearance of a region of this field itself, the determinate appearance of something in the field of our experience is attended by the appearance of some determinate region in this field itself, as a "place" in the field of our experience in which we can put the determined thing. Before a need is ever satisfied, we feel only a vague sense of loss without any definite idea of what it is we are missing, what would remove the sense of loss. We feel only vaguely uneasy, wanting to inquire into this need but without any definite expectation of what we will find there. This character of needs that have never been met is exactly the same as the character of those spatiotemporal regions beyond the horizon of the occupied field of our experience, those regions previously described as having the "emptiness of place-lessness." If we have never had experience of anything in them, we feel there only a vague sense of emptiness without any definite idea of particular empty places in them that could be filled by apparent things of a certain kind. A need, like the field of experience, can appear definite only to the extent that its filling appears possible. Localization, as the finding of satisfaction for a need through the determination of an object of experience as capable[52] of satisfying that need, is the closing of the gap between oneself and the field of one's experience in the midst of which one finds oneself.

These very needs that appear as our experiential field originally opened the gap between us and this field by prompting us to move in the first place, and thus to generate this field in which we "find our self" both as somewhat at a loss and as finding satisfying objects in it. The original needs that drove us to generate a spatiotemporal life-field in which we cannot help seeking to find our self so long as we live, are given, through the original emptiness of this field, as originally concealed; and, through the equally original openness of this field, they are given as determinable and capable of being revealed. But so long as the field of experience is not completely filled up, these original body needs that both prompt the movement by which the field is generated, and themselves appear as the generated field, appear as only partially revealed, remaining and appearing as also partially concealed. But this "partialness" is not to be understood partitively, as though one part of the field were revealed and another concealed. As we have seen, the apparent spatiotemporal field of active felt experience is an indivisible whole. It has no separable parts though it has distinguishable regions. Satisfaction is also global. The measure of our satisfaction in one area is a sense of satisfaction about our whole world, so that if the local satisfaction is extreme, we lose—at least temporarily—all sense that there is still *anything* left to be done. Likewise with dissatisfaction and disappearance. Local dissatisfaction gives us a sense of dissatisfaction with our world. Local disappearance appears as a hole or defect in our entire world, and, if the local disappearance is of something very important, with it we lose, at least temporarily, all sense that there is still *anything* left in the world, and therewith we lose, at least temporarily, our sense of the world itself. When one no longer has any felt needs, any motivation, in a given area, one is incapable of responding to anything in that area and one consequently no longer feels certain about determinations of things of that sort. Apathy, frustration and satiation, by making one incapable of responding to anything through lack of felt want, are alike in dis-solving one's sense of conviction about the characteristics of the things in question. However, one cannot find oneself in a pure field of experience empty of all determinate, regularly appearing, objects. The field of experience must have at least some de-termination if it exists at all, by the very fact that we *find* our self in it.

Failure of response

We have so far considered a satisfying response, i.e., one that meets (encounters and satisfies) a pre-existent and previously unmet need. In such a case, I know what I am doing just insofar as I am really doing it. However, if my response is unsatisfying, meets no needs, then I determine nothing by it, and have not really done anything I was trying to do though I may have done something *to* what I was trying to do something *with*. I did not really know what I was doing because I did not succeed in really doing it. I did not succeed in doing what I was trying to do. I did not succeed in meeting, with my response (my doing), one of the needs that clamored to be met at the initial appearance of the anticipated object and that by so clamoring first moved me to do something, viz., to respond when the anticipated object arrived. It is only in failure of response, and loss of poise, that a distinction appears between what I was trying to do and what I did. When I act in an effective, poised way, it is not merely that what I was trying to do is in *agreement* with what I (distinguishably) did do. Rather, there is no gap at all between my own action and what it made of my surroundings, so that no agreement or disagreement could be noticed; there were no two things to compare, but only the *perfect fit* of me-in-my-circumstances. Whenever there is a distinction in active felt experience between what I try to do and what I do do, it is because I fail to do what I am trying to do, and because I thereby, to some extent, and at least momentarily, lose my poise—becoming disoriented in my circumstances, losing track of, and thereby losing, both myself and my circumstances, and dimming the entire world of my experience.

The poise of inactive experience

But insofar as I have a world of experience at all, dim or bright, I necessarily to some extent know what I am doing, because I am necessarily, to some extent, really doing it in poised responsiveness to the objects about me. Even in my inactive, spectatorial experience, some element of poised responsiveness remains. Even though I withdraw from the things I am observing, by sitting or standing still as a mere spectator, nevertheless, in order to be at ease in my inactivity in respect to what I see, I must maintain a reliable actively responsive sense of poise and balance in the place where I am standing or sitting, in the place *from* which I am inactively observing.

We necessarily know to some extent what we are doing because we are necessarily to some extent really doing it, and thereby making our world habit-able, if we have a world of experience at all. This is the rock of our knowledge on which all scepticisms and dogmatisms are shattered, even those scepticisms and dogmatisms to which, as we will see, the capacious and elaborate Kant was not immune.

2.6 Reconsideration of Hume

I have now concluded my long digression from Hume that began in an attempt to answer the question, how does the wholeness of the movement-generated field of our experience guarantee any ("necessary") connection, such as Hume sought and thought impossible, between the things appearing in this field? To answer this question I have tried to develop some of the implications of the fact that *the field of our experience is a life-field*.[53] Now I will try to clarify some of my conclusions by commenting, in terms of them, upon some lines from the *Treatise*.

2.6.1 The nonvariability of the human body unnoticed by Hume

Hume writes that "there is no impression constant and invariable."[54] Now for the active man, his body through which he has impressions is nonvariable—*neither variable nor invariable.* His body serves rather as the center or norm of his life. His body is his way of measuring whether or not a variation has taken place in something around him; things around him appear variant or invariant depending upon whether or not there is a variation in his bodily response to them. But he has no way of responding *to* his body, whether variably or invariably. All his bodily response is *with* his body, to things around him. Therefore his active body cannot appear to the active man as either variable or invariable in nature,[55] but merely as the condition of the possibility of things appearing variably to him. The active man has a sense of his body as such a normalizing condition of his life. For him it is therefore a *non sequitur* to follow Hume in concluding from the variability of all impressions that "it cannot be from any of these impressions . . . that the idea of self is derived; and consequently there is no such idea,"[56] or there is only a fictional idea of a supposedly invariant impression, "or of something mysterious."[57] His body is something of which he does have an idea, yet it is neither a variable impression nor a fictionally invariant impression, nor yet something mysterious and inexplicable.

2.6.2 Observation, perceptual inference, and poise: Hume's view criticized

Hume frequently writes that the *observation* of constant union of objects *produces the inference* of the mind from objects resembling the constantly conjoined antecedents to objects resembling the constantly conjoined consequents.[58] The implication of our analyses is that the *inference, equally, produces the observation* of the constant union, for we can see as determinate and uniform in their appearance only those objects that we are in some way *prepared* to see, namely, by way of the bodily inferences of poise that we make from the anticipated appearance of those objects to their actual appearance. The actual "observation" is, of course, also necessary to produce the inference, in that the actual observation is necessary in order retroactively to complete the inference. Poise is lost as soon as anticipations cease being met as rapidly as they are made. *There is no time interval between the having and the meeting of the anticipation of poise.* Poise functions exactly at the threshold of response-time. Poise functions at that level of our experience where the flow of appearances is perfectly smooth and continuous. Beneath this level, that is, with a shorter interval between the appearance and the arrival of objects, the flow of experience becomes turbulent and disorderly; we become disoriented as the appearance of things is continually aborted, in that objects seem to be "gone" before they have "come," as if their disappearance preceded their appearance. But at the level of poise, things appear only insofar as they have been inferred by our bodily actions to appear; and, equally, things are inferred to appear only insofar as they actually do appear. This is just another way of saying that, at the level of poise, I know what I am doing just because I really am doing it.

2.6.3 Critique of Hume on pleasure and pain

Another of Hume's recurrent themes is expressed in the following pair of quotations:

Pain and pleasure (is) the chief spring and moving principle of all actions (of the human mind).[59]

If we believe that fire warms, or water refreshes, it is only because it costs us too much pain to think otherwise.[60]

On my view, both these conclusions are substantially correct, but for a reason that Hume never suspects, because it is not even formulable in terms of his philosophy. Pain and pleasure move the human mind in all its particular actions by which it makes and unmakes the whole *world* of experience *in* which all particular actions occur. The human body is first prompted to be a moving body at all, and thus to generate the spatiotemporal field of appearances (which is the apparent world of our needs), only by its needs that, literally, move the body to find pleasure (satisfaction of its needs), and to avoid pain (dissatisfaction of its needs). Pleasure (or satisfaction) and pain (or dissatisfaction), then, are not merely certain experiences among others *in* the world of our experience; they are the experiences of making and unmaking the very world in which particular experiences are first possible. A degree of pleasure and of pain, of satisfaction and of dissatisfaction, thus pervades every possible experience in virtue of its being in the world of experience. Pleasure and pain are not particular experiences among others. In virtue of being the experiences of the *world* of experience, they are *apparent forms of all experience.* If Hume had recognized this, he would not have written, "if we believe that fire warms, or water refreshes, it is *only* (my italics) because it costs us too much pain to think otherwise." If pleasure and pain are apparent forms of our experience as, broadly speaking, completed and destroyed, what *better* reason could there be for maintaining a belief than its satisfactoriness? Hume inserts this "only" because he believes that, while we somehow cannot in fact help maintaining those beliefs accompanied by the particular impression of satisfaction, the truth of those beliefs is logically quite independent of their satisfactoriness. On my view, the occurrence of a determinate impression must satisfy the general requirement that we appear able to live with such things. But on Hume's view, such occurrences[61] need satisfy only the determinate character they exhibit; possible determinations are not themselves constrained by any character of the human world.

2.6.4 Critique of Hume on the uniformity of nature

Hume assumes that sense experience (of impressions) is *immediately determinate* rather than initially determinable—as expressed, for example, by his previously footnoted statement that "all impressions are clear and precise." He concludes that there is no justification for our habitual tendency to believe that instances, of which we have had no experience, must resemble those of which we have had experience, and that the course of nature continues always uniformly the same.[62]

I will argue in this section that if Hume were right in his assumption, his conclusion would indeed follow; not only this conclusion, however, but a still more radical conclusion that Hume does not suspect, and that would render his entire position incomprehensible. I will try to show, however, that Hume's assumption (for which he never gives any arguments) is false; and that the corresponding truth is such as to provide grounds for a justification of the view that the "course of nature" is at least likely to be generally uniform.

Consider Hume's interpretation of "uniformity." Hume is mainly concerned to show that there is no justification for expecting that impressions will be regularly *associated* in the future as we remember them to have been in the past. "Uniformity" of experience means for Hume primarily regularity of spatiotemporal association between *distinct* impressions. Thus, for example, the endurance of an identical object (substance) means for Hume the continued coexistence of the same *set* of contiguous impressions, as revealed by looking back and forth among them and noting the regularity of what Kant calls their "reciprocal succession." For Hume, thus, the "uniformity" of nature lies primarily in the regular way it *changes* appearance time after time. He tends to ignore the "uniformity" of unchanging appearance through a period of time. This is in consequence of the fact that Hume *starts* with an elementary determined object (impression), and thinks there is no problem as to how perception of its initial determination is achieved or retained. Hume's assumption of initially determinate impressions, and his interpretation of the "uniformity" of nature, offer a striking parallel to the corresponding assumption and interpretation of the popularized Newtonian science of his day, which Hume greatly admired.[63] Like the atoms of the physicists, with their fixed and definite mass, size, and shape, Hume's impressions are initially determinate "atoms" of perception subject to change of their external relations ("associations") with other such atoms, but not subject to change of their internal characteristics. And as the physicists' laws described the surprisingly invariant character of change (e.g., the invariant value of the acceleration of a freely falling body), so Hume concentrated on investigating the invariant character of perceptual changes. This parallel is noted in an attempt to provide some explanation for what otherwise seems to be an oversight in an acute thinker. Perhaps Hume thought (or felt) that the impressiveness of Newton's achievement was of itself sufficient justification for the application of Newton's method to the analysis of evidence and belief. At any rate, for Hume *the determinacy of our experience poses no problem, and is logically independent of the uniformity of our experience.*

Kant tries to answer Hume by showing that this separation between determinacy and uniformity is impossible on the level of our *theoretical* judgments about experience. Kant tries to show that the very *form* of a definite theoretical judgment about experience implies the uniformity of determinate experience from time to time. He tries to show that, contrary to Hume, lack of uniformity in our determinate experience is not even possible—because this possibility does not make sense. According to Kant, the possibility is inconceivable—not because we find it psychologically too hard to entertain, but because the judgment asserting this possibility contradicts the implications of applying logical forms to temporal intuition, i.e., the implications of making a definite theoretical judgment about experience. Kant thus holds that the judgment, "Determinate experience lacks uniformity," is self-contradictory (since it implies by content what it denies by form); hence, that it is false in principle. Kant's answer, as I will discuss later, shows at best that our perceptual experience must be uniform *if* it is to be theoretically intelligible.

My answer to Hume parallels Kant's, but is made on the *perceptual* level. It thus provides, if valid, a more complete answer to Hume, by showing that our experience must be not merely *conditionally* uniform (depending upon the theoretical intelligibility of our perceptual experience), but *categorically* so (assuming only that we have some determinate perceptual experience). On the other hand, my general line of argument is merely an imitation of Kant's. My innovation consists wholly in applying Kant's general argument at a different point in experience. If I claim to have achieved a stronger result than Kant, it is only in virtue of more effectively applying a lever that he first made and left for our use.

I will try to show that *the very determinacy of perceptual experience implies the uniformity of that experience from time to time.* The complete irregularity of determinate perceptual experience is impossible—not merely psychologically too hard to believe, but *impossible to perceive,* hence impossible in principle. This is so because of the *form* of perceptual experience, because the anticipatory and responsive *way* in which perceptual experience is made determinate implies the likely stability of these determinations over time. Perception is conservative by virtue of its form alone; the way an object is perceived to be determinate in the first place implies that it must be presumed unchanged unless there is additional perceptual evidence to the contrary. If without subsequent evidence, we are doubtful that some initial determination of an object is likely to continue, then we are also doubtful that the object was correctly determined to begin with.

Let us first turn to a criticism of Hume, trying to drive him even further into skepticism. Consider the question: How do we know that our past experience as remembered remains uniform with what it was as first experienced? Suppose we have some present perceptual experience. With the passage of time, the given experience appears gradually to recede into the past; later memories (memories of later events) accumulate, and interpose themselves in an ever-thickening set between our present experience and our initial remembered experience. How do we know that our initial experience will remain stable and identifiable during this recession? How do we know that our ever changing memory-perspective of it (as if it were continually being seen through an ever-longer series of translucent pieces of vari-colored glass, each nearer piece representing a later remembered experience) will not be associated with a random change in it? Hume takes it for granted that our memory of a given event is stable and unaffected by its temporal recession in respect to later events. He must take this stability for granted in order to make sense of his basic question: What justification do we have for our expectation that our future experience will resemble our past experience? The question can be meaningfully posed only if it is therewith presupposed that our past experience exhibits a *fixed* pattern of stably identifiable impressions to which new patterns can be compared. If our memories changed at random we could not legitimately regard our memories as of past events; nor, therefore, as really *memories*. The hypothesis that our memories change at random implies that we do not really remember anything. But in that case, short of a remembered past, we would not be able even to expect (not to mention, know) that our future experience will resemble our past experience. Hume, however, always assumes without argument that we certainly *can* expect this resemblance, even though he concludes that we can not justify this expectation.

By assigning a fundamental role to the function of expectation, Hume assumes without argument that there is another mode of stability in our experience. The very meaning of our "expecting something," implies that *what* we expect does not change while we are expecting it. "Expecting something" *is* a way of keeping the *same* thing in mind *throughout* some period before a certain event. Hume holds that we certainly *do* continue for a time to expect events of a certain fixed kind, granted our fixed memories of our past experience. Yet how do we *know* that we stably expect a certain fixed outcome all the while we await a certain event? We are in fact led to *believe* that we often continually expect a single outcome while awaiting a certain event, but what *justification* do we have for this belief? Perhaps what we expect continually changes at random, and perhaps our memory of what we have been expecting continually changes in exactly the same way. Hume writes as though he *knows*, rather than merely believes, that we often continually expect the same thing—yet he never offers the evidence or justification for this belief in virtue of which it has title to knowledge. Nevertheless, there seems to be something foolish rather than profound about raising a serious doubt on this point. I do not raise the question of this belief's justification for the purpose of showing that it is *un*answerable, but rather for the purpose of showing the importance of the kind of answer that *can* be given.

The justification for our common belief (uncritically shared by Hume) that our impressions often remain uniform (stable) while we expect some-thing, is, I believe, two-fold. (1) The activity of expecting-something does not make sense without this assumption. Expecting-something involves waiting for it; hence, it involves continually expecting that same thing for some period of time. We may, of course, first expect one thing and then come to expect something else, thus changing our mind about what we expect while waiting for it to happen. But unless we expect one thing for at least a *little* while, we have not settled our self into really "expecting" anything at all. (2) The activity of expecting-something is so basic and pervasive in our experience, that every statement about our experience implies its occurrence. Thus no *meaning* can be given to the suggested possibility that "experience" (which we understand to *involve* expectation, hence some stability in what we expect) might be *without* the stability required for expectation, hence also without other characteristic functions such as our perceptual sense of a definite future. Making this hypothesis, we cease to speak about experience. We continue to use the *word*, "experience," but shorn of its meaning. We are, in effect, hypothesizing that experience is something other than experience; that experience is not experience. Is that not *possible*? No. Why not? Because it does not make sense.

Now the point in beginning with this criticism of Hume is to show that we can justify our common assumption (which Hume uncritically shares) that our impressions remain uniform *while* we expect something *in just the same way and measure* as we can justify our common assumption (of which Hume is so critical) that our impressions are likely to remain uniform *when* something finally happens.

The form of argument is simple. It is impossible in principle that any function definitive of "perceptual" activity be inoperative in perceptual experience; for the possibility in question is self-contradictory. The likelihood that what has been proven by experience in the past will be corroborated in the future, is definitive of "perceptual" activity; hence, it is unquestionable that this likelihood obtains for perceptual experience. The difficulty and interest of the matter lies, of course, in the specific analysis of the network of activities characteristic or "definitive" of perception. In offering this analysis, and showing that it implies the uniformity of our perceptual experience, I will assume the validity of the phenomenological analyses given in the preceding sections.

Perception is determination of an object through an effective response that forms a skill in the percipient. The whole spatiotemporal field of perception is organized about the active percipient who evidently retains his identity in the course of his activity. The percipient himself comes to be characterized by the skills he acquires. Through discovery of determinate objects, the freely self-moving percipient creates his own determinate skillful self.

(1) Now as the percipient accumulates skills proven effective by his past perceptual experience, *his* perceptual field (evidently generated by *his* capacity to perceive) must reflect this enrichment. To *have* a determinate perceptual field (of one's own) *is* to have evidence of one's general, though not unerring, capacity to effectively determine objects with one's present skills.

(2) A percipient can have a determinate perceptual field only by being *poised* in it. But we have seen that poise is possible only so long as one's anticipations, based on the continuity of immediately past impressions, are met as soon as they are made. *Our poise is sensuous proof that the perceptual experience of our immediate future conforms to that of our immediate past, and without poise no determinate perception is possible.* Consider for example our condition while tripping, and up to but not including the point when we catch our self. In this interval we have lost our balance; in one fell swoop, our entire stock of poised responses (employable only on condition that we are balanced) is thereby rendered inoperable. For the moment, accordingly, we are not aware of knowing anything. We are not even aware that we are tripping. We catch our self by an instinctive (rather than self-conscious) re-action, and only then come to realize what *did* happen to us. On our view, it is not just a familiar and seemingly insignificant fact that we cannot consciously know anything while tripping; it is a *necessary fact* because implied by the form of perceptual knowledge.

(3) We can determinately perceive only what we can *anticipate.* And we can anticipate only what is indicated by, and will bear out, our past and present experience up to the point of anticipation. Thus *if an impression is to be determinate, it must conform to our previous experience.* This does not mean that our anticipations must always be met, and that experience must always be uniform. It only means that if the uniformity of our experience is disrupted, determinate perception of the novel course of experience must be preceded by some *failure* of determinate perception produced by acting on the

old anticipations (which this failure renders in-operative, thus making way for new anticipations). For example, suppose we are given a jug to drink from, and suppose it is so constructed that its liquid contents are concealed from us. Suppose we are told by friends that it contains our favorite liquor, though it really contains milk. We will take a draught from it in anticipation of the liquor. Our first taste is that something-or-other undetermined is horribly wrong with the liquor. Only *then*, activating our whole gamut of taste-anticipation in order to determine what it is, do we determine that it is familiar milk. This shock of disbelief, attendant upon our unmet anticipation, may be quite brief, but it is noticeable. Thus Hume, as see saw, has only half the story in noting that the observation of constant union of objects produces our inference from objects resembling the constantly conjoined antecedents to objects resembling the constantly conjoined consequents. The implication of our analysis is that the perceptual inference (anticipation) also produces the observation of constant conjunction. For we *can* determinately perceive only what our anticipation *prepares* us to perceive.

(4) Because perception is anticipatory; because we can determinately perceive only what our foregoing experience prepares us to perceive, perception is *habit-forming*. For example, very crudely counterfeited bills are often passed for a surprisingly long time, because people are so used to receiving genuine bills that they seem to see "D-O-L-L-A-R," even though "D-O-L-A-R" is printed on the bill. Similarly, the most punctilious proofreader occasionally "sees" what he "knows" to have been written, though it is not there. It is a familiar fact that perception is habit forming in this way. But in my view, this habit-forming character of perception is a necessary, not merely contingent, fact because it follows from the anticipatory function requisite to make perceptual sense. The intrinsically habit-forming character of perception acts to stabilize our experience, minimizing the discrepancy between new and old experience, making forthcoming determinate perception more likely than not to conform to our past perceptual experience.

(5) Because perceptual determination is the outcome of anticipated response, it is intrinsically retroactive, determining not merely what the object *is* (as manifest upon conclusion of the

determining response), but also what the object *was* (what it turns out to *have been* during the period required for determination of it to take place). What we determine is evidently the *same object* we anticipated; and what we determine it *as*, is likewise the *same* as what we anticipated determining it as. Therefore perceptual determination of an object, in its capacity as responsive, at once presupposes and proves the *stability* of the determined object for at least the period of perceptual response-time. Therefore impressions can be determinate only if they turn out to have been uniformly so for at least a minimal period of time.

(6) The field of our experience can endure in intelligible form only so long as our experience in it is endurable, i.e., not "unimaginably" or "inconceivably" horrid.[64] It is the field of our *needs* and the *manifestly possible meeting* of them—which takes place by the determination of an object as something we apparently can live with. The field of our experience can thus endure only so long as we, by responsive action, can make it *habitable*: habitable, as our habitation, or dwelling place, *where* we live: and habit-able, as a place to which we can become *accustomed* as the determinately skilled percipients (marked by our past experience) we gradually create ourselves to be. In order that the field of our needs endure, we must be able to accommodate ourselves to it as the particular percipients we are, with our particular needs being uniformly discovered and met in at least a minimal way. Our desires are somewhat restricted by the facts, which eliminate unrealistic desires. But what can be countenanced as a perceptual fact is also limited by our indispensable human needs. Hume would agree that the percipient and his impressions would cease to be, if his needs were inadequately met. But for Hume this would be no more than an (unjustifiable) empirical generalization. He does not hold that the perceptual field is intrinsically a field of need—as evident from the way it appears, and from the way objects appear determinate in it.

(7) We saw that determination of an object in our perceptual field of needs involves a form of *satisfaction* that is not merely with the given object but also with our whole world of experience in which that object appears. Since we as percipients are indivisibly satisfied by the determination, the global field of our experience

(whose unity is correlative with our own as its percipient) is also indivisibly characterized as one in which a certain skillful response is successful. The global character of the satisfaction attendant upon perceptual determination of an object implies that what satisfies us here and now is also likely to satisfy us there and then in this same perceptual world. The well-known habit-forming character of skillful action in general and of rewarded action in particular, is not just a fact about our experience, but is implied by the definite form or structure of our perceptual experience. It is implied not only, as we saw above, by the anticipatory character of perception, but also by the global character of perceptual satisfaction, which serves to generalize the evident employability of a locally effective response.

(8) Objects determined in a certain way thereby appear capable of being later perceived in the same determinate way because the original determination was made possible only under the condition that the object was apparently *movable* or *variously approachable* without loss of identity or change of determination. The expected stability of a determinate perceptual object is not, as Hume thinks, merely an *additional* supposition subsequent to the determinate appearance of the object; it is rather a supposition necessarily accepted and acted upon in order to produce the *initial* determinate appearance. For the immediately apparent mobility (unrestricted in principle) of the stably determinate perceptual object, comes from the *free* manner in which the initial determination of the object is responsively made. The object anticipated as determin*able* appeared capable of being met or avoided by us, without change of its discoverable determinations; it appeared susceptible to being responsively approached from this side or that, without change of its discoverable determinations; it appeared as subject to either being determined there and then or being waited out for determination under other more favorable conditions, without change of its discoverable determinations. Uniformity of the future determinations of a perceptual object with its past and present determinations is thus implied to begin with, in the very determin*ing* of the object; the uniformity supposed to attend a manifestly determin*ed* object is merely a *continuation* of a belief already accepted with the determining of the object, and already proved as

soon as the object is evidently determined. If belief in the stability of the manifestly determin*ed* object is dropped, then this belief must also be dropped about the determin*able* object, for the latter belief reciprocally implies and is implied by the former upon completion of the determining activity in the concluding and conclusive proof of poise. However, if the belief about the determinable object is *really* dropped (i.e., if it is dropped in practice as well as theory), then no determinate perception is any longer possible, for we cannot engage in the free self-movement (of anticipation and response) necessary for determining an object without making the practical assumption that the same object is discoverable by a *variety* of approaches to it under a *variety* of field-conditions. Such real loss of perceptual faith implies catatonia.

2.6.5 Critique of Hume on the foundation of probability

The preceding discussion implies an objection to another remark of Hume,

Probability . . . must, in some respects, be founded on the impressions of our memory and senses, and, in some respects, on our ideas.[65]

I have argued that our memory, our sense, and our ideas *presuppose* in our experience a probability of order founded on the condition that all our experience occurs in a holistic spatiotemporal life-field generated by our holistically active body in its attempt (which must be at least minimally successful) to meet its needs unified as all its "own, all belonging to its singular bodily self. When active, we do not "have" our body by having a memory of it, or by having an idea of it. Rather, *through* our body movement (or preparedness to move), which is the same as our *own* movement (or preparedness to move), we are first able to have memories or impressions of something as having happened *to us* in our single *world* of experience; and through our body movement we are first able to have ideas of something occurring *to us* in *our* reflections about them if, as Hume holds and we agree, abstract ideas are derived from experience of apparent objects. For it is only through being active that we first have a single world of experience in which particular experiences can occur, with or without probability. And it is only through experience taking place in the world generated by our own active body, that this experience is "our" personal experience rather than being the impersonal experience of a dis-embodied point of view; so that, "*our* memory and senses and. . . ideas" could exist as "ours," with whatever any antecedent degree of probability, only in virtue of our bodily action. Further, it is only through having active bodies that we make it probable that there will be a (satisfying) order among these memories, senses, and ideas, whose occurrence, whose existence as in a world, and whose character as "ours," have also first been made possible by these active bodies.

Hume writes that "All reasonings are nothing but the effects of custom."[66] The argument of this book is in substantial agreement that all reasonings are the effects of custom. But Hume's evaluation of this is held to be incorrect. That the world of experience, insofar as it is an ordered world, is a world of custom, tells us not, as Hume supposes, merely what happens so far to be the case, but what *must* be the case in this world. For the world of experience is the world we live in, in the full and active sense of being "lively." That means it must be a habit-able world, which is to say, a world to which we can become ac-customed. Therefore, insofar as reasonings are about the world of experience, the fact that they are effects of custom or habit does not in the least make their validity suspect, but is rather the source of their validity. Hence, Hume's expression, "nothing but," is out of place here, much as his previously cited remark that we "only" believe certain things because it costs us too much pain to think otherwise.

2.6.6 Clarification of Hume's view of belief

Elsewhere we read,

[B]elief is some sensation or peculiar manner of conception, which it is impossible for mere ideas to destroy.[67]

The foregoing analyses suggest that the "peculiar manner of conception" that Hume here despairs of explaining is the way in which body activity leads us to a basic kind of understanding of the world around us that cannot be gained by merely standing still and observing. This peculiar manner of conception, which is or culminates in a felt belief, cannot itself be destroyed by mere (abstract) ideas, for, as will be shown, it is rather presupposed by them; the abstractly conceived universe is an idealization rooted in the world of active, felt experience. Hume later amplifies his notion of belief:

Belief, being a lively conception, can never be entire, where it is not founded on something natural and easy.[68]

Agreed. But liveliness is founded in the life of "having" a body naturally, that is, of being at ease with one's body rather than "having" it in a diseased way. To be at ease with one's body, one must have a lively sense of its unity, be well-coordinated, and be skillful in dealing with things around one. Taken all together, one must, in a word, have poise. Belief then is founded on body poise, with all those attendant functions previously shown to be unanalyzable in terms of Hume's philosophy of impressions and ideas striking upon the mind.

2.6.7 The problem of the continued existence of unobserved objects

Hume asks, "why do we attribute a continued existence to objects even when they are not present to the senses?"[69] He answers, because we cannot help having the unjustified habit of doing so. I have been arguing that we attribute continued or enduring existence to all and only those objects the assumption of whose continued existence helps make the world itself endurable as a place to live in. This is not merely in virtue of an unjustified habit. Those "objects" that "would" make the world unendurable, *cannot* be recognized in the first place. Those that turn out to make the world unendurable, though they did not appear to do so as first recognized, *cannot* be allowed to endure, and are accordingly unmade, repressed or suppressed, depending upon just how unendurable they are. Objects that merely make the world less endurable, though still endurable, merely tend (fallibly) to be excluded from the world. Though we tend to assume such objects do not exist, they still can "force themselves" upon our attention, force us to recognize them. Relying upon our assumption that they do not exist, we may nevertheless come up "against" the fact that they do exist, which makes further reliance upon their nonexistence unendurable, however painful (though endurable) the resultant belief in their existence may be. Our desires are restricted by the "facts" that may not be in accordance with them, so that we may be forced to recognize that what we desire to be so is not so; and further, so that we cannot really desire what we find in fact to be impossible. But the "facts" are also restricted by human needs. A need is stronger than a desire; a need is a "desire" that needs to be satisfied if the world of our experience is to endure. While we may *desire* what is in fact not so, we cannot recognize as a fact in our world what we *need* not to be so, i.e., what *must* not be so. Nothing can be known as a fact, hence nothing can be a fact, which is *absolutely* at variance with basic human needs. For example, if this analysis is correct, we can never know it to be a fact that we cannot possibly survive. We may know it to be unlikely but, so long as the strength of life endures, we cannot help seeking, hoping against hope, and therefore believing it possible, to find some way to endure. Completeness hopelessness is the surrender of life, and therewith, of all experience of truth. We cannot knowingly die in peace, realizing that we personally are dying, unless we do so hopefully.[70] The religious sense of immortality is a perennial faith rooted in this felt necessity, though it is usually a faith perverted into a dogmatic conviction. On the view here expressed, the Stoic attempt to put a merely factual face on death is a refusal to face death as it really is, and as all of us, Stoics included, cannot help *feeling* it to be, namely, not as merely one particular fact among others but as somehow entering into the definition of facticity, and bound up with the fate of the whole world of facts of experience.

2.6.8 Hume's admission of an inadequate account of the active life

The whole tenor of this book is to agree with Hume's view that "the philosophical system acquires all its influence on the imagination from the vulgar one . . . it has no primary recommendation to the reason or the imagination."[71] But this view seems to imply the non-Humean conclusion that, in order to produce a philosophical system more influential and with better credentials than Hume's, one must fashion it from the vulgar sense of the importance of active as well as of inactive experience. Indeed, *Hume finds that the experience of activity makes his philosophy seem ridiculous even to himself.* For he writes,

Most fortunately, it happens that since reason is incapable of dispelling these clouds, Nature herself suffices to that purpose... . I dine, I play a game of backgammon, I converse, and am merry with my friends; and when ... I would return to these speculations, they appear ... ridiculous.[72]

This is certainly one of Hume's main reactions to the results of his epistemological inquiry and it informs all his writings in moral philosophy as well, where we find the same thought expressed again:

When we leave our closet and engage in the common affairs of life, the conclusions (of philosophy as a kind of abstruse reasoning) seem to vanish like the phantoms of the night on the appearance of the morning.[73]

While meant by Hume as a genial criticism of philosophy, I have argued that such observations express in fact a criticism of an inadequate philosophy such as Hume's own, which is so "beside the point" of our lives because it denies the fundamental role that our active bodies play in our lives, and in all our experience.

2.7 Conclusion

I have now considered two main views of the human subject and the way he has his human body. First was the classic view of Plato and Aristotle, in which the human subject is considered to be a migrant, able to identify himself closely with his body as merely one material thing among others in the world, and able to free himself from his body to become, through his mind, closely identified with the ordering unity of the world. Second was the view of Hume and Leibniz, that the human subject is identified only with the function of explicating the unity of the world, and is never identified with the human body, which is regarded as merely one material thing among others in the world. I have interpreted Descartes's position as an unstable way-station between these two points of view; a station, though, clearly on the way to the consideration of the human subject as a pure world-subject. Both the classic view of the human subject as a migrant-subject and the post-Cartesian view of the human subject as a world-subject are, however, fundamentally in agreement that the human subject cannot *both* be in the world as one thing in the midst of others, *and thereby*, in the same way, be a function of the unity of the world itself. Both views are in fundamental agreement that these two relationships of the human subject to the world are mutually exclusive; on both views, the human subject could have the one relationship, if at all, only insofar as he did *not* have the other. The purpose of this book is to demonstrate that this agreement reflects a common fundamental error: *the misinterpretation of the human body as merely a material thing in the world.* In the present chapter I have expounded in an introductory way the fundamental contention of this study that the human body is not merely a material thing found in the midst of other material things in the world, but that it is also, and moreover thereby, that material thing whose capacity to move itself generates and defines the whole world of human experience in which any material thing, including itself, can be found. The contention is thus that the human body is indeed a material thing in the world, as all agree, but that it is so in such a unique way that it is thereby the defining subject of the world. In short, in direct opposition to the fundamental agreement of the classic and world-subject views of the human subject, it is the fundamental contention of this book that *the human body is the material subject of the world.*

2.8 Transition to Chapter 3

We saw earlier that both Leibniz and Hume were driven to give up Descartes's identification of the human subject with the ordering unity of the world, because, following Descartes's lead in severing the human subject from all definitive relation with his natural body, they both came to realize what Descartes had not, namely, that they could not understand how anything could come "into" the world of experience and thereby first receive its order, rather than merely come to display the order it had antecedently received. These philosophers ceased, accordingly, to regard experience as representational, in the Cartesian sense, of nonexperiential elements having "effects" in experience, and came to regard experience as representational, instead, of other experiences. The resulting philosophies of a world-subject reached, as we have seen, incredible extremes. Whereas Leibniz was driven to an incredible doctrine of the *full* implication of all experience by each experience, Hume was driven to the equally incredible doctrine, which he himself admitted he could not believe in practice, of *no* implication of any other experience by any given experience.

The next major event in the history of philosophy was the work of Immanuel Kant. He found each of the foregoing extremes untenable, considering one to be the untenable extreme of dogmatism and the other to be the untenable extreme of scepticism. He sought a synthesis. In doing so, the old Cartesian problem, of how something could possibly come "into" experience, reappeared. For the separation, so untenable to Kant, of the empiricist and rationalist elements in Descartes's philosophy, *was*, as we have seen, basically the way of denying that anything ever did come "into" experience. It was Kant's major achievement to find a new answer to the question posed by Cartesian philosophy: how do things come "into" experience? Kant's new answer was to distinguish between subjective and objective forms of sensory experience, and to undertake the analysis of how our subjective experience comes to be cast, by the human subject himself, into objective form. Thus, the two great systems of thought flowing from the troubled headwaters of Descartes's mind emptied at last together into the single current of Kant's attempt to understand not merely how the human subject *makes explicit*, but how he *makes* in the first place, the world of his objective experience.

3

Introductory Discussion of Kant's View That the Human Subject Makes the World of His Experience

3.1 The Development of Kant's Thought

In his *Inaugural Dissertation* of 1770, Kant distinguishes phenomena from purely intelligible things in themselves, holding that mathematics is the a priori[1] science of the world of phenomena in space and time; and that metaphysics provides the science of the intelligible world by means of pure concepts of the understanding. Scientific principles by which these concepts are applied to the world of phenomena are regarded as no more than heuristic fictions, not themselves strictly true of these phenomena, but serving effectively to guide us in the discovery of phenomenal truths. For example, the principles that every event has a cause, and that total energy (of the community of interacting substances, as Kant would later express it) in the world is conserved, are regarded as fundamental, metaphysical, nonmathematical principles helpful in determining objects of experience, but not strictly true of them. In the *Critique of Pure Reason*, however, Kant assimilates the applicability of pure concepts of the understanding to the applicability of spatial, temporal, and mathematical relations, holding them all to be objectively valid of phenomena and inapplicable to purely intelligible things in themselves.

Thus Kant in the *Dissertation* still followed Leibniz in holding that there are two radically different ways of knowing objects. He had moved away from Leibniz only in re-grouping these ways of knowing according to the regions of their strict applicability. The spatial and mathematical ways of knowing, which Leibniz had grouped with metaphysical principles, were shifted by Kant as strictly applicable to objects appearing in such a manner that our temporal way of knowing was also strictly applicable to them. As Leibniz had excluded *temporal* functions (perceptions) from the theoretical (scientific) understanding of objects,[2] Kant in the *Dissertation* excluded the traditional *metaphysical* concepts from such understanding. Metaphysical principles, for the Kant of the *Dissertation*, like temporal functions for Leibniz, were regarded as giving helpful clues to scientific understanding but not as constitutive of it. Like Leibniz, the Kant of the *Dissertation* believed that there were two fundamental ways of knowing. The four ways of knowing were considered to be: by traditional metaphysical principles–mainly, the principles of noncontradiction, a cause for every event, and an identical substance as undergoing every change; by mathematical relations; by spatial relations; and by temporal relations among perceptions. Like Leibniz, Kant at this time tended to regard one kind of knowledge as less trustworthy by restricting it to only *one* way of knowing; and he tended to regard the other kind of knowledge as more trustworthy because formed by a confluence of the *three* remaining ways of knowing.

In the *Critique of Pure Reason* Kant shifts for the first time to holding that there is but one kind of knowledge, viz., that of something as an "object of experience"; and that all four different ways of knowing cooperate as alike strictly applicable to this region of knowable objects, that is, to objects appearing in this way. The older problem, the problem for Descartes, Leibniz, and Hume, had been to understand the interdependence of two fundamentally different kinds of knowledge–perceptual and conceptual knowledge. According to Descartes and Leibniz, we know objects conceptually in the clear, distinct, and possibly indubitable ways of metaphysical principles, spatial relations, and mathematical relations; and we "know" objects perceptually only in the confused and never indubitable[3] ways of time. According to Hume, on the other hand, we know objects (single impressions) perceptually in a clear, distinct, and indubitable way that is not, however, in virtue of any form. All forms of our experience that seem to give us knowledge concern the connection among distinguishable and separable impressions, and control our relatively faint and wholly unjustifiable conceptual inferences in accordance with the merely presumed relations of space, time, and the metaphysical concepts of substance and cause.[4]

By shifting for the first time to the position that all four of our ways of knowing converge in a complementary way as strictly applicable to the same object appearing in a single fourfold way, Kant changes the fundamental epistemological problem. Prior to Kant the problem was: *How do we come to know initially knowable objects?* The problem was basically understood as the problem of how we relate our perceptual kind of information about the object to our quite different conceptual kind of information about it. So long as we seem to know objects in relatively different and independently applicable ways, the knowability of objects seems to be attested to but not dependent upon our ways of knowing. When Kant removes this apparent independence by analyzing all knowledge as the convergence of a single fourfold synthesis of ways of knowing, each way being strictly applicable to the same object appearing the same fourfold way, he makes the knowability of objects seem not merely attested to but produced by our single complex way of knowing. He thereby changes the fundamental epistemological problem to: *How do we make objects knowable ?* The problem for Kant becomes, How do we put our initially unintelligible experience (sensations) into knowable form? How do we apply our temporal, spatial, mathematical, and conceptual forms to the matter of experience in order to *make* this matter intelligible?

Kant is thus able to bring into focus the new problem of how things come "into" the world of experience as *capable* of being objectively known in the first place, *coming* thus to meet, rather than initially meeting, an objective pre-condition of their actually being known. But in doing this, Kant simultaneously tends to obscure a point that was appreciated in the older formulation. There does seem to be a difference between what we pre-verbally understand of matters of fact in ordinary perceptual, perspectival experience, and what we verbally understand about matters of fact in conceptual, nonperspectival ways. Kant may be right that we do not in these two cases understand (to whatever degree) different *objects*, as was sometimes thought before him, e.g., by Descartes, holding that the perceivable object is a confused effect of the clear conceivable object, and by Plato, holding that the perceivable object is a changing image of the unchangeable conceivable object. But even so, even if Kant is right that we do understand the same objects in conception and perception of matters of fact, it still seems plain that we understand them in very different ways that can be pursued in relative, though perhaps not in complete, independence of one another. Perceptual clues may help us to think abstractly in an objective manner, and conceptual clues may help us to explore and cope with perceptual objects. But it does not seem, on the face of it at least, that we must include perceptions in all abstract thought about matters of fact, or that we must include abstract conceptions in all acts of veridical perception. Certainly there are cases of seeming knowledge of matters of fact in which the perceptual contribution is very small, as when we calculate further information on the basis of given information about absent conditions; and others in which the conceptual contribution is very small, as when we make quick movements to avoid a present danger such as falling from a ledge; and the "flavor" of the knowledge in these contrasting cases seems to be quite different. But because Kant first made all ways of knowing so thoroughly interdependent, he was least able to understand how there could be more than one kind of objective knowledge of matters of fact. Thus it is not surprising that Kant tries to show that there is only *one* kind of objective knowledge of matters of fact, which all our ways of knowing conspire to produce. I wish to demonstrate that there is *more* than one kind of objective knowledge of matters of fact; that Kant fails in his attempt to show that there is only one kind; and that Kant's failure comes to a head in a concluding invalid reversion to his Leibnizian origins.

Kant had learned of Leibniz through students of Wolff (e.g., Knutzen) who had de-emphasized Leibniz's account of the internal horizon of a Monad in favor of Leibniz's logical account of inter-Monadal Space. This left a relative void in theory of perception. Kant's development can be regarded as starting with the filling of this void by the insertion of a Humean interior into the Leibnizian Monad that had been emptied of content by the Wolffian interpretation of it. Kant's development up to the *Dissertation* can be regarded as the additional internalization of Leibnizian Space and mathematics in to the Monad drained by Wolff. Kant's further development up to the *Critique of Pure Reason* can then be regarded as the culmination of an established trend in his thought by the additional internalization (into the Monad) of Leibniz's last remaining way of knowing, viz., by metaphysical principles. The fundamental problem that then besets Kant is that of the "affinity" of the Humean matter of appearance to being ordered by the Leibnizian forms of experience (the temporal, spatial, mathematical, and metaphysical or "categorial" forms). In trying to establish this affinity, Kant finally resorts to a Lebnizian ideal of pure reason. I try to show, however, that the "regulative solution" that Kant develops in this way is invalidated by the Humean analysis he retains for the matter of appearance.

On my view, in sum, Kant tries to synthesize the philosophies of Leibniz and Hume but fails because he seeks to synthesize them in an account of only *one* kind of knowledge of matters of fact, whereas this synthesis requires the interrelating of *two* such forms of objectivity: a form of perceptual knowledge, with which Hume was mainly concerned; and a form of conceptual knowledge, with which Leibniz was mainly concerned. The "affinity" of Kant's Humean matter of experience to being ordered by his Leibnizian forms of experience can be demonstrated only by first isolating a mediating *objective form of perception*, and then showing its affinity to the objective forms of conception.

This formulation of my general criticism of Kant can be clarified by reference to what is admittedly new and important in Kant's work. Kant himself writes that he was able to suggest and to solve the crucial problem of our a priori knowledge of objects of experience, only because he was the first person to whom it occurred "that the senses themselves might intuit a priori."[5] How can I reasonably claim that Kant's basic error was the denial of an objective form of perception when one of his central contributions was his recognition "that the senses themselves might (and do) intuit a priori?" The answer is that, according to Kant, "the senses intuit a priori" insofar as they have an objective *imaginative* form, but they have no objective *perceptual* form at all. For according to Kant in his first Critique (and in his *Prolegomena* version of this Critique), our a priori sensuous intuition is that of our productive imagination. This crucial new role Kant gives to the productive imagination in his first Critique can be better understood in the broader context of some of his other works. The Critique depicts a priori sensibility, or the faculty of productive imagination, as the distinctively human faculty of sensibility by which men are distinguished from animals and from all other beings so far as we know. In this depiction, Kant expresses one of his central and lasting convictions. For what is here depicted as basically distinctive about productive imagination is its being the sensible condition of our self-consciousness.[6] And Kant, like Leibniz before him, held for a period of at least 36 years that what distinguishes men from animals is man's self-consciousness. As early as 1762 Kant raised the question of what sort of "secret power" it is through which judging is possible, and hence through which rational animals capable of judging are distinguishable from nonrational animals incapable of doing so. "My present opinion," he writes, "is that this power or capacity is nothing but the faculty of inner sense, i.e., the faculty of making one's own representations the objects of one's thought."[7] He also writes, "Distinguishing things from one another is something quite different from recognizing the distinction among things. The latter is only possible through judgment and cannot be done by a nonrational animal."[8] Kant thus seems to arrive early at the view that our ability to think is founded on our ability to recognize as such our *own* experience, and our *own* contributions to our experience. This is close to the view that Kant held at the end of his productive life, "the ability to think 'I' distinguishes man from all other living beings."[9] Now in the *Critique of Pure Reason*, which falls between these two dates, productive imagination is our sensory way of making our own (spatial and temporal) contribution to the objective experience in relation to which "I think" is first possible. And "the senses intuit a priori" insofar as we can be self-conscious of this contribution.[10] The point is that, for Kant "the senses intuit a priori" insofar as perception takes place in an *imaginative* field of experience, but Kant has no notion of a *perceptual* field of experience in which perception may take place.

3.2 Summary of My Kant Criticism: That Kant Imaginizes Perception

Kant wrote that "Leibniz *intellectualized* all appearances just as Locke *sensualized* all concepts of the understanding."[11] Kant would have grouped Hume with Locke in this respect, and considered that he himself had corrected the complementary errors of both Leibniz and the British Empiricists by effectively synthesizing their views. The thesis I wish to develop in this chapter can be similarly expressed in the objection that Kant's purported synthesis failed because he *imaginized* all appearances in order to make them intelligible in a purely theoretical way. Convinced that sense experience is in fact not originally given in the way Leibniz supposed,[12] Kant concentrated on showing how sensation must be transformed into the kind of sense experience that would be intelligible in the way Leibniz supposed. Kant meanwhile retained Leibniz' conviction that sense experience is intelligible only insofar as it is theoretically (conceptually) intelligible. Kant's fundamental advance beyond Leibniz was not in what he counted as intelligible experience, but in his realization of how much had to be done in order to transform given sense experience ("sensation") into experience intelligible in this way. Kant never noticed that while sense experience is indeed not given as intelligible in the way Leibniz supposed, it is given as intelligible in some other way, namely, as *practically* intelligible. Since Kant regarded sense experience as intelligible only in a theoretical way, he was led, in his moral philosophy dealing with our practical reason, to disregard altogether the character of sense experience as determinative of intelligent or rational action. Sense experience, Kant held, might to be sure provide evidence that there is an occasion for action of a kind independently known to be intelligent, but it can never provide evidence for the intelligence of the action called for on this occasion. Kant had in short no notion of "sensible" action.

Kant's criticism of his predecessors enables us to put our point in another way. Kant criticizes traditional philosophers on the grounds that "since the oldest days of philosophy . . . appearance and illusion were identified."[13] Kant himself did indeed differ from traditional philosophers by elaborating, in his account of imagination, a fully objective form of sensory appearance. He is, nevertheless, on my view, still too much in agreement with the tradition he criticizes, and is himself to some extent subject to the same criticism he levels against it. For he holds that the imaginative forms of space and time are intelligible only through the application of concepts to them, and he thus agrees with the philosophic tradition in denying that there is any form of veridical sensory appearance independent of the employment of abstract concepts. Though he holds that we possess an objective sensory imagination that mediates the application of abstract concepts to perception, Kant like the tradition holds that, divorced from abstract concepts, all sensory experience, all intuition, is "blind"[14] and unintelligible.

Kant sought to synthesize Leibnizian rationalism, emphasizing the role of necessary and indubitable truths in all our knowledge, with Humean empiricism, emphasizing the merely de facto character of sense experience. He sought to do this by introducing the mediating notion that there is something necessary and indubitable not merely in human reason but also in human sensibility, at least in respect to its form. Kant's contribution was to view theoretical knowledge as based in a distinctively human form of sensibility that is itself the source of necessary and indubitable truths. In the following chapters I try to carry Kant's insight further by showing that this distinctively human form of sensibility, the form of our productive imagination, is in turn based on a more primitive kind of human sensibility, viz., that of active human perception. I try to show that this more primitive form of human sensibility also yields knowledge of necessary and indubitable truths, though in this case not merely as to the *form* of experience, but also as to its *content*.

To raise here at least the suspicion that our very ability to form theoretical concepts may be derived from more primitive perceptual functions, it is sufficient to note that theoretical thought is possible only in terms of words, and words in turn can be understood as having a definite meaning only insofar as they can be correctly read or heard, that is, correctly sensed. We may plausibly expect that our way of seeing and hearing objects conditions our way of seeing and hearing words, and thus conditions our way of thinking abstractly. But just how does our way of perceiving things condition our way of conceiving of things? In the following chapters, I try to develop and substantiate a general answer to this question.

In clarification of the thesis that there is a priori sense content, I refer once more to Kant's dictum that "the senses themselves intuit a priori." Defining "a priori" intuition as intuition of truths that are necessary and indubitable because without intuition of them we could not make sense of knowing or doubting anything,[15] my thesis is that Kant's innovation that "the senses themselves intuit a priori" in respect to their form, should be carried further to the conclusion that the senses themselves intuit a priori also in respect to their content. I wish to show that although the senses *imaginatively* intuit a priori only in respect to their form (just as Kant thought), they nevertheless *perceptually* intuit a priori in respect to their content as well (which Kant never suspected). Further, I want to show that since imagination makes sense only on the basis of perception, even imaginative intuition is indirectly founded on an a priori intuition of the content as well as the form of sense experience. In short, I seek to show that all human knowledge is based on knowledge of some *necessary facts* such that without knowledge of them we could not make sense of knowing or doubting anything. Necessary facts are those facts that we must know in order to be sufficiently balanced to have objective experience of any kind, perceptual or imaginative. Some necessary facts vary with our circumstance, and remain necessary facts only so long as the given circumstances in which they are necessary are actual. But some necessary facts are invariant with change of circumstance for they help to form our circumstancedness itself, i.e., our circumstantial way of being in the world. Though we may change our circumstances by modifying them or going elsewhere, we cannot change our circumstancedness by whatever we do. Rather, we take our circumstancedness with us, we take it invariably for granted, in taking any action at all. Central among the necessary facts that help characterize our circumstancedness is the fact that we have a human body that functions as the material subject of the world. Kant wrote that "life is the subjective condition of all our possible experience."[16] I wish to show that human life is also an *objective* condition of all our possible experience in that the way we appear to ourselves to be humanly alive constitutes part of the evidence for the truth of all our tested beliefs.

Kant's project is the synthesis of the philosophies of Hume and Leibniz. This project can be formulated in four generally equivalent ways: as the project of synthesizing comparatively *contingent* with comparatively *necessary* forms of experience; as the project of synthesizing the conditions for the unity of *actual* experience, with the conditions for the unity of *all possible* experience; as the project of synthesizing the unity of experience *in the world*, with the unity of *the world* in which experience takes place; as the project of synthesizing the conditions for the validity of *perceptual* experience with the conditions for the validity of *imaginative* experience. My thesis is that Kant begins with a *false dilemma* that forces him in the last analysis to fail in his attempt at synthesis, by forcing him surreptitiously to assimilate perception to imagination; to assimilate the unity of experience in the world to the unity of the world in which experience takes place; to assimilate the unity of actual experience to the unity of all possible experience; to assimilate the conditions of contingent experience to those of necessary experience; and in general to assimilate the insights of Hume to those of Leibniz.

Kant sees clearly that the reconciliation of this fourfold divergence poses a difficult and important problem. I try to show how he wrestles with this problem in an original, persistent, and provocative way; and how, though he eventually goes down to defeat, he manages to teach us a great deal. We learn not merely from his conclusions, which represent a too one-sided victory (and therefore also a defeat, by distortion) for the imagination, but also from the misleading way he states his problem, a way that forces him into a doomed though dogged fight to avoid his distorted conclusion. Kant drew philosophic attention to the human imagination as a source of justifiable belief. Our greatest indebtedness to him is for the philosophic knowledge he gave us of the objective imagination. But Kant's instruction in respect to the imagination is to be found in two forms: only one explicit, the other implicit; only one intentional, the other unintentional. In trying to synthesize the philosophy of perception with the philosophy of conception, he formulates his *problem* in terms of the imagination, as well as giving his *solution* in terms of the imagination. Kant seems to believe, however, that he refers to the imagination only in the solution of his problem. I try to show that his implicit and unintentional framing of his *problem* in terms of the imagination invalidates the general conclusions of his philosophy of "transcendental idealism" and "empirical realism." In the end we learn as much about the imagination from the insidious way in which it shapes the formulation of Kant's problem, as from the explicit characterization Kant gives us of it.

Kant attempted to understand how the functions of perception and imagination are effectively synthesized in actual human knowledge, as, somehow or other, they plainly seem to be. His attempt to do this, however, allowed for only *one* level of objective experience, so that the claims of conceptually imaginative experience had either to subordinate or be subordinated by the claims of perceptual experience. Because of the way Kant posed his basic problem, he committed himself to the former alternative, which, like its opposite, results in doing justice neither to the claims of conceptual imagination nor to the claims of perception. My solution is to show that there are two levels of objective experience: the ground floor of perceptually objective experience; and the upper storey of imaginatively objective experience,[17] which presupposes for its objectivity (i.e., for its dependability as living quarters) that the ground floor onto which it is built is itself on firm foundations. I attempt to show *that* the imaginative objectivity of theoretical knowledge presupposes a pre-imaginative, perceptual form of objectivity, by showing just *how* this is so. I attempt to characterize the a priori defining forms of *perceptual* knowledge, and to indicate what *systematic transformations* of these forms yield the a priori forms of *imaginative* knowledge exhibited by Kant. I attempt, in addition, to show the *objective need* for these transformations. Further, I attempt to show just how Kantian *dogmas*, inevitably attending any mistaken characterization of imaginatively objective experience as self-founding, are systematically replaced by *justifications* when forms of imaginative knowledge are understood as objectively founded, in accordance with objective need, in corresponding forms of self-founding perceptual knowledge.

3.3 Phenomenological Studies To Be Used in Support of My Kant Criticism

In my interpretation of Kant I will try constantly to focus the *double-image* in his thought produced by his persevering attempt to do justice to the claims of both *perception* and *conceptual imagination*. I will attempt to trace just how the claims of perception are gradually denied, and just how they implicitly return to distort the usurping image of the imagination. But in order to focus this double image, I have to bring to Kant's thought some knowledge of the structure of perception and imagination that Kant himself lacked. This knowledge, which we derive from phenomenological analyses of perception and imagination, guides me in my interpretation, telling me what to look for as crucial in Kant's account of these functions. Accordingly, as a prelude to my Kant interpretation, I now turn to such analyses.

4

Development of the Phenomenology of Practical Perception, as a Prelude to the Criticism That Kant Imaginizes Perception

4.0 General Statement of Problems Considered in This Chapter, and of the Conclusions To Be Demonstrated

The phenomenological analyses in chapter 2 were made by way of a data-gathering excursion. Their organization was somewhat loose, but this was unavoidable in a preliminary investigation. Without a body of phenomenological data to refer to, we cannot make sense of the more systematic phenomenological themes. But now, being in possession of this body of preliminary data, we are prepared for a more systematic comprehension of it, which will in turn lead to its elaboration as data. In the present chapter, the preliminary analyses of perceptual experience will be brought into sharper focus, and others added to them. In chapter 5, building on these results, the main contrasts between perception and imagination are developed. Finally, in chapter 6, in the course of a detailed critique of Kant, all analyses are brought to a head in a deduction of the categories of practical perception and an analysis of the relation between these categories and those of theoretical imagination.

This chapter has four main themes:

(1) Justification of the assumption that the percipient is a self-moved mover. I have made this assumption in all of the foregoing analyses. It is, however, in need of justification—not only on general philosophic grounds requiring the justification of assumptions so far as possible, but also because a great philosophic tradition stemming from Aristotle actually holds that a self-moved

The Phenomenology of Practical Perception

mover is impossible. Thus I am faced with two tasks. I must first counter Aristotle's proof of the *impossibility* of a self-moved mover. This task is taken up in the first subsection. I attempt to show that Aristotle's contention that the notion of a self-moved mover is self-contradictory, resting upon a mistaken analysis of body-movement on the model of object-motion. Secondly, there is the positive task of showing that the percipient is *necessarily* a self-moved mover. The rest of the chapter is, in effect, a demonstration of this thesis. The argument is twofold. On the one hand, it rests upon a reductio ad absurdum of the antithesis. For I show how we make sense of our perceptual world and the characteristic orders of determination in it, only in terms of our self as a self-moved mover. Hence, if we cannot make sense of a self-moved mover, we cannot make sense of practical sense experience. And this conclusion is manifestly absurd. On the other hand, my thesis that we are, as percipient, a self-moved mover, rests upon a positive appeal to the *felt* unity of our active body in its freely directable activity.

(2) A systematic analysis of the perceptual sense of the passage of time. The problem is to understand how the passage of time is not itself a perceptual event, though it is a sensible condition for the perception of all events. From a theoretical point of view, what passes is not Time itself, but only our experience in Time. From a perceptual point of view, however, Time itself passes with the passing of experiential events. What I *mean* by a perceivable "event" is: something that takes place under this condition. My analysis is directed toward the conclusion that the passage of time is perceived as the objective correlate of the self-activity of the percipient, both conditions taken together making possible all determinate perception of matters of fact.

(3) The perceptual world as a field of fields-within-fields. Every perception is a perception of an object by a percipient who thereby finds himself together with that object in a common world. But the perceived object appears to be in the percipient's world only *in*directly. The object appears to be directly in its place, appearing there in a certain orientation delimited from a field of possible orientations in which it evidently might also be made to appear at that same place. This place in turn appears in the percipient's circumstantial field of places, appearing in this field in a certain

direction and at a certain distance from the percipient—the distance and direction being delimited from a field of possible distances and directions in which this same place evidently might also be made to appear in the given circumstances of the same percipient. The percipient's circumstantial field in turn appears in his general horizontal field, appearing within rather than beyond the horizon of this field—this inner field being delimited from a field of possible inner fields (all others lying beyond the horizon) in respect to which the same circumstances might also be located in the given horizontal field of the same percipient, i.e., being in a given circumstance, the percipient is aware that this circumstance is only a delimitation of a general horizontal field such that, advancing beyond the horizon of the given circumstance, he can place it beyond the horizon behind him. The percipient's general horizontal field in turn appears in a general vertical field—which does *not* in itself appear variable. Going beyond the horizon, I appear to change my ground, but to retain my sky. The vertical field is accordingly the world-field[1] in which all other perceptual fields are contained, and in which the percipient finds himself together with every perceptual object. Every object is thus perceived to be *in*directly in the world, through being perceived to be in-its-place (by virtue of a delimited orientational field); which is in turn perceived to be in-the-percipient's-circumstances (by virtue of a delimited field of distance and direction); which is in turn perceived to be in-the-general-horizontal-field (by virtue of a delimited horizontal field); which is in turn perceived to be in-the-world (by virtue of a nondelimitable vertical field). The percipient is always aware of himself, on the other hand, as *directly* in the world.[2] For this relation is given by his sense of balance. And every perception of an object is a function of the percipient's poise, of which the percipient's sense of balance is a necessary (though not sufficient) condition.

The first question I consider in this connection is, What is the general significance of the fact that the world of practical perception is a field of fields-within-fields for the object, but directly contains the percipient? My general answer is that perception is essentially characterized as the culmination of the percipient's *search* to find himself in the world in which he originally (without an object) senses himself to be lost, but in which he can find himself in the midst of his circumstances in respect to some object he finds there with him. With or without an object, found or lost, the percipient always has a sense of his individual self in the world. But an object is something to-be-found, and without the finding there is no sense of the particular object. The object lies hidden in the world; in fields within fields, i.e., in recesses within recesses. And the practical percipient ferrets it out.[3] The second question I take up in this connection is, What is the epistemological significance of the fact that the world is a field of just *these* four fields in just *this* order of inclusion? My general answer is that these four ordered fields of our activity as percipient bear (correspondingly) the four ordered senses of the passage of time that enable us to make sense of the fact that an object is perceived. These four orders of sense are, respectively: the sense of the *primary field* of all passage of time, borne by the world-field; the sense *that* there is some passage of time, borne by the general horizontal field; the sense of *where* this passage of time is taking place, borne by the circumstantial field; the sense of *what* has taken place with this passage of time, borne by the place the event has taken. Following from the discussion of the second section, (2) above, each sense of the passage of time borne by one of these inclusive fields of our activity, is found to be correlative with some sense of our free activity as percipient, viz., our balance (and ability to turn in place); our movement (from place to place); our anticipation; and our response. The whole discussion is conducted not merely on an abstract dialectical level, but in terms of phenomenological analyses of four paradigm cases, each exhibiting only the prior but no subsequent senses of the passage of time and of the percipient's self-activity.

(4) Why the percipient is satisfied with the perception of an object. Practical perception is the percipient's search to find himself in the world. A perceptual object is the object of this search: finding a perceptual object terminates the search. What is it about an object that makes perception of it satisfactory, as providing a kind of perceptual answer—whereas the appearance of mere fields is like a question, only prompting the hunt for the object? How does the percipient find *himself* through finding an object? My general answer is as follows. Our world-field is correlative with our need to

find our self as percipient. Prompted by this need, we search for our self through the three other fields of our activity. These fields are all *freely reversible*; that is, we can at will so act as to reverse the left-right and front-back order in which its regions appear to us. Consider for example an object's orientational field. An object is perceived as having a near (or front) side, facing me; and a far (or back) side facing away from me. The object is perceived in its near side orientation. Simultaneously it is perceived as having a field of possible orientations, ordered by accessibility, and such that the far side is the least accessible. By passing around the object, I reverse its field of ordered orientations, making the least accessible most accessible, and vice versa. Similarly with the circumstantial field of ordered places, and the horizontal field of ordered circumstances. An object, however, is a whole composed of ordered parts. And its order is *irreversible* by my activity in respect to it.[4] Its order is revealed to me in a reversible *way* (i.e., in this orientation or turned about, placed to the left of me, or to the right, etc.); but *what* is revealed is a set of parts in a *fixed* order. An object's irreversible order distinguishes it from the fields in which it is sought and in which it appears. In this irreversibility, we meet a *match* for the irreversibility of our own front-back body directedness. To be freely active is to be able to reverse our activity; to go back and forth, at will. This ability to sensibly reverse *direction*, however, presupposes an invariant *sense of direction*. We have this sense of direction in virtue of the functional asymmetry of our front-back structured body. Our body asymmetry and the free reversibility of our activity bear the significance of our activity as a *seeking*. But we cannot *find* our self in this search without encountering something, viz., an object of irreversibly ordered parts, which mirrors our own irreversible body structure. This theme is substantiated and augmented by phenomenological analyses of: how the *irreversibility* of perceptual time is grounded in the irreversible functional asymmetry of our forward directed body; how *passing an object*[5] gives it a concrete unity; how the satisfactory character of our perception of an object is expressed by our sense of *practical self-composure*—by which we are fulfilled as percipient, gaining a sense that our concrete skillful activity is unified correlatively with the object successfully perceived.

4.1 Defense against Aristotle's Thesis That a Self-Moved Mover Is Impossible

Aristotle holds, "It is impossible that that which moves itself should in its entirety move itself."[6] He concludes that "in the whole of the (self-moved) thing we may distinguish that which imparts motion without itself being moved and that which is moved: for only in this way is it possible for a thing to be self-moved"[7] Aristotle arrives at these views by the following argument. Movement is change. Self-movement would be movement by something that endures unchanged, as the self-same thing, through this movement. "Self-movement" would thus be a contradictory notion of an unchanging thing changing itself, *if* the entire thing participated in this movement. Therefore only part of the thing can participate in this movement, and in such a way that the motion of this moving (hence changing) part is caused by *another* part that does *not* move (hence does not change).

For Aristotle, nothing can change itself because nothing can remain the same *by* the way it changes. "That which produces the form is always something that possesses it (to begin with)."[8] Something can indeed remain the same by the way it produces change, but only by the way it produces change in something *else*. Thus Aristotle concludes that nothing can move itself as a whole. This view is expressed very clearly when Aristotle writes,

Everything that changes must be divisible, since part of that which changes must be at the starting point, and part at the goal of the change (what it is changing to).[9]

This analysis of change of position[10] is adequate for the motion of objects, but inadequate for the movement of subjects. It distorts the latter on the model of the former. This can be seen in three ways. First of all, it fails to take account of the peculiar role of the percipient's position in structuring the field of places in his experience. All stationary objects are located in relation to our central position as percipient. Sometimes, an object appears to be located in relation to some other object, some landmark. But the landmark, at least, appears to be located in respect to our self. So the object is also so located, at least indirectly. We may not always appear to be the centrally important *content* in our perceptual field. But we do always appear to be its *locational* or perspectival center. All motion of objects is accordingly perceived as a change of that object's position in respect to our central position, provided we are stationary. Awareness of our *own* movement implies a pervasive and systematic change of *all* circumstantial positions in respect to our own. As we move from "Here" to "There," we change "Here" to "Back There," and we change "There" to "Here."[11] In doing so, we also change every other position in our field. By moving, we transform our field of perceptual positions; we map it onto a new origin. Our own movement as percipient is thus perceived in a very different way from the motion of the object. We perceive our own movement in terms of the perceptual field as a whole; but we perceive the motion of objects in a *delimited* way, as a local change *in* the stable field of positions. The motion of an object does to some extent *make* a place for itself where it goes; and it does to some extent erase the place from which it starts. But the percipient *changes* the apparent location of a place by moving toward or away from it. The active body of the percipient is thus the special kind of body that, in moving, *takes its apparent point of origin with it.* Thus Aristotle's analysis that "part of what changes must be at the starting point, and part at the goal of the change," does not apply in the special case of the active percipient.

Secondly, Aristotle's analysis fails to take account of the individuality of action. As a pure spectator, we may regard our body as a divisible object, or we may so regard the body of another. But as practical percipient, we cannot regard our body in this way. Though "headed," like objects, in a certain direction, we are not divided like them in the course of our movement. Our trailing members do not appear merely to follow our leading members, as in the case of an inert object thrown through the air. Nor do our trailing members push our leading members on ahead, as in the case of a boulder rolling downhill. Rather all our members appear concentrated, they all appear, in a functional sense, to be "there" in active support of our instrumental members with which we are carrying out our action. This is so even if the instrumental members are not the leading ones, as, e.g., in the case of a runner whose whole body is adjusted to facilitate the action of his legs.

Consider the case of a track race. In a photo-finish, the winner is the runner possessing the body-part that first passes across the finish line. A race-horse, considered in this way, may thus win "by a nose." For such purposes of measurement, the runner is indeed regarded as a whole composed of parts. And Aristotle's analysis seems correct. But from the vantage-point of the active percipient, from the vantage-point of the runner while running, this is a distorted analysis. As a runner, he perceives himself as a functional "individual," in the etymological sense of that term, i.e., as an undivide-able. He senses himself to be in *one* place—not "part" here, "part" there. He senses that he has body *members, not* body *parts*. To perceive his members as parts, is to dismember them in appearance. For parts, unlike members, appear capable of being taken a-part without losing their identity.[12] If, at the last moment, the runner stretches or flings himself forward, in order to cross the finish line first, he does not fling his *member* across (he does not throw his member away!), he flings *himself* across in a certain unusual posture. He seems to be in only *one* place—either across the finish line, or not across it. Now an object, to be sure, *passes across* a line—first its leading part, then its trailing part, doing so. But a runner, to himself, and to those empathizing with him, simply *crosses* the line—as an individual, in an all-or-none-way. Aristotle's analysis that only "part" of the runner can reach the goal at a time, distorts the individual character of the victory or defeat.

Thirdly, Aristotle's analysis fails to take account of the fact that the identity of the active body is an *identity of changeability*. The active body of the percipient is the special kind of body that retains its identity not merely *through* change, but *by* the way it changes. It has just the kind of identity that Aristotle believes to be impossible. The unity of our active body is felt as the bare unity of our free activity, conditioning whatever particular activity we may turn to. No activity appears to be ruled out as incompatible with this felt unity. Rather this unity is felt to *be* precisely that in virtue of which *all* coming and going is in principle open to us. It is the form of the wholly free variability of our activity, whose identity as "ours" implies no particular activity, and is thus not the identity of any content. The felt unity of our active body is the identity that characterizes all our activity as "ours" *in virtue* of its free variability. *We* do it, only when we do it *freely*, that is, in virtue of the felt original unity of our spontaneous vitality, our self-movement. As Aristotle might well express it, the felt unity of our active body is the identity of our freely changeable activity *qua* freely changeable. The identity of the self-moved mover is pure activity, just as Aristotle thought. It is not, however, the identity of pure thought thinking itself at the furthest remove from matter, as he supposed, but rather the identity of pure freedom freeing itself at the heart of the material world.

4.2 The Perceptual Sense of the Passage of Time: A Correlate of the Self-Activity of the Percipient

The passage of time is not itself a perceptual event, though it is a sensible condition for the perception of all events. It is not *something that happens* in time, but is rather *the happening* of everything that happens in time. My problem in this section is to determine how we make sense of something "happening"; what perceptual meaning we give to "the happening" of something. Consider, for example, two elementary kinds of perceptual event: rotation and translation of an object. How do we actually perceive these events to "happen?" I perceive, e.g., see, an object rotated. What exactly do I perceive? I see it, before it is rotated, in a certain orientation. I see it after rotation in another orientation. I see that it has rotated continuously. Therefore I must see it in an intervening series of orientations. NO! I perceive a *flow of orientation* from the initial to the terminal orientation. But I do *not* perceive a *series of orientations* between these extremes. Look and see! The terminal orientation is perceived as the *outcome* of this flow; and the initial orientation, as its origin. The flow is directional: *from* the initial *to* the terminal orientation. The terminal orientation appears as that orientation in which the flow of orientation is arrested; and the initial orientation as that in which it is begun. Instead of the flow being made up of a series of orientations, the extreme orientations are perceived merely as *limitations of the flow*. Instead of a series of discriminable orientations making up the flow, the flow first differentiates the pair of orientations limiting it. The flow makes and marks the difference between them. The initial and terminal orientations are commensurable with one another because they are perceived to be

The Phenomenology of Practical Perception

connected by this bridge of flow between them, through which one has been turned into the other. This flow is thus a common ground or path at once relating these orientations and keeping them apart, as exchanged *opposites*. This unitary flow bears the identity of the happening, and signifies that something is happening to . . . something enduring the change. In the case of an orientational flow, the enduring vehicle of the continuous variation is an object-in-a-place.

A parallel analysis holds of translational motion. It is a flow of location, not a series of locations. The terminal location *is* where the motion is arrested. The motion makes and marks the difference between its initial and terminal locations; it differentiates these locations from one another. The continuous path of motion relates these locations to one another, connecting them and making them commensurable; and at the same time it intervenes between them, keeping them apart and distinguishing them. It does so by showing that the terminal location has replaced the original in some respect. The flow of location bears the identity of the event, a change of location. The enduring vehicle of this continuous variation is an object-in-a-field-of-places.

A parallel analysis also holds of the translation of the circumstantial field of places as the percipient moves from place to place. A particular such field *is* where-the-percipient's-movement-is-arrested; it is a delimitation of his movement. His movement bears the identity of the event of his going from place to place. The enduring vehicle of this change of perspectival origin is the percipient-in-the-general-horizontal-field.

Notice in each case that an e-vent is an out-come of a flow of passage; a delimitation of this flow, by which it is differentiated from something else for which it can be exchanged in some respect. The flow of passage, which differentiates its limits, has no internal content of its own. It *is* simply the-way-of-exchanging-one-thing-for-another. This is one reason perceptual events appear to be reversible by succeeding events taking place in the opposite sense: the way one thing is exchanged for another, being itself empty of content, can offer no resistance, hence seems equally permeable in the opposite direction. The flow of change *is* nothing but the apparent *ex*change; it is like a *hollow* pipe for conducting the exchange.[13]

This empty continuity that characterizes all flow of passage is like that characterizing all perceptual fields of activity. Unlike perceptual objects, such fields are not composed of a finite set of connected elements. In this negative respect, they are like a theoretically continuous series, e.g., the series of points making up the Space of Kant's "productive imagination." The difference, plainly, is that imaginative Space is continuous because of the way it is composed of a series of discriminable points, whereas the perceptual field and flow are continuous because they are *not* composed of any discriminable elements at all. They rather *underlie* (as field) or *connect* (as flow) the elements they serve to relate as discriminable.

Thus, for example, the single continuous circumstantial field underlies and relates all the places in it. These places are not *parts* of the field; they are not "in" Space the way parts are "in" an object. For the field is not composed of the set of places in it, as the object is composed of the set of its parts. This can be seen from the fact that the set of places in perceptual Space is discontinuous, whereas perceptual Space is continuous. Perceptual places can be erased if emptied of objects.[14] Yet perceptual Space is not normally interrupted by this loss of place. Still, places do not quite *occupy* Space either, the way objects "occupy" their place in Space. The latter relation connotes a "belonging" that is absent from the former relation. Furthermore, without objects *fully* occupying them as "their" places, places tend to cease to exist. But Space[15] cannot be fully covered by any place; places are not in Space as "their" Space; and the erasure of places does not normally jeopardize the perceivability of Space, even locally, not to mention as a whole. Places, then, are "in" Space neither as parts are in objects nor as objects are in places. Like every perceptual order, they have their *own* way of being "in" what contains them. Places seem to be "in" Space by *covering* a region of it. They cover the continuity of Space, *without* interrupting it. Parallel analyses reveal that orientations are, in their own way, "in" an orientational field; also, without interrupting its continuity. And similarly for the circumstantial field "in" the general horizontal field.

An e-vent is in general perceived as a shift (flow in place) or jump (flow from place to place) of objects. Practical perception, as perception of events, is of *finite* events, i.e., of local, and finitely analyzable events. For the apparent state of an object is the outcome of a *discrete* shift or jump that is not further analyzable in a perceptual way. An event is a perceptual quantum jump. But it is not an indefinitely rapid *series* of such shifts or jumps. The appearance of a *definite* shift carries the sense that the appearance is of something happening to an (identical) *object*. As a bridge of flow between origin and outcome, it exhibits the identity of what continuously changes. Without this manifest bridge of flow, an appearance would not be of something happening; it would not be of an outcome. It would simply be an *appearance-in-itself*. On this static view, what passes with passing appearances is only *our experience*, as identical observer making a successive series of different observations. But there is no passage of events themselves. There is a subject-passage, as a condition of our experience; but no object-passage, as a condition of the world in which our experience takes place. On this view, Time is; our experience passes in Time; but Time itself does not pass. Both ignoring the flow or passage of perception, and constructing perceptual objects in an imaginative way (i.e., as forming a dense series), have this common result, viz., a "sense data" analysis of perceptual experience as a series of appearances-in-themselves. But our sense of the passage of time, as I will try to show, is correlative with our sense of our active body. This, if true, would make it understandable that a philosophy of atomic impressions (such as Hume's) eliminates *both* the passage of time[16] and, as we have seen, the sense of our active body. One cannot be eliminated without the other.

I will now try to show that the passage of perceptual time, and the activity of the percipient, have a correlative sense. I will consider the matter here only in a rather formal sense. In the next section I will take it up in a more concrete and more interesting way. The perceptual sense of passage is made up of four ordered senses, each presupposing the one before. The most concrete sense is the sense of *what* has come to pass. It includes a sense of *where* this has come to pass. This in turn includes the sense *that* something has come to pass, which in turn presupposes a *primary field* in which passage in general may take place. I have noted these senses in the order in which each presupposes the next. I will take them up, however, in the reverse order; the phenomenological order in which each conditions or helps make sense of the next.

(1) *The primary field.* The primary field in which passage in general may take place, is the world. But the world is the field of all fields *of our activity* as percipient. It is the field of all fields whose apparent (front-back, left-right) order is reversible by our free coming and going. Now our activity, too, has its primary condition, viz., the *felt unity of our active body*. Coming and going in general is simply an expression of this primary unity of our activity. The world, as a function of fields of our activity, is inseparable from the sense of our activity. In particular, the world, as the field of all fields of our activity, is correlative with the felt unity of our active body, as the condition of all conditions of our activity.

(2) The sense *that* something has come to pass. This is simply the sense of that of which the primary field is the condition. It corresponds to the sense *that* we are active; the sense conditioned by the primary condition of our activity.

(3) The sense of *where* something has come to pass. Something can come to pass only in a stable field of locations, in which the "where" can be located. But the stable field of perceptual locations is centered in the action-station (or position) of the percipient. Thus there can be no sense of "where" something has come to pass except in terms of the vantage point of the active percipient.

(4) The sense of *what* has come to pass. This has the sense of an outcome; of an e-vent, as what-comes-out-of some passage of time as the difference made by it. But an outcome is perceivable only as successfully *tracked* by an active percipient. Thus, once again, we can have a sense of what has come to pass if and only if we also have a sense of our self as active percipient.

4.3 The Perceptual World as a Field of Fields-within-Fields: The General Significance of This Fact, and the Significance of the Particular Order of Field-Inclusion

I will again take up in phenomenological order the four senses implicit in our concrete sense of the passage of time. Once again, I will try to determine the correlative function of the percipient's activity. But this time I will do it in the context of an analysis of particular types of experience. This will allow me to make a more detailed correlation, and to discern fairly readily some fundamental implications that otherwise remain obscure. It will be helpful to bear in mind one of our conclusions from 4.0. Every object is perceived to be indirectly in the world through being in-its-place (in a delimited orientation); in-the-percipient's-circumstances (at a delimited distance); in-the general-horizontal-field (within a delimited horizon); in-the-world (in a nondelimitable vertical field).

(1) Our sense of the primary condition of passage and activity. We saw above that these are: the world, and the felt unity of our active body. In what *experience* is all order of perceptual determination stripped down to this bare bone? We do not seek a negative form of experience; one that involves the *dis*appearance of perceptual forms. We seek rather an *elementary* form of experience in which we do know our self to be an active agent in the world, but in which we know only this and nothing more. This is the case in *vertigo*—taken just up to, but not including, loss of balance.[17] We are then aware of the invariant vertical world-field; and of our self in it, as a bare and empty agent doing nothing; and of a wholly undifferentiated, general horizontal field. Since the experience of vertigo carries the unadulterated sense of our-being-in-the-world, and since its sense of activity is that of *turning*, we learn that turning is the phenomenologically elementary form of activity.

(2) Our sense merely *that* something is coming to pass, with no idea where or what. Our formal analysis did not provide much insight on this point. We remain ignorant of the concrete form taken by this sense of passage, and by its correlative sense of our activity as percipient. Let us then seek the incomplete, pre-objective *experience* that bears in pure form this sense implicit in all objective perceptual experience. If there be such an experience, its possibility must be implicit in all perception. Perhaps we can find inscribed upon the flesh of experience some answers hidden from the logic of the mind. The experience we seek is, I believe, that of *rushing*, considered as taken to an extreme. We have then the sense that something-or-other is immediately following something-or-other, while no lapse of time gives us the chance to anticipate or respond, so that we have no idea what is happening or where. Now let us try our detailed question again, this time in terms of the pure experience, *that* something is happening. What form of passage and activity correspond to the sense merely *that* something is happening, and how are they related? Rushing is the sense of changing our circumstances without having a sense of the circum-

stances changed. It is thus the activity of moving from place to place so rapidly that, while we have a sense of the general horizontal field, we have no sense of a circumstantial field delimited within it.

(3) Our sense of *where* something is coming to pass, but not of what it is. We saw, even logically,[18] that this sense of passage implies a relation between an active percipient and a stable circumstantial field of places. But we received no instruction on the particular kind of activity characteristic of the percipient at this phenomenological stage. Consider now the experience of this pure sense; the experience of making-sense-up-to-this-point, which is necessary but not yet sufficient for all perceptual knowledge of matters of fact. We sense where something is coming to pass, but not what it is, when *startled*. In this case, our attention is caught so quickly or so violently that we do not have time to abet it and actively *pay* attention. Our attention is wrenched by something, so that what catches our attention is not that thing but our-attention-being-caught by that thing. This is half of what frightens us; being startled is just the violent form of being distracted. When startled, our attention is arrested by—the arresting of our attention. That is why we are made aware of the *flow* of the particular e-vent, without being made aware of its *outcome* (what the e-vent is). The outcome is what finally arrests the flow (the passage) of the event. The flow normally *draws* our attention to what eventuates from it, and there leaves us satisfied as to what it is. But if the flow *wrenches* our attention to its eventuation, we balk, we are frightened and angry (our perceptual freedom is very dear to us!), and we turn our attention upon the offending flow itself. So when startled we perceive pure happening, shorn of its normal completion in *what* happens.

What does the startle-experience teach us about the passage and activity functions of the "where" of events, shorn of their "what"? The passage function is flow-without-outcome in a circumstantial field. We knew that already. But we learn something about the corresponding activity. It is that of initiating *anticipation*: the startled percipient is caught in the act of making the initial movements of anticipation (which must precede any determinate and determining response) while already faced with the need for a response. The localization (as distinct from determination) of an object thus seems to imply the rousing of our anticipation of it.

(4) Our sense of *what* has come to pass. This is our full sense of perception. Our technique of seeking the pure experience phenom-

enologically presupposed by all normal experience is of no use here since we are here dealing precisely with normal experience. Falling back upon previous analyses, we remember that what has finally come to pass is an object-in-its-place, as determined there by the successful *response* of a percipient who has tracked the happening to its outcome.

What may we conclude about the general significance of field-inclusion, and about the significance of its particular order? To sense that we are *in* the world is to sense that we can *turn*. But if this is our only sense of activity, we feel utterly *lost* in the world. We have no more than the need to find our self; we lack the ability to do so. In order to find our self, we must have the ability to *seek* our self, which implies an ability to *move* in search. This ability is correlative with our sense of the flow or change of circumstances *in* the horizontal field *in* the world. If this is our only sense of activity, we still feel lost (disoriented), but have at least the sense of a capacity to do something-or-other about it. We can do something specific only by *encountering* something somewhere *in* our circumstances *in* the horizontal field *in* the world. This sense of encounter is correlative with the sense that we are prompted to *anticipate* what we encounter. Our sense of an ability to anticipate is thereby added to our sense of an ability to turn and to move. We have still not quite found our self, but we sense that we are at least about to do so. We actually *find* our self in the midst of circumstances by *responding* so as to determine something present *in* some place *in* our circumstances *in* the horizontal field *in* the world. Thus we see that *the order of finding our self in the world is correlative with the order of field-inclusion in the world. And the perception of an object is the successful outcome of the percipient's search for himself.*

4.4 Why the Percipient Is Satisfied with the Perception of an Object; How It Fulfills His Active Body

We have just seen *that* the perception of an object is the successful conclusion of the percipient's search for himself. I am now concerned to determine what there is about a perceptual object that *enables* the percipient to find himself by finding it. Some additional phenomenological studies are necessary for this investigation.

4.4.1 The bodily basis of the irreversibility of perceptual time

We have seen that the passage of time is a function of our activity as percipient. But I have until now concentrated on the reversibility of this activity; on the fact that it is felt to be *free*, so that we can at will go back and forth in all our activity. This raises a problem. If the passage of time is correlative with reversible activity, how are we to explain that this passage itself appears to be *ir*reversible? We will now see how this irreversibility of time is not only compatible with the reversibility of our activity, but is furthermore inseparable from it as correlative with it.

All flow or passage is a change taking place in some *direction*. In order to perceive this change, we must keep track of it, we must continually adjust our self so as to follow it. To make sense of directed passage, then, we must be able to perceive it in a directed way. But we are aware that we can in principle perceive the directed passage of events in *whatever* course it may take. This implies that we are able to follow it in a *freely* directed way—a way changeable at will with any change noted in the event.

Granted, then, that the perceivability of the passage of events implies the free reversibility of our activity, how is the irreversibility of this passage perceivable? This question falls into two. How is the direction of passage perceivable? And how is the irreversibility of this directed passage perceivable? Let us ignore events for a moment, and attend to our sense of movement. Consider the analogous questions for our movement. How do we know the direction of our movement? And how do we know that this direction is reversible? We know the direction of our movement by knowing that our body is *itself* functionally directed. Our body is built with a front-back asymmetry such that effective activity is directed toward what lies ahead. The direction of our oriented movement *is* the way we are "headed." Now suppose we turn, so as to reverse the way we are facing; or suppose we turn back, so as to reverse the way we are going. How do we know that we have reversed our self? We must somehow keep track of our turning; we sense our reversal of direction. But we cannot do so without some invariant sense of what direction has been reversed by this activity. We can sensibly reverse our *direction*, only by keeping our *sense of direction* invariant. And this sense of direction is provided by the functional directedness fixed in the structure of our active body.

Now to return to events. How is the direction of passage perceivable? Our own body-directedness is responsible. It enables us to perceive the direction of the event by enabling us to sense the direction in which we follow its occurrence. How is the irreversibility of this directed passage perceivable? Our ability to keep track of the reversal of our own movement is responsible. This enables us to distinguish an *initial* movement from a *reversal* of a prior movement. In walking to and fro, for example, I can thus distinguish the initial character of my walking "to," from the reversal character of my walking "fro." In the same way, I can distinguish my initial tracking of a directed event from my *subsequent* tracking of a reversal of it. Therefore, even if some directed passage were succeeded by an equivalent passage in the opposite sense, the latter would not appear to have *undone* the occurrence of the former, but only to have *added* a second occurrence to it. In sum, the irreversibility of the *occurrence* of events is perceivable only because the irreversible directedness of our body enables us to keep track of a reversal in the *sense* of directed events.

4.4.2 How passing an object enables the percipient to determine it as a concrete unity

Consider an object lying ahead of us. It appears to have a left side, a right side, a facing side, and a far side. Its orientational field appears thus to be divided in quadrants. This field may be represented by a set of Cartesian co-ordinates considered as fixed to a central vertical axis in the object. Now of course no side of the object is intrinsically its left side in such a way that this side can never under any circumstances be made to appear on the right. The virtual set of orientational co-ordinates is *mobile* around its vertical axis. We can also lift an object, or turn it over, so as to shift its vertical (above-below) axis as well. But with many objects this is impractical; while it is rarely impractical to shift an object's horizontal axes. Thus the characteristic shift is horizontal. I will confine the discussion to this case, though the line of argument is clearly extendable. In particular, I will investigate how our perception of a *passing* object is influenced by the attendant rotation of these orientational co-ordinates.

As we pass objects and leave them behind, we *retain* a sense of their nature and disposition. This is why we normally do not feel threatened by that half of our circumstances on which we turn our back. We retain not merely a memory of objects just passed, but a sense of their continued *presence*. If I walk down a street, passing stores and people, I do not merely think, but *sense* that they are *there* behind me. Moreover, that they are there as the same concrete ones I passed. But if they are sensed as concretely there, they must be sensed as having some particular orientation there. A problem thus arises. The last time I *actually* perceived them, they were before or beside me, and oriented accordingly. My virtual sense of their presence cannot consistently retain this orientation. What then does happen? Consider a case. I pass a girl. A moment later, I am still aware of her being there. In what orientation? Not facing me, as I last saw her, but (alas!) with her *back* to me. What we pass and leave behind is virtually sensed in that orientation it *would* actually appear to have, *if* we turned around and faced it.

A technical distinction will prove helpful at this point. Our body, as noted above, is functionally directed. Literally, as well as figuratively, we must normally face things in order to "handle" them; in order to deal with them effectively. By our *effective stance* in respect to some present object, I will accordingly mean the stance (defined by set and direction) we must assume in order to deal with the object effectively. By our *actual stance*, I will mean the stance we do presently assume. Now our sense of the presence of all objects is had in terms of our effective stance in respect to them. When first coming upon something, our actual stance coincides with our effective stance. As we pass it and leave it behind, our actual stance diverges more and more from our effective stance. But throughout, the object is sensed in terms of our effective stance in respect to it. My actual stance can never enable me to handle all my circumstances simultaneously. Nevertheless, I possess, when well-oriented, a global sense of my circumstances. Possession of a circular series of effective stances, directed at a circular series of circumstantial objects from around my present position, makes this possible. My actual stance appears like a selector, moving among them and activating now these now those, as the need arises. My virtually effective stance for a passed object varies *by itself*, deviating, as I have noted, from its form when last actualized. This keeping-up-to-date is advantageous; it keeps my effective stance ready for *instant* use if necessary. Effective stance is "instant-stance." Just add need, and you get actuality of effective deployment.

Now let us reconsider what happens when we approach an object, pass it and leave it behind. The orientational axes of the object sweep out a half-revolution, so that *each part of the object passes through all four orientational quadrants*. What was at first actually perceived as facing, is finally virtually sensed as facing-away, and vice versa. What was at first actually perceived on the right, is finally virtually sensed on the left, and vice versa. In the course of passage, each part of the object passes around to the opposite region of the orientational field. In doing so, it passes from, through, or into each quadrant of this field.

The passed object is thus a compound mirror image of the object before us. If we stand between an object and a mirror, the left-right distinction in the object is reversed in the reflection. But the near-far distinction remains invariant. If we place an object between our self and a mirror, the near-far distinction in the object is reversed in the reflection. But the left-right distinction remains invariant. Compound mirroring is peculiar to perceived motion. It is the perceptual work of motion through time. It cannot be brought about by instantaneous reflection. Passing *is* the compound mirroring of objects.

Now the immediately foreseeable future seems to concern the objects to which we are paying attention, the objects lying ahead of us. And the immediately sensed past seems to concern the objects we have just turned away from after having dealt with them, the objects we are "through with" for the time being, the objects lying behind us as passed by or passed over. The immediately sensed present seems to concern the objects we are engaged in dealing with, normally close by. Passing is then that function by which an object in the immediately foreseeable future passes into the immediately sensed past. The immediately sensed present may than be regarded as the motion-mirror through which immediately-future objects pass in becoming past. But in the case of unfamiliar objects, this is also the "mirror" through which merely determin*able* objects pass in becoming perceptually determin*ate*. The process of motion-mirroring may thus be expected to throw some light on just how a percipient's experience of a passing[19] object allows him to determine it.

By virtue of being motion-mirrored, a passed object has a kind of concrete unity that a merely anticipated object cannot have. This is not just because the passed object has appeared in a *greater* orientational range. It is more fundamentally due to the *way* we have seen the passed object oriented. In a merely anticipated object, left-and-right, near-and-far, are only opposites. They are simply opposed, i.e., placed against one another. There is a concrete difference between them without any concrete unity among them. They are given only as appearances of a determin-able, i.e., concretely unifi-able, object. These oppositions are perceptually reconciled by passing the object, for passing the object gives a perceptual demonstration of the reversibility of these oppositions within the comprehending unity of a single orientational field. The *variation* of orientation, the half-sweep of orientational co-ordinates, integrates the *opposite* sides into parts of the *same* object by demonstrating the *interchangeability* of these sides in a single orientational field whose unity is given by its continuous flow.[20]

4.4.3 The vertical field

In practical sense experience, the vertical field appears to be the field of the common world in which we find ourselves thrown together with objects. And the horizontal field, by way of contrast, appears to be the field of our experience in this world. We orient ourselves in our horizontal field by orienting ourselves in respect to *objects* we find in this field, which is itself *centered in us*. But we orient ourselves in our vertical field by orienting ourselves in respect to the *field* itself, which is *not* centered in us; we find ourselves near the ground, near the bottom of the vertical field, in like manner with the objects around us. As active percipients we are, to be sure, at the center of a low-ceilinged practical field of vertical movement. What we must stoop to reach, appears "down;" and what we must stretch or leap to reach, appears "up." But the point is that this entire practical field of vertical movement is itself perceived to be at the lower end of a downgraded vertical field directed from the heavens to the earth.

Being oriented in respect to the vertical field itself, we can be properly or improperly so oriented. That is, we can be right-side-up or up-side-down in it. The vertical field is the field *in* which our body direction is oriented. On the other hand, being oriented in respect to objects in our horizontal field but not to the horizontal field itself, it makes no sense to speak of a generally proper or improper horizontal orientation. That is, it makes no sense to speak of our being left-side right or front-side-back. For our orientation in our horizontal field, whatever it may be, is what first gives this field its order; its order must be consonant with our orientation in it. What is to our left *is eo ipso* the left-hand region of our horizontal field, and so for the other quadrants. The horizontal field of objects *is* the field of our body direction.

We may be improperly oriented in respect to objects in our horizontal field, not facing them when we should; but we cannot be improperly oriented in respect to our field itself. We may, moreover, be *dis*oriented in respect to some objects in our horizontal field, lacking all sense where they are while still retaining a sense of an ordered horizontal field about us. A disorientation of this sort is the only failure of orientation possible in respect to our horizontal field. Any further disorientation involves a disappearance of the field itself; a loss of the sense of its order, not merely a sense of the loss of our right order in respect to it. I may sense that I am upside-down in the vertically ordered field; and I may try to "right" myself, bring myself into an upright, proper and effective orientation in this field. But I can have no corresponding sense of an ordered horizontal field in respect to which my body direction is out of order.

Objects thus appear to be encounterable and determinable only in virtue of our appearing to be thrown together with them, stuck with them for better or worse, in the vertical field of a common world. Active determination of an object in the horizontal field of our experience is our way of accommodating ourselves to it as in the same vertical world-field with it. The particular determination or significance that is effective is the one that meets the requirements of our living with the object in a common vertically ordered world. It is *our* contribution to actually bestow this significance on the object. But it is the world's contribution to set the heaven-earth ordered stage on which, and conformably to which, this bestowal is possible.

There is then a phenomenological priority of the world-field—in which we must orient our off-centered selves—over the horizontal field of our self-centered experience in the world. This priority is reflected by the phenomenological priority of balance over poise; that is, the priority of our capacity for proper vertical orientation, in the world, over our capacity for effective orientation toward objects in our horizontal field of experience in the world. Balance in the vertical dimension may exist without poise in respect to circumstantial objects; but poise in respect to circumstantial objects is impossible without balance. Poise is our capacity to cope effectively with circumstantial objects. We first have this capacity in virtue of our ability to stand erect, to balance ourselves in the vertical world-field. The equi-poise of balancing ourselves makes us capable of the directed-poise for responding effectively to our circumstances. Directed poise flows from equi-poise as from a gyroscopic center of our activity. As soon as we lose the central equi-poise of balance, our directed poise issuing from it flies off into an uncontrollable clumsiness. But our central equi-poise need not be lost by withdrawal back into it of all circumstantially directed poise. Our capacity to stand up[21] normally gives us the capacity to act; but not vice versa. An effective poise or stance *is* an effective balanced poise. But good balance *is* not a well-balanced poise (in respect to something in our circumstances).

Let us consider more closely the peculiar nature of this vertical field of balance that conditions the practical capacity for poised response by which we determine objects in the horizontal field of our experience. The vertical field of experience is an apparent field of influence distinguished by its influencing its contents (ourselves as well as objects) without any possibility of resistance on their part.[22] The influence of the vertical field on its contents is in this way sharply distinguished from the influence of one object on another, or indeed of ourselves on objects or of objects on us. The influence of the vertical field on its contents is not *a* particular influence *on* its contents *to* which they react in any way—either by conformity or by resistance. It is a *field* of influence *in* which its contents first have and can exert their *own* various kinds of influence on each other.[23]

This vertical field is applied not *to* us, as active percipients, but *through* us. Our initial problem is to balance ourselves upright in this field of influence. Our problem is neither to conform (accede) *to* this influence, nor to offer resistance *to* it—neither of which makes perceptual sense. Our problem is to orient ourselves effectively rather than ineffectively *in* this field of influence; to align ourselves in this field in such a way that it dependably enables us to do what we need to do in it. Balancing ourselves upright, we depend upon the vertical field of influence to steady us for whatever we may have to do; to keep us well-balanced on the earth—instead of drifting away from it, falling on it, or inclining at some angle to it. Balancing ourselves we *are held* vertically upright by the way we *hold ourselves* upright in relation to the steady vertical field of influence in which we stand. Balance is neither purely active, like moving, nor purely passive, like being moved. It is both active and passive, and one only through the other. We balance ourselves only by actively orienting ourselves so as to be held in balance by the pull of the earth drawing down through us from the heavens above us.

Each moment we effectively orient ourselves in the vertical field in which we move, we seem to tap from the heavens above an inexhaustible spring of effective energy. No matter how much we have already drawn upon this steadying downward source of influence, it seems to remain permanently available for us to draw further upon it, so as to remain ready for effective action so long as we remain in an upright position. When active, we seem to draw energy from this perpetual field of vertical influence. This energy seems to flow down through us as through a pipe. We seem in our poised movements merely to direct this flow of effective energy upon the things about us in the horizontal field of our needs. Irrigating these things with this flow, we produce in the field of our needs a goodly crop of determinate objects making the world of our experience habit-able for us.

The horizontal field presents us with *our* needs for useful objects. These needs are evidently neither satiable in quantity at a given moment (since the spatial horizontal field is evidently limitless), nor permanently satiable (since the temporal horizontal field is evidently limitless). But the vertical field presents us with the requirement to meet *its* conditions for effective balanced action in it. This requirement can be completely met, at least for the moment. In effective action we are thus ourselves continually normalized (i.e., continually meeting the vertical demands of balance placed upon us), while we progressively normalize things in our general field (i.e., progressively make things meet the demands we place upon them). First setting ourselves right (normally, upright) in the given vertical world-field running through us, we then set about setting things right (making them available to met our needs) in the horizontal field we ourselves generate about us.

The active percipient takes his bearings in respect to circumstantial objects by bearing body skills directed toward these objects; skills that are inscriptions carved in his flesh by the balanced poised responses he has made. Insofar as these object-determining skills are a function of the percipient's own response, the percipient himself *conveys* determination to his object by exercising these skills. But insofar as these skills are conditioned by the percipient's balancing himself in the given world-field, their effectiveness does not spring from the percipient himself but *originates* in the world-field in which the percipient has accommodated himself.

The percipient appears to *discover* objects in the horizontal field of his experience, rather than to create them there. This is not because these objects appear to be independent of all possible activity by the percipient. For the object appears to have to be something capable under some conditions of being made manifest in the percipient's field of activity. What an object is, appears somehow to have to be within the limits of what some percipient activity can make manifest in such a way that the object *itself* is thereby *presented*, rather than some *sign of it* being thereby made to *represent* it. If an abnormally undeterminable "object" seems to flout this condition of perceptual decency or normality, we tend to read it out of the perceptual world as an intolerable deviationist; we begin to regard it as "unreal"; we begin to suspect that its appearance is an "illusion" to be explained by still unnoticed but conventionally noticeable behavior of other objects in the neighborhood.

The Phenomenology of Practical Perception

Our sense of discovery testifies that objects are "independent" of ourselves as percipient in the sense that they are (retroactively) revealed to have been that way *before* their manifestation, and (prospectively) revealed to be capable of remaining that way *after* their manifestation. It thus testifies that an object can be a certain way without *actually* appearing that way, so that it is independent of our *actual* activity as percipient. But this same sense of discovery testifies that an object cannot be a certain way without meeting the general conditions for appearing that way, and without showing up as consequence of some possible activity of the percipient—so that the object is not independent of our *general* and *possible* activity. In the phraseology of the last chapter, the characteristics of perceptual objects appear to be invariant whether our actual stance in respect to them is an effective one or not; but they appear to make sense only as circumstantial objects in respect to which some effective stance or other can be taken. Objects, then, do not appear to be completely independent of percipient activity. Why then do they not appear in this measure to be created rather than discovered by the percipient? Why does it not appear that the perceivability of the object is created by the percipient? Because the significance of the percipient's activity, from which the object's perceivability is indeed derived, appears to be merely conveyed rather than originated by the percipient. In making objects perceivable, the percipient merely bears, expresses or conveys the inexhaustible vitality of the vertical world-field from which his effectiveness evidently flows, and to which it is due owing to his self-accommodation in this field. This does not mean that the percipient appears to be moved by the world-field, but only that the effectiveness of his self-movement in generating a horizontal field of experience in which he can find himself, is apparently due to his ability to accommodate himself in the vertical world-field. The percipient is the world's messenger to objects. He delivers perceptual orders to objects, but does not make up these orders by himself. He merely receives them from the world-field in the course (and as the reward) of his upright conduct in this field.

Our sense that the effectiveness of our movement is derivative from the vertical world-field *in* which we live, is therefore what makes us conveyors rather than originators of practical perceptual significance. Thus, though all experiential significance is *contributed by* the human subject (as signifying something in *his* world of experience), it does not follow that all experiential significance originates in the human subject.

4.4.4 Perceptual fulfillment as practical self-composure

A perceptual object differs from perceptual fields in two respects: (1) its order is irreversible with varying activity of the percipient in respect to it; (2) it is brimful of content. In both cases, the uniqueness of the object is due to the fact that it is *composed of parts*. The ordered set of parts that comprise a perceptual object is perspectively revealed, but it is revealed *as* perspectively invariant. As brimful of parts in a fixed order, a perceptual object is not an open field of our activity; it is what our activity finally reveals by coming up against. Now the percipient, too, as we saw in 4.4.1, has an irreversible order, viz., his body-direction. This order is not changeable by any activity, but is rather presupposed by all activity. So the percipient and his object are initially matched in this respect. But in respect to fullness of content, the percipient and his object are initially unmatched. The percipient begins empty of content, lost in the world, having only the need for content. The percipient has to *achieve* fullness. He does this by determining a passing object. His activity in doing so acquires unity and specificity from the concrete unity of the object that he skillfully determines in this way. In the completed perceptual object, the percipient perceives a reflection of his own momentarily completed activity.

The percipient's sense of the integrity of his perceptual activity is a sense of achievement, of *practical self-com-posure*, of having put-himself-together, integrated himself, by his skillful practice. This sense is derived from the verification of his anticipations, which allows him to rest assured. It takes the form of an ease, or, at best, grace, of poise and movement. He feels, at least momentarily, the absolute master of himself as practical agent. He is fully occupied with his sensible circumstances, but in such a way that he is thereby also fully occupied with a sense of himself as responsive percipient of these circumstances. But this form of fulfillment is manifestly *only momentary and local*. He knows that it may at any moment be lost.

The Phenomenology of Practical Perception

This is its flaw with which we cannot humanly rest content. Indeed, as we will now see, we set about with our imagination to represent the world as a place in which this difficulty does not obtain.

5

The Phenomenology of Imagination, as a Final Prelude to the Criticism That Kant Imaginizes Perception

5.0 Introduction: Restriction of the Topic

Since I will try to show how Kant distorted experience by interpreting all experience on the limited model of imaginative experience, some of what I have to say about the phenomenology of imagination can best be brought out in the immediate context of a detailed analysis of Kant's thought. There are, however, some considerations that it is most convenient to undertake in a preliminary way, and to these I now turn.

I use the term, "imagination," in a semitechnical way. My usage of the term is, I believe, approximately that of ordinary language, but it is definite in some places where the ordinary usage is ambiguous or unclear. By "imagination," I mean that form of experience by which we represent to ourself that something is possible. By "perception," I mean that form of experience by which we are presented with something actual. I can perceive something only if it actually exists; otherwise, I can at most merely seem to perceive it. I can, however, imagine something even if it does not actually exist; my imagining it connotes merely that it might possibly exist. What strains my imagination to the breaking point (e.g., imagining a round square) thus seems also to limit what can possibly exist. Perception is *self-evidence*—in the literal sense that something is *itself* made evident to us by this way of experiencing it. But imagination is *proxy-evidence*—in the sense that only a representation of something is made evident to us by this way of experiencing it.

The Phenomenology of Imagination

Now in this sense of the terms, it is, for example, by *perception*, rather than imagination, that we are aware of the (hidden) far side of a perceived object. Suppose you are walking down a street and begin to overtake what looks like an attractive person. You do not seem to perceive that you are overtaking the *back* of an attractive person; you seem to perceive that you are overtaking an attractive *person*, merely seen *from* the back. What seems presented to you is not merely the person's back, but the *whole* person from the back. *The person*, not merely his or her back, is evidently *there* in the flesh. Most sense-data epistemologists would say that the back is "perceived," but that we do not "perceive" that the person is attractive as seen from the front. They would say that the latter is merely inferred or "imagined" as perceiv*able* if one were to go around the person. But in our sense of "perceive" and "imagine," that the person is attractive as perceived from the front is actually perceiv*ed* from the back. Of course, we are aware of the person's back in a definite and detailed way; of the person's front, only in a vague and general way. Furthermore, we are *immediately* aware of the person's back, and only *mediately* aware of the person's front—as revealed *by* the appearance of his or her back. But this is not a distinction between what is represented to us as actual and what we merely represent to ourself as possible. The appearance of the person's back is in fact not wholly distinguishable from the appearance of the person's front. The back *looks* like the back of an attractive person who would also appear attractive from the front. Thus if the back is perceived, so is something of the front. For suppose one overtakes the person and glances at him or her from the front (since one seemed to see that such a glance would be worthwhile). And suppose one finds that the person is unattractive, so that the appearance from behind was, after all, illusory. If the person forges ahead once more, he or she now *looks different* from the back. The back now looks like the back of an *unattractive person*. What seems now to be presented as actually ahead is an unattractive person seen from the back—seen in such a way that though the unattractive face appears to be *averted*, it plainly appears to be *there*. All perceptual objects are given as partially revealed (on their near side) and as partially concealed (on their far side). But in both ways the object is sensuously *given* (rather than produced by us) as wholly *there* (rather than absent, or merely possibly there).[1]

Images, i.e., what we entertain in our imagination, are given as "representations." In this capacity, they are given as related to the perceptual world in general, if not to particular circumstances in it. They are given as representations of possible, though not necessarily actual, perceptual conditions. There is always *some* sensible relation between our imagination and our perceptual world—merely in virtue of the fact that they are both sensibly *ours*; and that we have a world of imagination only by sensibly *withdrawing from*, hence, standing in relation to, our perceptual world. The particular form of this sensible "representational" relation between our perceptual world and the world of our imagination, is difficult to discern, however obvious the general character of this relation may be. To begin with, though, this relation is responsible for the sense in which we "have" both our imagination, and our active body. We *have* rather than merely *are* our active body and our imagination, because we are individuals who belong to *two* worlds. Insofar as we belong merely to our perceptual world and are merely percipients, we simply *are* our active body—or else, as pure spectators, we are nobody in particular. But insofar as we belong to the world of our imagination, we divest ourselves of our active body and assume another identity as particular beings characterized by our productivity. As a *single* human being capable of transforming himself at will from an active percipient into a productive creator of his own imagination, and back again, we are individuals who "have" both our embodied perceptual selves and our disembodied imaginative selves, viz., our imagination. This sense of "having" does not connote that we are fundamentally some third man separable from our perceptual and imaginative selves, but only that we *are* our ability to transform ourselves reversibly between these two forms of ourself. This self-transformability reflects, however, a phenomenological priority of our percipient over our imaginative self. For it is sensed as our ability to imaginatively "represent" in a derivative way, functions of our perceptual experience that are presented in a primary way. Hence, even our final ability to reversibly transform ourselves between these two forms of ourself, is phenomenologically founded in our primary self as an active percipient. The imaginatively perceptual self that we finally are, is our way of signifying to ourself that we are capable of growing at will out of the simply perceptual self that we originally are.

The Phenomenology of Imagination

5.0.1 Restriction of the topic in respect to the mediation of perception and imagination by inactive spectation

How, more particularly, do we remain our individual perceptual selves while transforming ourselves into predominantly imaginative selves? For after returning from a sojourn in the world of our imagination, we do not re-alight just anywhere in the perceptual world, but always sensibly reassume our perceptual attitude as the very *same* percipient whose functions have been sensibly held in abeyance throughout our imaginative flight. Our imaginative activity does not, however, appear to take up or use any perceptual space, even though, upon reassuming our perceptual attitude, we perceive ourselves to have occupied a perceptually spatial position throughout the duration of our imaginative flight. We apparently need, so to speak, no "elbow-room" for the work of imagining something. Our circumstantial space, and the central position we occupy in it, appear irrelevant to our imaginative activity. Our imaginative activity does, however, seem to be perceptually *temporal*. We seem *now* to be imitating something instead of perceiving something. By imagining something, we seem to be occupying the very same time that we might otherwise spend in practical perception. Imagining something thus seems to preclude perceptual events from the time during which it lasts, but it does not seem to preclude perceptual content from any spatial position. Imaginative activity seems in this way to take up perceptual time, but to be irrelevant to perceptual space. Throughout our imaginative flight, we sense the enduring, albeit suspended, animation of our individual perceptual self by sensing our willful preclusion, for the time being, of perceptual events from our individual perceptual time.

Though our imaginative *activity* seems to take up perceptual time, *what* we imagine does not. Though my imagining the centaur appears to occur after my perceivably getting dressed, and before my perceivably going to work, the centaur I imagine does not seem to so occur. In fact, my imagining of the centaur signifies that the centaur does not "occur" at all, in the sense of occurring in this perceptual world. Regarding our imaginative activity as our way of intentionally giving sense to the image that we productively entertain in our imagination, and regarding the image as the referent of this intentional signification, we may sum up these points as follows. *In terms of perceptual space and time, our imaginative activity appears to be intentionally temporal, but not spatial; and referentially, not even temporal.*

What, more particularly, is this mediating vantage point *from* which we may imagine, and *from* which we may return to our perceptual world after an imaginative interlude? It is the vantage point of our *spectatorial attitude*.[2] Our spectatorial attitude is given as privatively *inactive*, and thus as presupposing the active attitude from which we stand back, from which we withdraw, in adopting it. But our active attitude as perceptual participants does not seem reciprocally to proceed from our inactive attitude as pure spectators. We seem rather to adopt our active attitude in a wholly original way, that is, in a way co-primal with our original sense of ourselves. Our spectatorial attitude in inactive perception thus mediates in a directed sense *from* our original attitude of practical perception *to* our imaginative attitude. It does indeed also mediate any application of imaginative content to the perceptual field, but such a turn of attention has the character of a *return* to our original field of experience, just as the turning of our attention from perception to imagination has the character of a *turning away* from our originally perceptual form of experience. Our spectatorial attitude mediates our reversible turning back and forth between imagination and perception, but the sense it gives to the turn, in whatever direction, is that perception is the primary form of experience and imagination is the derivative form of experience. This is true whether our imagination is "idle," so that we turn to and from it without cross-fertilization of imaginative and perceptual content; or whether it is "objective," so that the content of our imaginative and perceptual experience is systematically affected by our turning back and forth between them.

Despite its interest and the crucial role it plays in our experience, I am not going to analyze the spectatorial attitude. I will restrict myself to a study of the contrast between practical perception and imagination, for this contrast, together with the evident condition that we somehow or other pass back and forth between these two forms of experience as the same enduring individual, prove sufficient to show in general how the human body is the material subject of the world.

5.0.2 Restriction of the topic in respect to the fusion of perception and imagination in imaginative perception

Perception is only of objects near enough to sensibly pose a practical problem.[3] We can determinately refer to absent objects only by use of our imagination: by use of our verbal imagination, whose verbal beliefs are hence sharply to be distinguished from the felt beliefs of practical perception; and by use of our practical imagination, whose purposive activity is hence sharply to be distinguished from the responses of practical perception. But only by reference to a character-of-this-world, as distinct from objects-in-this-world, can we have any ground for holding such imaginative verbal beliefs about, or undertaking such imaginative purposive action in respect to, objects *not* in our perceptual field. For such long-range suppositions and purposes pre-suppose that the concrete as well as formal kinds of order self-evidently manifest to us *within* our perceptual field (in virtue of our centrally habit-forming active body), generally hold also in the apparently placeless regions *beyond* our perceptual horizon—merely in virtue of the fact that these regions are also regions in the same world as the perceptually present region.

By the imaginative character of the world, the human subject *represents* to himself *absent* conditions in the world. By perception of objects in the world, the human subject *presents* to himself *present* conditions in the world. We produce this representation from this presentation by the mediation of our spectatorial attitude. By spectation, we first disengage perceptual objects from their practical circumstantial *presence-with* us, i.e., from the form of their presence correlative with our poise in respect to them. What remains to perceptual objects is then no more than a spectatorial *presence-before* us. This prepares them for their imaginative transformation into images having a representational *presence-to* us, as images of what seems at once possibly-perceptually-present and possibly-perceptually-absent, whether or not the represented objects are actually perceived to be present.

Normally, human perception takes place in such an atmosphere of an imaginatively characterized world. Normally, furthermore, there is some precipitation from this imaginative atmosphere onto the perceptual field, producing in our experience not merely a *juxtaposition* of imaginative representations and perceptual presentation, but a positive *fusion* of these two forms of experience in some single object that *presentatively represents* some absent condition. This can occur, however, only when there are in the object certain present perceptual signs or *traces* of the absent condition, which permit the imaginative precipitation onto the whole object containing these signs, so that the whole object concretely manifests what is imaginatively known to be absent. An illustration will be helpful here. If I make a wax apple so realistically that, though I know it is a wax apple I do not by looking detect any sign that it is, it nevertheless looks waxy to me. This is because its waxiness, as present, is something for which I can have a body set (something in respect to which I can take an effective stance). And the sense of this set in me, e.g., my foretaste of the waxiness if I were to bite it, is sufficient to make the apple manifestly waxy to me even when no verification of this set is at the moment apparent. But, by way of contrast, if I know a pewter plate to be old, I must detect some present perceptual sign of its antiquity such as tarnish or signs of wear—or else it *fails to look* old to me. This is because its distant past, as absent, is something for which I cannot have a body set (something in respect to which I cannot take an effective stance). Hence without verification of its antiquity being momentarily apparent, I have nothing else to provide me with a perceptually presentational sense of its antiquity. I may of course *know very* well that it is a genuine antique, but it will not really *look* that way to me in the sense that a worn or battered antique will look old.

Everyday human experience is normally replete with such fusions of perceptual and imaginative experience. In order to trace the combination of perception and imagination culminating in such a fusion (i.e., in such a presentative representation as an antique looking old), we would have to trace how each form of imagination generates a specific form of quasi-perception by which it manifests itself in the perceptual world. In particular, we would have to show the following. (1) How the practical imagination is expressed by determinative *purposive activity* directed toward absent goals; and how these absent goals are related to circumstantially present objects that are alone capable of provoking determinative bodily responses. (2) How the conceptual imagination is expressed by *words* (or other written or spoken symbols); and how words (as pure face, without any parts even virtually concealed) are related to perceptual objects (which always have parts that are at least virtually concealed). (3) How the aesthetic imagination is expressed by *works of art*, which, unlike words and purposive activity, do not represent possibly absent perceptual conditions *in* the world, but an absent, perfected perceptual *world*;[4] and how the structure of this perceptually represented world is related to the structure of the perceptually presented world in which it is able to appear.

Fortunately, my thesis does not require us to trace all these ways in which the fusion of our perceptual and imaginative experience takes place, producing the richly significant experience we first recognize as fully human and familiar. In order to prepare for my Kant critique, and for the general development of my thesis that the human body is the material subject of the world, it is necessary to understand only those main differences between perception and imagination that set the conditions for their combination and make possible their eventual fusion. I have taken this sidelong glance at presentative representation only so that the reader may be forewarned that I do not purport in this study to describe normal experience fully, but only to describe the phenomenological foundation on which it is built.

5.0.3 Restriction of the topic to the single modality of conceptual imagination

I have considered three main ways in which our imagination lays claim to an evidently valid relationship to perceptual conditions, in terms of a characterization of the world in which these conditions occur—by way of the conceptual imagination (of what is abstractly true of things in the world); by way of the practical imagination (of what ought to be done to make a better world); and by way of the aesthetic imagination (of a perfectly beautiful world). My particular problem, however, is to understand the role of the human body in objective (i.e., evidently valid) experience by means of a phenomenological critique of Kant's *Critique of Pure Reason*. Since Kant in this work is concerned only with the conceptual form of imagination, I will also restrict my phenomenology of imagination, in its more specific aspects, to this one form. This restriction exacts a certain price in adequacy, even within the limits of my narrowed topic. For some of my analysis concerns the imagination in general, and is as applicable to the practical and aesthetic forms of it as to its conceptual form; while some of my analysis concerns only the conceptual form of imagination. And without undertaking a systematic discussion of all three forms of objective imagination, I cannot adequately distinguish between the general and specific levels of analysis of conceptual imagination. This seems, however, a price well worth paying in the interest of a decent brevity.

5.1 The Imaginative Transformation of Our Relation to the World

Perception is of something encountered in our actual experience *in* the world. Imagination is of something entertained merely in our own imagination, and not in the world. What we imagine may objectively pertain to the world as representing something about the world, but it is not itself in the world. Correlatively, neither do we seem to be in the world, in our capacity as imaginative subjects. Our activity of imagining something seems to take place in perceptual time. But what we produce by that activity is an image entertained in the world of our imagination. This extra-perceptual extra-terrestrial world of our imagination appears to be, furthermore, nothing but our capacity as imaginative subjects to entertain images.

Our imaginative capacity to experience an object (entertain an image) *is* the world in which that object is experienced, viz., our imagination. On the other hand, our perceptual capacity to experience an object, viz., our poise, is merely *in* the world together with the object so experienced. In imagination, we are left alone with our object, or, equivalently, as imaginative subjects we are the world of our object. In perception, however, the world encompasses both the object and our capacity to experience the object; the world being a condition of the possibility of the existence both of the object and of our capacity to experience it.[5]

5.1.1 Our imaginative capacity is its own initial field of productivity

Our imagination, in which what we imagine appears to us, is a global field of our *own* imaginative productivity. The image is imagined as in a field of our general capacity to produce images, but it is not imagined as in any field that permits us to exercise this general capacity. Rather, our capacity freely to imagine or not to imagine, permits *itself* to be exercised. Our imaginative capacity is therefore its own initial domain. The domain in which our imaginative capacity finds itself is itself. In exercising our imaginative capacity by producing and entertaining images, we do not penetrate further into previously hidden recesses of the field of our imaginative productivity. Our imaginative productivity, being to begin with wholly in itself as its own field, remains a single kind of field "in" which all content appears in a uniform way.

The field of our imaginative productivity is united by nothing more than our reversible capacity to produce in it, and extinguish from it, any specifiable image. As I can move in any sensible direction, then back again, or not move at all, but cannot extinguish my freedom to do (or attempt to do) whichever I choose; so, I can produce any sensible image, then extinguish it, or not produce any image at all, but I cannot extinguish my freedom to *do* (not merely attempt to do) whichever I choose. True, some things are more difficult to imagine than others (e.g., because too complicated, or too horrible). But this corresponds to movements that are difficult to make because they involve bodily contortion. The faculty of imagination, like the poise of the active body (our capacity for practical perception), has limits to the kind of productivity (or, respectively, activity) that it can manage. But the point of difference we are emphasizing here is that *within* these limits of what is normally manageable, our movement may encounter obstacles, but our imagination is in principle free from obstacles. *The only possible obstacle to imaginative productivity is the imagination itself.* This is just another way of saying that our imaginative capacity (i.e., our imagination) does not appear in a domain permitting its exercise, but rather permits itself its own exercise, and is hence the initial domain of its own productivity.

We may notice, in this context, how Kant's often mentioned "faculty psychology" is a sign that he has imaginized perception. Our imaginative experience does take place in the world of our imagination, i.e., in the field of our imaginative capacity. But our perceptual experience is merely made possible by our perceptual capacity, which reveals this experience as taking place in the world-at-large—that is, in the world *in* which we find both ourselves as percipients and our perceptual object. Our perceptual experience thus takes place *by way of* our perceptual capacity, whereas our imaginative experience takes place *in* our imagination. Yet Kant holds that sensation takes place *in* our sensibility ("inner sense") as well as holding that objective empirical events take place *in* (the spatiotemporal field of) our productive imagination.

5.1.2 The imaginative transformation of balance and poise

It may at first seem that the functions of balance and poise, so crucial in practical perception, have no place in imagination. If "balance" and "poise" are concretely defined in terms of their detailed perceptual functions, this is so. But if they are more formally defined, they turn out to be functions necessary for experience-in-general, and they accordingly play a role in imaginative as well as in perceptual experience. In this section, I will distinguish between the formal and the concrete senses of balance and poise in order to point out a formal sense that remains invariant in the change from perception to imagination, and to show in what way the concrete sense undergoes a transformation in this change.

Balance and poise are: (1) functions of our relation to the *content* of our experience; and, (2) functions of our relation to the *world* of our experience. (1) As functions of our relation to the content of our experience, balance and poise may be regarded both formally and concretely. Formally regarded, balance is the sensible form of our ability to control *ourselves* by ourselves *alone*, without reference to anything outside us; poise is the sensible form of our ability to determine something *other* than ourselves *presented* in our experience. Concretely regarded, these formally common content-functions of balance and poise are embedded in one way in perception,

The Phenomenology of Imagination

and in another way in imagination. Balance in perception is the sensible form of our ability to control ourselves . . . *in* the world . . . by ourselves alone, without reference to anything outside us; in imagination, it is the sensible form of our ability to control ourselves . . . *as* the world . . . by ourselves alone, without reference to anything outside us. Poise in perception is the sensible form of our ability to determine something else presented in our experience . . . by *anticipatory response* to it as something *outside us.*; in imagination, it is the sensible form of our ability to determine something else presented in our experience . . . by *spontaneous production*[6] of it as something *in* our own imagination.

(2) As functions of our relation to the *world* of our experience, balance and poise may likewise be regarded both formally and concretely. Formally regarded, balance is the sensible form of our immediate relation to the world; whereas poise is the sensible form of our relation to that content of our experience *by* which we find ourselves in relation to the world.[7] Concretely regarded, these formally common world-functions of balance and poise are also, like the content-functions, embedded in one way in perception, and in another way in imagination. Perceptual balance is the sensible form of our immediate relation to the world . . . achieved by our *internal activity in* the world. Imaginative balance, on the other hand, is the sensible form of our immediate relation to the world . . . achieved by our *spontaneous production of* the world. In our poised relation to that content of our experience by which we find ourselves in relation to the world, that content is presented in perception as something *present with* us in the world; but in imagination, it is presented as *represented to us* in the world.

Our perceptual ability to balance ourselves in the perceptual world thus has the same general sensible form as our imaginative capacity to be (as imaginative subjects) the world of our imagination. And our perceptual poise in respect to objects in the perceptual world has the same general sensible form as our imaginative capacity to produce and entertain images in the world of our imagination. So the change from perception to imagination preserves at least the formal functions of balance and poise, both of which seem essential to having any kind of experience at all. All experience seems to require a subject who is initially free and self-controlled in his immediate relation to his world, and who is able to find himself indirectly by giving determination to something presented in that world.

The change from perception to imagination does, however, involve significant changes in the specific character of balance and poise. First of all, this specifically imaginative function of balance, our sense that we *are* the *self-producing* world of our imagination, is unprecedented in perception in which we appear as merely *in* the perceptual world *given* to us, correlatively with our active selves, as the open field for our activity. Secondly, *the specific character of the imaginative function of poise is simply taken over from the perceptual function of balance.* For our *poise* (i.e., our ability to find ourselves in immediate relation to our world by means of determining something other than ourselves presented in our experience) is concretely exercised in imagination by our ability to produce an *image* that is made to appear in our imaginative world in exactly the same detailed way as our *balance* makes *us* appear in our perceptual world. (1) For the image, like ourself as percipient, appears *directly in* the world. The image need not be sought and found, is not initially hidden, in some internal domain of our imagination. The image is immediately revealed, as soon as it exists, in the initial domain of our imagination. The fact that the image appears directly in the world of our imagination does not signify that the image is immediately related to its world, even though our appearance as percipients directly in the perceptual world does have such a significance. This is because our imagination *produces* its content as in itself, so that even its directly contained content is only mediately related to it, as produced in our imagination *by* our imagination. Our perceptual world, however, does not produce its content but appears only correlatively with ourself as its directly contained content; it is no more than the field of activity for ourselves as active percipients in it. (2) Secondly, the image, like ourself as percipient, appears directly in the world *through our internal activity* in the world. Since the world of our imagination is nothing but ourselves as imaginative subjects, all our activity productive of images in the world of our imagination, is activity internal to ourselves. The third main change in detail from perceptual to imaginative balance and poise, is that the detail of perceptual poise (i.e., our anticipatory response to something as outside us and present with us in the world) is altogether *eliminated* in imagination, since as we have now seen, the details of imaginative balance are unprecedented in perception, and the details of imaginative poise are taken over from perceptual balance,hence, there is no functional room left in the imagination for the details of perceptual poise.

It is thus as if we lifted ourselves up by our imagination into union with the world in which we were perceptually balanced. And as if we drew objects half-way up after us, to occupy our own former position as appearing directly in the world, instead of their former position as appearing in our experience, which in turn appears to be in the world. The difference of course is that images do not balance themselves in our imagination, however directly they appear there. Rather we are responsible for orienting our images in our imagination. But being our own imaginative world, we cannot be disoriented in it. Hence we can have the further capacity unfailingly to orient normally imaginable images in it, in contrast to our merely precarious capacity to orient ourselves in the perceptual world. For we infallibly imagine normally imaginable images in just the way we mean to imagine them; never upside-down in respect to our intention; never too far from our imaginative area of attention to be immediately fixated as they first appear.

5.2 The New Kind of Series Possible in the World of Imagination

Determinate images are *immediately produced* by the imaginative subject instead of being anticipated by him, as perceptual objects are anticipated by the practical percipient. The image is determinately imagined as soon as it appears in our imagination, which is to say, as soon as it appears to exist. But the perceptual object is not determinately perceived as soon as it appears to exist in our perceptual field. It first appears as merely determin*able*. Its initial appearance merely signals that it is something-or-other attracting our attention to it for its determination as something-in-particular. In order that it be made determin*ately* manifest as something-in particular, we must first so act as to *lead* to its determinate appearance. Appearing in this anticipatory way as initially no more than determinable, a perceptual object also appears retrospectively to have existed determinately before its determinate appearance. It appears as to-be-determined by us in the way it already-is in itself. The way a perceptual object appears thus dismisses any suggestion that the final determinacy of it appearance is merely *ex post facto*. Nevertheless, because of the anticipatory way in which perceptual objects are determinable, we cannot *perceive* any succession of determinate events as having taken place in less than reaction-time, i.e., in less time than it takes for us to anticipate and effectively respond to this change so as to make it determinately manifest. Our perceptual determining of an event is not always itself perceived as taking time,[8] but it nevertheless places a lower limit the duration of the event we can determine to have taken place. We must miss any faster change as come-and-gone before we have had a chance to determine it.

On the other hand, because of the immediately determinate way in which an image is manifest, it appears not to have existed determinately before its determinate appearance. The way an image appears makes its appearance not *verifying* (as for perception) but *constitutive* of its determinacy. The image *is* exactly the way it is immediately imagined. Thus there is no imaginative threshold of determinability below which we must miss events as happening too rapidly for our ability to determine them. There is no minimum of reaction-time between various imaginably determinate events, as there is between various perceivably determinate events. Instantaneously determinate images thus immediately fall through the sieve of practical space-time, which cannot hold events shorter than its holes of reaction-time. This is a way of understanding how images appear to be "outside" the perceptual world.

Being instantaneously manifest as whatever they are, as soon as they exist in that form, images can sensibly represent determinate events as instantaneous in occurrence. For we experience determinately only what we determine to *have* appeared to us. Thus if the determining of what appears to us requires a passage of time, as in perception, then we can determinately experience only an event of a duration not less than that which could have been brought about by this passage of time. But if the determining of what appears to us does not require any passage of time (so that what we determinately experience seems to have appeared to us instantaneously), then we can determinately experience an event of any duration, however short. An "instantaneous" perceptual event has to last at least as long as is required to "catch a glimpse" of it. But an "instantaneous" imaginative event is without any minimally discriminable duration. We can *imagine* a succession of determinate events taking place in as short an interval of time as we please.

Thus the content of the imaginative world can be dense. That is to say, we can imagine (as positive content) a successive series of determinate events such that given any pair of them occupying an interval of time between the start of the earlier event and the termination of the later event, we can imagine some other event of the series occurring between the given pair of events. As there need be no next-instant for a given instant in instantaneously determined time, so there need be no next-event for a given event in an instantaneously determined series of events. In perception, however, no such dense series is possible. The perceptual world, as we saw in the preceding chapter, exhibits only the unstructured continuity (i.e., the continuity of the undifferentiated ground on which differentiated contents may appear) of a reversible flow or field of activity (e.g., a spatiotemporal field in which perceptual objects are differentiable); or the discrete continuity of an irreversible end-domain brimful of determinate content (i.e., the continuity of the finite, contiguous parts composing a perceptual object).

5.3 The World of Imagination as a Field of Explicatable Images instead of Determinable Objects

We cannot be surprised by what we find in our image,[9] even though we may occasionally be surprised to find ourself imagining such a thing. For the existence of an image is not distinguishable from its significance made up out of independently existing constituents. The wholeness of an image is not an outlying wholeness produced by its contents, but an indwelling wholeness thoroughly pervading its contents and indistinguishable from them. As the perceptual object is a whole (passively) composed of the parts in it,[10] the image is a whole (actively) disposing the elements in it. Therefore an image, unlike a perceptual object, does not have a hidden side, though it has an implicit side. That is, we cannot be mistaken about what seems to be implicit in the image, though we may be mistaken about what seems to be hidden of the object.

Now we may imagine the same thing in a number of different ways, so that the manifestation of something imagined may be in some sense incomplete. And any perceptual object may also be perceived as the same thing appearing in a variety of orientations, so that the manifestation of something perceived must include at least some perceptual implication of what is hidden in it. Still, there is a difference between the kind of incomplete manifestation of something imagined and something perceived; and between the kind of implication of what is implicitly imagined and what is implicitly perceived. In order to perceive an object as the same object appearing in a different orientation, there must be some change from implicit in explicit of our sense of the newly revealed sides of the object; and there must be some change from explicit to implicit of the newly concealed sides of the object. For we must know at least *something* of an object's general proportions in order to have the sense of volume swept out by its internal axes that gives us our sense that this identical object has undergone a change of orientation. But something imagined remains the same through any variation in the way it is entertained only if this variation is *altogether* one of rendering explicit what was implicit. Varying orientation of an evidently identical perceptual object may reveal new details (e.g., scratches) not implicit in an earlier manifestation of that object. The evident identity of the object through a change in orientation can be borne by an invariant perceptual *sketch* of the object. But in the case of something imagined, even the imagining of new details not implicit in our earlier imagining signifies that we are imagining something more and different than we previously imagined. If we perceive new details not previously implicit in our perception of a given object, then we perceive *more of* that *same* object. When we perceive more of an object, no more is thereby added to it. But when we imagine more of an imaginary object, more is thereby added to it.

What we imagine is merely what we represent it to be. What we imagine is entirely a creature of our own making: it is no more than we mean it to be; and we are always capable at will of rendering explicitly manifest whatever is implicit in it. Such a spontaneously produced and in principle freely accessible object can exist in our imagination only because our imagination is a global field of activity in which we ourselves make way for the presentation of material to ourselves; a field of activity in which we can encounter obstacles only by getting in our *own* way.[11] Because the world of our imagination is nothing more than our own imaginative capacity, we are sovereign in that world; our word or thought is law, legislating the content of our imagination; our will is instantaneously carried out, whatever in our imagination we wish brought before us being immediately presented (i.e., made explicitly manifest) to us. Because our perceptual world, on the other hand, is evidently given to us as a world in which we are merely permitted to make our way as best we can, it can contain external obstacles not always in fact freely presentable to us, hence evidently not of our own making, and capable of holding surprises in store for us.

The evident incompleteness of something imagined is thus the incomplete *explicitation* of something given as determin*ately* implicit. The evident incompleteness of something perceived, on the other hand, is the incomplete *realization* of something given as determin*ably* realizable. What is imaginatively implicit about something *fully* implies how it is imaginatively explicitizable, whereas what is perceptually implicit about something only *generally* implies how it is perceptually realizable. Thus, in referring to a perceptual object we *always* mean more than we (determinately) imply; but in referring to an object of our imagination, we *never* mean more than we (determinately) imply. The distinction between the possibility and the actuality of something imagined, is simply this distinction between the implicit and the explicit way in which it is determin*ately* imagined. But the distinction between the possibility and the actuality of something perceived is the distinction between the determin*able* and the determin*ate* reality of that thing.[12]

These contrasts between perception and imagination are reflected in the contrast between ordinary and technical language. Ordinary language is meant for communication in practical circumstances. As such, it has *two* layers of meaning. First there is the meaning that the *words* have by themselves. This is the standard, dictionary meaning, which renders ordinary words fit for use in situations of a general kind, as having a common meaning in all such situations. Second there is what *we* mean *by* using ordinary words in a certain way. This personal meaning, which is what ordinary language finally communicates, fills out the standard meaning of the words we use. This personal meaning is *first made determinate in the course and particular context of our actually giving expression to it,* and only thereby fully realizing it. Technical language, on the other hand, has only *one* layer of meaning, viz., the meaning of its words alone, which are not in any way filled out by the personal situation of the one who uses them. The meaning finally communicated by technical language is no more than the meaning *initially fully implicit* in the language in which the words used make sense. We do not ordinarily *say in so many words* what we mean to express by our words. Our meaning cannot ordinarily be fully understood from a mere transcript of what we said, without any description of the circumstances and way in which we said it. But when we use technical language, e.g., give a mathematical proof, we do say in so many words what we mean to express by our words, so that our meaning can be fully understood merely from a transcript of what we said. Although what we mean by using the words we do is not normally put into so many words, it can be normally understood—if one is acquainted with the way we use these words, and with the practical context of our using them. For the literal meaning of the words we use is noticeably augmented by our gestures, facial expression, tone of voice, and general bearing while speaking; as well as by evident circumstantial conditions, which we take for granted in saying what we do.[13]

These contrasts between perception and imagination are also reflected in the contrast between factual and fictional stories. If we are told of something interesting that someone has actually done, we are aware that we are being told about someone who exists also in other connections of which we are ignorant. In thinking about this person, we are aware of referring to someone who is further determinable and not yet completely determined in our experience. It therefore always makes sense to ask, concerning actually existing persons, for some further information not provided in the story told us about them. But the grave-diggers in the play, *Hamlet, are* no more than the dramatic depictions of them. Bearing the play in mind as a whole, we may ask ourselves many questions about the implicit significance of their dialogue. But all these questions must be such as to be completely answerable in terms of the given fictional material. If they are not so answerable, then either they lose their sense as questions not really raised in the play; or else the play loses aesthetic rightness by seeming to make something significant without implying what that significance is.[14] But in any case, it *makes no sense* to ask a question not raised in the play. Thus, for example, there is no answer to the question, "How many children did the first grave-digger have?" And it makes no sense to ask this question.

5.4 The Imaginative Transformation of the Extent to Which the World Can Be Filled

The field of our experience represents our capacity for experience. Our field of practical perceptual experience is always given as more capacious than its actual contents. This is because the actual content of this field is given as determinable by our free activity in respect to it. And if the world were filled with content, we would be cramped by it and lose our capacity to maneuver freely in the world. Hence such "content" could not appear to be determinable; nor could it therefore really appear to be the content of the world. Thus our perceptual experience can never exhaust our capacity for perceptual experience. As we saw in the previous chapter, our capacity for perceptual experience can never be more than *momentarily* filled, just as the perceptual world can never be more than *locally* filled with content, viz., with perceptual objects. Our question in this section is whether it is possible for our experiential capacity and its world to be more completely filled in imagination than in perception.

A permanently full use of our practical perceptual capacity is not possible because any possession of this capacity is based on our ability to move freely in a world given as permeably open to further movement. We must continually take this permeability of the world for *granted*, in being aware of our own ability to move freely. We can neither *achieve* this permeability nor *eliminate* it by any exercise of our motive freedom. In perception, local mastery is possible; world mastery impossible. But our imaginative capacity is itself the world of our imagination. Our imaginative productivity makes way for itself; it makes room for neither more nor less than its own exercise. The objection in principle to the filling of the perceptual world, and to the permanent filling of our perceptual capacity, is therefore inapplicable to imagination.

We saw in the previous section that our imagination is only a single stage or place. No external distinction can be drawn between it and some other place to or from which identical content can be displaced. Thus our imagination is *momentarily* fully occupied by *every* image it entertains, but only in the sense that the content of our imagination is exactly what we imagine it to be; nothing more, which the given content merely leads us to suspect; nothing less, for there is no such thing[15] as an illusory imaginary object. This still leaves us with the question of whether there is any sense in which our imagination may be *permanently* occupied by its contents. Every image fills imaginative space, i.e., fully occupies our imagination as produced by it. But what sort of image can fill imaginative time, i.e., fully occupy our imagination forever?

Our imaginative capacity is exhaustible by a content evidently imaginable in an endless variety of ways. An imagistic representation of an endlessly and nonrepetitively explicatable idea, e.g., that there are any number of dots, is a content of this sort. We sense immediately that our imagination could be continually and endlessly employed merely in rendering explicit what is already implicitly given in such an imagistic representation. For we sense immediately that we could go on indefinitely imagistically representing that same idea in the countless other ways represented as possible in the given imagistic representation. It could evidently be a permanent occupation for us to follow out the determinate internal cues for representation presented to us by such an image, without possibility of being mistaken about what we thereby came to present to ourselves.

Full use of our imaginative capacity does not then consist in imagining at once, or even successively, everything we can possibly imagine. Even our imagination seems incapable of such completion; fullness of imaginative content is possible only in reference to some particular imaginative idea. If we dispense with it, we start again empty of content, and without limit as to what we can imagine. Full use of our imaginative capacity consists rather in an imagistically representative *way* of imagining an inexhaustible idea. The imaginative idea is in this way represented at once as entire, and as further imaginable with endless variation in the same entirety. Through the representing image, or explicit variation, the implicit variations are represented as definitely imageable in like manner with the arbitrarily chosen representing image. Such an imaginative content constitutes and fills up an imaginative world with an inexhaustible spatiotemporal order and content of its own. The only unfilled (and unfillable) field in such a world is the "orientational" field of the possible imagistic representations of this world; each imagistic representation, however, revealing this world in the entirety of its explicatable order. Even one such experience is sufficient to give us a sense of the permanent fullness possible for an imaginative world, in contrast to the merely momentary and local fullness possible in the perceptual world.

I will refer to such a content evidently imaginable in an endless variety of ways, as an *objective* content of our imagination. An image representing such a content will accordingly be considered an "objective" image; and an imaginative idea represented in such a content an "objective" imaginative idea. The perception of an object is considered an "objective" perceptual experience because it is an experience of the kind of completion possible in perception. The imaginative experience we are calling "objective" is, analogously, an experience of the kind of completion possible in imagination. Objective perceptual experience gives us a sense of the unity of our activity as percipients, making us concretely self-conscious with a sense of practical self-composure.[16] Objective imaginative experience, analogously, gives us a sense of the unity of our productive activity as imaginative subjects, making us concretely self-conscious with a sense that in our imaginative capacity we have ourselves produced a limitless yet perfectly ordered world. Objective imaginative experience is something from which we can stand back; which we can behold as having a structure of its own independent of the arbitrary imagistic orientation through which it may be viewed. From imagining such a production that can in this sense stand independently "on its own feet," we first derive a sense of the integrity of our own productive capacity. In idle fancy, we are aware of ourselves as capable of imaginative production. But it is only in the disciplined imagination of something that appears to have a structure of its own independent of its imaginative orientation, that imagination seems to be a form of *self-discovery*. In idle fancy we seem to *lose* ourselves in what we imagine. But in disciplined objective imagination we seem to *find* ourselves as imaginative subjects. The unity that we imagine through our imagistic representation of it serves reciprocally to unify our imaginative act of representing that unity. It allows us to orient ourselves (as imaginative subjects) by what we have produced.

In an objective imaginative experience, we regard the world of our imagination as implicitly completed. In such a world there is no room for an active self-moving body—for the same reasons that the perceptual world cannot be completed because it does contain such a body. *The* body—whose active unity is correlative with the unity of the perceptual world—is imaginatively regarded as no more than *a* body, i.e., as one thing among others in the world of our imagination. The other fields of perceptual experience correlative with the body inhabiting them, are likewise transformed. *The* horizontal field of the earth comes to be regarded as *a* cosmic body, *a* planet; *the* sky, as *an* atmosphere; *the* heavens, as *a* galactic region. The perceptual contexts or conditions of the appearance of particular objects do not themselves appear as particular objects, but only as the fields in which the appearance of particular objects is possible. Their sense, however, is correlative with that of our active body. Thus when the active body loses its sense in the completely filled world of our imagination, these fields of our body activity likewise lose their sense. Together with the body, they come to be imagined as one kind of thing among others. The function of perceptual conditions was to make possible the appearance of perceptual objects. This function, as we have seen, is exercised in imagination by the imaginative idea. But the order of the imaginative idea, unlike that of the perceptual field, *is* the explicatable order of its content. Hence imagination eliminates the fundamental perceptual distinction between an ordered field and its ordered content.

5.5 The Imaginative Transformation of Our Role in Contributing Significance to Our Experience

Objects appear to be encounterable and determinable only in virtue of our appearing to be thrown together with them, stuck with them for better or worse, in this *one* perceptual world. If an object repeatedly resists every attempted determination of it until we are left utterly at a loss, and can no longer think of anything it might possibly be, it begins to seem "weird." It begins to give the impression that it is like nothing in this world; that it does not belong in this world. Our feelings about such an abnormally undeterminable perceptual object are suggestive of magic, and akin to our feelings about spooks. Of course, we may not for one moment lend *credence* to such feelings; nevertheless, we cannot help *having* at least a twinge of them, in such a case. The initial appearance of an object as encounterable and determinable *implies* that we are thrown together with it in a common world. A successful perceptual encounter with an object, terminating in a perceptual determination of it, appears to *verify* this implication. And an abnormal failure to determine an object appears accordingly to throw *doubt* on this implication.[17]

All perceptual significance as well as all imaginative significance is contributed by some activity of the human subject that permits this significance to take objective shape in the field of his experience; a field whose sense is correlative with the sort of activity the subject undertakes in it. But only the imaginative subject appears to *originate* the significance he contributes to his experience—producing it *ex nihilo* in the world of his own imaginative capacity; being *himself* the world of imagination in which this significance originates. The active percipient, however, appears merely to *convey* the significance he contributes to his experience—comporting himself toward circumstantial objects as demanded by his need to get along *with* them *in* a common world that itself originates and lays down through him the conditions of his satisfactory co-existence with his circumstantial objects.

The main implication of the imaginative transformation of our relation to the world, discussed in Section 5.1, is that we thereby shed our humbler perceptual role as conveyors of experience, and assume a more imposing role as originators of experience. This is a crucial distinction that we will have several occasions to use. A technical handle for this distinction therefore seems excusable. By *subtentional experience*, accordingly, I will mean all experience in which the subject makes sense out of his object by conveying that sense to his object, but without originating that sense. Practical perception is subtentional. By *intentional experience*, I will mean all experience in which the subject produces his object by originating the sense he gives to it. Imagination is intentional.

5.6 Summary of the Main Contrasts between Imagination and Perception

(1) The world of imagination is the subject's *own* imaginative capacity. But the perceptual world is the world *in* which the subject is capable of perceiving objects.

(2) The imaginative world can be *dense*. But the perceptual world exhibits either the *unstructured* continuity of a perceptual field or flow of activity, or the *discrete* continuity of an object finally revealed to the practical percipient in the field of his activity.

(3) The world of imagination is a field of *explicatable* content that is, to begin with, completely determined by the imaginative subject. But the perceptual world is a field of *determinable* content that is, to begin with, undetermined by the percipient.

(4) The imaginative world can be *permanently* filled as a *whole*. But the perceptual world can only be *momentarily* and *locally* filled.

(5) Imaginative significance appears to be originated by the imaginative subject who contributes it to what he imagines. But perceptual significance appears to be merely *conveyed* by the percipient to what he perceives, without being originated by him. In both cases the significance appears to originate from the world in which the significant content is experienced. But since the imaginative subject gives himself his world, he also originates the significance of its content. And since the percipient merely finds himself thrown together with objects in a given world, he can do no more than convey to these circumstantial objects that significance by which he can live successfully with them under their common given world condition.

6

Development of the Thesis That the Human Body Is the Material Subject of the World, as a Critique of Kant's View That the Human Subject Makes the World of His Experience

6.0 The *Critique of Pure Reason* in the Light of a Phenomenology of Impure Experience

In this chapter I will consider in detail only Kant's first critique, the *Critique of Pure Reason*. I will try to show that Kant's analyses in this work are invalid because he tries to understand the universal and necessary applicability of the forms of conceptual imagination to perception, while dogmatically assuming that these imaginative forms make sense independently of any particular perceptual sense. Imaginative forms making sense in this way are considered by Kant to be "pure." Without first adequately examining the possibility of their existence, Kant seeks to single out such "pure" forms of sensibility, which he claims to find in the Space and Time of our productive imagination. Kant likewise dogmatically assumes the existence of "pure" concepts of the understanding, which he claims to find in the categories of our conceptual imagination in accordance with which we form particular concepts tailored to particular perceptual contents of imaginative Space and Time. Kant takes it too easily for granted that there are "pure" forms of our conceptual imagination, although the first Critique is principally devoted to an isolation and study of such forms, uncontaminated with perceptual sense. The *Critique of "Pure" Reason* is a critique of reason[1] purified of all perceptual sense.

Using the phenomenology of perception and imagination developed in the last two chapters, I will try to show that no such "pure" forms of the conceptual imagination exist. I will not attempt to do this by showing that some particular content is indispensable to our imagination. Kant seems correct in denying there is such a content. It seems moreover plausible to suppose that the very insight into the dispensability of any particular content of our imagination is what led Kant to so readily assume the complete independence of the forms of conceptual imagination from all definite perceptual sense. This insight first gave Kant the opportunity to interpret the evident distinction between imagination and perception in terms of[2] the distinction between imagination and its content. I will attempt to show that there are no "pure" forms of conceptual imagination by showing that the whole *level* of our conceptual imagination (form as well as content) makes sense only in terms of a primordial level of perceptual experience. It does not do so in the same way that some imaginative concept makes sense only in terms of some other such concept. Such an internal relation in our conceptual imagination is *logical*. I hope rather to demonstrate an external *phenomenological* relation between our conceptual imagination as a whole and our perceptual form of experience as a whole. Conceptual imagination will be seen to make sense only in terms of perception, the way a solution makes sense only in terms of a prior need it meets. The forms of our conceptual imagination singled out by Kant as the "pure concepts of the understanding" and the "pure forms of sensibility" will be seen to represent the systematic fulfillment of the objective needs presented by corresponding perceptual forms. I seek in this way to show that the sense of our conceptual imagination *is* its representation of the fulfillment of our perceptually presented kind of need. In other words, the very "purity" of the forms of our conceptual imagination (as logically independent of all perceptual sense) makes sense only as the result of an objectively needed *purification* of our perceptual forms (and hence as phenomenologically dependent upon a complex of perceptual sense). Our conceptual imagination can be logically pure of perception only because it is phenomenologically impure, as tainted with perception.

6.1 Kant's False Dilemma of A Priori Knowledge: How It Arises from Imaginizing the World

Kant frequently writes that his central problem in the first Critique, i.e., in the analysis of human understanding, is the problem of how synthetic a priori judgments are possible.[3] He holds that a set of principles of a peculiar sort play a crucial role in human knowledge of matters of fact. The truth of these principles, he holds, is not logically demonstrable, for their negation is not self-contradictory. Yet, he holds, these principles are known to be true "a priori"; that is, they are known to be true independently of the evidence of any particular matters of fact (i.e., independently of any particular perceptual evidence); and they are known to be universally and necessarily true (i.e., necessarily true of all possible experience). Kant's central question is, How can we come to have such knowledge? He is, of course, not concerned with the psychological question of how we come to have such *belief*, but with the philosophic question of the source of our evidence for this a priori *knowledge* that he holds to be presupposed by all our knowledge of particular matters of fact. The dilemma, and the interest of the matter, arises from noting that the two traditionally accepted sources of (secular) knowledge cannot be the source of our knowledge in this case. Since the principles in question are synthetic, their validity cannot be *logically* demonstrated. And since the principles in question are necessarily true of all possible experience, they are presupposed in our knowledge of particular matters of fact, and cannot be proven by any intrinsically limited actual *experience*; all actual experience, all knowledge of particular matters of fact, simply begs the question of their validity.

Once it is recognized that these principles are neither logical nor empirical, there is, according to Kant, only one possible interpretation of their source. Kant's entire philosophy follows from his opting for this source, and his only argument for this option is that no alternative exists for consideration. I will attempt to show in this section that there is another alternative unsuspected by Kant; that Kant failed to see this alternative because he considered only imaginative as distinct from perceptual experience in formulating his problem; and that this alternative is superior to Kant's because, while Kant's view does not provide a completely satisfactory answer to Hume, this alternative may do so if the thesis of Section 6.7 can be proved.

Kant writes,

There are only two possible ways in which synthetic representations and their objects can obtain necessary relation to one another.... Either the object alone must make the representation possible, or the representation alone must make the object possible. (B124)

Kant has already made it plain that, since he is here speaking of synthetic representations, there is no logical ground for any necessary relation into which they may enter. He then proceeds to rule out the first of these "only two" remaining possibilities by holding that if the object alone makes the representation possible, there is ground only for an empirical, but not for an a priori relation.[4] Victory then goes *by default* to the only remaining alternative, and Kant accepts the view that in the case of universal and necessary propositions the representation alone must make the object possible. "Only through (such a) representation is it possible to *know* anything *as an object*."[5] When Kant writes that the representation "alone" makes the object possible as a knowable object, he means that this representation is produced or originated by ourselves alone as knowers. Kant's general, and oft-repeated position, is that "we are adopting as our new method of thought that we can know a priori of things only what we ourselves put into them."[6] Kant sums up this "Copernican revolution" that serves as the starting point of his philosophy as follows.

Hitherto it has been assumed that all our knowledge must conform to objects. But all attempts to extend our knowledge of objects by establishing something in regard to them a priori, by means of concepts, have, on this assumption, ended in failure. We must therefore make trial whether we may not have more success... if we suppose that objects must conform to our knowledge. (Bxvi)

This was a bold "revolution," a bold break with tradition, to conceive man as the legislator instead of a citizen of the world of his experience. It implied a radical separation in empirical knowledge between the matter of experience (sensation), which we *receive* willy-nilly as having a nature of *its* own, and the forms of experience (categories, Space and Time), which we spontaneously *produce* in accordance with *our* own nature. The weakness in Kant's position is the difficulty of understanding how elements from sources that may be (so far as we can know) wholly divergent, must nevertheless have an affinity for one another. Once the matter and form of experience are so completely separated in origin, it becomes a serious problem how they are intrinsically fit for one another; how the matter of experience has an affinity to being ordered by the form of experience.

In opting for his "Copernican revolution," Kant does not envisage the possibility that a priori knowledge of objects may be possible because both objects and our capacity to deal knowingly with them necessarily conform to some *third* element. He does not seem to have believed that there was any third element to be considered. As we saw in the preceding chapters,[7] there is indeed no third element so long as one restricts his analysis to imaginative experience. For imagination is only a two-term relation: a relation between an imaginative subject and what he imagines. In practical perception, however, there is a third element, viz. the *world*. Practical perception is a three-term relation: a relation between a percipient and what he perceives in a common world in which he is thrown together with his object. Imagination is only a two-term relation, as we saw, because the imaginative subject is identical with the world of his imagination instead of being in the world of his experience, the way he is as percipient. Kant's inability to see a third possible resolution to his dilemma testifies to his general identification of the knower with his world in *all* human experience. This in turn indicates that Kant assimilated perceptual to imaginative knowledge. Even Kant's metaphors at times betray his confusion of the heaven-earth world-field *in* which we encounter objects, with the objects so encountered. He thus confuses, for example, the *ground on* which objects may resist us, with the *resistance* so offered, by writing of "meeting no resistance that might as it were, serve as a support upon which he could take a stand."[8]

From my phenomenological investigations, it seems that the world provides not merely a logical, but a plausible, third possibility for what makes our knowledge conform to our object. There is positive phenomenological evidence that the active percipient (if not the imaginative subject) makes sense out of his object by conveying to that object a sense originated not in himself, but in the common world-field that embraces him together with his object. In the case of practical perception, at least, the conformity of knowledge to object seems to derive neither from the subject nor from the object but from the commonality of the world condition under which they exist together. The commonality of the world-field in which we are thrown together with our circumstantial object implies *that* this object is determinable by us, and also implies *how* this object is determinable by us, since the world *is* the common field in which the object as well as our self behaves characteristically, however limited our experience of this behavior may be. Furthermore, the horizontal field of our experience in the world, being the field of our needs, implies by its very appearance that the objects in it are at least minimally determinable—for without this minimal determinability, the field itself would prove unendurable and disappear. The very appearance of the perceptual field carries with it the promise of contents determinable as sufficiently satisfying to continue to make that field endurable, as its present contents appear to do for the time being.

The mediating role of the world, in implying the conformability of perception to object perceived, thus obviates for practical perception the weakness inherent in Kant's general position, viz., that it is inexplicable how the matter of experience has an affinity to being ordered by the forms of experience. Hume's view posed this same problem, with the difference that Hume simply denied the problem was soluble. He held, using Kant's terminology, that there were no synthetic a priori propositions; that there were no a priori propositions about matters of fact. Kant disagrees with Hume in two ways, which he does not seem to distinguish. First, he holds that there are specifiable limits to the kinds of relations by which the matter of experience *might possibly* be intelligibly ordered. Secondly, he holds that the matter of experience *is actually* capable of being made intelligible in this way. Kant has several strong arguments to substantiate his first disagreement with Hume, but none, so far as I can see, to substantiate the second. He seems to assume that his second view follows from his first. But suppose we agree with Kant that we cannot conceive of any experience that does not exhibit logical relations in a temporal form; suppose we agree that anything not so ordered would be intrinsically unintelligible to us; and suppose we accept Kant's deduction of the categories as establishing that the categories are the logical forms of judgment (the forms of giving unity to our thought) considered in reference to temporal events. Still, all we can justifiably conclude is that the matter of our experience must be conformable to our categories *if* it is to be capable of being made intelligible. But what guarantee is there that the matter of our experience *is* capable of being made intelligible? So long as Kant holds that we can be aware of (i.e., represent and intuit) the form of our experience independently of any content in it, he cannot explain how there *must* be some content conformable to this form.

The forms of practical perception (i.e., the functions of perceptual fields) themselves imply that some factual content is determinable in them. But the forms of our conceptual imagination do not by themselves imply that any factual content is determinable under them. In employing our conceptual imagination we do indeed *suppose* that it is applicable to matters of fact. But the justification for this supposition cannot be found in the sense of conceptual forms themselves, as it can in the sense of perceptual forms. We perceive matters of fact themselves presented to us in a self-evident way. But we conceive only our representations presumably true of matters of fact. Perception reveals the actual and evident accessibility of objects. But conception reveals only how objects may presumably be made accessible to us. We somehow *bring to* our imaginative thought the assurance of its applicability to matters of fact. We cannot *derive* this assurance from our imaginative thought.[9] But from where, and with what right, then, do we bring this assurance to our imaginative thought? I will try to show[10] that this assurance comes from the forms of our practical perception. These forms, which imply their own applicability to matters of fact (i.e., objects) can lend some of this applicability to imaginative forms because the latter are nothing but representations answering to the objective needs presented by the perceptual forms as more or less meetable. The factual rootedness of these formal perceptual needs gives some factual relevance to the formal imaginative representation of their fulfillment.

6.2 The Ego, According to Kant: Its Three Stages of Self-Evidence

Knowledge, according to Kant, is justified belief in necessary connections of experience. These necessary connections may be demonstrable either a priori or a posteriori; they may concern, respectively, either the form or the content of our knowledge. But in either case, according to Kant, to know something, as distinct from merely feeling something, is to make a judgment "containing a ground for necessary universal validity and thereby for a relation to the object."[11] Whether or not a judgment represents necessary connections among sensations is what distinguishes objectively valid "judgments of experience" from subjectively valid "judgment of perception."[12] In this section we will see that for Kant knowledge is, in the last analysis, self-knowledge; that it is based on evidence of our self to our self: that it is in this sense based on "self-evidence."

Kant writes that,

[W]e cannot represent to ourselves anything as combined in the object which we have not ourselves previously combined.... [Such combination, or synthesis is] an act of the self-activity of the subject.[13] (B130)

And, according to Kant, *all* our knowledge consists of representing something to our self as formally or materially synthesized in the object. Therefore according to Kant all our knowledge consists of representing to ourselves some "self-activity" of our own. Kant thus regards the intelligibility of everything as a function of the intelligibility of our own self-activity. He regards our self-activity, however, as perfectly intelligible, for he takes it as axiomatic that,

What reason produces entirely out of itself cannot be concealed, but is brought to light by reason itself immediately the common principle has been discovered. (Axx)

By "reason" here, Kant means our self-activity as thinking subjects in general, whether occupied with logical, mathematical or empirical thought. For he holds in the same vein

That logic should have been thus successful is an advantage which it owes to its limitations ... leaving the understanding nothing to deal with save itself and its form. (Bix)

Likewise, writing of the mathematician,

If he is to know anything with a priori certainty he must not ascribe to the figure anything save what necessarily follows from what he has himself set into it in accordance with his concept. (Bxii)

And similarly, writing of classic scientific experiments such as Galileo's and Torricelli's,

> [R]eason has insight only into that which it produces after a plan of its own . . . constraining nature to give answer to questions of reason's own determining. (Bxiii)

All our knowledge, according to Kant, is a product of our self-activity as thinking subjects spontaneously responding to received sensation. This self-activity takes the form of synthesizing representations (for which sensations provide the ultimate filling); it takes the form of unifying them in accordance with a synthetic (as distinct from analytic) rule. The product of this synthesis is what Kant means by "experience." According to him our minds are such that for us only "experience" in this sense is intelligible. What we can know is limited by the range of our possible experience. "Things-in-themselves," i.e., things considered independently of the successive, fragmentary appearances that we receive and make sense of by spontaneous synthesis are in principle unknowable by us. And the factor in experience that makes things knowable by us is our own rational self-activity that goes into it. Experience is intelligible to us because we know what we think merely by thinking it, and experience is in part what we think.

But though Kant holds that our self-*activity* as thinker is perfectly intelligible to us, he denies that our thinking *self* is intelligible to us. We know *that* we exist as a thinking subject because we are aware of the spontaneity (the self-activity) of our thought. But we do not know *what* we are as a thinking subject. We have no intuition into the source of our thoughtful activity. We know our self as think*ing*, but not as think*er*. What then do we know our self to be thinking? According to Kant, we do not think our self, as, for example, Aristotle says the Prime Mover does, and as Kant supposes God does. We are not capable of rational intuition. No explanation of this incapacity is possible; it is simply so, a kind of a priori fact. We rather think *about* our passive self. As a passive consciousness we have an "inner sense," a time field in which we receive sensation. We are aware of our self as spontaneous thinker by being aware of how we apply our active intelligence to the problem of making sense out of the contents of our own field of passive sensibility. By succeeding in this attempt, we come to know both the objects by which we have been externally affected, and our self as the passive creature who has been affected by these objects in his characteristic temporal way. Kant thus holds that "we intuit ourselves only as we are inwardly affected *by ourselves*" (Kant's emphasis).[14] And that "time . . . is the mode of representation of myself as object."[15] A condensed, if rather cryptic, summation of his view is given as follows:

Since I do not have another self-intuition which gives the *determining* in me . . . prior to the act of *determination*, as time does in the case of the determinable, I cannot determine my existence as that of a self-active being . . . [but only] as that of an appearance. (Kant's emphases, B58n)

We are considering Kant's view of the sense we have of our self, of our own ego. We have seen that for Kant our logically initial sense of our self is in the form more of a question than of an answer. As passive sensibility we are incapable of knowledge; we undergo sensation without understanding it. Kant does not speak this way, but it seems consistent with his account to add that, as a passive sensibility we are utterly at a loss, aware only of *ignorance.*

We have an additional sense of our self, as actively thinking, only on condition of having a sense of our self as passive sensibility. For thinking is essentially our way of responding to our self as sensibility; it is our way of making sense out of what is initially given to us. Even in this second stage, "I am conscious of myself, not as I appear to myself, nor as I am in myself, but only *that* I am."[16] I first become conscious of *who* I appear to be, by actually and successfully exercising my spontaneous thought upon the materials of my passive sensibility. But, according to Kant, the very form of my knowledge is such that I cannot rest rationally content with any partial knowledge of myself as appearance, which is all I can ever achieve by the actual exercise of my understanding. Even my ability to partially understand myself as actual appearance presupposes a further measure, viz., that I project before my mind's eye an *ideal* understanding of my experience made wholly determinate.

Our sense of our self, according to Kant, is bound up with our sense of knowledge. Our sense of knowledge is the sense of a quest

Development of the Thesis

beginning with the awareness of self-ignorance and directed toward knowledge that implies self-knowledge. Throughout this quest, according to Kant, our goal is to understand the contents of our *own* field of experience, which is not itself knowably contained in any larger world. Our goal is to understand the world of our experience whose unity is provided by our self as thinking subject. Now the practical percipient *in* the world gives unity only to the *actually* perceived content of his body-centered perceptual field.[17] He gives unity only to *his* experience in the world, whereas the world itself appears to give unity to all content, to *all possible* experience, in the world. But Kant's thinking subject is an imaginative subject who *provides* the unity of his world rather than finding himself in it. As such, he provides the unity of *all possible* experience in this world. Thus the fundamental problem for Kant's thinking subject is to understand himself in terms of the unity of all possible experience.

I will now attempt to trace in some detail the three stages of the solution of this problem. These three stages follow the order of Kant's categories of modality.[18] (1) The first condition of any knowledge is knowledge of all possible experience in respect to its *possibility*; in respect to it as determin*able*. Such knowledge is of our self-activity as thinker. It is knowledge of our self as the formal "transcendental unity of apperception." (2) The second condition of any knowledge is knowledge of all possible experience in respect to its *actuality*; in respect to our incompletable determin*ing* of it. Such knowledge is of the partial effects actually produced by the intelligent self-activity we directed upon our passive sensibility. It is knowledge in terms of our self as an actual "empirical ego." (3) The third condition of any knowledge is knowledge of all possible experience in respect to its *necessity*; in respect to it as wholly determin*ate*. Such knowledge is of the total effects ideally producible by the intelligent self-activity we direct upon our passive sensibility. It is knowledge of the ideal "transcendental object = X," which is the objective correlate of our initial self-activity.

If any "judgment of experience" is analyzed, and the elements of its complex sense given the order in which they presuppose one another, the first sense, according to Kant, will be of our active thinking self as capable of knowing our passive sensing self. The second sense will be of some empirical knowledge we actually do have of our passive sensing self, i.e., of our self as object, in virtue of the activity of our thinking self. In these first two stages, our knowledge is *reflexive*. That is to say, it is knowledge *of* our self in one respect, *by* our self in another respect; it is knowledge of our self as object, by our self as subject; of our self as known, by our self as knower; of our self as receptive, by our self as spontaneous. As such it is intrinsically imperfect knowledge. For our self in one respect, our self as spontaneous knowing subject, remains unknown.[19] Despite Kant's "faculty psychology," he never loses sight of the fact that we are somehow *one* ego merely appearing in two ways. Full knowledge would accordingly be knowledge of the one ego closing the gap between the two halves of the split ego of our appearance to our self. This gap is reflected in the difference between Space and Time. The spatialization of our experience is, according to Kant, the work of our spontaneous thought, while the temporal character of our experience attests to its source in our passivity.[20] The fact that all our experience is both spatial and temporal thus attests to its "reflexive" character and to our active-passive ego split. The unachievable ideal of knowledge would be to know our self as a purely spontaneous subject. The objective correlate of such knowledge would be to know our experience as entirely the work of our spontaneous self; i.e., to know our experience as entirely spatial, and nontemporal. Such knowledge would represent an active interpretation of passive experience so complete as to remove any traces of the original passivity. It would represent a work of thought on sensibility so complete as to restore thought to itself; thereby undoing, so to speak, that original exercise of our thought upon something *else* that limits us to the knowledge of our mere appearance. Now the "transcendental object = X" is in fact just such an ideal of an exclusively spatial understanding of our experience. Hence it represents an immediate understanding of our self as active thinker by our self as active thinker, whereas our empirical ego represents a mediate understanding of our self as passive sensibility by our self as active thinker.

In the remainder of this section I will relate our phenomenological analyses of the last two chapters to Kant's analysis of the three stages of self-knowledge. Kant believes, as we have just seen, that these three

Development of the Thesis

stages characterize all knowledge as a quest of the following sort. (1) We begin with a sense that our true nature as a single ego is hidden from us; that we are, as a split ego, in search of ourselves and capable of discovering ourselves. (2) We go on to partially mend this split by empirically discovering something that is in fact true about ourselves. (3) But such discoveries make sense only in the context of a greater hope, viz., that we can discover ourselves completely, and so become outwardly and manifestly one with ourselves just as we are somehow inwardly and hiddenly one with ourselves. (1) We thus start with a split ego: a sense of self-alienation, self-concealment, *loss of self.* (2) We are then objectively impelled (in order to know anything) to gain a merely *de facto reflexive self-awareness.* (3) This, in turn, objectively impels us to hope, albeit unrealistically, for a thoroughly necessary *manifest unity of the self.* As Kant holds necessity to be that actuality produced by its possibility alone,[21] so he holds in effect that the transcendental object = X is the representation of an ideal necessarily existent ego (of stage (3)) whose actuality (unlike that of stage (2)) is produced by its possibility (of stage (1)) alone. The transcendental object = X also represents Kant's goal of knowledge in general, viz., the understanding of the necessity in experience. In the transcendental object = X, Kant's goal of knowledge coincides with his goal of self-knowledge.

(1) The first condition implicit in all knowledge is knowledge of the a priori conditions of the possibility of experience. All such conditions, as conditions of the possibility of synthesis, depend upon the transcendental unity of apperception, which has the function of giving unity to all syntheses. This transcendental unity is the master unity of our ability to have "experience" (in Kant's sense of the term) because it is the source of our ability to form judgments, i.e., to give unity to diverse representations in accordance with a rule. It is presupposed even by the categories, including the category of Unity.[22] For the twelve categories form a diverse set that can be entertained in our single consciousness only in virtue of our ability to judge each of them a "category," and thus to unify the set of categories in accordance with the rule giving the concept of a category, viz., the rule that a category is a kind of unity exemplified by all intelligible judgments of matters of fact. "We must ascribe all employment of the understanding, even the whole of logic (to this transcendental unity of apperception)."[23] This

transcendental unity also makes possible our *knowledge* (as distinct from global intuition) of Space and Time, for such knowledge is possible only by a synthesis of productive imagination.[24] Our transcendental unity of apperception "is that self-consciousness which, while generating the representation 'I think' . . . cannot itself be accompanied by any further representation."[25] Considered as a form of self-knowledge, it is the sense of our identity as subject, as one consciousness.[26]

For Kant, thus, the spontaneity of our activity as thinking subject makes us self-conscious of the unity of our consciousness, and is thereby the fount of the possibility of all our knowledge. We saw in chapter 4 how the self-movement of the percipient plays a similar role in practical perception. Let us now compare more closely the role Kant assigns to the self-activity of the thinking subject, with the role our phenomenological analyses have attributed to the self-movement of the percipient.

Kant holds that we produce the apriori forms of intelligibility by a spontaneous act of the self not elicited by anything other than the self. This corresponds to our phenomenological account of how all practical perception presupposes our ability to move ourselves by ourselves alone—in response to our internal needs, but not in response to any external object. For Kant, it is only on condition of our self-activity as thinker that objects of experience are made conceptually determinable for us. Similarly on our phenomenological account, it is only on condition of our self-movement as percipient that objects of experience are made perceptually determinable for us—in the front-back field generated by this movement. For Kant, our self-activity as thinker first reveals our self and our objects as determinable in a temporal field, and determinate in a spatiotemporal field. We saw, likewise, how our self-movement as percipient first reveals our self and our objects as determinable in our front-back temporal field, and as determinate in our circumstantial spatiotemporal field.

Contrasts are also instructive. Since the self-activity of the Kantian subject is entirely formal it does not imply the (spatial and temporal) sensuous fields upon which it happens to be directed. On the Kantian view, it is simply a kind of "a priori fact," so to speak, that our intuition takes these rather than some other forms. On our phenomenological account, however, the self-activity of the percipient is felt as the self-movement of his substantive body. The fields in which this self-movement is directed are therefore felt as the fields of direction of the very body that is self-moving. The structure of the body, which is both self-active and in-the-perceptual-field, mediates between our self-activity and the field in which that activity is directed; it is so structured as to make one conformable to the other. Our spatial and temporal fields of practical perception have their characteristics in terms of the front-back, left-right, up-down characteristics of our self-active body.

(2) The second condition of knowledge is that of some actuality. Regarded as a condition of self-knowledge, it is knowledge in terms of our empirical ego. Knowledge in terms of our empirical ego is actual, though incompletable, determining of what our transcendental unity of apperception first makes determinable. The distinguishing feature of the empirical ego is that all empirical knowledge must be in terms of it. Among all empirical objects, it and it alone *must* be to some extent understood if *any* object of experience is at all understood; and, further, if it is at all understood, some other object of experience must also be to some extent understood. This is so because the empirical ego is the representation of inner sense as an object.[27] It is to some extent understood if and only if any temporal perceptions are lawfully ordered. All other objects of experience are objects of the outer sense. They are understood if and only if certain spatial events are lawfully ordered. But the perceptual material of *all* experience, spatial as well as temporal, is itself temporal, and thereby a content of the empirical ego. This material is lawfully ordered in a temporal way if ordered by a rule of succession; and in a spatial way if ordered by a rule of reciprocal succession. It is thus plain that, for Kant, all spatial ordering implies a temporal ordering. He also believes that all temporal ordering implies a spatial ordering. For he writes,

[My empirical ego] is determinable only through relation to something which, while bound up with my existence, is outside me... [It] is bound up in the way of *identity* with the consciousness of a relation to something outside me. (My emphasis, Bxl*n*)

This implication is more complicated to demonstrate. It is perhaps most simply done by reference to the *Anthropology* where Kant indicates, in effect, his belief that psychological understanding is psycho-physio-logical understanding. The temporal perceptions of an empirical ego are understood (i.e., unified under a rule) when they are understood as causes or effects of events in spatial sense organs. In sum, Kant seems to hold that all spatial understanding implies some psychological understanding (of regular sequences possible for the empirical ego) of perception; and all psychological understanding implies some spatial understanding (at least in the form of physiological understanding).

Let us now turn to a comparison between Kant's analysis of the role of self-knowledge in the thinking subject's actual determining of some object of experience, and our phenomenological analyses of the role of self-knowledge in the percipient's actual determining of some object of experience. Kant holds that an empirical determination of our self by our self as thinking subject implies and is implied by some empirical determination of an object outside us. We have come to a similar conclusion about perceptual experience. In practical perception, the determining of an object proceeds by way of some effective response to that object, and culminates by determining it as circumstantially outside us. This response, however, determines not merely the perceptual object upon which it is directed, but also the percipient from which it issues. The effectiveness of the response institutes or develops in the percipient a certain perceptual skill that characterizes him empirically, i.e., as having become a particular kind of percipient as a result of his experience. The determinations of the object and the percipient imply one another because they both stem from the sense of the same effective response.

Kant holds that the actual determining of objects of experience by a thinking subject is in principle interminable, due to the temporal character of our experience—which makes our actual experience receptive, successive and fragmentary in respect to its matter, and always less than all possible experience. We have been led phenomenologically to similar conclusions about perceptual experience. All possible experience is contained in the world-field. Actual perceptual experience is limited by the horizon of our horizontal field in the world; and first of all by the front-back temporal field through which content appears to enter our horizontal field. The horizonality of our horizontal field appears, furthermore, to be ineliminable. It characterizes our circumstanced way of being in the world. We can never come *to* the horizon of the temporal field beyond which lies the unforeseeable future. We can only advance *toward it* while it recedes from us in a compensating way. The very structure of our forward-oriented active body always produces a future-field in which objects may appear ahead of us as still-to-be-encountered—no matter how much we have already experienced.

For Kant, as we have seen, inner sense (the time-field) is "the mode in which the mind is affected through its own activity."[28] In actually determining any object of experience, we know something of the empirical ego, "the subject, which is the object of the inner sense."[29] In all empirical determination, therefore, we somehow make ourselves passive objects of our own spontaneity. According to Kant, the common root of our split ego is inaccessible to us, and we can never understand the generation of our epistemological schizophrenia. But in terms of our phenomenology of practical perception, some understanding does seem possible of how our spontaneous activity makes us passive. By *active* self-movement the percipient first generates his spatiotemporal field. But as soon as he does so, he is *passively* thrown into the middle of it as an arena in which he must fend for himself as vulnerable, and seek to find himself, though subject to failure.

(3) The third condition of knowledge is that of necessity. What our transcendental unity of apperception makes determinable, and what we actually though partially determine in relation to our empirical ego, we must represent to ourselves as ideally completely determinate. The conditions of the determinability of experience are necessary, and their necessity can be known beyond doubt. But they provide the necessity only of the form, and not of the content of experience. Actual empirical determinations concern the content as well as the form of experience, but they are only presumably necessary. Further experience may always falsify them. Kant believes he has shown that there must be *some* universal and necessary empirical laws; but he does not believe we can ever know that the

particular laws we believe necessary are necessarily the necessary ones. This distinction between the certainty with which we can know the necessary form of our experience, and the uncertainty to which we are limited in knowledge of the necessary content of experience, raises, according to Kant, an objective need for its eradication. That is to say, considered purely as knowers (disregarding psychological interests) we cannot rest content with this distinction. For this distinction represents our ego-split as knowers.[30] We can know the form of our experience with certainty because it is given by our spontaneity. But we cannot know the content of our experience with certainty because it is given by our receptivity. So the distinction between the certainty of form and the uncertainty of content represents the distinction between our spontaneity and receptivity as knower. This distinction, as we saw, implies our ignorance concerning our self; it implies that the subject we *are* is hidden from us, and that we know only our self as we *appear* to our self.

Since this ignorance affects the form of our knowledge we cannot, considered purely as knower, deny or disregard the need for its removal. Accordingly we always project before our self as knower the ideal of "the complete experience of the object,"[31] such as we can never in practice obtain. This is necessary in order to "prevent our modes of knowledge from being haphazard or arbitrary."[32] For what makes experience knowledge, according to Kant, is the necessary agreement with one another of the representations synthesized in this experience. And since our actual experience can be no more than partially synthesized, it can lay claim to knowledge only by being understood in relation to its completion, i.e., as presumptively completed. This representation of the complete experience of the object is what Kant calls the "transcendental object = X." This transcendental object is, on the object side, what the transcendental unity of apperception is on the subject side. Each represents, from its respective side, the unity of our experience—which is, according to Kant, the fundamental condition of its intelligibility. Each is "transcendental" because each, from its respective side, is the unintuitable condition of the possibility of intelligible intuition.

Kant's notion of the transcendental object suffers from an ambiguity deeply rooted in his philosophy. On the one hand, Kant

Development of the Thesis

sometimes writes as if this notion were intelligible in terms of *perceptual* experience; as if what he meant by the "transcendental object" were the whole of *particular objects*[33] that we can intuit only in successive snatches. For example, Kant holds that the transcendental object is what a judgment of experience is about. It is the unity of the subject-matter of the judgment; that to which both the subject and the predicate of the judgment apply, even though subject and predicate are logically independent of one another. He notes that we may refer to objects by concepts (e.g., "body") that do not imply all the characteristics (e.g., "weight") of these objects. Yet in doing so we mean to refer to the objects as wholes, including all their characteristics. In such a case, he holds, "the (subject) concept indicates the complete experience through one of its parts (*sic!*); and to this part, as belonging to it, I can therefore add other parts of the same experience."[33] But Kant's stronger tendency is to write of the transcendental object in terms of *imaginative* experience. In these contexts, the "transcendental object" means the represented unity of all possible experience. This is the unity of a *single object* in which all separate, perceptual objects are merged. Kant writes in this vein that the transcendental object "in reality throughout all our knowledge is always one and the same."[34] Intuitable objects "in turn have their object which cannot be intuited by us... the transcendental object=X."[35] The transcendental object is then the single object of all separably intuitable objects. It receives its unity from the transcendental unity of apperception. But can Kant account for the unity of a local object, also somehow known to be more than we know of it? Kant can make sense of the global determinability of intuition, characteristic of imagination. But can he make sense of the local determinability of intuition characteristic of perception? Can he in the last analysis *distinguish* particular objects, "each" having the transcendental object as its object?[36]

6.3 Phenomenological Criticism: Kant Imaginizes the Ego

In this section I will argue that Kant has no sense of the formative influence of action *on the active agent;* that he has no sense of how practice makes the practitioner. Kant does keenly sense some ways in which activity may be formative. For he holds that by our self-activity as thinker we make the whole knowable world and all objects in it. But he interprets our making this world of experience as simply our way of holding a mirror before our mind, so that we could ideally see a representation of our self as we are "in-our self" *independently* of that representation. For Kant, in short, *we discover our self by making our world*. This is an accurate analysis of objective imaginative experience. For we create the world of our imagination; and if we do so in an objective way, we thereby achieve self-expression and self-discovery. But this is not true of practical perception, as our phenomenological analyses have shown. As skillful percipient, on the contrary, *we make our self by discovering our world*. On our view,[37] imagination presupposes practical perception because we must first become somebody by practical experience in the given world, before we can achieve self-expression and self-discovery by making a world of our own. In any case, whatever the true relation may be between these two forms of experience, Kant's view that *all* our knowledge has the form of self-discovery by the making of our world, shows that he has imaginized the perceptual factor in our self-knowledge. In this section I will consider the formative influence of practice on the practitioner, in order to bring out the contrast between the perceptual way we make our self by discovering our world, and the imaginative (and Kantian) way we discover our self by making our world.

In practical perception, the subject is in search of himself. What he *seeks* is, indeed, to find himself, not to create himself, in the midst of his circumstances. But what he *achieves* in the course of this search is the capacity to find himself. By seeking to find himself he first makes himself capable of finding himself. His need-prompted self-movement is directed toward the self-discovery that comes with the discovery of what one finds satisfying. By his self-movement directed toward his self-discovery, the percipient is self-made as capable of self-discovery. Self-movement is required in order to transform the *need* for self-discovery into the *capacity* for it. The self so produced is thus a *creative discovery*.

This is true both of our general and our particular capacities as practical percipient. Our particular capacities are particular skills for effective response to circumstantial objects. The sense of these

Development of the Thesis

skills as "effective" implies that they have proved themselves in actual practice. Our sense of our general capacity to determine circumstantial objects likewise stems from our sense of effective self-movement. The general notion of "capacity" implies a distinction between a determinate state of actuality and an antecedent state of the determinate possibility of that actuality. But this distinction does not even make sense unless we comprehend some *activity* by which the possibility can be transformed into the relevant actuality; by which the actuality can be made to issue from that possibility. A capacity is a capacity *for* something that can be realized by making use of that capacity. A sense of capacity thus presumes a sense of its realizability, which comes only from experience of its effective deployment. The distinction between possibility and actuality that defines a capacity thus makes sense only as the distinction between the availability and deployment of that very activity whose effective deployment first produced that distinction. Our general sense of capacity therefore issues from and presupposes our general sense of activity. Our general sense of activity is of something-or-other-taking place in the field of our experience; and in practical perception, as we have seen, this field is a function of our sense of self-movement. Therefore, our sense of activity is founded on our sense of self-activity. So long as we are conscious, we cannot evade the sense of our self-activity. Whether we hold still, or move, or struggle to move—we must always appear to be doing something or to be actively refraining from doing anything. So long as we are conscious, it does not lie in our power to give up our self-determination to action or inaction. On the contrary, all our power (capacity) lies in our self-determination to action or inaction.

In the case of the practical percipient, therefore, self-activity helps to *make* the active self. It transforms the active self from a creature of needs into a creature of capacities to satisfy these needs. This creative function of practice is, by the very nature of perception, hidden; it must be hauled to light. What we perceive is what we discover. Because perception does not create what is perceiv*ed*, it easily goes unnoticed that perception does in some measure create the perceiv*er*. What we perceive is something whose significance we have merely conveyed to it. We notice the object as having this significance we have not originated, but only discovered in it.

We tend to overlook the change that has been brought about in us by the exercise of bestowing the proper significance upon objects. What, more particularly, is this change, and why do we tend to overlook it?

Perceptual objects have a certain sense: that they are in the world; and what they are. We as percipient have a sense of this sense. Our sense has two phases: what it is; and the way it seems to be "of," i.e., have reference to, the object's sense. Our sense of the object's sense is our bodily skill[38] for determining the object to have this sense. Our skill seems to have reference to the object's sense by way of the horizontal field we generate about us through our self-movement. Our skills make furrows in our horizontal field, and give it its texture of relevance, as to what sort of thing goes on and is to be found there. The sense of objects is disclosed "in" our experience "of" them, because it is disclosed in our horizontal field through which we make skillful reference to them. Perceiving thus brings about two changes in the practical percipient. It brings him a skillful sense of the sense of objects; and it brings him an orderly way of making reference to objects as having this sense. The practical percipient merely conveys rather than originates the sense he gives to objects; but he must originate rather than merely convey his means of conveying sense to objects. To be sure, the world of human experience is the humanly habitable world, not just because we make it so, but because the world enables us to make it so. Nevertheless, the world does not compel us to make it so. Our actually making it so is internally prompted by our own needs; and our way of making it so (our skill and oriented horizontal field) is our own production within the merely limiting world.

Why do we tend to overlook this change produced in ourselves by our exploration and discovery of the perceptual world? Our quest is directed toward the self-discovery that comes with finding what satisfies us as percipient. But not everything satisfies us. And we somehow recognize ourselves by the practical self-composure we gain through finding something that does satisfy us. This seems to indicate that we discover rather than create our self, just as in the case of objects. The difference can be made plain only by recognizing that we begin as a creature of *need* rather than *desire*. A need, unlike a desire, is originally given as a pure restlessness; as the consciousness of one's *un*directed activity. It beings with the sense of a lack in oneself, *without* any sense

Development of the Thesis

of what would remove that lack; it begins with the sense of an *in*determinate lack of something-or-other, but nothing-in-particular. It begins with a sense of loss of something one has never had; whereas the "loss" of desire is always of something once had. Now the whole sense of our exploration and discovery of the world is prompted by the sense of having been initially lost in the world. We came into the world "lost." It was not that we *had* lost something; but that we *were* lost. If we had lost something, it would have been something we previously possessed. But we were initially lost in the world without having ever previously found ourselves. Our whole quest of discovery is thus initially prompted by need rather than desire.[39] It is initially "directed" not to get what we want but to discover what we want to get. Desire is first roused by an anticipatory interpretation of need, a feeling for what we need. And just as the initial demand raised by a need differs from the initial demand raised by a desire, so the meeting of a need differs from the satisfaction of a desire. The meeting of a need, unlike the satisfaction of a desire, always involves a confirmatory *recognition* of the need met, a recognition that retroactively determines the true nature of the need that prompted the activity culminating in its filling. The meeting of a need first makes the need recognizable for what it is; whereas the satisfying of a desire merely assuages the desire, without aiding us in its recognition. It was a "desire" only because there was no problem of recognition; we recognized what we wanted by it even before its satisfaction. We can thus be disappointed by getting what we desire; it may not prove as satisfying as we anticipated, so we conclude it is not what we needed even though it is certainly what we felt we needed, i.e., what we desired. What is at stake in the satisfaction of a desire is not what the satisfied desire was, but whether it was worth satisfying, how deeply satisfying the satisfaction of it is, how fully we desired what we needed. We cannot, in contrast, be disappointed by the meeting of our needs. For the whole enterprise of exploration and discovery of the world only makes sense as an attempt to meet our needs; the meeting of our needs is what we *mean* by "gratification." Unlike desires, needs as such need to be met. We may become disenchanted with life and the world, and cease to care about meeting our needs. But in such a case it is not the *result* of meeting our needs that fails us (there is nothing of which gratification could appear to fall short), but the life-*source* that gives vigor and vitality to our needs.

The retroactive determination of needs by their being met covers up the fact that they first become determinate by being met. The meeting of a need first fixes it; but it is fixed retroactively as having been that determinate need all along. Meeting a need, we first recognize it for what it is; but we spontaneously proceed to recognize it for what it was. We cannot do otherwise, for our experience *is* nothing but our quest to meet our needs; to proceed from being lost in the world to finding our self in the world. Whatever we find in this quest is *ipso facto* what we have been looking for all along. What we finally perceive an object to be is also what it retroactively turns out to have been determinable as all along. But there is a crucial difference. The determination of objects is retroactive because it culminates, and thereby gives final sense to, our prior *anticipation* of the sense these objects have. And this sense, as we have seen, is merely conveyed rather than originated by us. So the object is finally perceived as discovered rather than produced by us. But the determination of needs is retroactive because it culminates our entire quest for experience, including the initial stages by which we first *become able to anticipate* the sense of objects; by which we first acquire a sense of the sense objects have. And this ability to convey sense to objects is itself *originated* rather than merely conveyed by us. So the need is finally discovered as having been produced by the way we discovered (but did not produce) objects. The need is discovered as a determinate need-for-something-in-particular. This determinate need is not produced just by the object needed; nor just by our self as lost in the world; nor just by the world, which merely enables us to determine our needs (whatever they may be) in it. The determinate need is produced by our-experience-of-objects-in-the-world. It is produced by the combination of our being thrown together in a common world with objects having a certain sense, together with our self-produced sense of the sense these objects have.

Let us now contrast the view developed here with Kant's view of the ego discussed in the preceding section. Kant held that "I cannot determine my existence as that of a self-active being, (but only) as that of an appearance."[40] He holds that we *have* some perfectly determinate and intelligible nature "in-our self," but cannot *know* more than an imperfect representation of it. Even the purely "spontaneous" activity of our understanding, as we can know it, is only the actualization of an antecedently determinate disposition. The categories are

> dispositions in the human understanding, in which they lie prepared, till at last, on the occasion of experience, they are developed, and by the same understanding are exhibited in their purity, freed from the empirical conditions attaching to them.[41]

Kant sees that self-discovery comes only as the result of considerable activity. But he believes as much as Aristotle that activity cannot be formative in respect to its source. Aristotle's statement, "That which produces the form is always something which possesses it"[42] might just as well have been Kant's. No matter how spontaneous the activity may be, whatever it produces must "lie prepared" to begin with as a wholly determinate disposition in the agent of this activity. Kant writes, for example,

> Before the artist can produce a bodily form he must have finished it in imagination. (*Anthropology*, p. 31)

Kant has no sense that the work of art is not finally planned to begin with, but is only worked out *in the act* of producing it. Some Aristotelian conviction of this sort seems to be one reason for Kant's conviction that our whole activity of knowing, by which we make the whole world of our experience, is merely a way of approaching knowledge of the self that we determinately are "in-our self" independently of all this activity.

But there seems to be another ground for the conviction; a specifically Kantian ground, which should perhaps be taken as more fundamental. Kant holds that the "absolute unity"[43] of the understanding is a condition of the possibility of knowledge. Knowing *is* simply our way of representing in intuition this unity of understanding. But this unity of understanding presupposed by all our understanding cannot itself be intuited in the world of our understanding The most we can do is to represent it by the "I think" that can accompany all judgments. Our understanding, in short, *presumes* a unity of our self as subject, but cannot *present* this unity; it can do no more than represent it. If the very form of our understanding makes it evident that we have a unity as subject not presentable in our understanding; and if, as with Kant, one believes all experience is that of our understanding (our theoretical imagination), then one has no choice but to believe that we have a unity as subject not presentable in our experience *at all*. According to the view developed here, however, Kant's conclusion (fraught with difficulties of meaning) is happily avoidable. For we deny his second premise. Our theoretical imagination does indeed presuppose a unity of our self as subject, representable but not presentable in imagination itself. But this presupposed unity of our self as subject *is presentable* in the perceptual world as the felt unity of our active body. Kant holds that

> creation ... cannot be admitted as an event among appearances, since its mere possibility would destroy the unity of experience. (B251)

This is quite true in a given world of our imagination. But the contrary is true in the perceptual world. A condition of the possibility of the unity of our perceptual experience is that we *do* create our self in the course of exploring and discovering our world. Our self-activity in doing so determines us not for the *second* time, as appearance, in recognition of determinations antecedently in us as subject; but for the *first* time, as subject who has made himself determinate by his active perception. By self-activity, we do not merely first *know* who we are by knowing what we are doing; we first *become* who we are by doing it. Exercise does not merely *employ* the skills that give us determinacy as subject; it also *develops* them in the first place. To be sure, we do not create our self arbitrarily. Those attempted self-determinations by which we can actually create our self are limited by the conditions that they must enable us to find our self in the midst of circumstances; to recognize our self in the meeting of our needs. Our self-creation must imply our self-discovery. But though we do not create our self arbitrarily, we do, in a certain sense, create our self *ex nihilo*, viz., out of a state of privation. Our activity first makes us a determinate subject. Nevertheless, this determinacy retroactively characterizes us "in-our self" as its source. For the source of our activity that defines us as a subject is our needs that prompt us to act. And these needs are first made determinate by being met.

Development of the Thesis

6.4 Kant's View of Spatial Objects: Spatialization as Conceptualization

Kant holds that,

intuition is that through which (knowledge) is in immediate relation to (objects), and to which all thought is directed as a means. (A19)

More particularly, he holds that,

the representation of the *outer senses* constitute the proper material with which we occupy our minds. (Kant's emphasis, B67)

Yet Kant is clear that the knowledge of inner sense (time) as well as outer sense (space) is first made possible by an imaginative synthesis[44] of the sensible form of intuition, which has the same kind of unity as the conceptual synthesis of the matter of intuition.[45] In sum,

It is one and the same spontaneity which in the one case, under the title of imagination, and in the other case, under the title of understanding, brings combination into the manifold of intuition. (B162*n*)

Thus Kant holds that productive thinking is required for an understanding of time as well as space. In particular, we know that "space and time are *quanta continua*,"[46] and this common condition makes possible the spatiotemporal character that Kant attributes, as we saw in Section 6.2, to all our empirical understanding. Nevertheless, though Kant holds that we have an understanding of time as well as space, and though he even holds that our *sense* of space is derivative from our sense of time,[47] he still holds that our *understanding* of time is derivative from our understanding of space.[48]

For all inner perceptions we must derive the determination of lengths of time or of points of time from the changes which are exhibited to us in outer things (B156)

My problem in this section is to understand Kant's view of spatial objects, so that I can criticize it in the next section. My method will be to inquire why Kant believes the ultimate goal "to which all thought is directed," "the proper material with which we occupy our mind," is spatial rather than temporal intuition. It is not, according to Kant, merely a psychological fact that we are more interested in the spatial than the temporal aspect of events. Somehow, what we mean by "knowledge" implies that a spatial rather than a temporal intuition is its goal. For Kant, all knowledge is conceptual knowledge. Our problem, then, is to understand why, according to Kant, the spatial ordering of intuitions is *more fully conceptual* than their temporal ordering. To this end, I will first investigate more particularly Kant's account of the threefold synthesis whereby intuitive content is spatiotemporally conceptualized as indefinitely divisible. I will then show how this account, combined with Kant's view of the relation between logic and understanding, enables us to understand why Kant believes that spatially ordered intuition, represented by the transcendental object = X, is purely rational because reversible, whereas a temporally ordered intuition is only *partially rational because irreversible*. I hope thereby to show that what Kant means by the spatial order of spatiotemporal objects is their *purely conceptual* order. This clarification of Kant's view of the spatial character of objects will enable us more effectively to criticize his view in the next section.

Human knowledge, according to Kant, is knowledge of an "object of experience." Referring to such objects, Kant writes, "an *object* is that in the concept of which the manifold of a given intuition is united."[49] Kant makes two central points about this unity of intuition given by an object of experience. First, it is correlative with our formal unity as spontaneous thinker.

> The unity which the object makes necessary can be nothing else than the formal unity of consciousness in the synthesis of the manifold of representations. (A105)

Secondly, it is a unity of rule.

> If we enquire what new character *relation to an object* confers upon our representations ... we find that it results only in subjecting the representations to a rule. (B242)

Our first problem is to understand the threefold synthesis of intuitions that *culminates* in relating them to an object by subjecting

Development of the Thesis

them to a rule. In his "objective deduction," Kant shows[50] that the categories are necessary to think an object in space. But we are now concerned with his "subjective deduction" in which he shows how the applicability of the categories to objects in space is founded on the nature of representations in time.

As (inner)[51] sense contains a manifold in its intuition, I ascribe to it a synopsis. But to such synopsis a synthesis must always correspond; receptivity can make knowledge possible only when combined with spontaneity. Now this spontaneity is the ground of a threefold synthesis which must necessarily be found in all knowledge: namely, the *apprehension* of representations as modifications of the mind in intuition; their *reproduction* in imagination; and their *recognition* in a concept. These point to three subjective sources of knowledge which make possible the understanding itself—and consequently all experience as its empirical product. (A97)

Let us now turn to these three syntheses in the order given, seeking to understand better what Kant means by each of them. (1) The synthesis of apprehension. The *manifold* of intuition can be represented only by a spontaneous act of the mind successively relating one intuition to another, for intuitions contained in a single moment have "absolute unity,"[52] but lack the unity of a manifold.

In order that unity of intuition may arise out of this manifold (as is required in the representation of space) it must first be run through, and held together.This act I name the synthesis of apprehension. (Kant's parentheses, A99)

The problem is to understand more exactly what is meant by "running through" (*das Durchlaufen*) and "holding together" (*das Zusammennehmen*) the manifold. By "running through" the manifold, Kant seems to mean the successive singling out or noticing of each of a scanned set of intuitive elements. By "holding them together," he seems to mean grouping them into a single appearance, as a *unit* of determinability. Thus, e.g., it is finally the *whole* line, made up of numerous parts, that is "straight" or "not straight."

(2) The synthesis of reproduction in imagination. Kant holds that "to know anything in space (for instance a line), I must *draw* it."[53] To know anything in time is also, plainly, to know something produced in succession. Thus Kant can argue,

If I were always to drop out of thought the preceding representations (... the first parts of the line, the antecedent parts of the time period ...), and did not reproduce them while advancing to those that follow, a complete representation would never be obtained ... not even the purest and most elementary representations of space and time could arise. (A102)

What I single out and group in apprehension as determinable, I must retain in my reproductive imagination as I go through the process of giving determination to it. Giving determination to a determinable appearance is a continuous activity. To give unity to this whole activity, I must each moment both apprehend the present state of determination of my intuition, and reproduce in imagination the continuous series of its previously apprehended states of determination. In this way I give unity to my act as that of giving determination to a retroactively *identical* determinable appearance. The synthesis of apprehension synchronized (i.e., spatialized) a series of successively apprehended intuitions, grouping them as co-existent in a single determinable object, and as collectively determinable by identical determinations, whatever they may be. The synthesis of reproduction treats appearances (the products of syntheses of apprehension) much as the synthesis of apprehension treats single intuitions having the "absolute unity" of single moments. It synchronizes (i.e., spatializes) a series of successively reproduced apprehensions, grouping them as co-existent in a single object in process of being determined by identical determinations of some sort. The fundamental sense of "co-existence" or "spatialization" here, is grouping diverse intuitions (or intuition-complexes) as having the same fate, whatever it may turn out to be, in respect of their determination. For a given intuition to be *spatialized*, to be intuited as *co-existent* with another intuition, is for it to be intuited as *determinable only in like manner with* that other intuition. The intuitions of inner sense are thus objectified by being quantized in determinable packages containing a *plurality* of intuitions. The manner of their formation thus insures that objectified, or spatiotemporal, as distinct from merely temporal, intuitions are in principle divisible. What is knowable or objective is analyzable and divisible; what is analyzable and divisible is so because it has been synthesized in the ways we are discussing. But why are space and time mathematically continuous, i.e., *indefinitely*

Development of the Thesis

sub-divisible? For this we must turn to the third synthesis.

(3) The synthesis of recognition in a concept.

> If we were not conscious that what we think is the same as what we thought a moment before, all reproduction in the series of representations would be useless. For it would in its present state be a new representation which would not in any way belong to the act whereby it was to be gradually generated. (A103)

The recognition-synthesis is the unity of the act of progressively giving some specific determination to a determinable appearance; it is a unity on the *subject* side. It is the correlative of the reproduction-synthesis that provides the unity of the *object* as progressively receiving this specific determination. The synthesis of recognition is the unity in the thinker of this act of determining in a specific way that identical object he previously assembled in apprehension as collectively determinable in some way or other. The synthesis of reproduction is the unity in the object of the process of its being so determined. This correlative character of the recognition and reproduction syntheses expresses the fact that in the determining of a determinable appearance, the determining subject and the object being determined reciprocally determine one another. The identity of the object thought is what makes the thinker's thoughts cohere with one another; it gives him his identity, his unity, as thinker, just as he gives the object its unity and identity in the same process. He is one and the same thinker only because he continuously thinks the same thought, as made manifest in the synthesis of recognition of an identical object being continuously determined in an identical way. Unity of consciousness in the subject *is* consciousness of unity in the object. It is then in this third synthesis of recognition that we finally produce our representable unity as thinker, through producing an intuitable unity[54] as object.

But Kant holds that this unitary consciousness of our self as thinker,

> may often be only faint, so that we do not connect it with the act itself . . . with the generation of the representation, but only with the outcome. (A103)

We therefore tend to think that the object has its determination independently of our thinking it; that we only notice, but do not produce its determination.[55] We tend to think that the determinacy of an object of experience is given to us, instead of produced by us. But a problem lurks here for Kant. Through synthesis of recognition in *a concept*, the final determination of an object is in terms of a general schema implying something about the content of all portions of an *indefinitely* divisible mathematically continuous space and time occupied by the determined object. How can we think this determination is given, when its *non*denumerable factual implications cannot be derived from the way the determinable object was first formed (in the synthesis of apprehension) around a *denumerable* series of intuitions (each having the "absolute unity" of the moment it occupied)? In the synthesis of apprehension, a determinable object was formed by an actually completed successive synthesis of separate perceptual intuitions. In determining this determinable unit in continuous space and time, however, we apply a general schema to it and retroactively determine it as continuous in intuitive content as well as intuitive form. When the object's determination *seems* to have been given (our actual determining of it "only faint"), this original denumerability of content must be lost sight of. But Kant's account here of our failure to notice our construction of mathematical objects does not explain our failure to notice our mathematization of perceptual objects. From the syntheses of apprehension and reproduction, we saw that the very way spatiotemporal objects are formed implies their *divisibility*. We have now seen, from the synthesis of recognition, how the very way they are formed implies the *indefinite* divisibility of spatiotemporal "objects of experience."

Until now we have been considering the spatiotemporal objectification of experience through the synthesizing of a manifold initially given in a merely synoptic, receptive way. Now let us turn our attention to the difference between the spatial and the temporal forms of this objectified experience. Now we are ready to understand why the spatial form of understanding is the more ideal one.

Kant constantly refers to time as "inner" sense, and to space as "outer" sense. What, more particularly, is "inner" about the one and "outer" about the other? Insofar as we know ourselves as objects, we are merely *in* time (as empirical ego) just as we are merely *in* space (as body). Yet somehow, for Kant, time does not

Development of the Thesis

range "beyond" us in the same sense as space. We seem to be in time in a delimited way, in the sense that there are regions of it in which we seem to be *absent*. But there are no regions of it, as of space, from which we seem to be *excluded* by the presence of something else. Kant's distinction between a "bound" and a "limit" is useful here.

> Bounds (in extended being) always presuppose a space existing outside a certain definite place and enclosing it; limits do not require this, but are mere negations which affect a quantity so far as it is not absolutely complete. (*Prolegomena*, 352)

Kant seems to regard time as our ego's empirical limit, and space as our ego's empirical bound. Space, as a bound, is, in respect to its form, *closed in* on something. There is nothing in its form to prevent it from being comprehensible as a complete whole in itself. But time, as a limit, is intrinsically *open-ended* and incompletable. Our understanding of space is incompletable only because of the incompletability (granted our temporal form of experience) of its *content*. There is nothing incomplete in its form as the reversibly orderable empirical bound that hems us *in*. But our understanding of time is incompletable in content and in *form* as well; as our irreversibly orderable empirical limit, it must continually lead us *on*, beyond where we are. It is noteworthy, in this connection, that in the first Antimony the impossibility of making sense of a whole of space is due to the corresponding impossibility for time.

> In order, therefore, to think, as a whole, the world which fills all spaces, the successive synthesis of the parts of an infinite world must be viewed as completed, that is, an infinite time must be viewed as having elapsed in the enumeration of all co-existing things. This, however, is impossible. (B456)

Our inability to understand all co-existing things as a whole follows not from their nature as co-existing, but from the nature of our temporal way of apprehending them by a "successive synthesis." A purely spatial, nontemporal world might be intuitable as a whole—though such a world would be difficult to distinguish from Kant's "purely intelligible" thing-in-itself.

In Kant's discussion of the logical employment of the understanding, he clearly implies, though without saying it in so many words, that a purely intelligible order is indeed a reversible one, just like the spatial order.

> As regards the merely logical employment of the understanding, it remains undetermined to which of the two concepts the function of the subject, and to which the function of predicate, is to be assigned. . . . But when the concept of body is brought under the category of substance, it is thereby determined that its empirical intuition in experience must always be considered as subject and never as mere predicate. Similarly with all the other categories. (B128–129)

The "other categories" of particular interest at this point are the categories of Cause and Reciprocity, since the former identifies a temporal, and the latter a spatial relation. Now in "*general* logic" any relation has a reverse formulation that is its equivalent, if appropriate changes of modality and quantity are made. Thus: the categorical judgment, "Some A are B" is equivalent to "Some B are A"; the hypothetical judgment, "If A, then B" is equivalent to "If not B, then not A"; the disjunctive judgment, "A or B" is equivalent to "B or A." Considerations of "*transcendental* logic" (concerning the thought of a temporal object in general), however, determine an *ir*reversible order for the terms of categorical and hypothetical judgments, thereby producing the irreversible categorical relations of substance-and-accident, and cause-and-effect. But the disjunctive judgment provides an exception worthy of note. The corresponding relation in transcendental logic is reciprocity-between-agent-and-patient. The order of description of the factors in such a communal relation is a matter of indifference because each is both agent and patient. As the real relation in the first two cases is asymmetric, so the proper subject-predicate order of relation is a matter of indifference because each is both agent and patient. As the real relation in the first two cases is asymmetric, so the proper subject-predicate order of description is irreversible, according to Kant. And, correspondingly, as the real relation in the third case is symmetrical, so the proper order of description is reversible.

Now the third category, Kant holds, "always arises from the combination of the second with the first,"[56] and thus represents the completion of our knowledge, much as the conclusion of a syllogism completes the two premises from which it is drawn. The presence of the asymmetric time-order is what fundamentally characterizes the rational weakness of our form of experience, as merely *de facto*, fragmentary and in principle not completely knowable. The order of Kant's three categories of relation, and the oddity of the transcendental logic of the third category, thus express a fundamental Kantian conception: the goal of the application of reason, through understanding, to intuition is to overcome the irreversible temporal order of experience by developing from it a reversible, rational, spatial order. We can see here how the spatialization of temporal events is inseparable in Kant's mind from their rationalization.

In our mind, all appearances, since they are contained in a possible experience, must stand in community of apperception. . . . If this subjective community is to rest on an objective ground, or is to hold of appearances as substances, the perception of the one must as ground make possible the perception of the other, and reversewise—in order that the succession which is always found in the perceptions, as apprehensions, may not be ascribed to the objects, and in order that, on the contrary, these objects may be represented as co-existing. (B261)

Insofar as our experience is objectified, all its parts are in thoroughgoing reciprocity with one another, and co-existent with one another. Our knowledge of unreciprocated causal relations between different empirical substances seems to be, for Kant, a half-knowledge of a true state of affairs represented by the transcendental object = X, a single object having many determinations each pair of which is reciprocally determining through some continuous subset of determinations. The fact that our actual knowledge always includes knowledge of irreversible causes among a plurality of empirical substances is but a sign of the incompletability of our knowledge.

6.5 The Missing Perceptual Stage: How Is a Local Object Determinable?

In this section I will subject to critical scrutiny the view of spatial objects just presented as Kant's. I will take up the question raised at the conclusion of Section 6.2. For Kant, as we have seen, the transcendental object = X is the common object of all intuitable objects.[57] He thus has an ambiguous concept of an object—as *a* substance, and as a characteristic of *the* (one) substance, the transcendental object.[58] The issue in this section is whether Kant's view enables him to maintain this ambiguity in a systematic and consistent way. We will see that it does not; that, in terms of Kant's dominant view, one cannot make sense of a locally determinable object. All paths lead into the den of the transcendental object, and none emerges. In the last Kantian analysis there cannot be any locally determinable *units* of experience; every "whole" of experience short of the complete experience of the single transcendental object is only an *arbitrarily* delimited fragment of experience. This is an internal criticism of Kantian philosophy, for Kant also holds that judgments about single objects *in* the world of experience express knowledge, hence they must be based upon an objective local unity in experience. Kant even implies that the number of such objects known is the fundamental (i.e.,categorial) sense of quantity in experience. For in his discussion of the quantities of judgment, from which his categorial quantities are derived, he writes,

If. . . we compare a singular with a universal judgment, merely as knowledge, in respect of quantity, the singular stands to the universal as unity to infinity. (B96)

The importance of the singular judgment, in Kant's philosophy, is further brought out by his explanation, in the same paragraph, that while singular and universal judgments are not distinguishable in general logic, they are distinguishable in the transcendental logic that we employ in our knowledge of objects of experience.[59] We will see that Kant's inability to account for the objective unity of a local (perceptual) object is what drives him to interpret all knowable objects on the model of a universal (imaginative) object, and so, to imaginize spatial objects, just as he imaginizes the world and the ego.

Kant begins with some appreciation that judgments of locally actual conditions of experience are judgments of a different *kind* than those of universally possible conditions of experience. But by the time of the second edition of the Critique, he realizes that his overall position does not allow him to make sense of this distinction; and, accordingly, he drops it. This distinction is formalized in the *Prolegomena* as the distinction between "judgments of perception" and "judgments of experience."

> Empirical judgments, so far as they have objective validity, are judgments of experience, but those which are only subjectively valid I name mere judgments of perception. The latter require no pure concept of the understanding, but only the logical connection of perception in a thinking subject. But the former always require [categories]. (*Prolegomena*, 289)

"Judgments of perception" are only subjectively valid because they merely express what a *single* percipient finds to be so in his *present* state. The unity of the judgment is provided only by the relation of diverse sensations to the same *de facto subject*. Hence it is not valid of the *object*.[60] "Perceptions are only usually conjoined in (the) manner."[61] expressed by judgments of perception.

> Judgments of experience are of quite a different nature. What experience teaches me under certain circumstances, it must always teach me and everybody. . . . Hence I pronounce all such judgments objectively valid. (*Prolegomena*, 299)

"When the sun shines on the stone, it grows warm," is a judgment of perception. "The sun warms the stone," is a judgment of experience. The latter is produced from the former by adding the categorial concept, cause, "which necessarily connects with the concept of sunshine that of heat, and the synthetical judgment becomes of necessity universally valid."[62] To state the matter generally, judgments of perception are about what is actually and locally present, here and now, to a single percipient. In them, "I merely compare perceptions and connect them in a consciousness of my particular state." Judgments of experience, on the other hand, are about what is necessarily and universally true of all possible experience. In them, "I connect perceptions in consciousness in general."[63]

Kant thus considers judgments of perception to be merely "subjectively valid."[64] But the point of most importance for my line of inquiry is that he does here acknowledge *some* form of validity possessed by perception alone, independently of conceptual imagination. This much is indeed required by Kant's view that he has performed a "Copernican revolution."

Proof of the invisible force (the Newtonian attraction) which holds the universe together . . . would have remained forever undiscovered if Copernicus had not dared, in a manner contradictory of the senses, but yet true, to seek the unobserved movements, not in the heavenly bodies, but in the spectator. [A] change of point of view, analogous to this hypothesis . . . is expounded in the Critique. (Bxxii*n*)

But how did Copernicus know what sort of unobserved movements to seek in the spectator? Granted that in some sense,

The senses represent to us the course of the planets as now progressive, now retrogressive; and herein is neither falsehood nor truth, because . . . we do not judge of the objective character of their motion. (*Prolegomena*, 291)

Still, in some sense of "true" and "false," in some other sense of "objective,"[65] we can distinguish *truly* between apparently progressive and apparently retrogressive motion. It is only because Copernicus had subjectively *reliable* data that he could work out the "objective character of (planetary) motion." Kant's Copernican revolution consists, analogously, in seeking the objective character of perceptual "motion" in general (i.e., perceptual order with the passage of time) in the unobserved movements of the spectator (i.e., in the unobserved self-activity of the thinker as transcendental unity of apperception, engaged in the spontaneous synthesis of perceptions under categories). The analogous query likewise arises. However subjective pure perception may be, it must be in some sense reliable as it is, in order to be objectifiable. We can give our perceptions a *particular* objective order, only if we know *what* we are ordering.

But Kant cannot consistently maintain this distinction between "subjectively valid" judgments of perception, and "objectively valid" judgments of experience. Even to Kant's contemporaries, it was clear that some such distinction was at once required by, and difficult to reconcile with, the burden of the Critique. Kant's attempted clarification of the matter in his *Prolegomena* (1783) is by way of response to this criticism. The need for the distinction between judgments of perception and judgments of experience was raised by the obscurity of the "subjective deduction of the categories," as given in the first edition of the Critique (1781).

Development of the Thesis

Evidence that Kant himself was dissatisfied with his attempted clarifications is given by the fact that he dropped the subjective deduction altogether in the second edition of the Critique (1787). The obvious inadequacy of the distinction, as Beck notes,[66] is that judgments of perception seem also to be categorial, even though Kant claims that only judgments of experience are categorial. It does not seem possible to form any kind of judgment about matters of fact, no matter how subjective a judgment, without judging, e.g., that some "substance" (object) has some kind of "causal" relation to (influence upon) something else, if only the percipient. Believing that there was only *one* set of categories governing objective experience and judgment; and seeing that one could not formulate any judgments except in terms of *some* categories, Kant apparently gave up the idea that there were any judgments of perception at all. We will see in the next section that Kant should not have given up this idea because, although he was right in his second view, he was wrong in his first. Judgments of perception, like judgments of imaginative experience, are indeed made in terms of "substances," "causes," etc. But there is a systematic difference in sense between each perceptual category and its corresponding imaginative category.

Let us now turn to the Critique itself, to trace the developing tension between the need for judgments of perception and the impossibility of making sense of them; and to show how the latter consideration finally wins out. Our problem is to understand, in terms of this tension, both the subjective deduction of the categories in edition A, and its elimination in edition B. The material has already been presented in the preceding section, in the study of Kant's threefold synthesis. My task now is simply to consider this material in the light of the possibility of judgments of perception. The point of the objective deduction, which Kant retains in B, is to prove that the categories are necessary in order to think an object of experience. But the point of the subjective deduction, as given in A, is that,

[S]ince in such a thought more than simply . . . the understanding is brought into play, and since this faculty itself, as a faculty of *knowledge* that is meant to relate to objects, calls for explanation in regard to the possibility of such relation, we must first of all consider not in their empirical but in their transcendental constitution, the subjective sources which form the a priori foundation of the possibility of experience (A97)

Kant thus sees that there is a problem of the affinity of objects of experience[67] to being ordered by the categories of the understanding. He sees that theoretical understanding presupposes but does not demonstrate this affinity. The purpose of the subjective deduction is to remedy this deficiency; to find in the transcendental constitution of subjectivity the missing a priori ground for this affinity. Our understanding is spontaneous. But in giving us knowledge of matters of fact, it is somehow applied to received matter of sensibility. Kant's problem is to understand how our receptivity is intrinsically tailored to our spontaneity. In the subjective deduction he tries to show (by way of the synthesis of apprehension) that this is so on the level of subjectivity (perception); and that objective experience grows out of subjective experience by the further application of the syntheses of recollection and recognition. Objective experience thus presupposes the synthesis of apprehension, even though, as we saw,[68] it tends to cover up this synthesis. Hence, the affinity that objective experience presupposes without being able to demonstrate, is nevertheless a priori demonstrable—in the transcendental constitution of subjectivity, if not of objectivity.

The success of the whole project of the subjective deduction hinges on finding some subjective function whereby the matter of experience is *spontaneously* received. Now, before going on, we must stop to rule out some plausible misunderstandings of the preceding statement. Obviously, Kant consistently denies that the matter of experience is "spontaneously received" in the sense of being productively imagined; in the sense of being an intuition we give to ourselves. This spontaneous receptivity of the transcendental imagination is Kant's *objective* mediator between sensibility and understanding.[69] It leaves the *subjective* problem untouched.

The subjective form of spontaneous receptivity is best expressed in the *Prolegomena*.

How are space, time, and that which fills both—the object of sensation—possible generally? The answer is: By means of the constitution of our sensibility, according to which it is *in its own way* affected by objects which are in themselves unknown to it and totally distinct from those appearances. (My emphasis, 318)

Development of the Thesis

The point is that the matter of experience enters the field of sensibility *as* capable of being "run through and held together" in this field. The (received) matter of experience is intrinsically apprehensible (by a spontaneous synthesis) as an appearance determinable in the field of sensibility. This is so because the constitution of our sensibility allows itself to be affected only "in its own way." Apprehended intuitions are not yet objective; they are only objectifiable. They consist of a finite set of actual, locally present sensations, successively singled out and grouped together as a determinable, but not yet determined, object. They are converted into objectively determined objects of experience only when two further syntheses are successful in applying a concept to them. The point is that sensations are synoptically received in sensibility *as* determinable in the field of sensibility. Perception is immediately of a determinable object. We perceive the unity of the object before we perceive its determinate totality. We comprehend the unity of an object, however, only by comprehending its determinate totality; until then we comprehend merely that the unity of the object is comprehensible. Perception of the unity of an object *precedes* perceptual determination of it. But conceptual understanding of the unity of an object *awaits* conceptual determination of it. Kant does not go into further detail, but our phenomenology of perception supports this analysis. We say that our ability to receive the appearance of anything in our perceptual field is always co-ordinate with our ability to spontaneously anticipate it as a determinable object. We can be receptively aware only of what we can at the same time spontaneously anticipate. This is not to say that our anticipation produces what appears to us, as our productivity produces what we imagine. It is merely to deny that appearance is possible without anticipation.[70] Reception of appearance and spontaneity of anticipation, in sum, are distinguishable but not separable.

What then makes Kant give up this solution (by way of the synthesis of apprehension) of the subjective problem of spontaneous receptivity? It is his conclusion that "all synthesis . . . even that which renders perception possible, is subject to the categories."[71] This follows from his basic view that synthesis is our way of unifying, hence getting to know, our experience. Since, as we have seen, it never occurred to Kant that there could be *two* ways of unifying and getting to know our experience; *two* systematically related sets of categories (perceptual and conceptual), he was driven to the conclusion that the (necessarily categorial) synthesis of apprehension could not after all be a pre-objective function of the transcendental unity of apperception. All connections we have called "perceptual implications" must be regarded as functions of the conceptual imagination. This forces Kant to change his conception of the synthesis of apprehension. In edition A, he held it had an a priori function in generating the objective order of space and time.

This synthesis of apprehension must also be exercised a priori, that is, in respect of representations which are not empirical. For without it we should never have a priori the representations either of space or of time. (A99)

But by edition B he assigns to the synthesis of apprehension only an empirical function falling under the categories, and taking place in a space and time whose order conditions it rather than being conditioned by it. Thus,

by *synthesis of apprehension* I understand that combination of the manifold in an empirical intuition, whereby perception . . . is possible. (B160)

Thus *unity of the synthesis* of the manifold . . . to which everything that is to be represented as determined in space or in time must conform, is given a priori as the condition of the synthesis of all *apprehension*—not indeed in, but with these intuitions. (B161)

But does this change eliminate Kant's problem? We have seen that in edition A he believes a pre-objective, locally determinable, perceptual order is presupposed by the objective, universal order of our conceptual imagination. In edition B he seeks to eliminate this presupposition of which he cannot make sense. But does he *succeed* in eliminating this presupposition? We will see that he does not; that he carries it with him despite himself, despite his admitted inability to make sense of it. For it remains implicit in Kant's distinction between a semi-objective spatiotemporal order and a fully objective purely spatial order. An empirical object is thought

Development of the Thesis

in terms of universal laws applicable to all possible experience, and is to that extent objective. But such an object is spatiotemporal, rather than "purely spatial" like the transcendental object = X. And this, as we saw in the preceding section, makes it less than ideally objective. I wish now to show that the local, separate determinability of semi-objective objects of this kind is possible only if we are capable of grasping some pre-objective perceptual order. If this is true, Kant's repudiation of the subjective deduction and perceptual judgments (based on his inability to conceive of more than one set of categories of knowledge) leaves him unable to make sense of these separate empirical objects as distinct from their single common object, the ideally comprehensible transcendental object = X.

For purposes of argument, we assume with Kant that reversible spatial order is purely conceptual. We assume further that all objects of experience are incompletely spatialized; that this is why all actual empirical knowledge is of locally distinguishable objects; and why knowledge of the transcendental object = X is an unachievable ideal. Now insofar as the matter of experience is merely temporal, it is not repeatable. If we repeatedly think the same thought of the same object, the occasion on which we think it is numerically different each time, though what we think is identical. If we repeatedly perceive the same object in the same way, however, not only the occasion of our perception but also the appearance of the object on each occasion is numerically different. A given thought, in short, is actually recoverable as that identical thought made present once more. But a given perception is only recoverable in memory as what has been perceived, as what can be repeated in a merely similar experience. But it is not actually recoverable as that identical perception made present once more. To literally re-perceive is to re-live, to go back into the past by recall; but we may re-conceive wholly in the present. In the "higher court" of reason, there is a *statute of limitations* on the re-occurrence and plasticity (as subject to correction) of perception, which does not hold for conception.

The temporality of perceptions therefore raises a special problem in the application of empirical laws, in Kant's sense, to the matter of experience; a problem that would not arise in their application to purely spatial material, i.e., purely logical matter, if there were such. The law or rule repeatedly applied is in each case the same, and so is its schema. But the filling is never more than similar from one occasion to the next. The problem therefore arises as to how sensations of the same schematizable kind are recognizable *in their distinctness* from one another. This distinctness is somehow recognizable, for we are as keenly aware of the nonrepeatability of particular perceptions as we are of the repeatability of perceptions of their kind. Our recognition of a temporal order is inseparable from this recognition of the unrepeatability of identical perceptions. In recognizing a temporal order we must therefore have the capacity to grasp a pre-conceptual, perceptual order.

Therefore Kant cannot consistently maintain that "all synthesis ... even that which renders perception possible, is subject to the categories";[72] and that there is only one set of categories, viz., those of empirical thought. The semi-objectivity of spatiotemporal knowledge, to which Kant himself believes us condemned, depends upon our ability to grasp a distinctively perceptual form of order (the temporal order) as a base from which we can develop a conceptual (spatial) order of matters of fact. On Kant's account, purely temporal knowledge would be purely perceptual, of inner sense alone; purely conceptual knowledge would be purely spatial, of the transcendental object alone. Neither pure type is possible. All our actual knowledge is a synthesis of the two. But to deny, as in B, that each type contributes to this synthesis an order of its own is to undermine the synthesis itself. Yet Kant is in a dilemma. He believes that all order in experience is the product of our spontaneous synthesis of it, which is to say, our way of spontaneously getting to *know* it. And knowledge by its nature has an invariant form; it is a justifiable way of ordering our experience; it operates under certain categories of synthesis. But Kant holds that only one set of categories is available to us. He is therefore forced to choose between holding that there are some distinctively *perceptual categories* as well as conceptual ones, and holding that there is *no distinctively perceptual order at all.*

Since his initial view in favor of a distinctively perceptual order was one he held explicitly as the result of having raised and pondered the question originally, he was intellectually free to change his mind about it. Since his belief in a single set of categories was, by contrast, a dogmatic belief implicitly held and never questioned, he was not free to change his mind about it. We can have a choice only by *facing* an alternative, and I know of no evidence that Kant regarded the possible existence of more than one set of categories as providing us with an intellectual alternative. In Kant's mind, therefore, the difficulty of specifying a perceptual order did not drive him forward to its solution in a systematic set of perceptual categories, but backward to its dissolution in the denial that there was any distinctively perceptual order at all.

Kant tried to meet the ensuing difficulties by adopting the view that empirical knowledge consists of an "approach" to a purely rational ideal represented by the transcendental object = X. This "regulative solution" was indeed consequent. It accepted the implication that the sense of all objects of experience is derived from that of the single, universal transcendental object. We will see in Section 6.8 that this attempted solution is a failure. But what concerns us now is only the internal difficulty in Kant's view of spatial objects—how this difficulty stems from his inability to treat the perceptual form of objects, because he never conceived of the possibility of perceptual categories by which this might be done; and how this difficulty culminates in his imaginizing objects, by deriving their sense from that of the imperceivable transcendental object of our conceptual imagination.

6.6 The "Common, but to Us Unknown, Root"

In the next section I will take up the possibility of perceptual categories, and try to show that there are indeed such categories complementary to the imaginative Kantian ones. But before doing so, it will prove profitable, by way of introduction, to consider a certain problem prominent in the history of Kant interpretation, viz., the problem of finding "a common, but to us unknown, root" from which the various faculties of human knowledge "perhaps spring."[73] The problem of the subjective deduction, as we saw, is the problem of understanding a subjective (i.e., perceptual) form of spontaneous receptivity. A solution to this problem may, as I believe, *lead on* to an understanding of this common root of all human faculties of knowledge—in the felt unity of the active body. But the two problems are nevertheless distinct. That this is so is witnessed by Kant's belief (in A) that he could solve the first, coupled with his consistent claim that the second could *not* be solved. Kant consistently holds that the source of our capacities is *in principle* hidden from us. Thus, for example, he writes,

> But how this peculiar property of our sensibility (that it is in its own way affected by objects unknown to it) itself is possible, or that of our understanding ... cannot be further analyzed or answered, because it is of them that we are in need for all our answers. (*Prolegomena*, 319)

In the Critique, too, Kant consistently[74] denies the possibility of our knowing the source and unity of our powers. Thus,

> Though logic is not capable of deciding whether a *fundamental power* exists (in the human mind), the idea of such a power is the problem involved in a systematic representation of the multiplicity of powers.... But this unity of reason is purely hypothetical. We do not assert that such a power must necessarily be met with, but that we must seek it in the interests of reason. (B677)

In the second[75] and third[76] Critiques, this remains for Kant no more than a *goal* of understanding.

For two centuries, distinguished Kant critics have belabored Kant's "dogmatism" in not understanding the unity of the ego, without coming to grips with the *obstacle* Kant saw in the way of doing so. Fichte, Schelling and, most decisively, Hegel, began this line of criticism. Heidegger has continued it in our own day with his book, *Kant und das Problem der Metaphysik*. Henrich is right in emphasizing against all these critics that Kant did not merely *neglect* to uncover the unity of the ego, but thought that it was in principle *impossible* to do so.[77] But while Henrich sees that Kant thought it impossible, he does not see Kant's fundamental reason for this conviction. Kant, unlike Hegel, saw clearly that perception involves a radically different function of experience, which cannot issue from reason.[78] Unlike Heidegger, he saw that reason involves a radically different function that cannot issue from any limitation of practical perception. Kant was obsessed with the realization that these two intrinsically *incommensurable* kinds of experience are nevertheless somehow or other fused in knowledge. But Kant, like his critics, assumed, as we have just seen, that we have only *one* basic form of worldly knowledge; only *one* set of categories of knowledge of matters of fact. Like his critics, he further assumed that our understanding of our worldly understanding is limited to the use of this single form, by which we view the relation between reason and perception *from the prejudiced vantage-point* of one of them. Thus, the combination of views that forced Kant to the conclusion that no insight into the unity of our ego is possible, was: (1) the view that our worldly understanding consists of a fusion of reason and perception, neither of which is derivable from the other; (2) the view that our understanding of the relation between reason and perception is from the viewpoint of one of them. For Kant, thus, the disparity between reason and perception cannot be understood because it is presupposed in all our understanding. Kant's great critics who have tried to reveal the unity of our ego that Kant thought hidden from us have all agreed with Kant's second view, and disagreed with the first, without ever seeing the strength of this first view and without adequately refuting it.

The direction in this study is just the opposite. I will here investigate how far we can get by agreeing with Kant's first view, and disagreeing with the second. Phenomenological analyses have shown that perception and imagination are radically different. We have two irreducibly *different* ways of experiencing things; by anticipation of them; and by immediate production of them. Neither capacity is derivable from the other. Yet we are *not* bound to understand one in terms of the other. We can pass back and forth between them as modes of understanding. Together with our two radically different ways of experiencing things, we have two basic modes of worldly understanding: we have, as we will see, *two sets of categories* of matters of fact. Thus we can *understand* each mode of experience from the vantage-point of the other. As we will see in the next section, we can indeed gain insight into the way one form of experience is systematically related to the other so as to produce the fusion patently exhibited in our ordinary experience. But as Kant, unlike his critics, saw, we cannot do this by *deriving* one from the other. One perceptual element may be implied by, or derived from, another; one imaginative element may be implied by, or derived from, another. But no perception implies, or is derived from, any imagination. The relation, as we will see, is rather that perceptual understanding *presents* the objective *need* for imaginative understanding; and imaginative understanding *represents* the complete *meeting* of this need. No perceptual need, however, implies its complete meeting; on the contrary, every perceptual need implies the impossibility of its being completely met. For the same reason, no imaginative meeting of a need implies any perceptual need met; no perceptual need could be so fully met. Imaginative understanding indeed *presupposes* perceptual understanding, but it does not imply or produce such understanding. Perceptual understanding, on the other hand, *requires* imaginative understanding, but remains itself incapable of implying or producing such understanding; it remains incapable of completely meeting, even in representation, the objective need it presents.

6.7 Kantian Categories as Imaginative Idealizations of Perceptual Categories

In Section 6.5 we saw that if Kant had recognized the existence of perceptual categories, he need not have given up his subjective deduction and his doctrine of judgments of perception. He could instead have developed them further, and avoided the over-rationalization of experience that is implicit in his "regulative" solutions. The project of the present section is to provide an outline of that "subjective deduction of the categories" for which Kant was groping. I will attempt to do this by going to the heart of the matter: first deducing the "subjective" (i.e., perceptual) categories; and then showing how they make the "objective" (i.e., imaginative) ones possible. Having seen that Kant imaginizes the world,[79] the ego,[80] and objects,[81] we will see in this section that he also imaginizes the categories of our experience.

6.7.1 Deduction of perceptual categories from the felt unity of the active body, as Kant deduces imaginative categories from the transcendental unity of apperception

Our topic in this section is "the condition of the possibility" of perceptual,[82] as distinct from imaginative, knowledge. We have already seen in several ways that, Kant to the contrary notwithstand-

Development of the Thesis

ing, there is evidence for some kind of distinctively perceptual knowledge. For without reliable perceptual data, no theoretical knowledge seems possible; and by centering his attention on theoretical knowledge, Kant seems unable to account for certain things that at least seem to be true of the practical world, our practical self, and locally determinable objects. We have accordingly good reason to set out to discover the presumably operative forms of perceptual knowledge. But we must remember that the difficulties inherent in denying perceptual forms are not conclusive proof of their existence. Both the affirmation and the denial of perceptual forms may be false. Perhaps the proposition that there are perceptual forms of knowledge is, in some undetected way, nonsensical; or a conjunction of several assumptions, of which some are true and some false. Thus, while we have reason to *believe* our assumption of perceptual forms correct we do not yet have reason to *know* it so. For that, we must actually find what we are looking for. First, we must discover the perceptual categories, and the perceptual justification for their necessary participation in all perceptual knowledge. Secondly, we must discover their systematic relation to the conceptual categories, if we are to be finally convinced of their validity. For our experience strongly attests that there must be some such relation. Our familiar form of knowledge is plainly, somehow or other, a systematic interplay between our disembodied imaginative thought and our bodily perceptual practice.

The first principle of perceptual knowledge

I will call a proposition "formal" if it is justifiable, but does not imply any particular matter of fact. All propositions Kant considers analytic are formal. They are justifiable as logically valid, whether or not they are true of matters of fact. I will call a proposition "factual" if it is justifiable, and does imply some particular matter of fact. All synthetic a posteriori propositions that Kant considers justifiable are factual. They are justified by actual experience of matters of fact. Unjustifiable propositions, I will call "mere assertions." Now by these definitions, all propositions that Kant considers synthetic a priori are formal. They are justified by showing that they express the "conditions of the possibility" of knowledge of matters of fact; by showing that they state the "forms" of empirical knowledge. They consist of: the principles of the forms of sensibility; the principle that all the manifold of intuition is subject to the conditions of the transcendental unity of apperception; and the categorical principles that enumerate these conditions of transcendental unity, viz., the definitions of the categories,[83] and the principles resulting from the application of the schematized categories to intuition. Though Kant believes our knowledge of these synthetic a priori propositions is first possible on occasion of their empirical use, he consistently holds that no particular matters of fact can provide evidence for their validity, and that they imply no particular matters of fact.

According to Kant, then, all conditions of the possibility of knowledge are expressed by synthetic a priori propositions that are formal in our sense. We have seen that his thought centered upon an analysis of imaginative knowledge. I now wish to show that the conditions of the possibility of imaginative knowledge are indeed expressed by formal propositions, just as Kant thought. But the conditions of the possibility of perceptual knowledge must be expressed by factual propositions. If this is true, we have another explanation for Kant's inability to raise the question of perceptual categories. He never imagined it possible that the conditions of the possibility of knowledge in any form could be factual. To such a suggestion he would no doubt have countered that a psychological analysis of *belief* was being proposed. But we will see how the existence of our active body is a condition of the possibility of perceptual *knowledge*.

Thought of an object does *not* imply the existence of the thinker. Kant is very clear on this point. His whole discussion of the Paralogisms centers on the insight that the thinker is merely a formal unity of thought, not a substance that is some *object* coherently thought to exist in a spatiotemporal region of the knowable world. To exist is to exist *in* the world. But, as we have seen, the thinker, as an imaginative subject, *is* his own world of conceptual imagination. Kant, who identifies the knower with the thinker, is therefore consequent in criticizing Descartes's "Cogito, ergo sum." *Perception* of an object, however, *does* imply the existence of the percipient in the world. Thus "Cogito, ergo sum"[84] as Kant saw, is false. But "Percipio, ergo sum," as Kant did not see, is true. More generally, conception does not imply the existence of anything conceptual—either of the conceiver or of anything conceived.[85] But perception does imply the existence of something perceptual, viz., both of the percipient and of something perceived. For I can conceive something even if it does not exist. But I cannot perceive something (I can only *seem* to do so) unless it does exist.

Kant seems to hold that the proposition, "I think," is synthetic because it expresses the form of a synthetic unity. But he holds that the proposition, "That I think, is an objective condition of all my knowledge," is analytic. For it simply makes explicit the self-conscious character of all knowledge, viz., that,

(1) We think all objects as thought by us.

To think of an object that might be experienced is already to think of it as thought of by us. We can make sense out of objects only by referring them back to our self as thinker; only by understanding them as making sense *for us*, in our single field of experience.

> The synthetic unity of consciousness is . . . an objective condition of all knowledge. It is not merely a condition that I myself require in knowing an object, but is a condition under which every intuition must stand in order *to become an object for me*. . . . This proposition [is] . . . analytic. For it says no more than that all my representations in any given intuition must be subject to that condition under which alone I can ascribe them to the identical self as *my* representations, and so can comprehend them as synthetically combined in one apperception through the general expression, "I think." (B138)

Now perceptual knowledge is also self-aware. But whereas the thinker, as an imaginative subject, is self-aware as world-centered (since he is the world of his imagination), the percipient is self-aware as self-centered in the world. The perceptual equivalent of proposition (1) above, is therefore,

(2) We perceive all objects as circumstantially related to our active body.

The circumstantiality of objects is not just a condition under which we happen to be (psychologically and/or biologically) adept at knowing them. That is to say, not all pervasive characteristics of objects concern their way of existing. We can distinguish between *what* exists (perhaps always and everywhere), and *how* things exist (e.g., as parts-in-wholes in a location in a spatiotemporal field in the world). Now my point is that objects are not perceived as merely existing in our circumstances. They are perceived as existing in a circumstantial way. Perceptual objects can become objects for us only by our perceiving them. And to perceive an object is to encounter it in this way; to find oneself in the midst of circumstances that this object helps to make up. We can have an object in perception only by becoming circumstantially self-aware. And we become circumstantially self-aware by becoming aware of the existence of our active body in the center of our perceptual field of objects.

We have, as we have seen,[86] three phenomenologically ordered levels of awareness of our active body. We sense the *skillfulness* of our body-activity in respect to circumstantial objects, as founded in the *coordination* of the activity of our various body-members in respect to one another, and this in turn as founded in the felt *unity* of our active body. In the last analysis, therefore, we can have an object in perception only by our whole perceptual field and all its contents being sensed as centered in the felt unity of our active body. Thus (2), the initial form of the first principle of perceptual knowledge, can be more precisely rendered as,

(3) We perceive all objects as circumstantially related to the felt unity of our active body.

In sum, we can have a perceptual manifold only by perceiving it as the manifold of *our* perceptual experience *in* the world. We can so perceive it only by relating it all to our identical self as an identical percipient capable of sensing this unity as his in the world. We meet these conditions by relating our perceptual manifold to our body as centered in the midst of it in the world. The kind of unity we must be able to perceive in this way is a synthetic unity (i.e., a unity of *separable* parts in *replaceable* objects in *different* locations, all comprehended in the *same* overall spatiotemporal field in the *same* world). We meet this condition by centering our body-sense in the felt unity of body-activity, by which the body is felt as capable of going from place to place and allowing us a synthetic grasp adequate to the synthetic manifold. We can perceive the manifold as a unified field of determinately but not completely manifest disparate things, only because we sense our self as an active unity inhabiting this single field and capable, *without loss of identity*, of passing from one disparate thing to another, so as to reveal the determinate character of each. If we changed with our changing perceptions, we could not make sense of determining the *very same object* that was previously perceived as merely determinable.

"I perceive" expresses the felt unity of our activity as percipient, just as "I think" expresses the known unity of our productivity as thinker. And (3) expresses how our self-awareness as percipient is an objective condition of perceptual knowledge, just as (1) expresses how our self-consciousness ("apperception") as thinker is an *objective* condition of theoretical knowledge. In each case, the kind of unity we have as subject is an objective condition of the corresponding form of knowledge, because without this unity as subject we could not be given, encounter or entertain, unified objects capable of being known. In each case, our unity as subject is not merely something in particular capable of being known, but something that must be known in the knowing of anything—as subject-factor[87] of what it is "to know" anything. For objects are known only when we know that we know them, by knowing our self as (percipient) knower or (conceptually) knowing, in the very same act by which we know them as known.

But within this similarity between the objective roles of the thinker and the percipient, a signal dissimilarity appears. For (1), the principle of the objectivity of the thinker in all theoretical knowledge, is a formal principle. Its justification is by thoughtful reflection on the conditions of imaginative thought. But these conditions, so considered, do not imply any particular matter of fact. Nothing is involved but our way of *representing the possibility* of matters of fact in general. Neither this proposition nor the evidence for its truth, implies any matter of fact. But (3), the principle of the objectivity of the percipient in all perceptual knowledge, is a factual principle. Its justification is by reflection on actual experience of matters of fact. The principle concerns our way of being *presented* with *actual* matters of fact, and implies the existence of our body as crucial for this presentation. Both this proposition and the evidence for it imply the existence of our actual body. Consider, in this light, Kant's fundamental view that,

> In inner intuition there is nothing permanent, for the "I" is merely the consciousness of my thought. (B413)

This is true of our imagination; both of what we entertain in imagination, and of our self as imaginative knower. But it is not true of perception; for it is not true of our self as percipient. As percipient, we are inseparable from our substantive body, which, however peculiarly, is sensed both as something *in* the time-field of knowable objects and as something to which *all* objects must be presentable in order to be perceptually knowable. As such, we are as permanent as the perceptual time-field of knowable objects. Kant's statement is simply one more expression of his fundamental tendency, viz., to imaginize perception.

Very well, then, the first principles of conceptual and perceptual knowledge state the respective forms of our self-awareness as knower. What is the significance of this essential reflexiveness of our knowledge? For example, we cannot perceive anything without knowing our self as percipient. To perceive anything we must orient our self in respect to it; to perceive where the object is, we must perceive where we are in respect to it; to perceive what the object is, we must have a sense of practical self-composure as percipient—a sense that comes with our objective satisfaction in perceiving the object this way. What does this self-awareness tell us, not merely about our psychology as believers, but about our knowing as of something known? We have given many phenomenological analyses showing that perceptual knowledge is reflexive because it is the *satisfaction* of an original *need* for self-knowledge; that it is the completion of a *quest* to find oneself that arises from an original need to do so. Knowledge is essentially an *answer*. An answer is to an antecedent *question* in terms of which the answer first makes sense. The fundamental question giving sense to all perceptual knowledge is. Who am I? This fundamental *question* of all perceptual knowledge is simply the expression of the fundamental *quest* of all knowledge of matters of fact, viz., the quest to find our self in the world, and thereby to overcome our initial sense of being lost in the world. True, we find our self only by finding something else; but what is fundamentally found is our lost self, because that is what is sought. And this is why knowing implies knowing our self as knower, because that is what terminates our quest to find our self in the world.

Objective versus subjective satisfaction

Kant agrees, as we have seen, that knowledge is self-knowledge. But he does not agree that knowledge is essentially a kind of satisfaction. I will now attempt to clarify the sense in which it is. Knowledge, as distinct from mere belief, affords a unique sense of "completion." This sense of completion irradiates the justification (verification or validation) of belief. It is a kind of satisfaction. When sufficient evidence is in, we are "satisfied" that our belief is correct. Thus, e.g., after twenty years of compiling evidence, Darwin was finally sufficiently satisfied with his theory of evolution to publish it. Similarly, after carefully checking it a few times step-by-step, we may finally be "satisfied" that a purported logical proof is valid. Conversely, if a proposition or theory is not in doubt, we speak of data as "satisfying" its general requirements. Thus, an equation in analytic geometry determines a locus of points that "satisfy" it. And in running a quantitative analysis in a chemistry class, "satisfactory" results are those implied by accepted chemical theory (given the nature of the initial compound, known to the instructor).

Mere conception of matters of fact is not knowledge, and does not have the form of satisfaction. To conceive of matters of fact is not thereby to have a true conception of them. Even if the conception is true, the evidence sufficient for knowledge of its truth cannot lie wholly in the conception itself, but must lie in part in perception. But perception alone, without conception, is a form of knowledge. To perceive matters of fact is to have a true perception of them. Perception thus, as a form of factual knowledge, is essentially a form of satisfaction.

"I perceive (that) . . ." *means* "I am satisfied that . . ." Thus, for example, "I perceive a house" means "I perceive that this is a house," or, equivalently, "I am satisfied that this is a house." It is important to distinguish two different senses of "satisfaction." In the objective sense, I am "satisfied" by *evidence*. I feel that I should be satisfied; that it is *necessary* to be satisfied by this evidence, and impossible not to be. *Objective satisfaction* is satisfaction *that* something is so. Now I may happen to be subjectively "satisfied" by flattery, beans, or power. These are then the things that make me content, and they therefore come to be *desired* by me. But this is not enough to make them seem necessarily satisfying; to make it seem that I should desire them, i.e., that they are intrinsically *desirable*—though it may be enough to make me try (e.g. by rationalization) to see them as *also* desirable. *Subjective satisfaction* is satisfaction *by* something.

"I am satisfied that my enemy is dead," is strikingly ambiguous out of context. The subject is likely to be doubly satisfied, and we are not sure which satisfaction is being expressed. The sentence may express the objective satisfaction of the slayer standing over his victim and satisfying himself with the perceptual evidence that his enemy is dead. Or it may express, in abbreviated form, the speaker's subjective satisfaction by the information that his enemy is dead. Objective satisfaction is satisfaction with the sufficiency of the evidence that something is so. Subjective satisfaction, on the other hand, is satisfaction by something being so—as illustrated by the second interpretation of our ambiguous statement. Thus subjective satisfaction generally[88] presupposes some objective satisfaction, but not vice versa.[89] Gratified by some objective satisfaction, e.g., that our enemy is indeed dead, we may then use this satisfaction to relieve ourselves of some subjective worry, e.g., that our enemy may do us harm. Our last example was of something both subjectively and objectively satisfying. If subjective and objective interests are opposed, their expression is less ambiguous. For example, "I am satisfied that my friend is dead." This sentence expresses an objective consummatory satisfaction upon investigating the evidence; coupled with a subjective distress brought on by the objectively satisfying proof. In such a case, the objective consummatory satisfaction is overwhelmed by the subjective distress and hardly noticeable. But it is there.

Whether it is the case of my friend's death or my enemy's death, if "I am satisfied that . . ." is regarded as a perceptually objective statement (meaning, "I perceive that . . ."), it expresses an *objective satisfaction* that comes from seeing the significance of *evidence*, and that has the character of a *consummation*. Similarly, "I am not satisfied that . . ." expresses in both cases an *objective dissatisfaction* in the form of a *lack of consummation* coming form seeing the *lack* of sufficiently significant evidence. If the statement is regarded subjectively (as meaning, "I do (not) feel satisfied by the condition that . . ."), it expresses either a *subjective dissatisfaction* in the form of *distress* from seeing the significance of the *belief*, or it expresses a *subjective satisfaction* in the form of *relief from distress*, which also comes from seeing the significance of the belief. Our subjectively desired satisfaction by something believed to be so is then to be distinguished from our objectively desirable satisfaction that something is so. But at times we feel satisfied without having any ideas what-by *or* what-of. This third kind of satisfaction seems neither desired (because unanticipated), nor objectively desirable (since without justification). It simply *is*. I will disregard it as not concerning my problem.

I am trying to distinguish the sense of "subjective" and "objective" forms of satisfaction in order to analyze perceptual knowledge as a function of the latter, but not of the former. I must elaborate this distinction a little more, before going on. Subjective as distinct from objective satisfaction is by something we merely happen to desire. It brings general relief from the bother of searching and also from the disagreeable uneasiness, frustration, and anxiety that impelled us to the search. It is primarily *relief* from distress. It is the enjoyment of relaxation; in it we move agreeably toward lassitude; it is akin to the pleasure of falling asleep after a tiring day. But if objectively satisfied by what we find intrinsically desirable, such as knowledge is to the knower, we feel primarily *gratified* by the outcome of our painstaking search;[90] the consummation of our exertion makes them all seem to have been worthwhile. Our discomfort and distraction is not merely relieved but rewarded. We are satisfied not merely with the cessation of our effort but also with its initial stimulation. We are led to desire not merely similar relief, but also similar *exertion* in the future. Our satisfaction is primarily a positive pleasure, rather than a negative relief from pain. Its general effect is to rouse us, to make us keener for experience, to heighten our sensitivity; not, as with subjective satisfaction, to deaden us, make us comfortably dull, listless, and even sleepy.

Objective satisfaction with what we find intrinsically desirable makes us feel heroic—desiring to desire again; desiring to do what is hard. Subjective satisfaction with what we merely happen to desire makes us feel cowardly—desiring not to desire again; jealous of our comfort, and afraid to be disturbed.

To sum up my main conclusions about perceptual satisfaction. *Objective satisfaction* is satisfaction *that* something is so. It comes from the *evidence* that it is so, and is felt as a *consummation*. It is a *positive* form of satisfaction. *Objective dissatisfaction* is *lack* of satisfaction that something is so, coming from lack of evidence that it is so, and felt as a lack of consummation. It is a *negative* form of satisfaction, consisting essentially of the lack of satisfaction. *Subjective satisfaction* is satisfaction *by* something's being (generally believed to be) so. It comes from the evident *conclusion* that it is so, and is felt as a *relief from distress*. It is a *negative* form of satisfaction, consisting essentially of the removal of dissatisfaction. *Subjective dissatisfaction* is dissatisfaction by something not being so, coming from the conclusion that it is not so, and felt as distress. It is a *positive* form of dissatisfaction.

The form of perceptual judgment

Perception then is a form of search for our self that terminates in self-knowledge by way of objectively satisfying knowledge of objects other than our self. This quest, and its completion in the perception of an object, is unified by the felt unity of our active body. The form of a perceptual judgement is, "I am (objectively) satisfied that . . . ." It is the perceptual "I" that perception satisfies. And this fundamental "I" that unifies all our perceptual activity is the bare felt unity of our activity. It is originally without any determination; it first makes possible determinate perception. It is to begin with nothing but the bare unity of need for self-determination in experience. Perception is then the satisfaction of our original *unity of need* for self-determination as percipient.

How is this need met in objectively satisfying knowledge? We have seen that perceptual determination takes place by way of perceptual *skills*. The skillful search for self-determination has two phases: exploration of the world, and finding our self in the world. Our quest for knowledge begins with exploration. In exploration our activities are *dispersed* in a comparatively random way. First here, then there, we explore our environment in a restless, trial-and-error way. We are lost in the world, and without any definite plan, because we are ignorant of our goal; our task is to find our goal, not merely to get there. Our activity is a *disconnected series* of uncompleted starts and probes. Yet it is all *our* activity. The unity of our disconnected activities is not any unity of content, but only the primary unity of need from which our activity is felt to issue. The phase of finding our self by gaining knowledge proceeds by reversing this dispersal; by *focusing* our dispersed activity of exploration on something known. The same function that gives unity to our activity finds an answering unity in the object determinately revealed by that activity. Our original unity is thereby re-achieved, but this time as revealed to us, not concealed from us; this time with the sense that we have found our self in the world, not that we are lost in the world. This time, in short, as a unity of *objective satisfaction* instead of a unity of objective need.[91]

A perceptual judgment has the form,

(4) "I am satisfied that . . . is so."

This judgment expresses three stages of knowledge. (1) "I": the "I" who receives satisfaction is "I" who, as felt unity of objective need, was originally without this satisfaction. This is the active "I" who finally puts himself in position to passively receive objective satisfaction. In expressing the "I"'s satisfaction, the judgment implies the existence of his need as that which was satisfied. (2) "that . . . is so": this is what satisfies the unity of need, "I." It is his objective correlative skillfully found. (3) "I am satisfied": this is "I" as unity of objective satisfaction. The creation of this "I" is the goal of perception. *The existence of "I" as unity of objective satisfaction is the conclusion of perceptual knowledge.* This conclusion is proved to the knower by his own self-consciousness. The proof of his belief is *that* he can believe it objectively. A judgment of perception is a compressed *argument* of objective motivation, conducted on the principle that the proof that the pudding was rightly assessed is in the objective satisfaction of the eater with himself as eater-of-this-pudding.

Kant believes that all knowledge is in the form of an argument—

but expressed in three judgments, not one.[92] Concepts, according to Kant, make sense only in judgments, and judgments only in the context of arguments leading to a proven conclusion. The whole thus precedes the part in thought just as in intuition, where particular times and spaces are intelligible only as delimited within an initial whole of Time and Space. But Kant thought this prior unity of argument had to consist of propositions syllogistically arranged (i.e., of belief leading to a demonstrated conclusion). He thought, indeed, that if the argument were optimally comprehended, it would always be in the figure, *Barbara*: "All A are B"; "x is an A";[93] therefore, "x is a B." The fact that the argument of perceptual knowledge is expressed within a *single* judgment makes Kant unable to notice it.

His conception of judgment affects Kant's view of the categories, so we must consider it for a moment. All empirical knowledge, according to Kant, has the following form.[94] (1) Through an abstract universal judgment, the relation between two concepts is abstractly understood as capable of being given sense. (2) Through an intuitive judgment, sense is then given to the subject-concept[95] of the abstract universal judgment. (3) Through a concluding intuitive judgment, sense is thereby also given to the predicate-concept of the abstract universal judgment. Beginning therefore with a merely abstract understanding that something is intuitively under*standable* in a certain way, we end with a concrete understanding of something intuitively under*stood* in that way. This final intuitive understanding of the schematized concepts, moreover, first grants us a clear understanding of the pair of abstract concepts with which we began.[96]

This, then, is Kant's conception of judgment, formed by analyzing theoretical judgment. A judgment is a step in a three-step-procedure of subsumption under a rule. Perceptual judgment, as we have seen, is not like this. A single perceptual judgment expresses a whole argument. A perceptual judgment expresses a determination arrived at by *skill* not by rule. The percipient, unlike the thinker, cannot form a judgment without expressing in it his own *satisfaction* with it. To elucidate this last point: the capacity to suspend judgment, to form a judgment without judging its truth, is a privilege of imaginative detachment. Judgment can be suspended in a world of our own making; but in the given world of perception we are restricted to balanced judgment. We may hedge and qualify, and come down on both sides at once—but come down we must, if we are to make any sense. The difficulty experienced by sense-data epistemologists in trying to formulate a neutral or suspended perceptual judgment expressed in "seeming" language, reflects the fact that we simply do not perceive things that way. "I seem to see a sailboat" is not a suspended judgment. It normally means, "I see something-or-other is there; I can hardly make out what it is; it looks like a sailboat, i.e., it is *probably* a sailboat." We can distinguish between the objective form and the truth value of a theoretical judgment, but not of a perceptual judgment. What finally gives a perceptual judgment its objective form *is*, as we have seen, the satisfaction that it is true. Since we cannot form a perceptual judgment without judging it true, it follows that we cannot perceive (as we can conceive) that there is something in particular of whose existence we are ignorant—for otherwise we would be capable of perceiving that we had to suspend judgment on this matter. We can make perceptual sense only of so much as we perceive. We can perceive that much lies concealed from us; but we cannot give more determination to what *may* be revealed there than we perceive to *actually* or *probably* lie there ready to be revealed. Conceptual possibility may be merely logical; but perceptual possibility is limited to *real* possibility. Say I see a cup. I *know* that it may or may not be spotted on the far side. I know that I don't know which. The case of its being spotted on the far side is perfectly intelligible, though I suspend judgment whether this *is* the case. But I do not *see* that the cup may or may not be spotted on the far side, though I do *see* that there is a far side. I do not see that the far side is spotted; nor do I see that it is not. That is all. I do not see any possible spots. I do not in any way see spots. I just see that I do not see the details of the far side, and that something-or-other is surely there. But I do not see at all *what* I may be missing.

The categories of perception

Now it is no accident that Kant's table of Categories is a tetrad of *triads*. This Table follows from the Table of Judgments, which directly expresses Kant's syllogistic (hence triadically organized) view of thought. He furthermore believes, as we have seen, that all valid thought, synthetic a priori and empirical, as well as logical, has the normal form of a syllogism in the single figure, *Barbara*. We are also told that each triad of categories does not merely comprise a list, but is ordered so that "the third category in each class arises from the combination of the second category with the first."[97] This is an obvious parallel to the way the third proposition (the conclusion) in each syllogism arises from the combination of the second premise with the first. The suggestion is difficult to resist that the forms of judgment and the categories in each triad are ordered not merely in the way that *guides* our syllogistic thought, but also so as to *exhibit* a meta-a priori syllogism. This syllogism would have to exhibit greater unity than the Tables themselves, according to Kant's usual procedure of regarding a meta-function as a unifying function. There is but one plausible candidate, viz., the single syllogism in *Barbara*, which could be repeated in each tabular triad. A test of this possibility shows that it works for the Table of Judgments, in eleven cases out of twelve. The test for the Table of Categories would be similar and show similar results. (1) Quantity. "All A are B" is a Universal judgment. "x is an A" is a Particular judgment; x is not yet wholly determined, therefore not yet wholly distinguished from similar x's. The conclusion, "x is a B," represents the complete determining of x,[98] hence the determination of it in its uniqueness, viz., by a singular judgment. (2) Modality. As a universal proposition, the first premise of *Barbara* has no existential implication, and is Problematic. The second premise is a mere assertion of fact, without proof, and is hence Assertoric. The conclusion, following necessarily from the premises, is Apodictic. (3) Quality. The first premise is Affirmative. The second premise has a Negative component in that it breaks the grouping of A with B made in the first premise, and ascribes only A but not B to x. The conclusion completes the singular characterization of x, and thereby first forms the distinction between one definite thing and everything else, so that an Infinite judgment first comes to make sense.[99] (4) Relation. The first premise is Categorical. The second premise of *Barbara* does not seem to be Hypothetical; the theory breaks down here. The conclusion, taken in the context of the syllogism as a whole, is Disjunctive in the sense of giving us a disjunctive knowledge of the exclusive, but all-inclusive, determinations of x as a singular object. The theory that Kant's thought is dominated by a meta-a priori syllogism in *Barbara* therefore more or less satisfies all but one out of twelve cases. We may well suspect that Kant *sought* a neater fit, but could not manage it.

Kant tells us in the "metaphysical deduction" that the list of categories is derived from the possible forms of judgment, where by "judgment" he in fact means theoretical judgment. We have just seen that the precise order of the categories is approximately that dictated by the primary form of theoretical argument, viz., the syllogism *Barbara*. Kant may or may not have been right in thinking that concepts make sense only in judgments; and judgments, only in the context of an argument. And he may or may not have been right in thinking that all arguments have a single normal form. But if he were right in thinking thus, he would have been right in concluding that the categories of thought (the articulated forms of thought) were derivable from an analysis of the primary form of conceptual argument. Kant's *method* is pertinent to our present problem (deriving the categories of perception), rather than his *right to use* this method in solving his problem (deriving the categories of thought). For it turns out that Kant's methodological suppositions about conception *do* hold of perception. We may *conceive* of properties independently of objects having them, we are capable of imaginative abstraction. But we do not *perceive* qualities. We perceive *objects* having certain characteristics; we notice characteristics *of* objects. We perceive always *that* something is so. "I see a chair," implies "I see that there is a chair." Perception is always *judgment*. Perceptual determinations make sense only in the context of a judgment. Furthermore, as we have seen, a perceptual judgment is an *argument*. It states that something has satisfied the demands laid down by our needs. So perceptual determinations make sense only in the context of a perceptual argument. We have, in addition, found the primary form of this argument.[100] It is a three-stage motivational argument: from our ineluctable unity of need that prompts all our activity, through our consequent finding of some unity of object, to a concluding unity of satisfaction derived from this object. All perceptual sense makes sense in the context of this argument. To determine the fundamental quantities, qualities, relation to an object, and modalities that characterize perception, we need merely to ask these four questions about each of the three stages of perceptual knowledge, in what we now see to be their phenomeno-*logical* order. The foregoing phenomenological analyses have already provided all twelve answers. The table of Perceptual Categories is accordingly as shown on the next page.

A cursory inspection is sufficient to reveal the general similarity of this table of perceptual categories to Kant's table of the categories of theoretical judgment. The main similarity of a triadic organization is, as already noted, due to the fact that both tables are modeled on a primary three-step form of argument. The main dissimilarity is that the perceptual table is of plus-and-minus categories, whereas the conceptual table in Kant offers no such distinction. In the coming subsection, we will examine this dissimilarity in some detail. But a general observation is in order here. The plus-and-minus character of perceptual categories expresses the fact that perceptual knowledge is *retroactive*. Perceptual knowledge is knowledge of what we turn out to *have been* deprived of, though *no longer* are to be deprived of. This is another way of saying that perceptual knowledge is the conclusion of an objectively "motivational" argument.

Now Kant's categories are also developmental.

> The combination of the first and second (categories) in order that the third may be produced, requires a special act of the understanding, which is not identical with that which is exercised in the case of the first and second. (B111)

Furthermore, Kant's categories, like the perceptual categories, apply all at once rather than singly; they form a twelvefold whole or network serving as the context within which any particular judgment first comes to have an objective sense. But Kant's categories do not form a developmental whole in the same sense as the perceptual categories. Consider, for example, the categories of Relation. According to Kant, we form a fully objective judgment of object-relation only when we conceive a set of objects as reciprocally influencing one another. This presupposes, but is not presupposed by, a (causal) conception of an object exerting influence.

TABLE OF PERCEPTUAL CATEGORIES

I. QUANTITY

− (1) Unity, of need.
o (2) Plurality, skillfully co-ordinated.
+ (3) Totality, of plurality integrated in a unity of satisfaction.

II. QUALITY

− (1) Deprivation.
o (2) Anticipation and Response.
+ (3) Satisfaction.

III. RELATION TO OBJECT

− (1) Lack of object.
o (2) (a) Anticipation of determin*able* object (Perceptual Substance).
  (b) Responsive determin*ing* of object (Primary Perceptual Cause).
+ (3) Reciprocity, between percipient and determin*ate* object of whose state percipient is satisfied.

IV. MODALITY

− (1) Lack of possibility. Lack of evidence for possibility of satisfaction. Action prompted merely by need.
o (2) Real possibility. Evidence that possible satisfaction may or may not be realized.
+ (3) Necessity. Evidence necessitates belief in actual satisfaction.

This causal conception in turn presupposes but is not presupposed by the substance-concept of a single object. But when we finally conceive of a community of substances, we finally conceive that there *are* (not merely have been) a set of substances acting as causes. Kantian judgment is developmental in the sense of progressively *realizing* what is rational. But this realization involves no *cancellation* of what is finally known to have been at first insufficiently known.[101] For Kant, thought is developmental in the sense of progressively augmenting, filling out, but never removing, an initially inadequate state of thought. Kant's philosophy is, in this respect, Aristotelian—though it is an Aristotelianism of the "active intellect" itself, not merely (as for Aristotle) of developing substances (entelechies) understood by an active intellect itself perfectly actual to begin with. Hegel's dialectical notion of Reason remains faithful to this aspect of Kant's thought. For Kant as well as Hegel, rational necessity "comes to be," merely in the sense that an initially undeveloped conception finally *comes-to-be-manifest*. Rational necessity is simply our coming to realize a rational necessity whose forms, to begin with, "lie prepared in dispositions of the human understanding."[102] But perceptual necessity "comes to be" in a more radical sense. It is the culmination of progress, not from an *inadequate* to an *adequate* perception, but from the total lack of perception to the *existence* of perception. Perceptual necessity "comes to be" in the sense that an undeniable perception *comes-to-exist* in the first place. What lies prepared to begin with in the dispositions of human sensibility is only the *need* for this necessity. The *form* of it is first *created* with the successful conclusion of the activity prompted by the need for it.

6.7.2 The concept of nothing (=0) versus the perceptual sense of nothing (=–x)

There are, according to Kant, degrees of reality. The degree of reality of a given object can vary. This variability is not unrestricted; it must be continuous. But reality is a matter of more or less. What concerns us here is the *range* of this variability; more particularly, its *lower limit*. According to Kant, the degree of reality ranges *upward from 0*. The degree of reality has apparently no upper bound. But

Development of the Thesis

it does not make sense to speak of a negative degree of reality. "Negation" of reality simply means no reality. Thus, Kant writes,

> Every sensation has a degree or magnitude whereby, in respect of its representation of an object otherwise remaining the same, it can fill out one and the same time, that is, occupy inner sense more or less completely, down to its cessation in nothingness (=0=negatio).... The schema of a reality, as the quantity of something insofar as it fills time, is just this continuous and uniform production of that reality as we successively descend from a sensation which has a certain degree to its vanishing point, or progressively ascend from its negation to some magnitude of it. (B182–183)

The same point is made in the *Prolegomena*.

> (Degrees of reality) can only be estimated quantitatively by the relation of 1 to 0, namely, by their capability of decreasing by infinite intermediate degrees to disappearance or of increasing from naught through infinite graduations to a determinate sensation in a certain time. (*Prolegomena*, 309 n)

Now Kant has to hold this view, because of his basic view that knowledge of matters of fact is possible only through the conceptualization of perception. The main result of Kant's Axioms of Intuition and his Anticipations of Perception, is that,

> All appearances, then, are continuous magnitudes, alike in their intuition, as extensive, and in their mere perception (sensation, and with it reality) as intensive. (Kant's parenthesis, B212)

It is essentially this result that Kant claims "as justifying the application of mathematics to appearances."[103] This result teaches us how,

> alike as regards their intuition and the real in their perception, [appearances] can be generated according to rules of a mathematical synthesis. (B221)

Kant believes that perceptual variation is intelligible only as a variation of intensive magnitude; that variation of intensive magnitude is intelligible only in terms of a corresponding variation of extensive magnitude (which is a priori intelligible by use of our productive imagination); and that variation of extensive magnitude is essentially continuous. Kant thus must hold that perceptual variation is intelligible *only if* continuous. Since he believes reality is indefinitely intelligible, and that its schema "is just this continuous and uniform production" of perceptual variation in time, he must, further, hold that perceptual variation *is* continuous. This is what makes Kant place the lower limit of perceptual variation at 0.

Conceptually, we can make sense of the existence of something as its having some positive force or influence of a continuously variable strength. And we can make sense of its nonexistence, as its having a zero, or vanishing, strength, which is the lower limit of its continuously variable strength. But we cannot make sense of its *failure* to exist, which implies a *negative* kind of existence. We cannot, without the aid of perception, conceive of the difference between nonexistence and failure to exist. The latter implies a disruption of existence, a kind of hole in existence, which makes existence *dis*continuous. In perception, however, as we have seen, we do make sense of negative existence. For perceptual knowledge is of the cancellation of deprivation. To know satisfaction is to know an end to deprivation. But Kant always regards perception from the vantage-point of the thinker; he never reverses the roles to regard conception from the vantage-point of the percipient. So he never notices the negativity of perception, which it is the function of conception to eliminate.

Knowledge of the cancellation of negative existence, which is included in all perceptual knowledge, brings with it the sense that this cancellation is only *provisional*. It is only for-the-time-being. It can never be made permanent. Deprivation as experienced in perception, is perceptual confusion; it is the perceptual form of ignorance. We *suffer* deprivation; but we do not *know* it, by itself. But satisfaction brings with it retroactively *knowledge* of the deprivation now ended. In so doing, it brings also knowledge that deprivation is possible. Perception is a precarious form of knowledge, which is apt to be lost and knows it. In my Table of Perceptual Categories, I noted that perceptual knowledge involves knowledge of negative existence. Each of the four dimensions of knowledge is made up of: a retroactive of knowledge of *lack* (–); an antecedent knowledge of the *possibility* (but not certainty) of filling this lack, designated "(0)" to indicate it is knowledge that our fate hangs in the balance and

TABLE OF PERCEPTUAL SENSE OF "NOTHING" AS LOSS OF KNOWLEDGE

I. QUANTITY

Disappearance (–x)

II. QUALITY *III. RELATION TO OBJECT*

Dissatisfaction (–x) Destruction of object (–x)

IV. MODALITY

Disillusion (–x)

might go either way; and final knowledge of a satisfaction that certainly fills this lack (+). Perceptual knowledge is thus self-aware of how it *came* to be. And with this awareness comes the presentiment that it may *pass away*. Knowing satisfaction, we know the end of deprivation—and thereby we know too that our objective satisfaction may be lost. Perceptual certainty is intrinsically provisional.

Just as there are four dimensions of the gaining of perceptual knowledge, there are four dimensions of its loss. Our sense of loss is not that of an argument but of the breakdown of an argument. It is not a sense of validity but of invalidity. Each threefold dimension of *justified* belief (belief justified by a three-step argument) corresponds, accordingly, to a onefold dimension of *loss* of knowledge. This loss expresses the perceptual sense of "nothing," insofar as it limits (rather than founds) the perceptual sense of "something." Even in the state of knowledge, this loss is sensed as a real possibility—casting doubt, not on the momentary validity of the knowledge but only on the permanence of this validity.

Perceptual knowledge implies the possibility of the disruption of existence, which takes these four forms. But conception supposes that existence is not disruptible; that only our perception of existence is disruptible. The contrast is brought out clearly by a comparison of the perceptual sense of Nothing with its conceptual sense. The latter is fairly represented by Kant's Table of the concept of Nothing, given in B348. There, in brief, Kant holds that the concept of Nothing has the following forms: Quantity: none (=0). Quality: absence (=0). Relation: empty (=0). Modality: impossible (=0). Now in each of these cases, Kant interprets (rightly, I think) the *concept* of Nothing as the concept of the minimal case of Something. But since he thinks that *all* sense we make of our experience is conceptual, he tries to make this single Table do also for what we mean by our *perception* of Nothing. Kant's general position, as we have seen, requires this. For if perception were intrinsically capable of going where conception could not follow, so to speak, it would have to make sense of *itself*. And this, perception is not supposed to be able to do. Kant concludes that *all* synthesis, *all* making sense of our experience, is conceptual, because he sees that he must otherwise make sense of local and provisional perceptual judgments—which he is unable to do.

But the fact is that in perception, if not in conception, there is a clear distinction between Nothing as the *minimal* case of Something and Nothing as the *limiting*[104] case of Something. Nothing as a minimal case is perfectly intelligible; just as intelligible as a "positive" case of Something. But Nothing as a limiting case is the breakdown of intelligibility; it is unintelligible—except from the standpoint of a recovery from it. Let us consider the matter for each type of Nothing in turn. (1) Quantity. None is the minimal case of what appears. It is, as Kant writes, the terminus of ceasing to appear. But this is quite different from dis-appearing. Ceasing to appear is a particular intelligible function of appearing. If we perceive something, then place something else in the way, the initial object ceases to appear. But it does not thereby disappear. Nothing, as quantity, is also perceivable without anything ceasing to appear. We may look for apples on the fruit dish and perceive that there are none. We may be satisfied that this is the case; there is nothing unintelligible about it. It does not imply the baffling fact that apples have disappeared, though their disappearance does imply that there are none. (2) Quality. Similarly, absence is minimal presence. It is a particular function of intelligent satisfaction. One can upon investigation be satisfied that there is an absence of tubercular symptoms in a certain patient. The absence of something satisfying certain conditions does not imply any objective dissatisfaction; though objective dissatisfaction does imply the absence of something satisfying certain conditions. (3) Relation. Emptiness is the minimal case of filling. It is a function of intelligible change in the motion of objects. If a place is empty of objects, no destruction of objects is implied, although the destruction of objects does imply a certain emptiness of place. (4) Impossibility is the minimal case of necessity. It is the perfectly intelligible case of what is necessarily not so. Impossibility does not imply any disillusion; though disillusion does imply a certain impossibility of objective satisfaction.

Kant, however, does not merely ignore the perceptual sense of objective loss; he denies that objective loss is possible. In this he is consistent. Whatever make sense, he holds, makes conceptual sense. Therefore, since objective loss does not make conceptual sense, it makes no sense. Perceptual disillusion is possible because perceptual judgment is of local, changeable conditions. But conceptual judgment is of universal conditions. It therefore lays claim to be true once and for all, if it is true at all. We are aware that our conceptual judgments are corrigible, *despite* their claims, because we are aware of their basis in our frankly corrigible perceptual judgments. We understand how our theoretical judgments are in one sense corrigible and in another sense not, because we recognize that they universalize our perceptual judgments and thereby represent these corrigible judgements *as if* they were incorrigible. But Kant was misled into taking the representation for the fact. He thought, in this vein, that the destruction of objects made no sense, because it made no conceptual sense.[105]

Kant does not seem to have noticed the perceptual sense of objective loss of quantity and quality, so he does not explicitly deny its real possibility. Nevertheless, as we have seen, his general position requires such a denial. For he holds firmly to the continuity of all experience, in respect to its matter as well as its form. Only thus can all sense be conceptualized. And objective loss is the sense of the disruption, the discontinuity of experience. Kant is driven, in effect, to the general position that the perceptual or apparent properties of objects vary exactly as their conceptual or physical properties. Thus, for example,

> I can determine a priori, that is, can construct, the degree of sensations of sunlight by combining some 200,000 illuminations of the moon. (B221)

Kant takes it for granted that if scientific instruments record sunlight as 200,000 times as intense as moonlight, then our sensations must vary in the same ratio. All modern discoveries of so-called constancy phenomena in perception would be inexplicable on Kant's account.

What then is the systematic relation between perception and conception? This relation must account for the fact that conceptual categories systematically omit the sense of negative existence implicit in perceptual categories. Perceptual categories, as I have shown, are categories of a merely local and provisional satisfaction. But we seem by nature unable to rest content with less than global and permanent satisfaction. Kant writes in this spirit of,

> that notable characteristic of our nature never to be capable of being satisfied by what is temporal (as insufficient for the capacities of its whole destination). (Kant's parenthesis, Bxxxii)

Our conceptual imagination can be understood as our way of representing to ourselves the global and permanent satisfaction of our needs; whereas perception is our way of presentatively satisfying ourself on a local and provisional basis. Kant himself believes that,

> [P]ractical principles, unless they find scope for their necessary expectation and hope, could not expand to the universality which reason unavoidably requires from a moral point of view. (*Prolegomena*, 363)

I am suggesting that the very same thing is true of those practical perceptual principles that lead to the universality of theoretical reason.

I have previously noted that my deduction of the perceptual categories is an attempt to go in a direction already indicated by Kant, though not taken by him. Some elements of my view of the relation between perceptual and conceptual categories may also be found in the body of Kant's work, if not in the first Critique. In the *Anthropology*, Kant realizes that the senses of pleasure and pain cannot be treated the way he treats perceptual sense. He distinguishes "interior" from "inner" sense.

Development of the Thesis

The senses are outer or inner according as the human body is affected through bodily things or through the mind. The "inner" sense ("*der innere Sinn,*" or "*sensus internus*") of pleasure and pain, through which the subject is led to preserve or defend against the circumstances of his representations, is to be thought of differently, as the interior sense ("*der inwendige Sinn,*" or "*sensus interior*"). (*Anthropology*, Section 15)

The reason for his dissatisfaction with treating pleasure and pain as he has treated perceptual sense, is even more intriguing from our point of view. It comes out only later, when Kant writes,

Pleasure and pain are related not merely . . . as plus and zero, as local opposites or contradictories; but as plus and minus, as real contradictories or opposites. (*Anthropology*, Section 60)

Kant thus sees the key difficulty of applying his interpretation of sense experience to the experience of pleasure and pain. But he does not see that this difficulty applies to the *whole* of our perceptual experience. For perception is, as we have seen, a kind of satisfaction cancelling a deprivation; a "plus and minus" rather than a "plus and zero" kind of experience. Kant never draws any consequences about the nature of our reason from this character he finds essential to pleasure and pain. This, despite the fact that he holds,

The final end of pure reason is in the sphere of the practical. (Bxxxviii)

And adds that practical principles of reason are inoperative "unless they find scope for their necessary expectation and hope."[106] This last point is perennial with Kant. For example,

No finite reasonable being can renounce its natural end of happiness. (*Über den Gemeinspruch: das mag in der Theorie richtig sein, taugt aber nicht für die Praxis.*)

Now Kant never indicates he means by "happiness" anything different from pleasure. Thus, in sum, he sees that a person's having pleasure has the peculiar character of being a "real contradictory" of its opposite, a person's being in pain. And the whole exercise of our reason, he acknowledges, is possible only with the hope of happiness. Yet he absolutely refuses to interpret reason in terms of this peculiar state whose representation (in hope) makes it possible. He insists that even a critique of practical reason proceeds "without reference to human nature."[107] The view developed in this section agrees with the importance of Kant's characterization of pleasure and pain as "plus and minus" phenomena. It agrees that our judgments could not "expand to universality" without the hope of happiness. But it attempts to achieve some understanding of *why* these connections obtain.

The answer is given by showing how the very rationality of our theoretical reason *is* a representation of a hoped-for-world, better than the one we live in. Reason is not just facilitated by hope; it is itself a way of hoping. We are vulnerable in the perceptual world we find ourself *in*. The possibilities of disappearance, dissatisfaction, destruction and disillusion can never be entirely driven away; we can never do more than hold them at bay, for the time being. Our knowledge is that of a precariously balanced judgment, which has to shift with shifting circumstances. It is a knowledge that requires all our skill, not merely to gain, but to retain. We cannot rest content with this epistemological "cold war" with reality. And we have the strange capacity to fashion an imaginative world of our own; a world we do not have to be in; a world we *are*. Here, instead of having to accommodate ourself to the world, we need only accommodate ourself to ourself. What wonder, then, that our imaginative thought represents a form of knowledge free from the disappearance, dissatisfaction, destruction, and disillusion that are the ever-present enemies of all our perceptual knowledge? This is not to say, of course, that we refuse to theorize *about* these epistemological dangers. These things are eliminated in the *way* we think; in the *categories* of our imaginative thought, so that everything we theoretically entertain denies these functions in the way they plague us perceptually, viz., as categories. Perception itself may be theoretically studied. But then the categories of perception, ineliminable in the perceptual world, are converted into mere contents of our imaginative world; they are represented as one more set of facts related each to each in accordance with imaginative principles of universal conservation.

Imaginative thought is an idealization of perception in the sense that it represents a world of global and permanent objective satisfaction, in place of the local and provisional objective satisfaction with which we are perceptually presented. This does not mean that imaginative thought is delusory; it is plainly a great source of our knowledge. It enables us to unify in great detail our past perception of objects now absent with our present perception of objects present. Also, since we are, as imaginative subjects, disembodied worlds, we are indistinguishable from one another as thinkers. And this helps us greatly in sharing the perceptual experience of others, and thus serves to vastly augment our knowledge of this world. In sum, though the forms of imagination are untrue to actual experience, they are nevertheless valuable instruments of knowledge, for they greatly multiply our ability to gain knowledge of the content of perceptual experience.

6.8 Kant's Dialectic: Perception Takes Revenge

Kant, as we have seen, imaginizes experience. The world, the ego, the object, and the categories of experience, in the Transcendental Aesthetic and Analytic, are imaginative in form; the corresponding forms of perceptual experience are entirely overlooked. Yet Kant retains some perceptual ingredient in experience, albeit merely as the formless matter of experience. For Kant's central insight has continually been that, somehow or other, we must understand our experience as a synthesis of receptive, perceptual, Humean experience, and spontaneous, imaginative, Leibnizian experience. His general conclusion, by the end of the Analytic, is that experience is a synthesis of perceptual content with an imaginative form. But in the Dialectic, the difficulties of this solution become apparent. Kant himself makes many of these difficulties explicit; and he is so rigorous in his thought, that even the difficulties he fails to see in his position are nevertheless implicit in what he writes, and can be mined from his own text in a surprisingly systematic way. In the present section, we will see that the main difficulty is this: emasculated perception, formless perception, cannot be unified by imaginative forms. The attempt to give perception a purely imaginative unity, leads to an irresoluble tension: if a perceptual ingredient is retained in knowable objects, knowledge loses its unity; if the unity of knowable objects is retained, they lose their perceptual ingredient. Kant is faced with a dilemma: *either* the unity of the knowledge of objects; *or*, the experiential character of objects known. This is a serious dilemma for Kant's whole philosophy. Now appearing in the Dialectic, in the guise of the discrepancy between reason and understanding, this is substantially the very same problem Kant first set out to solve by his "Copernican revolution"; his transcendentally subjective resolution of the problem of a priori knowledge. This re-appearance of his basic problem is a reductio ad absurdum of his whole philosophy of "transcendental idealism" and "empirical realism." We saw in Section 6.1 that Kant's original mistake lay in his formulation of the problem. By this formulation, he restricted the world of experience to the world of imagination, although he recognized that experience was also perceptual. Eliminating the perceptual setting from his consideration of experience, he was bound to eliminate all perceptual forms. Now in the Dialectic, Kant's blind dismissal of perceptual forms comes back to plague him. If the only forms of experience are imaginative, then knowledge of experience is in the last analysis impossible. And the whole work of Kant's philosophy fails to achieve its purpose. This, at any rate, is what I will try to show in the present section.

We learn early in the Transcendental Dialectic that the universal premisses of understanding *help* to unify experience, but they cannot do so *completely*, because they are synthetic judgments and hence themselves incompletely unified. Their synthetic character of course comes from the fact that they are principles of possible experience including a receptive perceptual factor. The principles of understanding, considered as having empirical reference, have a merely conditioned unity, and stand in rational need of an "unconditioned unity" from which they may be derived. It is the function of "reason" to provide this unconditioned unity for the understanding.

[T]he principle peculiar to reason in general, in its logical employment, is: —to find for the conditioned knowledge obtained through the understanding the unconditioned whereby its unity is brought to completion. (B364)

Thus Kant began by seeking to find the unity of perception in understanding. He now sees that this theoretical understanding of matters of fact presupposes some unity it does not provide. So he

Development of the Thesis

seeks to find the unity of this unifying faculty in a third faculty, reason. We have seen that perception has its own unity, viz., the felt unity of need of our active body; and we have seen that theoretical understanding of matters of fact presupposes a unity of experience that it does not provide. But Kant is wrong in the direction he takes seeking to find that unity. Instead of looking still further away from perception, he should have looked back to perception. But doing that, of course, would have meant starting all over again. Within his initial framework, the course Kant takes is the only one open to him. He seeks the unity of understanding in concepts of reason that are not even about possible matters of fact.

> If the concepts of reason contain the unconditioned, they are concerned with something to which all experience is subordinate, but which is never itself an object of experience. (B367)

We have an ineradicable tendency to think that all principles that make sense are in some way about what exists. But this tendency, when effective in matters of reason, is the seat of "transcendental illusion." Since principles of reason do not have "the unity of a possible experience,"[108] and since we cannot avoid the tendency to suppose they are about *something* knowable, we are misled into supposing they are about knowable nonexperiential objects, i.e., knowable "things-in-themselves." Transcendental illusion is the delusion that principles of reason, as knowable by us, have a *transcendent* employment beyond the limits of possible experience; whereas in fact all our knowledge is limited to a *transcendental* form, as applicable only within the limits of possible experience. The truth is that a principle of reason is,

> only a logical precept, to advance towards completeness by an ascent to ever higher conditions and so to give our knowledge the greatest possible unity of reason. (B365)

The concepts of pure reason give the rule for this "advance," and are what Kant calls "transcendental ideas."[109] We saw from Kant's general doctrine of judgment, that the orderly employment of categories consists in forming judgments in the context of empirical syllogisms. We now learn[110] that empirical syllogisms of the understanding are themselves made in the larger context of a train of syllogisms ordered by transcendental ideas of reason, and directed toward the comprehension of "experience in its totality."

Reason thus guides an "advance towards" completeness by understanding. And this completeness approached by understanding is the condition of "experience in its totality."[111] Let us stop for a moment to distinguish two possible kinds of "approach" to a given condition. (1) A may "approach" a *limiting* condition, C, such that "A reaches C": is consistent; implies no loss of identity of A; implies that A is in the condition, C. (2) A may "approach" an *impossible* condition, C, such that "A reaches C": is contradictory; implies that A is not A; implies that A is transformed into the condition, C. A limiting approach may be incompletable in fact, but it must be completable in principle. A contradictory approach, however, is incompletable in principle as well as in fact; and furthermore the "approach" is itself contradictory, so that it cannot even get started. Something having the characteristic, A, can approach a state of not having that characteristic. But something, A, or a characteristic, A, cannot itself approach being not-A. Yet Kant implies it can—in the particular case where A is experience, and C is the unification of experience in its totality.[112] For experience *is*, according to Kant, a spontaneous synthesis of successively received sensation; and the successive reception of sensation implies that we can never have experience in its totality, as "all in." The temporal form of inner sense in which sensation is received, is in principle indefinitely extensible as a form for *further* possible experience. And the receptivity of sensation implies that we can never know for sure that our further anticipations will be met, for it implies that the source of sensation is something other than ourself, hence (according to Kant) something into which we can have no insight, as it is "in itself." No matter how fully all previous experience is understood as of a community of substances, the temporality of experience insures that it is possible to look indefinitely back and forth among these substances, and so to perceive each of them anew an unlimited number of times. And the receptivity of sensation insures that each new perception *may* be unexpected. The very nature of experience thus implies that it is open to revision, incompletable, *un*totalizable. Hence, "experience in its totality" would not be *experience*.

Development of the Thesis

We can certainly understand our experience better, so as to give it *more* unity. But we can never advance one step toward giving it a different *kind* of unity. Yet this is what Kant proposes, for he admits,

> The unity of reason is therefore not the unity of a possible experience, but is essentially different from such unity, which is that of understanding. (B363)

The systematization of judgments of experience can never make their kind of unity approach that of reason. It can only give these judgments of understanding a greater unity of the kind they already have. Theoretical understanding, in its synthetic application to intuition of matters of fact, may well suppose a unity of experience that it does not itself manifest. But if so, this unity is not to be found, as Kant thinks, in something outside of experience, something "never itself the object of experience."[113] Such a thing could not fulfill its function by being brought to bear upon experience, with its "essentially different" type of unity. Something might (as we believe) provide the unity missing from the theoretical understanding of experience, if it applied to experience in some other way. But if it does not apply to experience at all, it cannot remedy the deficiency in theoretical understanding of experience. It simply adds a second difficulty of how such a contradictory application would be possible.

From our point of view, the pattern of Kant's analysis is clear. Perception provides the missing unity of our experience of matters of fact. Theoretical imagination presupposes this unity and borrows on it in the formal idealization of our experience, representing our experience as taking place in another world,[114] yet in such a way as to be re-interpretable in this world. Great dividends in knowable content accrue from our imaginative employment of the borrowed factual unity of perception, and give imagination its relevance to reality. We can borrow knowingly in this way, because we know we are the identical subject who freely transforms himself from percipient to imaginative subject and back again. Kant is correct that our understanding of matters of fact borrows a *kind* of unity that it does not itself possess. It borrows a perceptual unity that differs in kind from that of theoretical imagination. The contents of the perceptual field are only loosely united by direct relation to one another. They are unconditionally united only in an indirect way, viz., by the switchboard of their common centering in the felt unity of our active body. Perceptual content has thus a *radial* unity, achieved by our active body functioning as parameter of all our perceptual knowledge of matters of fact. Imaginatively known content, on the other hand, has the direct unity of content filling a world. It has the unity of a *plenum of content.* There is no distinction between total imaginative content and the imaginative field. Kant himself, writing from an imaginative point of view, frequently expresses this fact. Thus, for example,

Space (may be) represented as *object*, as we are required to do in geometry. (Kant's emphasis, B160*n*)

Intuitions in general, through which objects can be given to us, constitute the field, the whole object, of possible experience. (A95)

Through this unity of consciousness an object (a determinate space) is first known. (Kant's parentheses, B138)

Kant's general way of referring to objects of experience as "parts" (*"Teilen"*) of space,[115] illustrates the same point.

Thus the unity of imagination is not commensurate with that of perceptual matters of fact. Imaginative reference to perceptual matters of fact, therefore brings with it the problem of the source of a pre-supposed kind of unity adequate to our *actual* experience as distinct from our imaginative representation of all *possible* experience. Kant of course cannot go to perception for this unity, since he holds that all perceptual unity is provided by our conceptual imagination. Unable to account in any way for the unity of our actual experience, Kant is driven to hold in the last analysis that unity is introduced into our experience by rational ideas for totalizing experience, i.e., making experience exhaustively determined by concept and judgment, thus draining it of receptivity and actuality. Purely spontaneous imaginative experience is unified in this way. Kant's view that the unity of our theoretical knowledge of matters of fact is derived from ideas of reason is thus equivalent to the view that the unity of our knowledge of matters of fact is derived from ideas of a *purely imaginative knowledge of matters of fact.*

Development of the Thesis

Experience, according to Kant, is a blend of spontaneous imaginative forms, and received perceptual content. In the Transcendental Aesthetic and Analytic, Kant establishes his conclusion that knowledge of matters of fact is purely imaginative and spontaneous in its forms, and is perceptual only in its received content. In the Dialectic, Kant sees that this merely formal imaginizing of empirical knowledge is not sufficient to account for its unity. Even if perception is reduced to providing the wholly formless material of knowledge, it still prevents spontaneity from being sufficient for knowledge. Productive imagination under the transcendental unity of apperception and the categories does not produce knowledge of matters of fact. Reproductive imagination working with perceptual matter, is also required.[116] This additional requirement changes the kind of unity our knowledge has. Productive imagination produces an intuition *following from* a rule. The intuition so produced is completely unified by the rule, because its "matter" as well as its form is determined by the rule. More accurately, it is nothing but pure form, infinitely detailed. Thus, the productively imagined form of intuition "contains nothing but mere relations."[117] Reproductive imagination of empirical content, however, produces an intuition merely *in accordance with* a rule. Real intuitions so produced, are incompletely unified by the rule of their production; they are unified in form, but not in respect to existence. And the relation between our receptive faculty (which gives rise to knowledge of existence in accordance with a rule) and our spontaneous faculty (which gives rise to formal knowledge following from a rule) is in principle hidden from us. The unity of the form and existence of things is in principle undiscoverable by us. Kant thus rightly sees in the Dialectic that the unity of our knowledge of objects can be made comprehensible on his view only by supplementing the *formal* imaginizing of experience (carried out in the Transcendental Aesthetic and Analytic) with a *factual* imaginizing of experience. Spontaneous understanding is an incomplete unity because it is conditioned by the incompletely unifiable sensory matter to which it must apply. To establish the complete unity of our knowledge, this conditioned unity of understanding must be shown to follow from an unconditioned unity of pure spontaneity, viz., the unity of reason capable of forming ideas of "purely intelligible objects."

But this conclusion gives rise to a fundamental antimony that pervades the whole of Kant's Dialectic, and is the net-result of the "transcendental idealism" of his first Critique. Kant has two basic premises. (1) Knowable objects consist of a purely perceptual diversity of real content and a purely imaginative unifying form. (2) Knowledge is possible only through an unconditioned unity in the act of knowing. In the Dialectic, Kant faces the fact that, on his account of the matter, the imaginative unity of perceptual content is merely conditional. It thus seems that we cannot have any knowable experience at all, for:

(I) Kant's Basic Antinomy:

Thesis: Knowledge of experience cannot have an unconditioned unity, and must have a receptive perceptual ingredient. For all perceptual content has only a conditioned imaginative unity. And without perceptual content there is no *experience.*

Antithesis: Knowledge of experience must have an unconditioned unity and must be purely spontaneous or imaginative. For all perceptual content has only a conditioned imaginative unity. And without unconditioned unity, there is no *knowledge.*

Kant's regulative "solution" to this basic antinomy is that in the unreachable limit, the perceptual content of experience is eliminable; in the unreachable limit, the antithesis is correct.

As construed by Kant, the "unconditioned unity" for experience turns out to be a contradictory notion implicit in all knowledge of experience. *Knowledge* of experience presupposes such an unconditioned unity; but *experience,* because of its perceptual elements, is held to lack such a unity. Now either there is such a unity of perceptual knowledge itself, and Kant is wrong in the latter supposition (my view); or else we do not have true knowledge of experience retaining a perceptual ingredient. This is Kant's final, but somewhat incredible view—of such experience, he holds we have at most something like true knowledge, something analogous to that noncontingent knowledge of a purely intelligible object that we cannot help seeking but can never attain.[118]

Kant would be rid of his dilemma if he saw that the unconditioned unity he seeks for experience is to be found in perception itself.

Development of the Thesis

But, once again, as in the case of his false dilemma of a priori knowledge, Kant's formulation of the problem is so strictly from an imaginative point of view that the possibility of a perceptual solution is ruled out to begin with. For Kant defines "the unconditioned" in such a way as to rule out its perceptual form.

The totality of conditions and the unconditioned (are) equivalent titles for all concepts of reason. (B380)

The unconditioned unity of all *conceptual* content does lie in the plenum-unity, the totality, of what is conceived. But the conditioned unity of all *perceptual* content lies in the felt unity of the active percipient who radially unifies what he circumstantially perceives; the unconditioned unity of determinate perceptual conditions lies not in their *totality*, but in *one central condition* among them. The general meaning of "the unconditioned," applicable both to imagination (as the totality of conditions) and to the corresponding function of perception (the central condition), is, simply: the condition of all knowable conditions.

We saw that Kant means in general by an "idea of reason," a rule for extending a train of empirical syllogisms "toward" the goal of knowledge of "experience in its totality." As the categories prescribe an iterable four-fold syllogistic form for empirical arguments, so ideas of reason prescribe syllogistic forms for the ordering of empirical syllogisms. An idea of reason is a rule of the form: given an empirical syllogism of kind A, find next an empirical syllogism of kind B. The direction of empirical inquiry is dictated by a syllogism having an idea of reason as its major premise; the knowledge of some empirical syllogism of kind A as its minor premise; and the directive to seek knowledge of some empirical syllogism of kind B, for its conclusion. Guiding his thought, as usual, by the categories, Kant notes that the three kinds of syllogism (from the Table of Judgments) are expressed in the three categories of Relation. There are, accordingly, three (and only three) ideas of reason generating, respectively: categorical prosyllogisms directed toward knowledge of the unconditioned condition of all knowledge in the thinking *subject*; hypothetical prosyllogisms directed toward knowledge of the unconditioned condition of all knowledge in the series of *objects*; and disjunctive prosyllogisms directed toward knowledge of the unconditioned sum of all possibilities in the *world* of objects, or in the universe of scientific discourse.[119] Knowledge of the unconditioned thinker, object(s), and intelligible world, can never be reached.

> The concept of the absolute totality of conditions is not applicable in any experience, since no experience is unconditioned. (B383)

Nevertheless, the ideas of them cannot be relinquished. It is only by their use "that we can have any faculty of understanding whatsoever."[120] The three kinds of prosyllogism our ideas generate to regulate our theoretical inquiry, correspond closely to, and seem to issue from, the three Leibnizian principles of reason that "prepare the field of the understanding," viz., the principles of homogeneity, specification, and continuity of forms.

In the remainder of this section, we will see in detail how Kant's basic antinomy[121] pervades the regulative employment of each of his ideas of reason. According to Kant, as we have seen, we are subject to transcendental illusions. We have an unavoidable tendency to misconstrue all our ideas of objects as referring to knowable objects, whereas they are in fact merely ideas of objects limiting our knowledge. Most of the Dialectic is devoted to unmasking these transcendental illusions. The idea of the thinking subject is discussed in this way, in the Paralogisms; the idea of objects, in the Antinomies; and the idea of the world-sum of all possibilities for objects, in the Ideal of pure reason. Kant himself believed that the Paralogisms and the Ideal were free of antinomies. Thus, for example, he characterizes the Antinomies as,

> the most singular phenomenon of human reason, no other instance of which can be shown in any other use of reason.[122] (*Prolegomena*, 340)

I will show, however, that the Paralogisms and the Ideal have suppressed antinomies of the same basic form as the so-called Antinomies proper. All of Kant's antinomies come from his imaginizing experience; his unsuccessful attempt to make imagination alone do work that it in fact shares with perception. Kant was well aware of the problem of relating perception to imagination, in the particular case of *objects*. So he was in this case able to discern the antinomies produced by his general point of view. But Kant had no notion at all of the percipient as knower; or of the knowable perceptual world. So in the cases of the Paralogisms and the Ideal, he was not even aware of the problem of relating perceptual to imaginative knowledge. How then could he possibly discern the particular antinomous shape this problem took in the context of his assumptions? He took it for granted, for example, that while the difficulty with the series of objects was that they could never be adequately given in experience, the difficulty with the subject and the world was that they could not be given in experience at all.[123] But while this is true of conception, it is false of perception.

Each idea governing a prosyllogism of empirical knowledge, does so in respect of Quantity, Quality, Relation, and Modality. The idea of the subject concerns not merely the first moment of Relation, viz., Substance, but also the first moment of each other categorial group. And similarly with the other two ideas. The four Paralogisms presented by Kant concern the first tetrad of categories; and the four Antinomies, the second. Careful reading of Kant's section on the Ideal, discloses that four transcendental illusions are also presented here, concerning the third tetrad of categories. I will consider each idea in turn; state its general form of the basic antinomy, (I); and then show how this general form is exhibited in each of the four categorial moments it governs. Thus, in sum, I will show that Kant has not merely four, but *twelve* antinomies; and that each one arises from the same basic antinomy, produced by imaginizing perception and thereby concealing the perceptual form of unconditioned unity.

6.8.1 The antinomies of the Paralogisms: the suppressed perceptual thesis vs. the imaginative antithesis

(IA) Kant's General Antinomy of the Subject

Thesis (suppressed): The knowing subject is a material subject who is aware of his own existence. Otherwise, he could not be the subject of *his actual* experience

Antithesis (expressed): The knowing subject is a purely logical subject spontaneously forming judgments. Otherwise, he could not give his act of knowing an unconditional *unity*.

Kant expresses this antithesis in such statements as the following.[124]

> We can thus say of the thinking "I" . . . that it does *not* know *itself through the categories*, but knows the categories and through them all objects, in the absolute unity of apperception, and so through itself. (Kant's emphases, A402)

Four such antinomies may be found in the Paralogisms, the thesis being suppressed in each case.[125]

1. Quantity, Unity:

Thesis: I am an identical knower in all my actual experience, and am thereby intuitively identifiable as existing.

Antithesis: I am an identical subject in all my knowing, and am thereby not intuitively identifiable as some particular existing thing.

2. Quality, Reality:[126]

Thesis: As knower, I am the functionally individual agent of all my actual experience, and am thereby inseparable from my functionally indivisible body.

Antithesis: As knower, I am the logically simple subject of every judgment I make, and am thereby not an indivisible substance, an object of judgment.

3. Relation, Substance:

Thesis: As knower, I am a self-determining skillful agent in all my actual experience, and am thereby a substantial being.

Antithesis: As knower, I am a self-determining subject of judgment, and am thereby not a self-subsistent substance determined in judgment.

4. Modality, Possibility:

Thesis: I am the recipient of actual experience, and must therefore have an actual capacity for experience, which exists in addition to what I experience.

Antithesis: I am the conceiver of all possible experience, and therefore cannot have an actual capacity for experience, which itself exists as some possible experience in addition to whatever I may conceive of.[127]

Development of the Thesis

By the four preceding antitheses, Kant seeks to deny the four transcendental illusions of "rational psychology." In B410–411, Kant offers a general explanation of the plausibility of these illusions.[128] They all depend upon a sophistic syllogism that plays upon the ambiguity of the word "subject"—treating the subject first as transcendental knower, then as something empirically known. The sophistic syllogism, or para-logism, runs as follows.

That which cannot be thought otherwise than as subject does not exist otherwise than as subject, and is therefore substance.

A thinking being, considered merely as such, cannot be thought otherwise than as subject.

Therefore it exists also only as subject, that is, as substance.

But why should it be that,

> there is nothing more natural ... than the illusion which leads us to regard the unity in the synthesis of thoughts as a perceived unity in the subject of these thoughts. (A402)

Why should human beings, who normally have little trouble distinguishing one empirical friend from another moving in the same social circles (and therefore quite similar in many ways), have such enormous difficulty distinguishing a purely logical subject from a radically different empirical one?

On my view, the answer is plain: the "natural" view is the *correct* one. If the burden of Kant's "para-logism" is taken to be this "natural" tendency, the "paralogism" only *seems* sophistic because there are some missing steps that depend upon the perceptual theses of the subject-antinomies. The full argument implicit in common sense may be stated on the model of Kant's "paralogism."

(1) That which cannot be known otherwise than as material subject, exists as material subject.

A percipient, considered merely as such, cannot be known otherwise than as material subject.

Therefore, a percipient exists as a material subject, that is, as a kind of substance.

(2) That which cannot be thought otherwise than as pure subject does not exist otherwise than as pure subject, and is therefore not a substance.

A thinker cannot be thought otherwise than as pure subject.

Therefore, a thinker exists as pure subject, not as a substance.

(3) An identical subject is one who retains an identical unity of consciousness (though not necessarily a consciousness of identical unity) through all transformations he undergoes.

The human subject consciously transforms *himself* from material subject to pure subject and back again.

Therefore the unity of consciousness of a pure human subject (a thinker) is identical with that of a material human subject(a percipient).

And the "natural" belief that the thinker and percipient are identical is proven correct.

In sum, Kant's "para-logism" is a *product* rather than a *discovery* of his philosophy. It expresses the vestigial form of common sense in one who has systematically ignored the percipient as knower in favor of exclusive concentration upon the abstract thinker.

Kant tells us that the plausibility of the paralogism depends upon failing to distinguish the subject "given in intuition" from the subject "in relation to . . . the unity of consciousness."[129] But the point naturally appreciated even by the unreflective but sensible subject, is that the percipient is "given in intuition" *as* providing a "unity of consciousness." The matter may be further clarified by recalling one of Kant's central theses, with which I agree, provided the following interpolation is made.

In inner intuition there is nothing permanent, for the "I" [*which*] is merely the consciousness of my thought. (B413)

For there is another "I" that is the consciousness of my perception. And in its inner (i.e., temporal) intuition there *is* something permanent, viz., the felt unity of my active body.

Development of the Thesis

6.8.2 The perceptual thesis vs. the imaginative antithesis of Kant's Antinomies; or, the fruitless question: Which form of objectivity is the right one?

I wrote that Kant's second idea concerns knowable *objects*; and that his third idea, properly understood, concerns the *world*. Yet Kant labels the second idea, "cosmological." This label is simply a misnomer in the light of the problems actually handled in this section of the *Critique*. The label is but one more expression of the fact that Kant imaginizes knowable objects. For he tells us that the expression "world"

> signifies the mathematical sum-total of all appearances and the totality of their synthesis. (B446)

Now it is true that in the *special case* of imagination, the unity of content is identical with the unity of the world. But in perception, all content is limited to appearing locally in the world; the world cannot be filled as a plenum of content, and always has a unity distinguishable from that of its content. Kant's Antinomies in fact center upon the series of objects of experience (and their spatiotemporal conditions), and are concerned with the way in which this series always falls *short* of the totality that would make it equivalent to a purely imaginative kind of empirical world.

Before examining the Antinomies in detail, we must be clear about one more point. We saw that the unconditioned unity of the content of theoretical imagination lies in the totality of this content. This totality is the condition of all knowable conditions; without comprehending it, one cannot comprehend anything theoretically; theoretical comprehension of a particular condition is in the context of a theoretical whole of all possible conditions of that sort. We saw on the other hand that the unconditioned unity of perceptual content lies in a central condition of this circumstantial content, viz., the felt unity of the percipient's active body. Except for his discussion of the Antinomies, Kant holds without apparent qualification that the idea of the unconditioned condition is equivalent to the idea of the totality of conditions. Thus, as I have noted, he imaginizes the unconditioned. But in the Antinomies he may *seem* to qualify this equivalence. For we are told that there are two possible kinds of unconditioned series: one in which each member is conditioned and only the totality is unconditioned; and one in which "the absolutely unconditioned is only a part of the series ... to which the other members are subordinated."[130] Is Kant here acknowledging a perceptual kind of unconditioned condition?

The answer is complicated; in a sense he is, and in a sense he is not. He is, insofar as he hereby acknowledges that the unconditioned condition may have its *source* in a privileged condition rather than uniformly in all conditions. He is not, insofar as he continues to imply that the unconditioned character of this privileged source condition includes its function of *passing on* its own unconditionality to all other conditions indiscriminately. While Kant's alternative kind of unconditionality is unique to the Antinomies, it does not qualify his basic view that,

This *unconditioned* is always contained in the *absolute totality of the series* represented in imagination." (Kant's emphasis, B444)

Nevertheless, the appearance of this alternative is of considerable interest for my analysis. Only in the case of our experience of *objects*, does Kant really face the problem of synthesizing perception with imagination. Perceptual form requires the centrality of the unconditioned condition present in the *midst* of the perceptual series of contingent circumstantial conditions. Imaginative form requires that the unconditioned condition be represented *throughout* the imaginative series as the totality of necessary members. Kant's question is: what may be required by formless perceptual content contained in imaginative forms? The burden of my analysis is that this question presupposes the truth of a self-contradiction,[131] and therefore admits of no satisfactory answer. Kant is caught in a dilemma of two unsatisfactory alternatives: to treat the experience as if it were purely imaginative (Antithesis); or to treat is as a weird hybrid—with a perceptual sort of finitude and point of origin, combined with an imaginatively unconditioned totality (Thesis). This hybrid is expressed as the thesis of a privileged unconditioned condition that bestows its unconditionality upon all members of its series from its position as the first member of this series.[132]

Development of the Thesis

The distinction between a uniquely unconditioned *central* condition, and a uniquely unconditioned *first* condition of a series of knowable conditions, is of crucial importance for understanding the weakness of Kant's Thesis in each Antinomy. This distinction is in fact the measure of Kant's having stripped perception of its forms; and of his having thereby prevented effective appeal to perceptual knowledge in support of the Thesis, with its emphasis upon the stake knowledge has in experience. Let us first consider this distinction in a preliminary way, postponing a more detailed examination until we take up the Antinomies singly.

The percipient unifies his series of circumstantial objects from his position in the *midst* of them. He leaves things behind him in perceptual time, and others lie ahead of him. He is not the temporally first thing in his perceptual field, although his position in the midst of the field makes the temporally first thing knowable as such, i.e., as that which is manifestly furthest back. Nor is he at the spatial limit of his determinate field, though his position in the midst of the field makes these limits knowable as such, i.e., as the most outlying discernible conditions. The percipient is not himself simple, but is a composite of co-ordinated body members. Yet simple circumstantial elements are perceivable only because of his ability to co-ordinate himself skillfully in the perception of them from his continually central action-station. Likewise, the percipient's self-activity is necessary for the series to be known; yet it takes place from the midst of the knowable series, not from its beginning.

It is a traditional philosophic maxim, stemming from classic times, that "the order of Being is the reverse of the order of knowing." The order in which we gain knowledge of various conditions is the reverse of the order in which we finally understand these conditions to condition one another. For example, we learn last to know God; or, we learn last to know the most powerful scientific generalizations. The maxim thus has the sense that, the order of the known is the reverse of the order of getting to be known; and the order of Being is the order of what is known as distinct from the order of knowing. The explicitness with which this view is held varies in the philosophic tradition. It is generally more explicit in more idealistic and more rationalistic philosophers, and less so in their counterparts. It is, for example, classically expressed in Spinoza's assertion that,

The order and connection of ideas is the same as the order and connection of things. (*Ethics*, Part Two, Prop. VII)

But I know of no philosophy built around the *denial* of this maxim.

Nevertheless, despite its noble lineage, this maxim is true of what we conceptually know to exist, but it is *false of perception*. Kant's notion of the unconditioned first member of a series, expressed in the Thesis of his Antinomies, follows this massive tradition—and prevents an understanding of the perceptual element in knowledge. Kant takes it for granted that in all experience, as in conception, the order in which objects exist is the same as the order in which knowledge of the existence of one makes possible knowledge of the existence of another. Kant takes it for granted that the order of existence is the same as the logical order of the knowledge of existence; or, more concisely, that the existential order follows the logical order. Imaginative knowledge of anything does indeed follow from knowledge of what precedes it, and implies knowledge of what succeeds it. For example, "If I knew the state of all particles in the universe at a given time, and the laws that govern their motion, I could in principle determine any *later* event." The difficulty with which the distinction between a logical and a real consequence emerged in the history of philosophy attests to the deep-seated strength of the foregoing conviction. In Descartes, for example, the distinction is still not clearly made. And even when it is made, as with Kant, the two orders are still regarded as parallel; they come together in an empirical law that refers *to* the order of a real consequence in matters of fact, *under* a logically ordered form of judgment. It thus seems that we can know the determining order of events only if it conforms to the logical order of our judgment. But perceptual knowledge of the determining order of events does *not* so conform.

Perceptual knowledge of any object reciprocally implies and follows from the self-knowledge of the skillfully determining percipient, whether he himself precedes, succeeds, *or* co-exists with the given object. Perceptual knowledge thus has, as we have seen, a phenomeno-logical (rather than a purely logical) form. An imaginative judgment expresses what simply *is* the case in the world; and the judgment is made from the panoramic, nonperspectival view of the world (our own imaginative capacity) in which this case is represented. A perceptual judgment expresses what is *found* to be the case in our circumstances; and the judgment is made from the perspectival center of our circumstances in the perceptual world in which this case is presented.

Now let us turn to a detailed consideration of Kant's four Antinomies.

(IB) Kant's General Antinomy of the Series of Objects:

Thesis: The series of knowable objects and conditions is limited. Otherwise, it could not be known by *experience.*

Antithesis: The series of knowable objects and conditions is an unlimited whole. Otherwise, there could not be an unconditional *unity* in knowing it.

Kant's regulative "solution": The series of known objects and conditions can be made to approach (can be extended "toward") the completeness of an unlimited whole; or at least, in the case of objects, we are rationally compelled to *seek* to do so. In the limit, objects would be truly knowable nonexperiential objects, "purely intelligible things-in-themselves." Actually, both objects and conditions must remain incompletely knowable elements of experience—though we are entitled, for purposes of enlarging our hope and understanding, to *suppose* that there are purely intelligible objects limiting our knowledge.

My solution: Recognize that we have, as identical subject, two supplementary forms of experience (perception and imagination), with two corresponding forms of apparent unity; and that the thesis partially represents the claims of perception, while the antithesis represents those of imagination.

First Antinomy: Quantity, Plurality.

Thesis: The series of knowable moments has a beginning in time, and a limit in space. Otherwise we could not complete the successive synthesis of intuition required for an intuitive knowledge of the whole.

Antithesis: Time is an unlimited whole of determinable moments; and Space, of determinable places. For any limit would be incomprehensible, as arising out of nothing.

Commentary. The perceptual field has the limited character defended by the Thesis. Kant later writes that for the Thesis of the first Antinomy to hold,

> we should be required to have a perception of limitation by absolutely empty time or space. But such an experience, as completely empty of content, is impossible. (B549)

True, such an experience would be required. Furthermore, it is possible because we actually have such an experience. Look, and see! It is the familiar experience of a placeless perceptual space and a momentless perceptual time that limits the local spatiotemporal field of determinate perceptual localities, meeting this local field at the "horizon" of our actual experience. Kant's argument of the Antithesis fails to demonstrate that this actual kind of perceptual knowledge is impossible. It fails because it does not take account of the central character of the unconditioned perceptual condition. Kant shows only that the *limiting* condition cannot be understood as the unconditioned condition of the series that it begins.

> No coming to be of a thing is possible in an empty time ... because no part of such a time possesses ... a distinguishing condition of experience. (B454)

Very well, empty time cannot posses a distinguishing character of existence. But it is the percipient's presently *filled* position in the midst of perceptual time that "possesses the distinguishing character of existence" setting the limits of determinable perceptual time. And the same argument holds for space. The limits of determinable perceptual space and time are set, not from *beyond* these limits, but from *within* them. Kant fails to see that *perceptual times and places, unlike those of the imagination, are determined in one order and exist in another order.*

Second Antinomy: Quality, Negation.[133]

Thesis: Knowable objects are limited in their divisibility. Otherwise, they would be composed of nothing and could not be given as actual objects.

Antithesis: Knowable objects are unlimited in their divisibility.

Otherwise, they could not be comprehended as occupying an infinitely divisible space.

Commentary. Again, perception exhibits the limited character of experience defended by the Thesis. The Antithesis is valid of purely imaginary objects entertained in imaginative space, but it fails against perceptual objects, for two reasons. First, perception demonstrates that it is not in fact the case that,

everything real, which occupies a space, contains in itself a manifold of constituents external to one another. (B464)

There are in fact minimal or simple perceivable parts of all objects in perceptual space. Objects are always perceived to be composed of a finite number of finitely subdivisible parts, such that further subdivision is imperceivable. Thus it is false of perceptual objects, though true of conceptual objects, that,

only the divisibility . . . is given—the whole is not in itself already divided. (B554)

Secondly, the Antithesis fails against perceptual objects because it is argued on the false premise that perceptual objects occupy imaginative space. The finite divisibility of perceptual objects is understandable because these objects occupy a distinctively *perceptual* space whose minimally determinable regions are *places*, not points. The basis for the comprehensibility of finitely divisible perceptual objects lies in the comprehensibility of finitely delimitable perceptual space. And this in turn lies in the felt *indivisibility* of our finite active body, with which all circumstantial perceptual determinations (of field as well as content) must be made commensurate.

Third Antinomy: Relation, Causality.

Thesis: The series of knowable events is limited in its origination by a spontaneous cause that is its first member. For events can be given as presently taking place, only if the series of conditions leading to them has been completed. This is possible only if it has a beginning that begins of itself.

Antithesis: The series of knowable events is unlimited in its origination, and all events are conditioned by prior events. For an original event is incomprehensible. It "abrogates those rules through which alone a completely coherent experience is possible." (B475)

Commentary. The Thesis argues that the actual experience of finite, determinable events implies the existence of a free or spontaneous original determination. It is in this respect true of perception, though false of conception.[134] However, the Thesis also argues that this free act is the *first* member of the series of knowable events. It is in this respect false of perception as well as conception; and is thereby open to the counterargument of the Antithesis. For it implies that the causing of the determinable series is itself an event in the determinable series. The first cause supposedly determines itself in a unique way, but determines its successor B in the same way as B determines its successor C. The first cause is, however, merely one event among others that have taken place. It must, accordingly, be knowable in the same way as other events, for,

> The causality of the cause through which something takes place is itself ... something that has *taken place,* which again presupposes ... a preceding state and its causality. (Kant's emphasis, B473)

Free causality, as that of a self-caused first cause, differs from conditioned causes in how it take place, but not in the more fundamental fact *that* it is merely something that takes place. This account of free causality is therefore open to the criticism of the Antithesis: if the first cause is an "event" in the same sense as other events (i.e., something that has taken place), then if the field of events is to be comprehensible as a whole, the first cause must be comprehended in the same way as all other causes (e.g., by rule); but if the first cause occurs in a different way than all other causes (e.g., spontaneously), it cannot be comprehended in the same way as the others. As an "event" in the same sense as other causes, a *first* cause is presumably knowable in the same way as they. But as a *self-causing* cause, it is presumably not knowable in the same way. A knowable cause might be either self-causing, or first cause, but it surely cannot be both.

The criticism of the Antithesis is thus well-founded. Speaking of events in the series of causes, Kant asserts,

[E]very beginning of action presupposes a state of the not yet acting cause (from which it follows in accordance with fixed laws). (B474)

Free causality of the series of causes, however, implies,

an *absolute spontaneity* of the cause [which] . . . *begins of itself*. (Kant's emphasis, B475)

If free causality of the series of causes is itself an event in this series (as it would be, if it were the first cause), Kant's objection would be cogent, viz., that,

This kind of connection . . . renders all unity of experience impossible. (B475)

Let us now leave the difficulties of Kant's thesis of semi-perception, and turn our attention to the free cause of perception itself. Our spontaneous self-movement, as we saw in Section 6.3, does not "presuppose a state of the not yet acting cause." It is not the exercise of an antecedent capacity, and does not presuppose a readiness to move on occasions of a given kind. Rather the reverse. The original spontaneity of our movement makes possible the acquisition of determinate capacities for skillfully determining activity of a certain kind, and thereby first establishes the distinction between the possession and exercise of a capacity. The spontaneity of our self-movement is thus the original condition of the knowability of circumstantial events. But our free determining of a circumstantial event is not itself an event *that takes place* in the perceptual field. It is rather correlative with *the taking place* of this determinable event with the passage of perceptual time. To be sure, the determination of the event is retroactive. By determining the event during passage of the time it is happening, we finally determine what it *was* in the completed time passed; and we simultaneously determine what we *did* in determining it. Our determination of an event is a future-perfect product of our present determining of that event. Our present determining will have been a knowable event of a certain kind. But we must distinguish our freedom as *act,* from our freedom as *product* of itself. Our freedom as act produces the knowability of circumstantial events, *without* itself being one among these events. It produces the knowability of circumstantial events with the present passage of time, without being something that has taken place in time. Events are determin*able* only because there is the possibility of knowing them determin*ately*. Our freedom as act bears that possibility. It is the possibility of converting determinable events into determinately known events. As such, it operates from the *midst* of the perceptual field. It looks to the future in order to eventually find the passed. It is our way of making things known by making them happen. It is our way of digesting our experience, by converting our determinable future into our determinate passed. Circumstantial events thus do indeed presuppose an original spontaneous determining of them, just as Kant's Thesis maintains. But this self-causing cause is not, as the Thesis also claims, a *first* cause in the series of events. Rather, its very function as the determining of events places it in the *midst* of the series of events—between those that are determinable in the future and those that are determinately experienced in the passed. Even when it has produced itself as a product, it will not appear as first cause, but only as one cause among others in the *midst* of the passed field of determinate events.

    Kant held, as we saw, that the "kind of connection" obtaining between a self-caused first cause and the other causes in the series of knowable events, "renders all unity of experience impossible." I agree. Nevertheless, Kant is wrong in concluding that no free cause of *any* kind is possible in experience. Kant dogmatically identifies a free or *self-causing* cause with a *first* cause in experience.[135] Thus he writes,

Assume that there is freedom ... namely, a power of absolutely beginning a state, and therefore also of absolutely beginning a series of consequences of that state. (B473)

And when he sees that a self-causing first cause "renders all unity of experience impossible," he concludes that freedom as such "is not to be met with in any experience."[136] But in perception, the "kind of connection" existing between objects and the free activity of the subject is precisely what "renders all unity of experience" *possible*. Perceptual freedom (self-movement of the percipient) exists at the phenomenological and perspectival *origin* of the series of perceivable events, but not at the *beginning* of this series. Because it occurs in the very midst of our experience, our perceptual freedom of spontaneous activity is itself *present* as a determinable content of our experience. It is, indeed, unconditionally present in all our experience of matters of fact; so fundamentally present that its presence is what makes *the present* present.

Fourth Antinomy: Modality, Existence

Thesis: The series of knowable events is limited in its contingency by something necessary that exists as a member of it. For the actual experience of determined conditions implies that the temporal series of their determining conditions is complete; hence that it is finite and has a first member that, as self-conditioning, is necessary.

Antithesis: The series of knowable events is unlimited in its contingency, and nothing necessary exists. For events are comprehensible only as determined by something else. Hence a necessary being is incomprehensible, and so is the action by which it might relate itself to contingent beings.

Commentary. The Thesis gives partial expression to the perceptual fact that the existence of the percipient's active body is necessary for the endurance of the series of perceivable events. The general difficulty with the argument, from our point of view, is the same as with the preceding Antinomy. Kant argues against the Thesis on the ground that it implies impossible alternatives.

Either there is a beginning in the series of alterations which is absolutely necessary ... or the series ... [is] conditioned in all its parts, nonetheless absolutely necessary as a whole. (B482)

Kant shows the second alternative is impossible because "the existence of a series cannot be necessary if no single member of it is necessary." And the first alternative is impossible because it conflicts with the "dynamical law" that "the beginning of a series in time can be determined only by that which precedes it in time."

This is an adequate argument against a necessary being belonging to the world of imagination. But it is insufficient against this thesis for the perceptual world, because it overlooks a third alternative that may, and in fact does, obtain. The active body of the percipient is necessary to determine the beginning of the series of perceptual events from its position in the *midst* of this series. From this central position, the percipient determines the limits of the determinable (foreseeable) future, and the determinate passed (the passed determinate in hindsight). The determinate passed beginning of this series is determined *by* the percipient as that which most *precedes* him. Kant's "dynamical law," while true of imaginative conception, is precisely *contrary* to the corresponding law for perception, viz., the beginning of a series in time can only be determined by that (the percipient) which *succeeds* it in time.

Concluding note on the Antinomies in general

Kant holds that the Thesis of the Antinomies always represents the "dogmatism of pure reason," and the Antithesis, its "empiricism."[137] My conclusion is that Kant is correct in these assertions, but wholly fails to notice that the dogmatism of pure reason expresses something of the *empiricism* of perception, despite itself; its dogmatic element is precisely the dogma that reason can be entirely "pure." Kant likewise sees correctly that the Thesis always represents,

a certain *practical interest* in which every . . . man, if he has understanding of what truly concerns him, heartily shares. (Kant's emphasis, B494)

But once again, he fails to understand the perceptual ground of this fact. He believes we can discern our practical interest only by "right thinking."[138] Kant displays here his blindness to the practical function of sense experience, which is part of his general blindness to perceptual form. He has no sense of our ability to know what we are doing merely by virtue of skillfully doing it. He thus declares,

An awareness of what man *does* belongs to the faculty of thought, to pure apperception; inner sense is an awareness of what man *suffers*. (Kant's emphasis, *Anthropology*, 24)

Development of the Thesis

For Kant, there is only one variety of practical freedom, having only one relation to sensibility, viz., freedom *from* being affected by sensuous motives—such effect being in all cases, "pathological."[139] Now the ability to "resist temptation" is commonly acknowledged to be a function of the objective personal will, under certain conditions; and this seems to be what Kant has in mind. But I have pointed out another kind of practical freedom, a perceptual kind of whose existence Kant seems entirely unaware. This is an objective freedom not *from*, but *of* and *for* sensuous motivation. It is the freedom of activity prompted by our unity of need, and leading to our unity of objective satisfaction as percipient. This book, being restricted to a study of issues in the natural philosophy of the human body, provides no scope for an investigation of the natural foundations of that personal form of freedom with which Kant was exclusively concerned. It is sufficient for our present purposes to recognize that we possess, as percipient, an objective form of natural freedom that Kant, who imaginizes experience, fails to notice. Kant holds that in the dynamical Antinomies,

> We are able to obtain satisfaction for *understanding* on the one hand and for *reason* on the other. (Kant's italics, B559)

Understanding is satisfied so long as no unconditioned element is admitted among appearances; and reason, so long as an unconditioned element is admitted in some way or other. Reason and understanding can thus reach agreement in supposing there is an unconditioned element of which no experience is possible. The burden of my analysis is that in this agreement between understanding and reason no satisfaction is obtained for *perception*. And this lack produces internal difficulties in Kant's "solution." For Kant sees that theoretical understanding of matters of fact represents itself as supposing a unity of experience it cannot demonstrate. This unity is in fact provided by perception. But since Kant can not make sense of perceptual unity, he must seek elsewhere, and purports to find what he seeks in "reason." But reason cannot provide the unity missing in our understanding of experience, for it represents the denial of experience rather than its completion; it represents a contradiction, rather than the limit, of understanding experience.

6.8.3 The antinomies of the Ideal of pure reason: the suppressed perceptual thesis versus the imaginative antithesis

The antinomies of the Ideal are more difficult to recognize than those of the Paralogisms and of the Antinomies proper. And after all their difficulty of recognition, they do not reward us by illuminating anything otherwise obscure. All we learn from recognizing them is that they seem to exist. From the other antinomies, however, despite their ease of recognition, we learn much about the subject, and about the determination of the series of objects of experience—both about their true nature, and about Kant's problems begotten by his failure to understand them. We will see the reason for this difference.

The Ideal of pure reason is founded on the proposition that "everything which exists is completely determined."[140] This gives rise to the

> idea of the sum of all possibility, insofar as it serves as the condition of the complete determination of each and every thing. (B601)

The Ideal is this idea of the sum of all possibility, considered as "the concept of an individual object that is completely determined through the mere idea."[141] The individual object conceived by the Ideal serves as the "archetype"[142] from which we derive the rules of reason for the complete determination of experience in its image. The Ideal is then the ultimate condition under which objects of experience *exist*; the source from which they derive the particular possibilities they exhibit—just as the transcendental subject is the ultimate condition under which they are *known*. It thus seems plausible to regard the Ideal as the *world* of knowable objects.

Though we cannot, as rational beings, give up the attempt to form our experience in the image of this Ideal "All,"[143] we can as little succeed. Unlike the categories of understanding, the ideas of reason are not schematizable in intuition. For ideas of reason we must be satisfied with a mere "analogon"[144] of a schema, given through the idea of an indefinite maximum in the systematization of empirical knowledge. Kant emphasizes that the completeness of the Ideal is immeasurably greater than that of any intuition.[145] Yet he also emphasizes that it is an effective guide in the organization

Development of the Thesis

of our actual intuition. A tension is thus traceable throughout Kant's discussion of the Ideal. On the one hand, he implies its *commensurability* with experience—as an *effective guide* for the progressive understanding of our actual experience. On the other hand, he implies its *incommensurability* with experience—as in principle *unrepresentable* in experience. Even the attempt to represent the Ideal in experience is "absurd."[146] The claims of the latter view remain in force, and a tension between the two views is present as a suppressed antinomy. Corresponding to the third tetrad of categories, four double-views of the Ideal are discernible: one emphasizing its relevance to actual experience; the other emphasizing its distance from all possible experience.

(IC) Kant's General Antinomy of the World:

Thesis (Suppressed): The condition of all possibility must be commensurable with the conditions of experience. Otherwise, experience could not actually exhibit any real possibilities.

Antithesis (Dominant): The condition of all possibility cannot be commensurable with the conditions of experience. For it has an unconditioned unity that cannot in principle be exhibited in experience.

1. Quantity, Totality:

Thesis: The condition of all possibility is wholly undetermined in its predicates. For it serves as the condition of objects of experience, which are contingent. (B601)

Antithesis: The condition of all possibility is wholly determinate in its predicates. For it is the condition of the intelligibility of an object's specifications (B602)

2. Quality, Limitation:[147]

Thesis: The condition of all possibility must be a manifold of distinguishable possibilities limiting one another. Otherwise, it could not condition the limited possibilities of experience.

Antithesis: The condition of all possibility must be absolutely simple and without limitation, an *ens realissimum*. For it is the condition of the intelligibility of all limitations.

3. Relation, Community:[148]

Thesis: The condition of all possibility is a distributive unity. For it is the condition of possibilities exhibited in experience in one horizonally limited region after another.

Antithesis: The condition of all possibility is a collective unity. For reason requires this greater unity, even though it cannot be represented in experience.[149]

4. Modality, Necessity:

Thesis: The condition of all possibility is a necessary reality. Otherwise, no real possibilities[150] could be given as existing under this condition.

Antithesis: The condition of all possibility is not necessarily a reality. For its intelligibility does not require this.[151]

Admittedly, I had to *pry* these antinomies of the Ideal out of Kant's text; whereas I merely had to *notice* the antinomies in the Paralogisms and the Antinomies proper. This difference, however, is not a partial disconfirmation of my general analysis[152] implying the existence of all three. It serves rather as added *confirmation* of that analysis. For *my* basic difficulty in interpreting the Ideal is inherent in *any* interpretation of it. It is, namely, the difficulty that Kant's third idea of reason is poorly developed; the contrast with the comparative clarity of the first two ideas is striking. And my view *implies this confusion*!

For what exactly is "the primordial being," "the highest being" that "has nothing above it," and to which everything conditioned is subject?[153] What exactly is this "simple" being that "must condition the possibility of all things as their *ground*, not as their *sum*" (Kant's italics), and in such a way that "the manifoldness of things . . . follows from it."[154] Kant expresses his own difficulty with comprehending exactly what he means, when he admits that its being a sum rather than a ground "is impossible, although in our first rough statements we have used such language."[155] Kant is never so "rough" with the first two ideas! Our interpretation of the Ideal as the world of perceptual experience is comparatively clear. The heaven-earth vertical field "has nothing above it," and is therefore "the highest being."[156] But it also has nothing below it; it is rather the "ground" conditioning the possibility of all things in it. It is given as the source of all empirical determinations; these determinations are merely conveyed by the percipient to the objects he finds in the world; the world is therefore perceived in such a way that "the manifoldness of things . . . follows from it." But though the vertical field is perceived as the source of all determinations, it does not appear differentiated in itself, and is therefore a "simple" being. Limitation is possible in the world-field, but the world-field itself cannot be delimited from anything else; it is the condition of all comparability, but is itself incomparable. It is in this sense a "thing-in-itself," having no "negative predicates" through which it would be determinable by its difference from something else. The *perceived* world is thus readily distinguishable from the percipient and the series of perceived objects. But the primary characteristic of imagination is the assimilation of the world to the subject. The *imaginative* world is indistinguishable from the imaginative subject. Now suppose someone imaginizes experience, trying to interpret all experience on the model of pure imagination. Where would the nub of his confusion lie? He could retain a clear distinction between subject and object, although a definite ambiguity would be discoverable in his conception of each. But his idea of the world, as third condition of experience, would waver between some idea and *no idea at all*, i.e., it would be a *confused* idea.

6.9 Summary, and Concluding Remarks

We have seen how Kant imaginizes the world, ignoring the perceptual world and interpreting the world of all experience on the model of the purely imaginary world. We have seen how this gives rise to a false dilemma of a priori knowledge, which shapes his whole philosophy. Working on the assumption of an imaginized world, he is forced to conclusions likewise imaginizing the ego, the series of objects, and the categories, of our worldly experience. We have seen how this oversimplification of experience produces various difficulties in his philosophy: insupportable dogmas and irresoluble antinomies, both expressed and suppressed. We have seen how to overcome these difficulties inherent in a philosophy of imaginized experience, viz., by comprehending the distinctively perceptual form of experience, and relating it to the imaginative form. Furthermore, we have deduced phenomeno-logically what this distinctively perceptual form is; and we have shown in a general way the relation it bears to the imaginative form as envisioned by Kant. My argument in this latter connection does not depend upon the accuracy of Kant's Table of categories, but only upon the accuracy of his general conception of an imaginative "category" as the form of a necessary and universal connection among events. I demonstrate the accuracy of this general conception by a phenomenology of imagination. Kant's own grounds for it are inadequate. He simply assumes it, on the implicit grounds that logical forms are of necessary (valid), hence exceptionless, truth; and that categories are the forms of the application of these logical forms to events. But it does not follow that the *particular way in which* categories are necessary and exceptionless is by being the forms of necessary *universal* connections among events. Kant never notices the logical possibility that categories might be the forms of necessary *local* connections among events. No purely logical considerations can tell us how its exceptionless connections are expressed in temporal intuition. It so happens Kant is right that in the imaginative time of our theoretical understanding, they are expressed universally (i.e., as functions of the world's total content). But Kant nowhere shows that he is right. And he has no inkling of the equally important fact that in perceptual time they are expressed locally (i.e., as functions of a local circumstance in the world). Therefore, he cannot make sense of a perceptual judgment.

The root of Kant's inability to understand perception is his failure to understand our *active body*, for this is what gives unity to a local circumstance in the world and thereby makes possible an objective judgment of it. The primary consequence of failure to understand our active body is failure to understand the basic role of *need* and *satisfaction* in perceptual knowledge. For this knowledge is essentially a kind of satisfaction that meets the need that prompts our body activity. Kant writes,

[F]eeling is not a faculty whereby we represent things, but lies outside our whole faculty of knowledge. (B633)

Development of the Thesis

But if he had understood perceptual judgment, he would have seen that the contrary is true. Our whole faculty of knowledge of matters of fact rests upon the feeling of objective satisfaction. Thus failure to understand perceptual judgment opens an unbridgeable gap between knowledge and feeling.

A feature of the present interpretation deserving notice is that it interprets Kant's Critique *as a whole*. Many critics, particularly Norman Kemp Smith, have been unable to find any unity in the argument of the Critique, and have consequently been satisfied interpreting it as a mere compilation of views once held by the author. Others, less outright in their criticism but implying something of the same sort, have been satisfied to interpret one particular view, considered apart from its context in the remainder of the Critique. These Kant critics may, of course, be right. But their very concern with Kant-interpretation testifies to their high regard for Kant's philosophic abilities. And he published the Critique as a *single* work, thereby implying that it is all-of-a-piece. Someone who bothers with Kant interpretation, therefore, should accept a piecemeal interpretation only as a last resort. Ours, then, has the merit of being, at least in this respect, the *kind* of interpretation every Kant scholar should find preferable. The Critique may have been *written* in chronological "layers"; but it was *published* as a whole—on my view, as a seamless web woven by a master craftsman who knew what he was doing and boldly drew the consequences, however difficult, of the only position he believed possible. If we read the Critique as a philosophic tragedy, a *reductio ad absurdum* of a false dilemma of a priori knowledge—it is not with any disrespect to the author, but rather with profound admiration. For Kant did not recognize that his "Copernican revolution," carried out in the Critique, was based on a false dilemma arising from the fact that the perceptual world was concealed from him. Nevertheless, due to his true intuition as a master craftsman, the influence of this *hidden* world is clearly traceable by the *manifest* perturbations in his course of argument taken as a whole.

General Conclusion

The phenomenological material presented in this study has been brought together in the last chapter. It only remains to state how it provides a solution to the problem of the unity of the world—the problem around which the historical material has been organized. The "unity of the world" is the evidence demonstrating the common-sense convictions that there is one and only one actual world, and that everything we can think of is in terms of this world's possibilities. The problem is to find the evidence. Now we have seen that the world is the field of all our fields of activity. It is correlative with the felt unity of our active body in it. Our sense of being an *individual* self-moved mover in the world is then our evidence that there is but *one* world. Our sense that all our experience presents or represents some way of meeting our *needs* is correlative with our sense that everything we can think of, everything perceivable and imaginable, refers to some possibility of this world in which we have the needs we seek to meet. The unity of the world therefore lies in our sense of life, our sense of being an individual self-moved mover seeking to meet our needs.

Appendix I

The Subject Body in Perception and Conception: A Brief Sketch*

We interpret everything we know, and over time different persons and different cultures and our selves, differently. But this does not necessarily mean that these variations have no constraints at all. The human body, I will argue, is uniquely placed to limit the range of these variations. The body itself is, of course, also an object of variable interpretation. But it is in addition the source of all our experience, that without which we could not possibly have any experience of even the least significance. And our body as source of our experience is cross-culturally and trans-historically invariant in the sense that it has not evolved in historical time, so that a naked Pharaonic man would not stand out for us, nor would we stand out nakedly among his crowd. Our idea of the "naked truth" about men and women would differ from theirs, but each of us would see our own truth exhibited in *all* of us. Modern evolutionary biology supports this contention that mankind has not evolved over historical time—that is, in the last five or ten thousand years—and makes it plausible that the species-specific character of the human body may condition all human experience within some broad but definite limits. A phenomenological analysis, I will argue, justifies our current biological belief by demonstrating how our sense of our body plays a basic formative role in our making sense of everything. And not merely in a culturally bound way. For historical knowledge, travel, reading, and imagination show that we can make *some* sense of different cultures. But the level at which our sense of our

---

* An unpublished note dated January 1993.

body enters into our sense-making is such that experience shorn of that body-sense is *unintelligible*. We cannot imagine having any sense at all of things without the participation of some specific body-sense appropriate to the experience of things of that type.

I will try to show this for perceptual objects, which *actually* present themselves to us, and for ideas or concepts, which we represent to ourselves as forms of *possibility*.

Perception is an achievement. It culminates in the determination of what has happened to an object *in* its place *in* our circumstances *in* the general horizontal field of the coming to pass of things *in* the vertical world of our perceptual experience. Perception thus singles out some determinate thing to which we pay attention in a nested context of fields within fields. We keep track of each of these fields in a co-ordinated fashion by virtue of some specific body-sense. The world as the field of all fields of our perceptual experience is sensed through our upright posture as our most general capacity to be up and about as an active percipient. The general horizontal field of the coming to pass of things in the world is sensed in our forward-directed movement to encounter the passing of events. Some particular circumstantial field in the midst of which we find ourselves is sensed through the arrestation of our movement. The location of what is happening at some particular place in our circumstances is sensed in our anticipatory attention directed toward that place as "there" from our bodily "here." The determination of what is going on there is sensed through a skillful bodily response by which the character of the thing is successfully grasped.

Phenomenology has discovered and stressed the contextual nature of perceptual experience as a figure-ground phenomenon in which the subject finds himself or herself situated. This is the core idea in Merleau-Ponty's work, and has become commonplace among philosophers today. All experience, it is now generally believed, is "context-dependent." But this contextuality is generally taken to be thoroughly open-ended, indefinitely variable, so that no form of it is discernible. We have just seen, however, that perceptual contextuality is analyzable as having a definite nested form. Perception is the revelation of what is actually revealed to *our* body with our senses in accordance with the basic forms of our bodily activity. We cannot make sense of *our* perceiving things that present themselves as actually having no determinateness whatever that we could figure out; as actually having no location to which we could attend; as actually not found in some array of locations in a circum-stantial situation in the midst of which we can take a stand in arrested movement; as actually having no place in the train of events that we can face in the course of our forward-directed movement in passing them; or as actually unlocalizable in the vertical world-field of our upright experience. Perception is the experience of what actually presents itself, and it is unintelligible without reference to the fundamental bodily activities that seek, solicit, find, and entertain that presentation as their object. Perceptual objects are thus discerned by the percipient not merely in fact, but *de jure*, as objects custom-tailored by and for him, as objects of, by, and for the body-subject. In this way the body contributes a categorical structure to perceptual objects, not in the Kantian sense of providing *forms for the possibility* of such objects, but by providing *forms of actuality* satisfied by the kind of object that distinctively presents itself as actually existing. Functioning in this way, the body progressively fleshes itself out, determining not merely things but also itself as a being together with them in a common world. Yet the body is never just one thing among others in the perceptual world. In this way, the self-moving, freely responsive percipient constitutes himself not merely as a fact, but as the *factory of all facts* in the perceptual world.

Merleau-Ponty is the first to discern the subject body, to see the body as ineliminable from all perceptual sense, not just causally or instrumentally, but epistemologically, that is, as ineliminable from the intelligibility of all perceptual sense made. Merleau-Ponty, however, only makes a start. In constant battle with his compatriot, Sartre, for whom *all* structure is on the side of the object, and for whom the subject is nothing but empty transparency to the object, Merleau-Ponty manages to salvage only pure motility as an ever-present perceptual content on the "hither" side of the percipient. Every perceptual figure appears on a ground and as soliciting the percipient to explore that ground with further free activity. But because the body proper is not further characterized and fleshed out as we have done, Merleau-Ponty repeatedly slides back into Sartrean formulations such as, "the perceiving subject is the perceived world." He holds in this vein that my subject hand with which I grasp and sense objects cannot itself be sensed. Here again Merleau-Ponty is too influenced by Sartre, though Husserl made the same mistake, in modeling our sense of feeling on our sense of sight. In the act of seeing something, I do not see myself seeing it. To see myself seeing, I must catch sight of myself doing so in a mirror reflection. But then I do not see myself catching the reflections, etc. However, I hold that in the *very act* of feeling something, e.g., feeling a smooth surface by moving my hand across it, I feel myself feeling it. In vision as in thought, in order to catch sight of myself making sense of things, I must do so in a second-order act taking my first as its object. I must do so, in short, reflectively. But feeling is *reflexive*; I make sense of my own making sense of something within the first-order act of sense-making. In feeling in all its forms—tactile, proprioceptively motile, and emotional—the thickly substantive character of the subject body is sensed and fleshed out in ways that Merleau-Ponty and the whole phenomenological tradition overlook.

In our purely visual capacity as inactive spectators, we appear to ourselves as an insubstantial *point* of view on our spectacle—a perspectivally central vantage point around which our scene is displayed. The thickly substantial body of the feeling percipient, in contrast, appears as a *voluminous* center of our phenomenal field, which we move as a whole and from which we deploy our members in a poised and co-ordinated way as sentient expressions and outreaches of a felt voluminous unity of bodily activity. This voluminous unity is felt as the *interiority* of our substantial sentient body. It is not sensed as an "inside," for it is not given as composed of parts outside of parts, like our body laid open to the objective gaze of the surgeon or autopsy examiner. Interiority is absent in things and distinctive of the lived body, as the phenomenon of its organic unity, the phenomenon of the body's all-in-all form of organization, with the structure and function of each member and each disposition implicate in all the others. At the center of our perceptual field of things-outside-of-things composed of parts-outside-of-parts lies our voluminous percipient body as a *central core without a center*.

The Subject Body in Perception and Conception

We are now prepared to consider the second of our topics: how the sense of our body is inextricably involved in our thought, in the conceptions with which we represent to ourselves forms of possibility that may or may not be actually exemplified anywhere at all at any time. How, in short, does our body underlie our mind, not merely causally, but as a sense inseparable from the sense of "mind," so that the idea of a mind is unintelligible without reference to the idea of a body? There is, of course, a mountain of literature that denies this is the case, most notably the work of Descartes but also prominent strains of Platonic, Gnostic, mystic, religious, Kantian, and Husserlian thought. All those who think the mind logically separated from the body regard the body merely as a thing, one object among others in the world discovered by the mind. They have no inkling of the subject body. When the subject body is recognized in its fleshed-out form, we can find *the origin of the mind in the interiority of the percipient body*.

Our skills are inscribed in the flesh of our percipient body as outwardly directed dispositions ready for deployment in grasping objects. As such, they are modifications of our interior readiness. If we inhibit our perceptual activity in its preparatory stage, short of its natural goal in the perception of an object, we bring our sense of the object, as distinct from the object sensed, into prominence as a sensuous abstraction shorn of involvement in the concrete object and its circumstance. Thus the gourmet does not taste to eat but eats to taste, savoring, in a kind of perceptual foreplay, not the food but its flavor. Thus one hears sounds, but listens to music; sees sights, but looks at paintings—remaining in a state of rapt attention by looking-at or listening-to things seen or heard with that attitude of attentiveness normally reserved for looking-for and listening-to things not yet seen or heard. In this aesthetic attitude, we "see" pictorial qualities rather than a colored thing hanging there, and we "hear" tonal qualities rather than things making sounds. Our percipient body's interiority becomes a sensorium, resounding inwardly with purified sensuous qualities derived from actual things around us but held somewhat aloof from them, withheld from full immersion in them, floating free by means of the tentativity of our own involvement with them.

This perceptual inhibition is the initial stage of withdrawal from perceptual involvement in the actual world. In this aesthetic stance, the phenomenal field is drawn back toward its core of interiority. Standing back more completely, in a fully detached manner, we represent to ourselves contents wholly detached from our immediate surroundings and having reference to our general horizon of all possible surroundings. We retreat into our own interiority, drawing on our skillfully digested experience as a whole, constituting ourselves as a sense-world within the world, as the world of our own imagination, in which we freely compose and rearrange representations of possibilities of the outside world, from which we have provisionally withdrawn into solitary meditation, but to which we may at any moment be recalled by any urgent objective signal.

The mind is the interiority of the body as it is made to appear by changing our initial perceptual stance of standing-in the actual world of our circumstances into our conceptual stance of standing-back from the actual world. Through this withdrawal, our outwardly directed interiority is introverted, turned outside-in, as in the ontogenesis of our spinal canal, and we come to dwell on the harvest of our skillful commerce with the actual surrounding world, as food for thought released from the comparatively narrow prejudices of merely factual involvement.

The mind so conceived satisfies Descartes's characterization as an indivisible whole replete with contents, yet not extended in space with parts outside of parts. And it does so without the intractable problems resulting from the counterintuitive divorce of mind from body. On this view, the mind as a sphere of reflective interiority does have a merely external relation to the body as an object, or indeed to any other object, as Descartes saw, but it has an internal relation to the body as subject. The subject body's interiority, whose sense is latent in the sense of a "mind," mediates the mind's relation to the actual world and undercuts the skeptical and solipsistic tendencies and conundrums of mind-body dualism. Wherever mind is, the percipient's body was. *Mind is the introversion of the subject body's interiority.*

Thus, in summary, all sense we can make, whether of what is actual as perceivable or possible as conceivable, draws on our sense of our subject body and is unintelligible without reference to it.

Appendix II

Sensuous Abstraction and the Abstract Sense of Reality*

Theoretical interpretation poses a paradox: it is somehow responsible both *to* and *for* the facts to which it refers, viz., facts consisting of what is shown by interpreted data. The interpretation is responsible to these facts since it may be true or false as fitting or failing to fit the data. Yet the interpretation is also responsible for the facts because interpreted data first gain factual significance (whether properly or misleadingly) by being subjected to interpretation. To be sure, we cannot in practice consider a datum (e.g., the color of a precipitate or the reading of an instrument or punch card) strictly by itself, apart from all interpretation. For we would have no stable context in which to identify "this" datum again and again over the course of one or more experiments. But we can distinguish the datum from its interpretation for purposes of understanding it as a datum even though we cannot do so for purposes of treating it as an objective event. So considered, apart from all interpretation, an interpretable datum is a purely qualitative presence (or, by extension, the record of such a presence). It is the presence of a nonqualifying quality. As such it has two striking features. First, it is thoroughly clear evidence, but it is evidence of nothing in particular. It is uninformative evidence pointing to no conclusion. It testifies not to elementary facts but to no facts at all. In short, apart from its interpretive context, it is unintelligible as a too-pure form of evidence. But the scientific datum, considered by itself, is

---

* This essay was published in James M. Edie., ed., *New Essays in Phenomenology: Studies in the Philosophy of Experience* (Chicago: Quadrangle Books, 1969).

equally unintelligible in a second respect, viz., as a too-isolated form of presence. That the theoretician is presented with certain data rather than others appears as a "brute" fact into which no insight is possible. Theory, of course, makes the internal relations in the body of evidence taken as a whole remarkably lucid. The data as a whole are strictly explicable as precisely coherent. The favorable comparison of theory to unaided perception in this respect is so widely recognized and honored as to be platitudinous. But a price is paid for this advantage, a price that goes generally unnoticed. *What* the facts are is made luminous by theory. But *that* these are the facts is plunged by theory into a darkness just as extraordinary as the light shed on their nature. Even a body of theoretically understood data remains a body of evidence for brute facts that we understand might just as intelligibly have been quite otherwise. Our hypothetical way of conceiving the given facts makes plain that they might equally conceivably have been quite different.

So in theoretical data pure qualitativeness is associated with brute givenness. Theoretical interpretation overcomes the former limitation by assigning to data a factual significance. But the latter limitation is not overcome; theoretical facts remain brute facts. There is something objectively unsatisfying about this. Philosophers have perennially sought to peek behind this "facade" of brute facticity to discover, like Leibniz, some sufficient reason for the facts being just as they are, or, like Plato and Descartes, some self-evidently necessary principles from which they follow. Nonphilosophers have been equally tenacious in seeking to understand the seemingly brute facts of life as deliverances of some God or Fate or Destiny working secretly behind the scenes of experience, though they avoid the question of the brute facticity of these agents themselves, these supposed puppeteers of existence. But many philosophers, like Hume, and many tough-minded nonphilosophers have insisted that whether it is satisfying or not, the existence of what exists, the existence of this world rather than some other, is unintelligible. Like it or not, facticity *is* brute facticity. This latter view is shared by all those who believe that all real or responsible knowledge of matters of fact is scientific knowledge.

Ordinary noncontrolled experience offers some reason to doubt this conclusion of scientism. To be sure, sometimes in the course of uncontrolled experience things appear as they do in science to be the brute facts of the matter. The facts in such cases may be reasonably clear. They may even display a consistent pattern such that any few are readily placed in light of the others. Still, in such cases, it seems strikingly unfathomable that the facts are just these rather than some others. We are struck at such moments not with our ignorance of why things are as they are but with our knowledge of the intrinsic unintelligibility of things being just as they are. But normally in our uncontrolled experience things appear somehow to be "naturally" there; the semiautonomous facts of our local situation do not appear to be "brutely" given. One must first adopt or fall into a special unnatural attitude in order that it come to appear startling, surprising, inexplicable that one's local situation happens to be the way it is rather than some other way. The very abnormality of this attitude renders the appearance suspect.

In particular, one must "step back" from one's situation through an inhibition or destruction of interest and involvement in order that the appearance of brute facticity pervade uncontrolled experience. With moderate inhibition or disillusionment, one's surroundings appear "curious" and perhaps "interesting" as an object for disinterested scrutiny. Severe disengagement, however, makes one's situation appear "strange" and even repulsively alien, so that its special character ceases to be noticed and tends to be submerged in the sheer obtrusive *presence* of the unwanted and not otherwise differentiated situation. Only extreme disaffection of this sort produces shocked awareness and surprised questioning such as, "What am I doing here (rather than elsewhere)?" "Why am I alive (anywhere) at all?" "Why here, not there?" "Why now, not then?" "Why me, not another?" "Why this, not that?" In sum, "Why are things the way they are rather than some other way?" Or, in the limit of disaffection from reality, "Why is there anything rather than nothing at all?" Under such conditions of abnormal disengagement, the fact or facts of one's personal life do take on the air of brute facts. But with normal concern and hope, and with the resulting normal degree of participation, the fact and facts of daily life do not seem arbitrary and surprising.

So the sense of brute facticity is normal in scientific understanding and abnormal in the everyday understanding of reality. Which sense of reality is more fundamental, which more to be trusted? Is our everyday sense merely an unreliable impression, or our theoretical sense merely an elegant fiction? Both senses of reality seem too weighty to be discarded. One is right at this point to be at least as perplexed about such questions as about their answers. For the connection between the brute facticity of science and the brute facticity of ordinary disillusionment is not yet made sufficiently clear to demonstrate any conflict or contrast between the norms of scientific and ordinary understanding. The brute facticity of science is bound up, as we have seen, with the abstractness of its data. But ordinary disillusionment seems to have nothing to do with abstraction. So perhaps its brute facticity is not significantly related to that of science. Perhaps the "natural" facticity of normal (as contrasted to disillusioned) experience is quite compatible with "brute" facticity in the specifically theoretical sense. The matter is decidable only by discovering how sensuous abstractions are produced; how we turn from perceiving things of a certain sort to entertaining just their sort, just the qualities they display.[1] For the question whether there is a significant link between the two modes of brute facticity is the question whether there is some function clearly related to ordinary disillusionment and also clearly essential to sensuous abstraction.

I shall try to show that such a function does exist. The pervasive appearance of brute facticity in ordinary experience is effected, as we have seen, by a comparatively rough or complete disengagement from one's situation. Sensuous abstractions with their air of brute givenness are effected, I shall argue, by a mild, incomplete, and delicately controlled inhibition of the perception of the particular object having the abstracted sense-quality. The "standing back" that produces sensuous abstractions is not the spontaneous total disengagement of a Husserlian or Kantian transcendental attitude, which is required rather for the theoretical interpretation of these previously formed sensuous abstractions. Nor is it the forced total disengagement effected by a loss of reality that for early Heidegger discloses the pure sense of what is lost. It is rather a "standing back" of the *bodily* man who remains, however tentatively, in touch with his real material rather than detached from it. Conceptual abstractions are formed by the transcendental subject, but sensuous abstractions are formed by the embodied subject in the world, viz., the percipient.

Perception normally has three stages: (1) In the first stage we prepare our self to perceive an object by getting into a proper position or attitude in respect to it. For example, we reach toward something so as to be able to touch it; we place something in our mouth so as to be able to taste it; we sniff to smell; we look and listen for something in order to see and hear it. (2) Having prepared our self to perceive it, we next ready the object to be perceived. This is done by "getting at" the object in some essentially preliminary, tentative, and easily reversible way that allows us with comparatively light consequences to go on to perceive the object fully. For example, we touch something preparatory to taking hold of it; we taste before eating; we get a whiff of something before smelling it by taking in a deep breath; we look at or listen to something in order to see or hear it. (3) In the third stage we finally perceive the object. We finally "get" what we have "gotten at." We finally receive what we have made receivable by establishing an affinity between our readied self and our correspondingly prepared object. Thus eating is the consummation of tasting what we have put in our mouth; getting hold of something is the fulfillment of having reached for and touched it; seeing is the fruition of looking at something looked for; hearing is the successful outcome of listening to something listened for. The second stage, getting-at things, gives us evidence for tentative conclusions. But the real nature of the object is not fully established until the third stage of getting the thing itself. Taste is a guide; but the proof of the pudding is in the eating.

So perception is a form of motivated objectification having a natural terminus. But man is no more a slave to his nature in perception than in his other affairs. We make a frequent, enjoyable, and highly significant practice of holding back the course of perception so as to prevent its natural completion. We indulge in a kind of perceptual foreplay, stimulating our senses for stimulation's sake without regard to their natural end of consummation in the founding of an objectified reality. The sensualist makes this practice a way of life. As a gourmet, he does not taste to eat but eats to taste. Such preliminary tasting, when done unnaturally for its own delightful sake, is called "savoring." Similarly the unnatural sensualist-lover concentrates as long as he can on the dallying touch. Nor is the method restricted to the practical arts of the contact-senses of hand and mouth. It is equally central to the fine arts of the distance-senses of sight and hearing. Not only the grossest sensualists but also the most refined do it. For sight and hearing, the method is practiced by retaining attitudes of looking and listening even after what is sought presents itself. Thus one hears sounds, but *listens to* music. And one sees things, but *looks at* paintings. One remains before a work of art in a state of sustained receptivity that at its fullest is wonder. This state of rapt attention is achieved by looking-at or listening-to things seen or heard with the attitude of attentiveness that is normally reserved for looking-for and listening-for things not yet seen or heard.

In all these cases of skillfully inhibited perception—perception carefully preserved, as it were, in a state of delightfully prolonged adolescence or immaturity—one becomes aware of *qualities* rather than things. Thus we ordinarily taste the food, but the gourmet savors the flavor. We ordinarily feel the thing, but the buyer may lightly stroke the fur to feel not it but its texture. To the aesthetic eye, similarly, a painting is not a material thing like what it is on but a pure surface of visual forms. And music is not listened to as a real sound made by real things but as a pure sound of tones and timbres sounding, as it were, by themselves. Savoring, stroking, looking-at, listening-to, and other forms of inhibited perception are "studied" ways of perceiving because they are ways of bringing out and noticing the forms of things while disregarding the things themselves.

So perception is a systematically achieved outcome of a multistaged effort, and sensuous abstraction is founded on the inhibition of this effort. Sensuous abstractions must therefore be deficient in whatever intelligibility comes to experience from the completion of normal perception. What sense does come from the completion of normal perception? "I conceive x" is quite consistent with "X does not exist." The same is true for "I imagine x," "I desire x," "I intend x," etc. "I *perceive* x," however, is inconsistent with "X does not exist." Acceptance of the latter statement requires correction of the former to "I *seem* to perceive x." "I remember x" also implies the (past) reality of x in all cases. But only if x is taken as *my previous consciousness* of something, rather than the thing itself.[2] Thus I may remember imagining y. This implies that I really did imagine y, but it does not imply the (past) reality of y. Perception, I conclude, is essentially and distinctively our knowledge of the *existence* of existing things. Perception is perception of existing things as existing as what they are. This knowledge of the existence of things comes, however, only with the completion of perception and must therefore be lacking in all experience of sensuous abstractions. Since sensuous abstractions in the form of "data" comprise the only scientific evidence of matters of fact, the theoretical sense of facticity must be deficient in the same respect. Sensuous abstractions occur, we have seen, when the normally transient stage of anticipatory presence is maintained. Thus for theory, which understands matters of fact only by way of such abstractions, facticity is understood in terms of the presence of a form (or sort) of possibility. But in perceptually rooted experience facticity is understood in terms of the complete presence of a particular actual thing.

Now the scientist is, of course, also a man. Though his perceptual knowledge cannot be cited as scientific evidence, it remains with him as his primary sense of reality. He understands facticity as brute facticity from a theoretical point of view only because he also understands perceptually that there is more to facticity than he can theoretically comprehend. Specifically he understands that the particularity and actuality of things, in general the "thisness" of things, systematically eludes his abstract comprehension. All perception is the coordinated knowledge of four particular actualities, four "thises": this thing in this local situation in this world as presented to this individual percipient. None of these "thises" is theoretically comprehensible. So theory assigns to "thing," "situation," "world," and "knower" a new sense, which (as the price paid for a wonderfully lucid insight into the nature of things) barters their natural facticity for a brute facticity. (1) The particular thing is understood as a purely logical, rather than real, conjunction of its properties. Its existence is therefore entirely unfounded in its nature. (2) The local situation is the context of relevance in perception; it is the vehicle of perceptual comparison among distinct perceptual objects. The "constancy phenomena" of perception depend on some pervasive character of the local perceptual field as a parameter in respect to which objects may be perceived to vary among themselves. Thus, for example, an object appears to be "bright" because it is *relatively* bright in a given field of illumination. But from a theoretical point of view the autonomy of a particular circumstance is as obscure as the particularity of a single object. So the formalization of things is accompanied by a universalization of their context of relevance. Objects are theoretically interrelated not by constancy phenomena of local range but by formal laws of universal scope. The local situation as a context of relevance *within* the world is simply eliminated. (3) The world is perceived to be "the" world—that is to say, the one and only actual world. It is not perceived to be a sort or kind of world. For a "sort" admits of a variety of possible specifications, and things of a given sort are correspondingly variable. But the world is perceived to be the unconditioned, hence invariant, condition of all variable conditions in the world. Since the actuality and particularity of "this" world are theoretically unintelligible, the real world is conceived as one sort of world among many other equally possible worlds. The actuality of this possibilized world rather than another is then understood as a brute fact—that is to say, as ununderstandable. (4) Perception understands "this world" as the setting of all settings, the context of all contexts. But theory understands "this world" as one specific context among others, viz., the context of possibilities conforming to certain universal laws held to be, in brute fact, true of Nature. The role of the context of all contexts is then assigned to the knower himself in whose mind the various possible worlds are envisaged. But the knower has no content of his own. Theory leaves the existence of the knower's formally all-encompassing mind not merely unintelligible but unacknowledged.

The sensuous abstractness of theoretical data is associated with a bruteness of fact because sensuous abstraction is produced by inhibition of the perceptual consummation in which our intelligible sense of reality is founded. The "natural" contingency of perceptual things and events does not imply that their existence is unfounded but only that it is *locally* founded in a certain highly skillful way.

Appendix III

Anticipatory Postscript*

This is a "postscript" because written 26 years after the bulk of the following text, rewritten here and there only to clarify and flesh out points made in the original. It is an "anticipatory" postscript because it introduces the text, not by a summary of it, which is given in the Introduction, but by offering a glimpse of what the text anticipates as following from it. *The Human Body as Material Subject of the World*, hereafter referred to as *Material Subject*, is about the neglected role of our subject body in our knowledge of things, written at a time when American philosophy was primarily concerned with epistemology. Since then, central concerns have shifted to moral, political and social philosophy, giving rise to views that similarly neglect the crucial role of the subject body. In *Material Subject* I show how conceptualization systematically covers up its origins in the *material* subject, misleading epistemologists to do the same. In this Anticipatory Postscript I will try to indicate how these errors in epistemology and illusions of conceptualization produce flaws in contemporary social philosophy and society itself as the price of a consequent neglect of the *social* subject body. For the social subject, the person, is today an outgrowth of both the material subject, the percipient, and the conceiving mind, as fused in a shared social body, in a manner further indicated in this

---

* This Anticipatory Postscript was written in 1990 for the Garland Press edition of Todes's dissertation, published under the title *The Human Body as Material Subject of the World*. Unfortunately, the sequel mentioned in the text, *The Human Body as Personal Subject of Society*, was never completed.

Appendix III

Postscript. A double cover-up is produced: society covers up, and in doing so arrests the development of, the individual person, who in turn covers up his own percipient body, thereby rendering himself hostage to society as nothing more than a moving image of it. In order sketchily to trace and untie this tangle of developments, so as to help free us in the realization of our personhood, I introduce a *noumenological* method based on the idea of the transformational freedom of the understanding subject. The gist of this noumenological idea will shortly be presented here, as the organizing idea of this Postscript. It will be fleshed out in a sequel, now in progress, *The Human Body as Personal Subject of Society*, hereafter *Personal Subject*. The present text, *Material Subject*, is to be read as a prolegomenon to the sequel that will both presuppose and retroactively clarify it, much as *Material Subject* itself shows perception to be a retroactive determination of what a determinably anticipated object turns out to have been.

Broadly stated, *Material Subject* shows how we must understand perception in its own terms in order to understand the reliability of observations, which accounts for how theory can be responsible *to* rather than merely *for* its data. In *Material Subject* we see how Kant is the first to face this problem seriously, and how he is finally defeated because he fails to catch sight of the percipient as bodily subject.[1] No one has succeeded since, but the problem has at least come to be generally recognized. Theoretically useful observations are evidently so theory-laden that it is no longer clear how data "confirm" our theory; how data are anything more than sophisticated Rorschach blots from which we read out only what we have first interpretively projected and read into them. The traditional correspondence theory of truth is on the defensive, and every notion of realism has become problematic in the philosophy of science. Feyerabend simply dismisses realism and affirms a projectionist theory of truth, but most are perplexed and still searching for a satisfactory resolution that preserves *some* sense of realism.

Social philosophy has reached a similar impasse. We have come to see that persons are heavily characterized by the social norms of the society to which they belong. This is especially true in modern and contemporary society, which has come to regulate, monitor, and standardize our behavior in ever greater detail. This social influence is so pervasive in customary practice and so interiorized in the governance of our thoughts, that it comes to seem we *are* no more than modulations of our society. The traditional democratic and even feudal idea that government is supported *by* and responsible *to* flesh and blood individuals, whose needs it must meet, as well as being responsible to some extent *for* what happens to them, is thrown in doubt. If all of us and all our institutions are governed and constituted by a single cohesive set of social norms, the very idea of individuals, as *sustaining* society and bearing its harsh or satisfactory *consequences,* is made incoherent. Individuals come to seem hardly more than "data" of their technologized society. And just as we have lost sight of how data can confirm or disconfirm a theory in whose light they are first intelligible, so we have lost sight of how the quality of individual lives can prove, as satisfactory, or disprove, as harsh, the validity of a social order in whose light the conduct of these lives is first rendered intelligible. The socialization of individuals has become so thoroughly complete that no standards remain by which we can judge society and critically evaluate it. Society is whatever it is; all applicable standards are but part of what it is.

The work of Michel Foucault depicts this contemporary situation. The spirit of his work protests it. But the content of his work simply displays it. What we can do about it is left to be seen, with the caveat that we do not presently appear able to do anything at all. At present we cannot help sadistically inflicting socialization in every pore of our being, while at the same time wincing in helpless masochistic rebellion against the outrage we have ourselves brought upon our own primordial flesh, reduced to the prime matter, *the brute sensing datum,* of technologized society.

Derridaean deconstructionists, especially the American variety, those scavengers of destructive skepticism—to be sharply distinguished from critical skeptics, like Montaigne—meanwhile flock to devour the dying body of traditional social values. Like Feyerabend in philosophy of science, they celebrate projectionism: the idea that nothing is intelligible but interpretations, which themselves are not of or for any not-purely-interpretive reality, but only of other interpretations, and for further interpretability, without end. At once playfully anarchic in rebellion against all authoritative ideas, and contemptuously de-meaning them in calculatedly reckless abandon of all established standards of interpretation, deconstructionists make equal room for every conceivable interpretation. They gleefully vaporize every presumption of social reality, turning it into a cloud of interpretation. Whereas Foucault presents us with the painful dilemma of individuals disappearing and taking with them the grounds for social criticism, Derrideans dance on the grave of responsible social criticism and prepare the ground for anything-goes, wherever it goes.

These philosophic developments in the recent thought of various philosophers of science, society and culture are not, I believe, coincidental or separately accidental. Western thought, impressed by the achievements of theoretical science in the 17th and 18th centuries, came to identify understanding with theoretical representation, and to construe nature as a theoretical object. Technological advances in the 19th and 20th centuries have so transformed our social life that we have increasingly come to understand society and *ourselves* purely rationally. The earlier shortcoming in our understanding of things as purely theoretical objects, which involved a flaw merely in our epistemology, as oblivious to our primary bodily understanding, has thus grown, as I will try to indicate, into the far more dangerous error of a way of life oblivious to its pre-reflective roots from which socialized rationality grows, on which it continues to draw, and to which it is intrinsically meant to return, bearing not only instrumental goods and services, but also the form of necessary freedom and understanding whose realization is definitive of the individualized embodied person, and impossible without impersonal socialized rationality.

The noumenological idea of the transformational freedom of the understanding subject

Judgment is an exercise of freedom. *We* decide, only if we are *free* to decide. Otherwise, the matter is decided for us, not by us. If we are free to decide, and we do decide under these conditions, then we are also free *in* our decision. For example, if we have to judge whether the universe will go on expanding indefinitely or start contracting at some point, we assemble the relevant available information, in light of the best available theory, and balance the likelihood of one outcome against the likelihood of the other. If we must judge whether a human foetus is a person, we again do so by balancing the strengths of the opposing arguments. We may be intimidated into behaving in accordance with one or another judgment, even constrained as to what issue we are forced to judge, but we cannot be forced to make a certain determinate judgment of an issue rather than some alternative one. For then the balance of judgment would be rigged, the issue not truly weighed, and only a pretension of judgment made. Such a "false" judgment, as extracted for example in a false confession made under duress, is not false as distinct from true—for what is said may well be true—but false in form, as a counterfeit rather than genuine judgment, as an utterance merely counterfeiting a judgment. Similarly, if a mugger threatens us, "your money or your life!," we are forced to address ourselves to this practical issue, and to take a certain course of action, but our doing so, by actually taking out our wallet and handing it to the mugger, is freely undertaken and executed by the free self-movement of our body, under these intimidating circumstances. Otherwise, if even our movement were unfree, the mugger would not force us to do anything, for we would not have done anything, we would not have moved at all. Our wallet would simply have been removed from us, perhaps by way of our protecting arm being moved and our grip being forced open, by the mugger. Nonreflex movement, like judgment, exists only as an exercise of freedom.

The text of *Material Subject* shows that the freedom of rational judgment is based in the free self-movement of perceptual judgment. For freedom in making any judgment, as freely coming to some conclusion, presupposes freedom *in undertaking* to exercise judgment by raising the issue for critical review.[2] We cannot come to any rational conclusion in the sciences, for example, without first rationally setting up controlled experiments and assembling relevant data to prepare the mental scene for making a rational judgment on the basis of reliable information. When judgment is made on the basis of given determinate material, such as reliable data, undertaking to make a judgment presupposes a prior free judgment that yields the given material as its result. This in turn presupposes freely undertaking to make that judgment, etc. This ordered set of free acts presupposed in any judgment continues till

Appendix III

we come to the original undertaking of judgment whose completion in making a judgment gives us our original determinate material. The text of *Material Subject* shows that this original material is a perceptual object determined by a perceptual judgment as the outcome of a specific, finite, ordered set of free bodily movements by which this judgment is originally undertaken.

Our original freedom, exercised in undertaking and making a perceptual judgment, is a *freedom of movement* of our percipient body as a self-moved mover. Our rational freedom, undertaken and exercised with a body of ideas, is a *freedom of productivity* through which we produce the very body of ideas we bring to bear in our determination of rational objects, which are not merely discovered to be already there, like perceptual objects, but are themselves formed by the application of our theoretical and practical ideas in the making of a rational judgment. We do not, of course, produce these rational objects ex nihilo, but only on the basis of evidence in the form of data refined from perceptual results. Still, the "packaging" and identity of these conceived objects, their properties, and the unity of what counts as a particular or singular object, are produced by and relative to the particular body of ideas we bring to bear in undertaking to understand them. Rational understanding is thus doubly productive, as the understanding of objects produced by a produced body of ideas.

Nevertheless, as demonstrated in *Material Subject*, it is as an *identical self* that we freely adopt one or another of these postures, and undertake to situate ourselves either in the perceptual world of our given local circumstances or in the rational world formed by our own global universal interpretations. We migrate freely back and forth between the actual world of our bodily movement and the viewed world produced by our ideas. In doing so, we transform not merely the objects of our understanding, but also the form of our understanding itself, all the while remaining an identical understanding subject.

Our freedom of understanding is thus multiform. We are free to move understandingly in bodily fashion and free to produce understandingly in rational fashion. But we are above all chameleons of freedom, free to undertake either form of understanding we choose—and free also to undertake a final third form of freedom, as we will see. However, though we may freely choose a certain posture or modality in which to practice our freedom, we must always be in one stance or another so far as we stand ready to understand at all, always free to transform our free self but never free-form in our freedom. Our freedom is the *transformational freedom* of our self as understanding subject. It can be developed and widened or arrested and restricted—by accident, history, education or temperament—in its range of available modalities as well as its range of exercise within a given modality. But the capacity for the three ordered modalities of freedom and understanding, as we will see, is definitive of our humanity as the ineliminable destiny of humankind without which we would no longer be human.[3]

But the philosophic tradition, and our social self-understanding as expressed and in turn influenced by this tradition, does not recognize the transformational character of our freedom, and repeatedly ties itself in knots, creating irresoluble dilemmas, by trying to work out the implications of the assumption that our *freedom is univocal*. The only generally recognized form of freedom is *rational* freedom, i.e., freedom to judge rationally and to act in accordance with a law intelligible only to the rational mind. Recognition of the alternative freedom of objective perceptual movement and judgment is not a traditional possibility, since this freedom is a new discovery of *Material Subject,* inspired and first anticipated by the fairly recent work of Merleau-Ponty. Philosophers of all schools have seen that we apprehend objects of very different sorts, from perceivable things to mathematical entities. But they have all held that our way of comprehending them, the structure of our understanding of them, is invariant. Classical, medieval and modern rationalist philosophers hold that we may understand dimly or clearly, but so far as we do understand at all, or at least clearly, we do so rationally. They generally believe this because most of them conceptualize the senses and consider perceptual understanding to be nothing but dim, latent, implicit or confused conception. Even empiricists who sensualize conception generally agree that clear understanding is conceptual, for they regard conception as merely the clear organization of associated perceptions. And even Kant and those post-Kantians who closely study our way of apprehension and recognize that the content of what we find cannot be derived from the form of our finding it, hold that the form of our understanding, while complex, is nevertheless invariant, and that it is dominated by the organization of perceptual material under a concept, something like a Kantian schema or an Husserlian noema, so that our comprehension of perceptual objects is formally identical with our comprehension of all other objects, including, for example, mathematical ones.

The only nonrationalist who is a post-Kantian in the above sense, is Heidegger. He replaces the invariant phenomenological structure of Husserlian consciousness with the equally invariant ontological structure of "existentials." He thereby founds our understanding neither on reason nor on perception but on our formally invariant *manner of social involvement,* within which the subsidiary alternatives of authentically free and inauthentically routine involvement always present themselves. In his later work, he seeks to found our understanding on the gift of some revelatory *Seinsgeschick* that lays down an invariant social form of understanding for a given epoch, implying at once an epochal transformation of our understanding and the ununderstandability of this transformation. Foucault's stress on the disjointed epochal character of our socialized understanding derives from this later Heidegger.

Beginning with Hegel and Marx, dialectical philosophers combine all the foregoing tendencies. They think of perception and conception as inextricably intertwined from beginning to end, the simplest perception fully pregnant with conception, and the most refined conception undetachable from its fully concrete sensible basis, the whole being always already socialized from the beginning of history to its end, continually exhibiting and demonstrating the invariant dialectical logic of the history of human freedom. This social freedom is considered to be already pregnant at the birth of history with its full development, the telos or goal of history that will become clear only at the end of history. Meanwhile, this telos or goal is read back into all experience as the supposedly ever-present invariant sense of free human understanding comprehended ever more clearly over the course of history.

This 19th century dialectical understanding of socialized man as headed toward some apotheosis of freedom, has been replaced in contemporary thought by Foucault's idea of a beheaded history whose merely epochal and disjointed transitions stamp socialized man with

Anticipatory Postscript

a merely provisionally invariant form of understanding, a form invariant for the time being. This development from the idea that human freedom and understanding are absolutely invariant, to the idea that they are merely provisionally invariant, is a decisive step toward the noumenological idea being presented here that they are transformationally variant, as *Material Subject* and *Personal Subject* argue, with pre-social forms in the percipient and imaginative individual, purely social forms in the impersonally socialized individual, and post-social forms in the personalized individual, allowing at all levels for variation within certain very broad limits.

This richly variegated tradition of rationally, dialectically, ontologically and epochally univocal freedom has managed to retain its dominance despite its history of begetting irresoluble dilemmas that constitute a reductio ad absurdum of its basic premise, and presage its imminent dissolution.[4] If there is only *one level of freedom* and we participate in *two worlds*, viz., those of nature and reason, then any account of freedom must truncate the person, enslaving one half to the other. Human understanding must be viewed as either natural *or* rational, either empirical *or* transcendental, either amoral *or* moral, either unfree *or* free, being in each instance "really" situated in one way despite a plethora of allegedly misleading evidence to the contrary. We are supposedly forced to choose between the heteronomy-from-below of an imperial Humean sensibility and the heteronomy-from-above of an imperial Kantian rationality. As in a Kantian antinomy, the best argument for each side is the reductio ad absurdum of the sweeping claims of the other. The only sensible conclusion from this interminable historical debate is that reason is part of the core of humanity, somehow beholden to sensibility, yet inexplicable by sensibility alone. Since we migrate freely between reason and sensibility, emigrating and immigrating at will and bi-locating with maturity, all the while retaining our identity, there must be *two levels of freedom freely translatable into one another*, accounting for the co-operation of our two natures in a single self capable of making itself whole. *Personal Subject* will show how the natural freedom of self-movement does not oppose the moral freedom of socialized self-determination, but rather promotes it and enables it finally to take root and be realized in the world.

These antinomies of reason and sensibiliity at the heart of traditional philosophy are today regarded as old-fashioned, for they assume a distinction between reason and sensibility that is denied now that both are seen to be fused in contemporary social practice. Socialization does indeed fuse them, radically so in its contemporary technological form. But without understanding *how* this is done, we lose sight not only of the original human material *from* which we are socialized, but also of the personalized individual who finally develops himself out of impersonal society as the end *for* which society exists. This double blindness, to both the alpha and the omega of human life, produces the distinctive mark and signature of contemporary thought: our being stranded in the midst of impersonal social norms whose provenance and destiny are manifestly unfathomable.

Material Subject provides the basis that *Personal Subject* will develop to analyse the beginning and end stages of human understanding in relation to the middle in which we now find ourselves stuck. For example, to indicate the sort of thing that needs to be done along these lines, it is now generally recognized that we cannot comprehend contemporary morality, bound up as it is with codified thought and principles, until we can somehow connect principled thought *intrinsically* with what has been variously called the "experience," "sensibility," "human nature," "human interests," or "human needs" to which it is responsible and meant to apply. But the many attempts to make this connection between morality and human experience, interests or needs *in general*, whatever they may turn out to be, have proven fruitless. The program seems right, but its execution produces no insight. It turns out that if we already know the content of the moral law, and how to think and communicate in principled fashion, we can then find the form and content of accepted morality more or less compatibly intertwined in our normalized social practice. Social normalization does somehow bring off the fusion of thought and sensibility in terms of human needs, but it does not show on its face how this is done, displaying merely the result while covering up the procedure.

Personal Subject will show how a more specific analysis is more productive. Our moral sensibility testifies to an internal connection between morality and *verticality*. Metaphors of verticality are unavoidable in moral intuition. This unavoidability bears witness not only to the general grounding of moral sensibility in motivated perceptual experience, but also to the *specific locus* of this grounding. We "look up" to the principles and practice of virtuous and moral behavior as "higher," and "look down" on vice and immorality as "lower" and "low-down" forms of behavior, while perfect justice reigns in Heaven "above" and pure evil in the nether-world of Hell "below." Empiricist utilitarians, who are at home on the ground of everyday sensible experience, and do not believe in the independent authority of a higher court of reason, tend to ignore the prevailing metaphor of verticality. But rationalist moralists, who do believe in the supremacy of principled behavior, while also ignoring verticality in formulating their theories—for no perceptual content can be normative *in* thought, which reduces all such content to data incorporated into a more comprehensive order of ideas—tend nevertheless to refer to it rhetorically in describing their inspiration for their moral conceptions. Is it really just coincidental that rationalist philosophers looked *up* for their inspiration in formulating their conceptions of guiding ideas of conduct and thought, Plato and Kant to the starry sky above, and Descartes to the ceiling as he lay in bed originating the Cartesian co-ordinates of a productively a priori geometry?

In *Material Subject* I show how our original sense of being in the world, our sense of being in a world before time, is our sense of verticality given by standing erect and balanced in the gravitational field of earthly existence. I then show how this elementary subject body is developed in specific stages, culminating in the perceptual understanding of a determinate perceptual object; and how this developed subject body underlies a pre-social individual mind that differs from it through a systematic transformation of our sense of verticality. *Personal Subject* will show more specifically how the exteriorization of the interiority of a completely developed subject body effects the transformational development of an individual mind; how the close, intimate encounter of developed bodies effects the transformational development of a shared social body, initially a family; and how specific further transformations, drawing on both individual minds and shared social bodies, produce a shared social mind whose full development is characteristic of contemporary technological society with its principled legalistic morality. With the development of a social mind, the imaginative transformation of verticality that inaugurated the individual mind is socialized. As our erect stance gave us our original sense of actually being in the natural world, our *possibility* of upright principled conduct comes to give us our sense of being in a moral social world. The fully developed shared mind of contemporary technologized society radicalizes this sense of social being. The fully literate society around us now demands codified conduct not only for high standing, but even for *membership* in it. If we do not *actually* manage such conduct most of the time, we are social and moral illiterates. As such, we are not merely lowly members of society, like traditional sinners or members of a despised underclass, but not members of society at all, merely *resident aliens* in it, like utterly helpless congenital cripples in the natural world. Traditional familial society, and extensions of it, made a place for black sheep, but contemporary fully mentalized society makes room only for white ones.

So the human self is not univocally but transformationally free in its understanding. By "noumenology" I mean the study of the developmental logic of this transformational freedom of the understanding human subject. Noumenology supplements traditional analyses of the stratified kinds of known objects with a correlative stratification of our ways of knowing them. Whereas traditional orderings of things known operated within a single, e.g. rational, modality of understanding, the idea of noumenology implies that understanding itself changes form understandably. Since understanding is essentially free, this understandable transformation of understanding must also be free, hence a self-transformation of the knower by the knower, for a free change is a self-made change. Our original freedom as the bodily freedom of free self-movement is familiarly transformational *within* its form. Dance is the exploration and celebration of these transformations in their own terms. But reason *canonizes* freedom. A given theory may be true or false, one cannot tell by its form alone, but it cannot possibly be either unless it meets certain criteria of a "well-formed" theory. Likewise, proposed societal rules, regulations and laws, whether moral, procedural, civil or criminal, may vary in content, but must meet certain formal standards in order to be even considered for adoption. A developed body of ideas exists in only one form if it is effectively deployable—on data or in practice—at all. Reason has only one effective stance, viz., for deployment on material synoptically presented before it with a high degree of precision and contextual completeness. Reason, as compared to perception, is both literally and figuratively *phenomenally free* to vary its content, but constrained to be *uniform* rather than multiform in its form. So the very idea of noumenology is doubly based in an understanding of the human body: since the transformational freedom of our understanding originates in the free movement of our perceptive body, all forms of our understanding are functions of our body, however transformationally remote; and our original bodily understanding is itself transformational in form, replete with many mutually translatable effective stances.

Understanding assumes three main stances, an ordered triad of basic postures. Each stance noumenologically presupposes those out of which it sensibly and sensically develops, and back into which it may always revert. But no stance initially implies, as sensibly foreshadowing, those into which it may turn out to have been able to develop. Such further development is always a creative discovery produced by a free response to completion and arrestation at the preceding stance. Generally stated, these three stances are: the *standing-up* of perceptual bodily understanding, which is analyzed in *Material Subject*; the *standing-back* of imaginative mental understanding, which is partially analyzed in *Material Subject* and considerably fleshed out in *Personal Subject*; and the *standing-for* of social understanding, which is first analyzed in *Personal Subject*. The end of social life is to fuse the divergent stances of standing-up and standing-back into the whole-some stance of standing-for. Standing-for begins with social identification as openly-standing-for-the-social-whole in the openness of the open behavioral field of society; it ends with closure in the close, standing-for the social whole in standing by the near and dear, the personally close.

The stances of understanding are transformations rather than variations of one another because they bring about or effect understanding in different ways, which constitute different *modalities* of understanding, each with its own modes. (1) Perceptual understanding is effected by actual *movement* centered in our being up and about, and ending in the determination of a perceptual object as actually there. As such, *perception is the form of actuality*. It is seen in *Material Subject* as arising out of actual need; as guided, when not aimless, by desire, the fallible feeling that we actually need something in particular; as completed in the perception of an actual determinate thing that might be needed; and as retained in memory, either in short-term memory as the lingering actual perception of the recent past, or in long-term memory as the stored actual perception of the distant past. (2) Imaginative or mental understanding is effected by the *production* of productive ideas, beginning with fantasizing, and ending with the formulation of objective ideas, which may or may not be true of actual objects. As such, *imagination is the form of possibility*. It is directed upon memory and desire in fiction; upon pure-face data in theoretical understanding;[5] and upon pure-facing activity in planning. (3) Social understanding is effected by the *realization* of significant ideas through their productive embodiment in actual movement. Social understanding is completed in rooted personal understanding, in which significant actuality follows from possibility alone. Once this significance is personally realized, we can no longer concretely imagine our life without it; the once-realized significant idea so captivates us by so completely organizing our life around it—in relation perhaps to other significant ideas forming a web of significance—that we cannot imagine what our life would be like without it, because we cannot conceive, plan or even fantasize any specific order in our lives without reference to it. An actual life without it comes to seem impossible for us; this significance rather becomes that possibility *from* which our life draws its actuality as livable. The once-realized significance is henceforth part of the "backbone" of our life, connecting the "head" of our mentality to the "legs" of our percipience. As culminating in an actuality following from its compelling possibility alone, *social understanding is the form of necessity*. Sheer or brute necessities of actual survival are instinctively rather than freely governed and realized, forming the boundaries within which freedom is possible.[6] Within these absolute boundaries, the significant necessities of rooted personal understanding are first made possible by governing impersonal social ideals; they are partially realized by society in ritualized institutional embodiments of these ideals; and wholly realized by individualized persons: in time, as captivated by a chosen significant life's work, in a vocation; in space, as made at home at a chosen significant place, in a home; in society, with a chosen significant few with whom we become our true selves, in true friendship.

Possibility, actuality and necessity, as modalities of rational understanding, are all subsidiary forms of the understanding of possibility. But rational understanding, in its seemingly bodiless stance as disinterested—not uninterested and passionless, but passionately dispassionate—is transfixed by its ideal object and blind to its bodily origin and destiny, to which it must be transformationally awakened by the individual thinker, perhaps at the prompting of some urgent circumstance. Otherwise, rational deliberation mesmerizes itself, as in a Socratic trance, into believing it can discern not merely the possibilities of actuality and necessity, but also actualities and necessities themselves. Traditional rationalist philosophy, accordingly, never catches sight of the understanding body, and regards reason as an original form of understanding founding and upholding itself. Hence, it regards actuality, the form of perception, as derivative from possibility, the form of reason; and since reason is supposed to be self-founding, possibility is in turn perenially traced to some supposedly original rational necessities. These purported necessities take the form of supposedly primary and self-evident laws of thought, supposedly primary and self-evidently final goals of action, or gods as supposedly primary and necessary rational beings on whose existence our own rational being is held to be necessarily founded. But reason is here an imposter, supposing, as Kant saw, what it cannot deliver. Rationality as such is beholden to actuality from which it refines the idealized and problematicized data it means to interpret. And it contains only mediating necessities that establish merely the *possibility* of necessary realization, in the form of a *promise* that may or may not be fulfilled or even fulfillable by given individuals, for whom these supposed necessities may, unbeknownst to rational society, or even intentionally, prove to be *im*possibilities, effectively *ex*cluding them from personal realization in significant freedom.

Thus noumenology reverses the traditional rationalist modal order. From a rationalist point of view, the stratification of objects of understanding depicts actuality as a delimitation of possibility founded in turn on necessity. The goal of ideal understanding is to see all actualities as following completely from possibilities established by necessity alone. Such is the rational kingdom of heaven. But from a noumenological standpoint, actuality is seen to be our original form of understanding, from which possibility arises, and to which necessity finally returns bearing and realizing significant possibility. We originate in the self-actualization of our perceptive body in the actual world, die the death of reason in the self-idealization of our bodiless mind, and finally return to our original world resurrected in the perfected body of an interiorized life of a rooted person who has found his own true place in the world, an extraordinary part significantly greater than the whole for which he stands.

Notes

Introduction I: Todes's Account of Nonconceptual Perceptual Knowledge and Its Relation to Thought

1. John McDowell, *Mind and World* (Cambridge: Harvard University Press, 1994), 46.

2. Maurice Merleau-Ponty, *Phenomenology of Perception*, trans. Colin Smith (New York: Humanities Press, 1962), 49–50.

3. John R. Searle, *Intentionality* (Cambridge, England: Cambridge University Press, 1983), 90.

4. "Poise," which usually describes a static stance, is a rather misleading term for the way skilled perceivers move successfully to lower the tension produced in them by the indeterminacy or disequilibrium in their perceptual field. The reader must always keep in mind that, for Todes, poise is a characteristic of skillful *activity*.

5. Merleau-Ponty sees this phenomenon but doesn't draw out the epistemological consequences.

6. For details, see Hubert L. Dreyfus, "A Merleau-Pontian Critique of Husserl's and Searle's Representationalist Accounts of Action," *Proceedings of the Aristotelian Society*, 2000.

7. Although the structure of the spatiotemporal field depends on the structure of the lived body, Todes is no idealist. In Introduction II, Piotr Hoffman shows how the fundamental phenomenon of balance, which is so close to us that no previous phenomenologist has described it, enables Todes to avoid the antirealism that threatens the philosophies of both Heidegger and Merleau-Ponty.

8. Aron Gurwitsch coined this expression. Todes uses the term on p. 196.

9. The indeterminacy of perceptual objects and their dependence on various situational and bodily capacities is argued for in detail in Sean D Kelly, "The Nonconceptual Content of Perceptual Experience: Situation Dependence and Fine-

ness of Grain," forthcoming in *Philosophy and Phenomenological Research* (with a response by Christopher Peacocke).

10. I owe this way of putting the point to Sean Kelly. See his "What Do We See (When We Do)?," *Philosophical Topics*, vol. 27, no. 2 (Fall/Winter 1999).

11. McDowell, *Mind and World*, 57. "We can ensure that what we have in view is genuinely recognizable as a conceptual capacity if we insist that the very same capacity to embrace a color in mind can in principle persist beyond the duration of the experience itself." McDowell doesn't speak of "reidentification." However, Sean Kelly argues that McDowell's "recognitional capacity" gives rise to a reidentification criterion. The reidentification criterion states that, for a subject to possess a concept of an object or property x, the subject must be able consistently to reidentify a given object or property as falling under that concept if it does. See Kelly's "Demonstrative Concepts and Experience," unpublished paper, University of California, Berkeley.

12. Maurice Merleau-Ponty, "The Film and the New Psychology," in *Sense and Nonsense,* trans. Hubert L. Dreyfus and Patricia Allen Dreyfus (Chicago: Northwestern University Press, 1964), 51. Merleau-Ponty develops this Gestalt account of the "synasthesia" of perception in *Phenomenology of Perception* (see esp. 229 and 313) and in "Cézanne's Doubt" in *Sense and Non-sense*. There he says: "Cézanne said that one could see the velvetiness, the hardness, the softness, and even the odor of objects. My perception is therefore not a sum of visual, tactile, and audible givens: I perceive in a total way with my whole being; I grasp a unique structure of the thing, a unique way of being, which speaks to all my senses at once" (50).

13. Samuel J. Todes, "Sensuous Abstraction and the Abstract Sense of Reality," in James M. Edie, ed., *New Essays in Phenomenology* (Chicago: Quadrangle Books, 1969), 19, 20.

14. If the spectator were to assume an even more detached attitude, from outside the world, so to speak, as an impressionist painter does, the object would be isolated from the context it shares with other objects. Then, the object's qualities would lose their perceptual constancy. What one would then see is captured by Monet's paintings of the Rouen cathedral at various times of day. The painter shows how the cathedral's purely spectatorially perceived color-qualities change with changes in the color of the illumination.

15. This important qualification is part of Todes's argument that, although neither of the two modes of intelligibility he distinguishes can be reduced to the other, embodied perception is more basic than disembodied thought. I cannot, however, deal with this important issue within the space of this Introduction.

Introduction II: How Todes Rescues Phenomenology from the Threat of Idealism

1. S. Todes, *The Human Body as Material Subject of the World* (New York and London: Garland Publishing 1990). In the text, the following abbreviations will be used: BT: M. Heidegger, *Being and Time*, translated by J. Macquarrie and E. Robinson

Notes to pages xxix–xxxv

(New York: Harper & Row, 1962); PP: M. Merleau-Ponty, *Phenomenology of Perception* translated by C. Smith (London: Routledge and Kegan Paul, 1962).

2. I am not speaking here of what has come to be known as the "late" Heidegger (after the *Kehre*), or the "late" Merleau-Ponty (of *The Visible and the Invisible*). For if, in those later periods of their development, both thinkers made significant moves beyond the idealistic implications of their earlier positions, they both did so at the price of abandoning the evidence, and the foundational status, of human subjectivity by subsuming it under a mysterious *Seinsgeschick* or *chiasme*. It is the strength of Todes's account that he avoids the pitfalls of idealism, without abandoning the phenomenologically accessible perspective of a lived, experiential reality of human subjects.

3. See, for example, A. de Waelhens, *La philosophie de Martin Heidegger* (Louvain: Editions Nauwelaerts, 1942; 5th ed., 1957), esp. pp. 309, 316. Recently, the charge has been renewed, and argued skillfully, by William D. Blattner in his *Heidegger's Temporal Idealism* (Cambridge: Cambridge University Press, 1999), esp. pp. 251–253.

4 For what follows immediately see BT, 38–40

5. M. Heidegger, *The Basic Problems of Phenomenology* (1927), translated by A. Hofstadter (Bloomington: Indiana University Press, 1982), p. 166.

6. Ibid., p. 170.

7. M. Heidegger, *History of the Concept of Time* (1925), translated by T. Kisiel (Bloomington: Indiana University Press, 1985), pp. 196–197. The first emphasis is mine.

8. Heidegger, *Basic Problems of Phenomenology*, pp. 168–169.

9. Ibid. p. 169

10. *Befindlichkeit (Geworfenheit)*. For all this see: M. Heidegger, *The Essence of Reasons*, translated by T. Malick (Evanston: Northwestern University Press, 1969), pp. 81, 83.

11. M. Heidegger, *What Is Metaphysics?* in M. Heidegger, *Basic Writings* (Harper & Row, 1977), p. 105, my emphasis. See also ibid., p. 111: "Only because the nothing is manifest in the ground of Dasein can the *total strangeness of beings* overwhelm us" (my emphasis).

12. Ibid., p. 103.

13. The mystical writer closest to Heidegger was Meister Eckhart, whose writings Heidegger knew thoroughly. Eckhart's idea of the transcendence of God does go so far as to deprive us of the very category of existence in our deepest relationship to God. "These three are far from God: 'good,' 'better,' 'best,' for he is wholly transcendent . . . or if I say that 'God exists,' this is also not true. He is being beyond being: he is a nothingness beyond being." Meister Eckhart, *Selected Writings*, translated by O. Davis (London: Penguin Books, 1994), p. 236. Could Heidegger have accepted some such view in the period of *Being and Time*? No doubt a lengthy and detailed discussion of a few scattered hints would be needed even to articulate the issue properly, and, even more so, to decide whether such

a view would be compatible with the framework of *Being and Time*. It seems that Heidegger took concrete steps to warn us not to understand him in that sense: "our investigation . . . asks about Being itself insofar as Being enters into the intelligibility of Dasein. The meaning of Being can never be contrasted with entities, or with Being as the 'ground' which gives entities support; for *a 'ground' becomes accessible only as a meaning, even if it is itself the abyss of meaninglessness*" (BT, 193–194, my emphasis). It is difficult not to read the last sentence as a gesture against some such view as Eckhart's.

14. PP, 320. See also M. Merleau-Ponty, *The Primacy of Perception*, edited by J. M. Edie (Evanston: Northwestern University Press, 1964), p. 16.

15. For example: "dialogue" (PP, 320), "symbiosis" (PP, 317), "sympathetic relation" (PP, 214), "synchrony" (PP, 211).

16. Merleau-Ponty, *The Primacy of Perception*, p. 16.

17. E. Husserl, *Cartesian Meditations. An Introduction to Phenomenology*, translated by D. Cairns (The Hague: Martinus Nijhoff, 1970), p. 78.

18. See, for example, R. Leakey, *The Origin of Humankind* (New York: Basic Books, 1994), pp. 13–16, 56–57.

19. For both Heidegger and Merleau-Ponty the worldly space stripped of its appropriate orientation would make the circumspective world unintelligible to us; for both Heidegger (BT, 143–144) and Merleau-Ponty (PP, the chapter "Space") the oriented space of the world (with its distinctions of "left-right," "top-bottom," "near-far," etc.) is derived from the spatiality of an embodied self actively involved in the tasks of daily life. While Heidegger's analyses are here no more than hints at a theory, Merleau-Ponty does show in detail how neither an intellectual calculation of distances and directions (the rationalist model) nor an association of some impressions with the impressions of various parts of our body (the empiricist model: say, an association between the impressions of my feet and the impressions of the floor) is sufficient to reestablish a sense of our body's directedness and spatial orientation after various disturbances induced by natural or experimentally created conditions. The body regains the sense of its own spatiality and reestablishes the oriented space of the world by plunging into skillful coping with the daily tasks. Analyses and arguments are offered to show that without the (practically achieved) appropriate position and orientation of the body, nothing at all would be intelligible to us. In some rare passages Merleau-Ponty goes farther and shows how the particular constitution of our bodily frame does condition some (to be sure, rather peripheral) features of experience. For example, the persistent perceptual illusion that the moon on the horizon is much larger than the moon above us is derived from the circumstance that the vertical movement is, for us, strained and artificial, while it is natural for us to move horizontally (PP, 304*n*). Not even this much is made of the inherent asymmetry between our backward- and forward-oriented motion (although, of course, Merleau-Ponty *describes* repeatedly both our motion and our perceptual exploration as forward-oriented); and it often seems as if Merleau-Ponty's body-subject were merely a pure power center (the pure "je peux," as he calls it) connected

with a body-object accidentally endowed with precisely such features as the human body happens to possess. This gap in Merleau-Ponty's account is all the more surprising since it was Merleau-Ponty himself who first demanded that the seemingly "contingent" facts of human bodily constitution be recognized as the necessary conditions of any *conceivable* human experience. "Everything in man is a necessity" (PP, 170); "a handless or sexless man is as inconceivable as one without the power of thought" (ibid.); and "it is no mere coincidence that the rational being is also the one who holds himself upright" (ibid.). But these principles and indications did not find a systematic phenomenological application in the concrete analyses carried out in the *Phenomenology of Perception*.

20. "[T]hrough movement we do not merely notice, but *produce* the spatio-temporal field around us" (49).

21. "[W]hen we are active our front and back generate and acquire a temporal significance. Our front apparently brings into appearance what is *coming* to be because of what we are (forwardly) going to do; it thereby produces the (future) field of what lies ahead. Our back apparently leaves behind what has appeared and thereby produces the apparent field of what is now *passed* (past), so that the front-back body distinction makes possible the passage of time" (49). "Compare: 'passed-past'; 'passé-passé'; 'vergangen Vergangenheit'" (ibid., n.). See also 112–113.

Author's Introduction

1. It is not easy, though, because the forms of our understanding suppose the full complexity of our experience.

Chapter 1

1. *On the Soul*, III, 5.

2. *Nicomachean Ethics*, X, 7.

3. "... I thought that I should ... reject as absolutely false anything (primarily any of the opinions he had himself formerly held) of which I could have the least doubt, in order to see whether anything would be left after this procedure which could be called wholly certain" (*Discourse on Method*, p. 31). The pagination for citations from Descartes is as given in *Oeuvres de Descartes*, ed. Charles Adams and Paul Tannery (Paris: L. Cerf, 1897–1913). Quotations according to the Lafleur translations of the Library of Liberal Arts Press.

4. "Nothing is in the intellect except the intellect itself," *New Essays on the Understanding*, Bk. II, Ch. 1, Section 2.

5. "... other things of which (men) might think themselves more certain (than of the existence of God and of their souls), such as their having a body, or the existence of stars and of an earth, and other such things, are less certain. For even though we have a moral assurance of these things, such that it seems we cannot doubt them without extravagance, yet without being unreasonable we cannot deny that, as far as metaphysical certainty goes, there is sufficient room for doubt"

(*Discourse*, pp. 37-38). Descartes never investigated whether this "moral assurance" might not be founded in a systematically undeniable necessity of some kind that was not purely intellectual; he assumed instead that it was founded in a merely *de facto* incredulity at the perfectly consistent "extravagance" of its denial.

6. *Discourse*, p. 33.

7. Ibid., p. 76.

8. Ibid., p. 18.

9. Ibid., p. 64.

10. *Meditations on First Philosophy*, p. 46.

11. Ibid., p. 64.

12. *Discourse*, p. 34.

13. Ibid., p. 32.

14. *Discourse*, p. 67.

15. E.g., *Meditations*, p. 37.

16. This "failure" is, however, so characteristic of Descartes's system of thought that it is not possible to determine what he would have thought without it. This is not so much a failure *in* his system, which Descartes could have "corrected," as a failure *of* his system as a whole. His system must be generally rejected or transformed insofar as the distinction between a real and a logical ground is upheld.

17. Such an interpretation suggests an explanation of Descartes's claimed fear that publication of his deduction of the first principles of his scientific investigations would encourage clever but hasty people in "building some extravagant philosophy on what they believe to be my principles." Was the extravagance Descartes feared the extravagance of an irrational instead of a rational subjectivity?

18. "If we did not know that all reality and truth within us came from a perfect and infinite Being, however clear and distinct our ideas might be, we would have no reason to be certain that they were endowed with the perfection of being true," (*Discourse*, p. 39.)

19. It is in this vein that Descartes, thinking of man as a fragment of the world, writes, "I am a mean between God and nothingness." Note he does not write, as a Greek theist might, "Between God and a thing in the world."

20. *Meditations*, p. 46.

21. *Discourse*, p. 36.

Chapter 2

1. The validity of algebraic and arithmetic implications, which are for Hume the only valid implications, is based on the relation of equality between two representations of the *same* unit, hence is not an example of a representation implying some other representation; that is, a representation of something *else*. Cf. *A*

Notes to pages 24–38

Treatise of Human Nature, Vol. 1 (London: Everyman's Library, 1939–40), p. 75, hereafter referred to as *Treatise*.

2. *Monadology*, paragraph 6.

3. *Treatise*, p. 248.

4. "God is not the author of His own understanding." *Theodicy*, paragraph 380.

5. The future, not merely the instant, as for Descartes, being included in this "all."

6. God's creation of Monads is, of course, not a creation *in* time, but a creation *of* time.

7. *Treatise*, p. 255.

8. Since for God—and for man, too, insofar as man knows—knowing is willing (judging).

9. *Monadology*, paragraph 7.

10. *Monadology*, paragraph 83.

11. *Treatise*, p. 71.

12. Note the temporal associations of logical inference.

13. He does this, as we will see, in order to find a substitute to take the role of the human body in our experience. For Leibniz had really given up the ordinary human body as playing a crucial role in experience, whereas Descartes had only given it up in theory but still depended upon the metaphor of an "intimate union" of body with mind to explain how perception was a representational "effect" of events taking place outside the human subject.

14. *The Principles of Nature and Grace, Based on Reason*, paragraph 24. All Leibniz quotations are taken from *Leibniz Selections*, ed. Philip P. Wiener (New York: Scribner's, 1951).

15. *Monadology*, paragraph 62.

16. *Monadology*, paragraph 14.

17. Without any additional intervening act of judgement.

18. *Monadology*, paragraphs 26-27. Leibniz's italics.

19. By "logical motivation" I mean that need for the solution of a verbally expressed problem which is produced merely by comprehension of a statement of the problem.

20. *Monadology*, paragraph 14.

21. Ibid, paragraph 15.

22. *The Principles of Nature and of Grace, Based on Reason*, paragraph 3.

23. For clarification, cf. Sections 2.5.1, 2.5.3, and 2.5.8.

24. *Monadology*, paragraph 19.

25. That is, to judge in conformity with the principles of non-contradiction and sufficient reason.

26. Ibid., paragraph 29.

27. Ibid., paragraph 83.

28. Equating both perceptual world and human subject to an Aristotelian organism.

29. *Treatise*, p. 11.

30. Ibid., p. 71.

31. Cf. Section 2.5.11.

32. *Treatise*, p. 184.

33. To the inactive observer, the "visual point of view" *appears* to have an immaterial, disembodied location that coincides with a tactually determinable location more or less in the center of the head, between where the ears can be felt with the hands and between where the forehead and back of the head can be felt with the hands. It is in relation to the position of this point of view that objects appear to the "left" or "right," "above" or "below," "far" or "near."

34. Objects are "external" to ourselves in virtue of being placed away from the point of view from which we regard them; but they are for the same reason "internal" to ourselves in being placed in the field (our "mind") that is organized in reference to this point of view.

35. *Treatise*, p. 185.

36. It was fundamentally Descartes's inability to comprehend the seemingly miraculous experiences of a human subject who "has" his body by being the mover of it that drove Descartes to seek some material instrument *by* which the immaterial mind might, through its will, affect material events. Descartes thought, in effect, that he had found such an instrument in the mind's capacity to alter the angular if not the rectilinear momentum of physical objects. *By* changing the direction of motion of extended objects in motion, the mind was thought to affect physical objects. But direction of motion, and its change was not *itself* a physical condition; it was not supposed by Descartes to "count" in the mathematical reckoning of what was happening in physical processes. The capacity to change at will the angular momentum of material bodies was thus conceived, in effect, by Descartes to be the mind's instrumental body function. However, this view could not have "saved" Descartes's philosophy even if it had not been quickly shattered by the rapid advance of physics in Descartes's day, for it was not comprehensible in terms of Descartes's philosophy how the mind, being utterly devoid of extension, could have *any* effect on extended matter.

37. Obviously, the stick is in my hand. But the point is that the *feeling* of the stick is not in my hand. The stick is felt *with* my hand (or arm) to be raised in my hand.

38. *Treatise*, p. 56.

39. Ibid., p. 46.

40. Compare: "passed"-"past"; "passé"-"passé"; "vergangen"-Vergangenheit."

41. Our sense of time as inactive percipients, and as active percipients of change occurring without motion, is here disregarded, because these senses of time are phenomenologically derivative from our primary sense of time as active percipi-

ents of motive change. The subject will be taken up again in Section 5.0.1, but the following considerations are adduced for the present. In the case of change through motion, the path of change remains apparent *after* the event has taken place. This permits later events to be *perceptually* related to the course of the earlier event. We can thus gain a *perceptual* sense of the earlier event receding into the past. Perceptual time in this case spans a future (of things whose arrival is anticipated); a present (of things actually happening); and a past (of events that have taken their course but left the course itself behind in the perceptual field). The case of change without motion, however (e.g., the case of a blinking light), is quite different. No perceptual trace is left of the course of the blinking. A blink, once blinked, appears utterly "gone." The perceptual time of such change is constricted to an almost specious present of perhaps a second or so. In this case the events alone appear to pass in time; but time itself does not appear to pass. Time appears like a narrow stage of the ever-present; and events, like actors in a pageant, seem to make their appearance, say their piece, and hurriedly exit to make room for their successors. This sense of time is akin to the pure spectator's sense of time. The active percipient's experience of inactive change in the object is in this respect similar to the inactive percipient's experience of active change in the object. Neither of these senses of time can be primary because our full sense of time is of a present bounded by a future and a past, and both our inactive senses of time are bounded on one side by what is simply non-existent, and on the other by what is non-existent because gone. Since our perceptual sense of inactive change tends to restrict our sense of time to the single modality of the present, it is essentially a *simplification* of our temporal sense of time that informs our fully active experience of change. This *tendency* of inactive perception to restrict our sense of time to the present is brought to *completion* in imagination. Inactive perception is thus the way-station between active perception and disembodied imagination.

42. Both are merely "impressions," "ideas," "qualia," "sense data," "phenomena," etc., in the same sense.

43. Mainly, those movements by which we touch them.

44. Or for those things by which we can be reached, possessed or used through movement or motion, e.g., other animals, or missiles.

45. For it is difficult in the last analysis to distinguish, on Hume's view, between regular succession of momentary impressions and "simultaneity" of point-impressions that must be temporally scanned.

46. The *disappearance* of things must be carefully distinguished from their merely *ceasing to appear*. Things disappear when we are unable to meet *any* of our needs with them; they merely cease to appear when we are unable to meet *present* needs with them. We will take up in detail this distinction and its consequences when we come to a detailed analysis of the work of Kant who fails to make this distinction, in effect treating disappearance as ceasing to appear.

47. As, for example, Elie Wiesel approaches doing in *Night* (New York: Hill and Wang, 1960), the moving account of his living death in Auschwitz.

48. Throughout this study, "movement" is always used to mean self-produced movement; "motion" is always used to mean externally-produced transposition. Thus inanimate things, such as stars and stones, are *in motion*, and animals are in motion when they are pushed, or when they fall. But only animals (or other live organisms) can *move*. To speak of the planets as "moving" is to use an animistic metaphor; it is to regard them for purposes of speech as moving themselves, e.g., intelligently. For a person to merely "go through the motions" of doing something, conversely, is for him to do it mechanically, i.e., as if he were an inanimate machine. Animals *move* quickly, but auto-mobiles *go* fast, etc.

49. In these cases, our "movements" do not appear to be produced by ourselves, to be intended by our own bodies; that is, to be poised. Instead, our "movements" appear to be produced in us by things in our circumstances that set off or "trigger" our "responses" —better called "reactions"—in a way beyond our control, as in the movements we make when startled. In awk-ward "movement" we feel the *loss* of control of our movement. Awkward-ness is the loss of real, or self-produced, movement. *Awkwardness is not a kind of movement, but the disappearance of movement.*

50. Literally, much more a motion than a movement.

51. This is the model of directed action that Hampshire employs throughout his book, *Thought and Action* (New York: Viking Press, 1960); see, for example, p. 84.

52. Our ability to localize objects thus demonstrates our ability to store up, rather than immediately consume, all available satisfactions.

53. In doing this, we have followed Heidegger's lead in arguing that the motivational significance of objects of experience is phenomenologically prior to their conceptual, or "objective" significance. We have differed from Heidegger throughout, however, in conducting our analysis wholly in terms of concrete features of the human body, rather than in terms of such abstract properties as "care," "in-ness," "being-there-ness," "thrown-ness," etc.

54. *Treatise,* p. 238.

55. Of course, one's body may appear to vary in sickness or in health, in effectiveness or clumsiness, etc. This appears, however, as a variation not in what one finds one's body to be, but in *how well* one finds it, or anything else, to be what it is. All body changes, including those of body maturation and of bodily aging, are of this kind. When the body changes it normally becomes more or less *itself,* i.e., more or less capable of revealing the circumstantial world to us through its poised response.

56. *Treatise,* p. 239.

57. Ibid., p. 241.

58. E.g., *Treatise,* Vol. II, p.114.

59. *Treatise,* p. 119.

60. Ibid., p. 255.

61. Hume believes that "all impressions are clear and precise." *Treatise,* p. 76.

62. Ibid., p. 76.

Notes to pages 74–94

63. Cf. e.g., Hume's *Inquiry Concerning Human Understanding*, Library of Liberal Arts, p. 24.

64. We may of course survive biologically for some normally limited time in a vegetative, tortured, nightmarish or dumbfounded state in which our field of experience is shrunken, decayed or disintegrated with consequent loss of full intelligibility.

65. *Treatise*, p. 92.

66. Ibid., p. 179.

67. Ibid., p. 148.

68. Ibid., p. 181.

69. Ibid., p. 183.

70. I think there is a way to do that without our hope resting on an after-life. We may so live *this* life that when it comes time to die, we can, out of a realized and substantiated love of life, kiss life good-bye, and know gratitude as the realization of hope for a life well-lived. Such gratitude is the final poise of a graceful death.

71. *Treatise*, p. 183.

72. Ibid., p. 254.

73. Ibid., Vol. II, p. 165.

Chapter 3

1. Since I wish so far as possible to reserve italics for indicating *emphasis*, I will not underline this phrase nor its correlative, "a posteriori," nor such other commonly used foreign phrases as "prima facie." I will treat such phrases as if they were English phrases.

2. Of course, he thought that as finite intelligences we have to rely somewhat on perceptual evidence in order to substantiate our detailed scientific conclusions. But the point being made here is that our theoretical understanding for which this perceptual evidence gives us a clue, does not itself *include* the perceptual clue but only a clear distinct conceptual idealization *prompted by* this clue.

3. For Descartes and Leibniz, dubitability and indubitability are functions only of reflective, self-conscious belief. Thus, although Leibniz holds that we have *petites perceptions* of the universal implications of each given perception, he does not hold that we have indubitable knowledge of any perceptual implications.

4. In addition, according to Hume, we have in arithmetical knowledge a purely formal, non-inferential kind of indubitable knowledge. This conceptual indubitability admitted by Hume differs, however, from that of Descartes and Leibniz in lacking any implication as to matters of fact.

5. *Prolegomena to Any Future Metaphysics*, edition of the Preussische Akademie der Wissenschaften, 1911, p. 374, footnote. Citations will hereafter be made to "*Prolegomena*" followed by page references to this edition.

6. It might be objected that the more distinctive character of productive imagination is the necessity of our knowledge of its field. However, Kant holds that this a priori character of our productively imaginative intuition is founded upon our even more basic self-conscious awareness that this intuition is our *own* contribution to our sensuous experience. Kant argues that we can be certain about what we imagine, only so far as we know that *we ourselves* produce it.

7. "Die falsche Spitzfindigkeit der vier syllogistischen Figuren," *Immanuel Kant, Werke,* Cassirer edition, Berlin, 1922, Vol. II, p. 65. My translation.

8. Ibid., Section 64.

9. *Die Anthropologie* (1798), Section 1. My translation.

10. Kant believed, of course, that we may be self-conscious of this contribution in particular cases, without being aware of its general philosophic significance. For, though Kant thought he first accomplished the latter, he did not think he first accomplished the former and thereby first made the sense intuit a priori.

11. *Critique of Pure Reason,* B327. Hereafter, references to the first Critique will be made simply by the standard first or second edition "A" or "B" numbers. The translations are from the version by Norman Kemp Smith (London: Macmillan, 1921).

12. B 61.

13. *Prolegomena to Any future Metaphysics,* p. 314. Quotations are from the translation of Mahaffy-Carus, as revised by Lewis White Beck (Liberal Arts Press, 1950), but page references are to the Preussische Akademie edition, volume IV.

14. B 75.

15. I disregard for the moment the qualification that Kant sometimes adds and sometimes implicitly denies, that such intuitions must be knowable without appeal to any sensory evidence, and also Kant's consistently added qualification that all such intuitions must be universally applicable throughout all possible experience.

16. *Prolegomena,* p. 335.

17. Of which theoretical understanding is one kind.

Chapter 4

1. In Section 5.5 we will see other, more detailed, reasons for this identification.

2. Though he *finds* himself *in*directly in the world—by finding himself in and through some relation to perceptually determined objects in his circumstances.

3. Does this structure of perception linger from our evolutionary past as small burrowing mammals?

4. Of course, I can so act as to rearrange the parts—but then it would become a different object. I am here concerned with the effect of my activity on the perceived order of the same perceptual element.

5. The percipient's passing by or around it; or its passing by or around the

Notes to pages 107–109

percipient.

6. *Physics*, VIII. 5. 257b. Quotations from Aristotle are taken from *The Basic Works of Aristotle*, edited and with an introduction by Richard McKeon (New York: Random House, 1941).

7. *Physics*, VIII. 5. 258a.

8. *Physics*, VIII. 5. 257b. We will see (in our discussion of Kant's conception of the ego) how Kant shares this notion with Aristotle, and how crucial it is for him too.

9. *Physics*, VI.4.

10. For Aristotle, change of position is one form of "motion." *Physics*, III. 1.

11. Husserl makes this point in *Cartesian Meditations. An Introduction to Phenomenology*, translated by D. Cairns (The Hague: Martinus Nijhoff, 1970), sects. 53 and 55.

12. The word "part" has many senses. In the loosest sense, everything that exists is a part, because it is a part of its surroundings, a part of what exists in its neighborhood. In this sense, even the active percipient's body and limbs are "parts". In the present context, however, I am considering a narrower sense of "part"—the sense that specifically characterizes an *object* as distinct from a *subject* such as the percipient's active body. This distinction requires elaboration.

To begin with, there seem to be two main senses in which we speak of a "part" of an object. The first refers to what I will call an *arbitrary part* of an object. It is the portion of an object occupying any arbitrarily chosen volumetric sub-section of the object. The second sense, which I normally have in mind, refers to what I will call a *natural part* of an object. It is the part bounded by lines of articulation with which the object is normally presented when used in a certain way. This sense of "part" is bound up with the appearance that, given its practical context, there is only *one* natural way to describe the articulation or subdivision of the object. Other ways seem arbitrary, determined by the choice of the percipient but not by the characteristics of the object; they do not "carve the chicken at its joints." It is in this sense that we ordinarily speak of *the* parts of an object—meaning that set of parts determined by the natural way of dividing the object. It is in this sense that the recruit can be legitimately asked *how many* parts there are in an M-1 rifle; and it is in this sense that an advertiser can reasonably claim that his machine has *fewer* parts than any other machine capable of doing the same job. Parts are the elements out of which an object is com-posed, i.e., out of which it is put together. Fabricated objects are literally com-posed by man, and the production process normally follows the lines of what I mean by a "natural part"; normally the natural parts are produced separately, and only later put together to form the final product that is the object. A natural part is normally *recognizable apart* from its object, to someone familiar with that object; but an arbitrary part is not normally recognizable in this way, or at least not so easily.

The distinction between a natural and an arbitrary part of an object may be more formally drawn as follows: Perceptual objects may be composed of parts (unless they are too small to be di-visible), and the parts, of course, may in turn be composed of parts. Now consider any perceptual object, O, and any two parts, P and P'. of that object. P or P' or both must be arbitrary parts of O if: some but not all parts of P are parts of P', and some but not all parts of P' are parts of P; in other words if P and P' overlap. Given *any* arbitrary divisible part, P, there is some other arbitrary part, P', which overlaps it. But *no* natural part overlaps any other natural part.

13. This metaphor for flow of location would have to be altered for flow of orientation (as a hollow sphere); and for flow of circumstance (as a hollow surface).

14. Compare the discussion of Section 2.5.6.

15. These statements about objects in places in Space can be fully paralleled by statements about events in moments in Time.

16. Only *our subjective* "felt determination to pass from one impression to another," is retained.

17. Cf. in this connection Kierkegaard's statement that "vertigo is under the rubric soul (psyche) what despair is under the rubric spirit, and is pregnant with analogies to despair" (*Sickness Unto Death*, Part I, Section B). Despair for Kierkegaard is the minimal sense of God and self, just as vertigo, for us, is the minimal sense of world and percipient.

18. Granted our data so far.

19. Note the ease of the *double-entendre* on "passing": as a particular event; and as the "passing" of events in general.

20. This *perceptual work* done by passing in the fashioning of perceptual objects has gone unnoticed. As a result, philosophers cannot explicate our sense that the near and far sides of a perceived object are not merely co-*meant* but co-*present* as co-*presented* (though one side is presented as revealed and the other as concealed). Attempts at explication generally imply that the far side is *represented* as what *would be* (but is not) presented if some *possible* (but not actual) way of viewing the object were adopted. Even the subtle Husserl is driven toward such a phenomenalism, in however sophisticated a form. Cf. e.g., his view that objects are "appresented" and "not strictly perceived" in respect to their far sides (*Cartesian Meditations*, Sect. 55).

21. Our sense of balance is generally most prominent when we are erect, but it is to some extent required even when we act effectively in other positions.

22. Even in such a highly unusual case as hanging onto a cliff to avoid falling, we do not, strictly speaking, resist our *falling*; we resist only the loosening of grip that would *result* in our falling.

23. Even if this field is without strength, as in the experience of weightlessness in outer space, it is *apparently* of this zero strength. It remains an apparent *field* of no influence *in* which, and not in reaction *to* which, objects and people first possess the particular determination characteristic of them. Weightlessness is essentially a *privative* experience for us.

Chapter 5

1. Firth makes this point for "ostensible objects." See his article "Sense-Data and the Percept Theory," *Mind,* Oct. 1949 and Jan. 1950. Merleau-Ponty makes this point for perceptual objects in his article, "Le Primat de la perception et ses conséquences philosophiques," *Bulletin de la Société de Philosophie,* Vol. XLI, 1947-48.

2. This equivalence does not imply that *all* spectation takes place in a perceptual time divorced from any perceptual space, but only that spectation does so in so far as it functions as a ground for a flight of the imagination from perception. Spectation may also be a detached way of regarding the field of practical perception. Spectation so directed *toward* the perceptual field takes place in a perceptual space as well as a perceptual time, albeit in a uniquely transformed perceptual space. We will, however, ignore this spectatorial space since its consideration is not essential to show that the human body is the material subject of the world.

3. The perception of celestial bodies may at first seem to be an exception. The sun, moon, planets, stars, and comets do not seem to pose practical problems for us. This is, however, because they are perceived entirely in the vertical field, and as not subject to relocation or reorientation by our movement in respect to them. We thus perceive celestial objects in a different *way* than we perceive ordinary objects. Furthermore, celestial objects may appear to be independent embodiments of the vertical world-field in which we are oriented; much as we appear ourselves to be embodiments of our horizontal field in which ordinary objects are dependently oriented about us. Now our poise, i.e., our capacity to have a horizontal field of determinable objects posing practical problems for us, is sensed as derivative from our balance, i.e., our capacity to orient ourselves in the vertical field of the world. Hence the celestial bodies that may appear to embody the vertical world-field may thereby appear to be the source from which we derive the effectiveness of our practical capacity. They may thus appear to give us our general field of practical problems with circumstantial objects, rather than to pose such problems in and by themselves. This is the phenomenological ground of the primitive tendency to worship "celestial" or "heavenly" bodies as divine; to regard our fortune as somehow fixed by our stars. In any case, whether or not they appear to embody the vertical field, the "objects" of the astronomer are not objects *in* the perceptual world, but heavenly bodies *at the limit of* the perceptual world itself. Heavenly bodies appear in the heavens at the limit of the perceptual world; not, like objects, *in the world* whose upper bound the heavens are.

4. Not a world moralistically perfected by the particular contents in it, but a world esthetically perfected by the *way* its contents are together as "in" it.

5. Though, to be sure, our own capacity for active perceptual experience in turn evidently conditions the possibility of the perceptual world, which is nothing but the initial domain making way for our reversible activity in it.

6. That is, production of the material as well as the form, so that the formed-material is not distinguishable into material "having" a form and the form "of" the

material. An image, unlike a perceptual object, is not a whole (passively) composed of its constituents; but rather a whole that is nothing but the way it (actively) disposes its constituents in it.

7. As distinct from feeling lost or empty in this relation. Thus, we may *sensibly* have an immediate relation to the world with or without *finding* ourself in terms of this relation. We may thus have perfect self-control without having determined any content in our experience. All our external senses may be stopped up and we may be taken to a strange place so that we do not have the slightest sense of our material circumstances. Totally lacking in poise (i.e., in set to meet circumstantial objects) as we must be in such a situation, we may yet be sensibly well-balanced. If we lose our balance, however, we lose *all* sense of our orientation in the world, i.e., we cease to have any immediate sensible relation to the world.

8. Sometimes, our perceptual determining of an event appears to be merely a function of the passage of time that *makes* determinate temporal intervals without appearing to *take* a determinate amount of time in doing so.

9. This is a point Sartre makes central in his book, *L'Imaginaire* (Paris: Gallimard, 1940).

10. The perceptual whole is *existentially* passive to the parts com-prising it; they can exist separately without it, but not it without them. But it is active in a *teleological* sense—the parts receive their role or significance in the object from the whole that they existentially comprise; if taken a-part, they lose their significance as parts.

11. As seen in Section 5.1.

12. A more detailed analysis of the comparatively loose nature of perceptual as distinct from imaginative implication is given in my article with Hubert Dreyfus, "The Three Worlds of Merleau-Ponty", *Philosophy and Phenomenological Research*, No. 4, 1962.

13. Merleau-Ponty makes much of this point in *Phénoménologie de la perception* (Paris: Gallimard, 1945).

14. Ingmar Bergman movies, for example, are criticized by many for raising the question of the significance of scenes obviously "symbolic" of something-or-other, but not providing the leads by which this question may be definitely settled.

15. That is, there is no such thing *within* the imagination—the field to which our discussion of the imagination is confined.

16. Section 4.4.3.

17. It makes no sense, of course, to speak of "verifying" or "doubting" a *logical* implication. We can only verify or doubt that there is a logical implication in a given case; not whether, as here, an admitted implication holds. But we speak here of a *perceptual* implication, which has the peculiar property of holding temporarily (i.e., making sense only if its consequent turns out to make sense; and capable of losing sense by its consequent turning out not to make sense).

Notes to pages 155–166

Chapter 6

1. In his *title,* Kant uses "reason" to comprehend both "understanding" and "reason" as this distinction is made in the *text.* "Understanding" is used in two senses: (1) as theoretical knowledge of matters of fact, i.e., as conceptual imagination, whose forms are the categories and the field of productive imagination to which they apply; and (2) in a narrower sense, as the spontaneous (in contrast to the receptive) functions of "understanding" in the first sense, having only the categories as its forms. The central problem handled in the text is an analysis of the scope and limits of "understanding" in the broader first sense; all problems, including those of "reason" as distinct from understanding, are broached only in relation to this problem. Thus the work might better have been entitled *Critique of Pure Understanding.*

2. "In terms of," though not as "equivalent to" this distinction. Although Kant holds that all objectified perception is in the field of imaginative Space and Time, he does not hold that all contents of this field are perceptual.

3. E.g., B19.

4. B125.

5. B125.

6. Bxviii.

7. Especially in Section 5.5.

8. B9. The important phrase is, *"keinen Widerhalt gleichsam zur Unterlage."*

9. Hume saw this was also true for our other form of inactive thought, viz., as pure spectator.

10. In Section 6.5.

11. *Prolegomena,* p. 299 n.

12. Ibid., p. 298.

13. ". . . ein Aktus seiner Selbsttätigkeit. . ."

14. B156.

15. B52.

16. B157. Italics mine.

17. He also gives unity to his limitless horizontal field. But our point here is that he does not give unity to any *content* that he knows may lie "beyond the horizon," in the placeless portions of his field. He lacks an effective stance of sufficient range to do so.

18. Our first sense of ourselves, as a purely passive sensibility, is a stage of pure ignorance. It *produces* the entwined problems of knowledge and self-knowledge, but is not a stage of their *solution.* So we will henceforth ignore it.

19. To know it would be to know ourself in ourself; to have the rational intuition that we in fact lack.

20. We will consider this matter at length in Section 6.4.

21. B111.
22. B130.
23. B134.
24. B137.
25. B132.
26. B133.
27. B54.
28. B67.
29. B68.
30. It is not a merely psychological ego-split because our character as having a "psyche" (i.e., an empirical ego) is only a *result* of this split.
31. A8.
32. A104.
33. A8.
34. A109.
35. A109.
36. This question will be considered in Section 6.5, and answered in the negative.
37. To be more fully developed in Section 6.7.
38. We also have a sense of our skill. This, however, is not our sense of the sense objects have, but our sense of *our sense of* the sense objects have. Effective deployment always awakens some sense of our skill.
39. Golden Age myths, like the lost Garden of Eden we supposedly seek to re-enter, implicitly misunderstand need as nothing but desire, and thus obscure this creative character of human questing—how, in discovering the answer to our *quest*ions, we first make ourselves answerable, create ourselves as responsible solvers.
40. B158n.
41. B91.
42. Aristotle, *Physics*, VIII 5.
43. B92.
44. The synthesis of productive imagination.
45. B160n, and 162.
46. B211.
47. In the order of the "subjective deduction of the categories," which is something like a phenomenological order of the generation of knowledge.
48. In the logical order of our achieved knowledge.
49. B137.
50. At least to his own satisfaction.

Notes to pages 183–194

51. That Kant is here writing of inner sense is first made absolutely clear in A99. "(All our representations) as modifications of the mind, belong to inner sense. All our knowledge is thus finally subject to time, the formal condition of inner sense. In it they must all be ordered, connected, and brought into relation…Throughout what follows (this) must be borne in mind as quite fundamental." A spatial manifold is an "empirical product" of synthesis; a temporal manifold is its synoptic condition.

52. A99.

53. B137.

54. Or the representation of such a unity.

55. Since Kant interprets the perceptual determination that we merely notice, on the model of the imaginative one we produce, he is bound to feel uneasy, and to feel that some explanation must be offered of why object determinations do not *seem* so completely produced as his theory implies.

56. B110.

57. A108.

58. B6.

59. It is only in logic of the latter kind that "we do not abstract from the entire content of knowledge" (B80), hence can estimate a judgment "not only according to its own inner validity, but as knowledge in general, according to its quantity in comparison with other knowledge…"(B96). The Table of Judgments is developed in the Transcendental Analytic of *Transcendental* Logic.

60. *Prolegomena* 299

61. Ibid., 301*n*.

62. Ibid., 301*n*.

63. Ibid., 300.

64. In this context, Kant attempts in effect to draw the conventional distinction between primary and secondary qualities, by distinguishing between those judgments of perception that can and those that cannot be converted into judgments of experience by the introduction of a categorial concept. Judgments such as "The room is warm," "Sugar is sweet," "Wormwood is bitter," could never become judgments of experience even with the introduction of a categorial concept, "because they refer merely to feeling, which everybody knows to be merely subjective, and which of course can never be attributed to the object." (*Prolegomena*, 299, 299*n*)

65. Corresponding to Kant's notion of "subjectively valid."

66. Beck's introduction to Library of Liberal Arts edition of *Prolegomena*, xvi*n*.

67. In respect to their matter.

68. On page 208.

69. The schema of transcendental imagination is the "third thing. . . homogeneous on the one hand with the category, and on the other hand with the

Notes to pages 195–211

appearance,"making possible the application of the former to the latter. (B177)

70. Though *dis*appearance is possible in this way.

71. B161.

72. B161.

73. A15.

74. Cf. also A398; B404.

75. *Critique of Practical Reason,* p. 163.

76. *Critique of Judgment,* p. 239.

77. Dieter Henrich, "*Ueber die Einheit der Subjecktivität,*" *Philosophische Rundschau:* 3. Jahrgang, Heft 1/2, pp. 30-58.

78. Or, to contrast him with Schelling, Kant saw clearly that perception is not derivable from imaginative intuition.

79. Section 6.1.

80. Sections 6.2 and 6.3.

81. Sections 6.4 and 6.5.

82. By "perception" I will continue to mean, unless otherwise stated, the primary form of perception, viz., active or practical perception. The inactive perception of the pure spectator is, as we have seen, a secondary form given as a withdrawal from the primary form, hence as presupposing it but not being presupposed by it.

83. Kant does not give these definitions in the Critique: "In this treatise, I purposely omit the definition of the categories, although I may be in possession of them." (B108)

84. Descartes, it is true, did not limit "cogito" to mean abstract thought, as I do here; but he included this as an alternative, indeed, as his paradigmatic, sense. So his "ergo" does not hold.

85. Though, as we will see, it does presuppose the existence of some things perceived.

86. Cf. Section 2.5.2.

87. Though not the subjective factor in contrast to the objective factor. It is the subject-factor, in contrast to the object-factor, in objective experience.

88. In case we know what is satisfying us.

89. No satisfaction from conclusions is evidence, though satisfaction with conclusions is.

90. This feeling of gratification may indeed be suppressed if we are subjectively distressed by what we discover. "Gratification" is too grandiose a feeling for simple perception; the feeling of completion is more characteristic. But I am here speaking of "objective satisfaction" in more general terms, to include for example the feeling of scientific discovery. There is, however, a continuum of objective consummation (as distinct from subjective relief) that stretches all the way from

the modest sense of completion characterizing perceptual objectivity, to the more dramatic sense of gratification characterizing more developed objective experience. Sketching the whole range of objective satisfaction throws light on the perceptual end of it.

91. An "objective need" is simply a need that can be met by an objective satisfaction.

92. The following account is taken from "Die falsche Spitzfindigkeit der vier syllogistischen Figuren" (1762), Immanuel Kant, Werke, Cassirer edition, Berlin, 1922, Vol. 11, pp. 49-65. A clear indication that Kant still held this doctrine at the time of writing the Critique is given in B141n. "The lengthy doctrine of the four syllogistic figures . . . is nothing more than an artificial method of securing . . . the appearance that there are more kinds of inference than that of the first figure."

93. Or, in place of the singular judgment, 'x is an A' (e.g., 'Socrates is mortal') a normally formed argument can contain a universal judgment, 'All x's are A's', where 'x' stands for an object representable in intuition. 'x' is not itself intuitable. We have only mediate, not immediate knowledge of objects. Knowledge is by judgment, which is the conceptual representation of an intuitive representation of the object itself. (B93)

94. This summary of Kant's view is derived from a synthesis of material from "Die falsche Spitzfindigkeit. . ." and material from the Critique, especially from "The Logical Employment of the Understanding," "The Schematism," Ch. 1, and B360.

95. According to Kant, this is not an arbitrary order. 'All bodies are divisible', and 'Every metal is a body', are in proper order (B94). The order seems to be: concepts appearing in synthetic a priori propositions; primitive variables in Newtonian theory; variables appearing in corollaries of this theory.

96. Hegel's "concrete Universal" looms on the horizon. But it is kept away by Kant's conviction that the receptivity of sense means that the clarification of concepts by their sensible application is not just a self-clarification. The aid intuition provides our thought is not just an indirect aid our thought provides for itself.

97. B110.

98. It represents the third category in each triad, which is the category of complete knowledge. We cannot reach this category in empirical thought, because we cannot complete the required iteration of the syllogistic form in an infinite "ratiocinatio polysyllogistica." But the conclusion of the meta-a priori syllogism in Barbara nevertheless represents the determination of this series, which is the ideal of knowledge, viz., knowledge of the transcendental object = X, in its singularity.

99. The fundamental form of an infinite judgment, for Kant, is the judgment that things-in-themselves are the limits of our knowledge; they are not-the-transcendental-object=X.

100. Cf. p. 302.

101. Perception, on the other hand, involves cancellation of a deprivation that we were originally at a loss to explain, but that we are finally able to understand as having been the lack of the object finally found.

102. B91.

103. B221.

104. This sense of a "limiting" case of intelligibility is not to be confused with Kant's sense of things-in-themselves as limiting cases of our ability to understand. Kant was thinking of the limits of the *range* of our knowledge; we are here considering the limits of its *endurance*.

105. Cf. "First Analogy of Experience."

106. *Prolegomena*, 363.

107. *Critique of Practical Reason*, Preface.

108. B363.

109. B597.

110. B378.

111. "*(der) Ganzen der gesamten Erfahrung.*"

112. Hegel takes up this implication as the starting point of a general logic, systematically assimilating the relation between *contradictory* states to that obtaining between *contrary* states.

113. B367.

114. I.e., the unreal world of our imagination; the conceptual universe in which laws never fail to hold, and in which nothing disappears, dissatisfies, disillusions, or is destroyed.

115. Eg., B234.

116. In the subjective deduction, edition A, Kant speaks of an a priori form of reproductive imagination, viz., the second-stage "synthesis of reproduction in imagination." In edition B, only the empirical, generally Humean, form of reproductive imagination is retained, viz., that taking place under the psychological law of association. But for both editions, our generalization holds true. Whether or not there is an a priori root of our psychological ability to associate sensations lawfully, we could not plot facts in the space of our productive imagination unless we were capable of such association. Suppose we discover that sensations A and B are lawfully associated in a certain way, and that they occur in particular at x1 and x2. We can then determine that if A occurs at x3, B must occur at x4. But such reckoning is possible only if we can regularly associate 'A' and 'B' with the kind of sensation they are meant to represent.

117. B66.

118. Cf. e.g., B594.

119. B379-380. Kant sometimes holds that the third idea is of God. But Kant means by "God," merely "the Supreme Understanding" (B374), "the condition of all objects of thought in general" (B391), in short, the world-subject of

Notes to pages 238–256

imaginative thought. Kant's second sense of the Ideal, as the world that is *not* subject, will be explained later.

120. B685.

121. Viz., (I), p. 264.

122. And he writes, "The transcendental paralogism produced a purely one-sided illusion in regard to the idea of the subject of our thought." (B433)

123. *Prolegomena*, 337.

124. Similar statements occur in B409, and B422.

125. B407-409.

126. "The simple here again corresponds to the category of reality." (A404*n*)

127. In this vein, Kant writes in the *Anthropologie*, "Dreaming is involuntary action of the imagination and must continue all during sleep although we may not remember it upon awakening" (Sect. 31). Thus we cannot "have" an unused imaginative capacity.

128. These "illusions" are really delusions. I retain Kant's word only for the sake of simplicity.

129. B411.

130. B445.

131. Since perceptual content *is* that content contained in *perceptual* forms.

132. E.g., B446.

133. "Negation," in the sense that division of objects implies taking away something real and leaving nothing in its place. The category of Negation is Nothing(0).

134. Conception, as an act of the imagination, implies a free or spontaneous origination of determinate representations. But this productivity does not imply the *existence* of anything, although it does suppose such existence.

135. Kant does distinguish self-determination from first-determination, in the case of practical reason—which he believes to be self-determining without appearing as a first cause in experience. But this conception fails to do justice to our perceptual sense of freedom: Kant's rational freedom is only presumable, but not *knowable* (even retroactively); and its relation to our *experience* is utterly obscure.

136. B475.

137. B494.

138. B494.

139. B562.

140. B601.

141. B602.

142. B597.

143. B604.

Notes to pages 256–275

144. B693.

145. E.g., B598.

146. B598.

147. Limitation, as a condition of all possibility, "is impossible, although in our first rough statements we have used such language." (B607)

148. "How does it happen that reason regards all possibility of things as derived from one single fundamental possibility, namely, that of the highest reality?" (B609)". . . Because we substitute dialectically for the *distributive* unity of the empirical employment of the understanding, the *collective* unity of experience as a whole." (B610)

149. Though this unity is readily provided by imagination representing a whole world of possibilities produced from a single imaginative idea.

150. It is a function of perception to provide real possibilities.

151. Imaginative reason, being purely representational, has of itself no presentational, or realistic, implications. "For reason. . . has used (the condition of all possibility) only as the *concept* of all reality without requiring that all this reality be objectively given" (B608, Kant's italics).

152. Viz., that Kant imaginizes (all) perception; hence, that he imaginizes the subject, the series of objects, *and* the world of perception.

153. B606.

154. B607.

155. B607.

156. Not, of course, as an object, as something that exists0, but as the "being of all beings" (B607), as that which *is* in such a way that "everything that is conditioned is subject to it" (B606-607). The vertical world-field has both these formal properties of "the highest being." And it is metaphorically associated with "the highest being" when we imagine God as "in heaven." If this common association is dismissed as merely metaphorical, it remains to be explained why the metaphor is so irresistible.

Appendix II

1. The question is philosophical, concerning the logic of the formation of sensuous abstractions; it is not psychological, concerning how we come to notice qualities initially given as such in sense experience. Kant, for example, considers sense experience to be initially given as sensation (*Empfindung*). For him the problem arises in regard to the constitution of appearance (Erscheinung) out of sensation. He treats the problem in the first portion of the subjective deduction of the categories.

2. In the special case in which my previous consciousness was perceptual, memory does of course imply the reality of a remembered thing. But only because it implies the reality of a previous experience that in turn implies the reality of its object or referent. But essentially—that is, in the general case—memory is not of

things but only our consciousness of things; the existence of a memory does not imply the reality of past things but only of our past consciousness of things. Memory may then be regarded as the "perception" (because implying the reality of its object) of our past consciousness of things.

Appendix III

1. I am grateful to Michael Friedman for drawing my attention to an article by Eckart Förster, "Kant's *Selbstzetsungslehre*," in *Kant's Transcendental Deductions*, ed. Eckart Förster (Stanford University Press, 1989). This article brings out evidence that Kant does eventually catch at least a glimpse of the Promising—albeit never Promised—Land of the bodily subject. In some passages cited from the *Opus postumum*, Kant seems to see that our spontaneous bodily movement as self-moving movers enables us to discern basic dynamical facts about the world that remain inaccessible to us, in their facticity as well as their necessity, so long as we merely *think* the world of our experience without also *moving* and thereby appearing *in* it.

2. We have just seen, however, that we may be forced *to* undertake the exercise of some judgment.

3. Some rare and remarkable individuals retain their full humanity, and even realize it all the more forcefully through their courage in doing so, despite being almost completely immobilized by a nerve disease. To the best of my knowledge, all such persons have lost a mobility they once possessed. On the view expressed here, they are drawing on the stored legacy of what was once learned by movement.

4. Or perhaps this tradition has retained its dominance precisely *because* it has continually shifted from one horn to another of the hopeless dilemmas it has generated, thereby giving at least the illusion of progress, until finally facing in our own day the incomprehensibility of a supposedly single invariant form of free human understanding that, as social, is provisionally invariant, internally coherent yet untranslatably changeable with every step from one historical stage to the next.

5. Cf. Ch. 5 in *MS;* and my articles, "Sensuous Abstraction and the Abstract Sense of Reality," reprinted here as appendix II, and "Shadows in Knowledge: Plato's Misunderstanding of Shadows, and of Knowledge as Shadow-free", in *Dialogues in Phenomenology*, ed. Don Ihde and Richard M. Zaner (The Hague: Martinus Nijhoff, 1975).

6. Cf. *MS*, Ch. 2 Sect. 2.5, and Ch. 6 Sect. 6.72.

Index

Abstractions, sensuous, 272–276
Abstract thought, and practical perception, xxiii–xxv
Acting, xvii
Active body, xi, 6, 64
  and circumstantiality of objects, 205–206
  as determining series of perceptual events, 254
  and experience, 83–84
  of space and time, xix
  felt unity of, 103, 109–110, 114
    as common root of faculties of knowledge, 199
    contents of perceptual field united in, 234
    deduction of perceptual categories from, 8–9, 202
    and local situation, 8
    objects as circumstantially related to, 206–207
    and perceptual quest, 212
    and unconditioned unity of perceptual content, 243
    and unity of self as subject, 180
    and world, 262
  and imagination, 132, 152
  indivisibility of, 249
  Kant's failure to understand, 260
  movement of, 108
  and perception, xxi
  and perceptual knowledge, 204
  and question of sensibility and inner sense, 29
  and sense of direction, 119
  and space/time, 48–52
  three functions of, 46–47
Actual a priori of poised response, 64–66
Actuality, 291
  from rationalist vs. noumenological standpoint, 291–292
Actual stance, 120
Aesthetic attitude, 267–268. *See also* Spectatorial attitude or view
Anticipation, xviii, 105, 178, 195
  and sense of encounter, 117
  and startle-experience, 116
  in Table of Perceptual Categories, 219
  verification of, 128
Anticipatory response, 141, 142–143
Antifacts, 61–62
Antinomies of Kant, 254–255
  basic, 236–239
  general antinomy of series of objects, 247
    first (Quantity, Plurality), 247–248
    second (Quality, Negation), 248–249

Index

Antinomies of Kant (*continued*)
    third (Relation, Causality), 249–253
    fourth (Modality, Existence), 253–254
    in Ideal of pure reason, 256–259
    in Paralogisms, 239–247
Antinomies of reason and sensibility, in traditional philosophy, 286
Antirealism, and balance, 293n.7
Anxiety, and Heidegger, xxxiii–xxxv
Appearance
    vs. appearing, 52
    veridical vs. illusory, 53–56
A priori conditions of possibility of experience, 167
A priori intuition, 97–98
A priori knowledge, Kant's false dilemma of, 156–161, 259
Aristotle
    and activity as formative, 179
    and "body politic," 3
    on human subject, 10–11, 12
    on judgment, xx
    and Kant on thought as developmental, 220
    and motion, 30
    and order in world, 25
    on Prime Mover, 163
    on self-moved mover as impossible, 102–103, 107–110
Art works, and aesthetic imagination, 137
Auschwitz, as artifact, 61–62
Autonomy, and circumstantiality (Kant), 7–8

Balance, xlv, 124, 125, 140–141, 142, 293n.7
    imaginative transformation of, 140–143
    and passage of time, 105
    and percipient as directly in the world, 104
Being and Time (Heidegger), xi, xxix. *See also* Heidegger, Martin

Beliefs
    Hume on, 84–85
    nonconceptual perceptual, xx
    and nonconceptual readiness, xxvi
    and poise, 85
Berkeley, George
    and "body," xlii
    and Merleau-Ponty, xxxvii
Body, xiii, xl, 1, 88, 266. *See also* Active body
    and circumstantial field of objects, 3
    in classic view, 11–12
    current interest in, xxvii
    and Descartes, 5, 14, 26, 46
    and desires, 37
    and experience, xlii, xliii, 263
    front-back asymmetry of, xix, xliv, 106, 118
    and gravitation, xlv
    and Heidegger, xliii
    and human subject, 32
    and Hume, 6–7, 26, 40–44, 46, 71
    and imagination, 152
    Leibniz on, 6–7, 26, 30–39, 40
    as limiting variations in interpretation, 263
    Merleau-Ponty on, xiii, xix, xxxviii–xl, xlii, xliii, xlv, 265–266
    and mind, 267–268
        Descartes on, 27
    misinterpretation of as merely material thing, 88
    necessity of, 64–65
    as object, 47, 54
    and perceptual world, xli, 265
    and permanence of percipient, 208
    posture of, xliii
    and regularity of experience, 41–42
    and self-activity of percipient, 169
    and social identification, 3
    as source of experience, 263
    and spatiotemporal field, xix, xxvii
    as subject of world, xl, xli, xlv–xlvi, 1–3, 88, 98
    as unified, 108–109

Index

and unity of the world, 5
  as veiled, 29–44
  world as function of, 42
Body-directedness, 65, 118–119
Body-direction, 49–50, 128
Body feelings. *See also* Feeling(s)
  of ache and pain, 59 (*see also* Pain)
  and active body, 46
  as objects, 44–46, 47
Body set, and absent conditions, 136
Bound, Kant on, 187
British Empiricism, 23, 96

Camus, Albert, xxxix–xl
Capacity
  sense of, 175
  and spontaneity of movement, 251
Carnap, Rudolf, 55
Categories, Kantian. *See under* Kant, Immanuel
Categories of perception. *See* Perceptual categories
Causality, in Kant's Antinomy, 249–253
Causal sequence, and logical sequence (Descartes), 20
Circumstancedness, 98
Circumstantial conditions, and ordinary language, 148
Circumstantial field, 103–104, 105, 106, 112, 264
  translation of, 111
Circumstantiality, 205–206
Circumstantial self-awareness, 206
Classic view of human subject, 10–12, 26, 87
  Descartes's rejection of, 13–22, 87–88

Colors, Merleau-Ponty on, xxxvi
Compound mirroring, 121
Conception
  and empiricists, 283
  imaginative, 254
  vs. knowledge (matters of fact), 209
  vs. perception, 161, 197, 205, 217, 223–224, 226, 239

for dialectical philosophers, 284
  and Kant, 93, 94
  and original determination, 250
  and sense of body, 267
Concepts, and intelligibility, xv
Conceptual imagination, 137–38, 156, 226
  and factual content, 161
  and Kant, 137–138, 155, 156, 234
  and perceptual implications, 196
Conceptual judgment, Kant on, xv, 225
Conceptual knowledge, and Kant, 94
Conceptual representation of goal, xix
Condition
  central vs. first, 245
  limiting vs. impossible, 232
Constancy phenomena, in perception, 226, 275–276
Contemplation
  Aristotle on, 12
  perceptual, xli
  in Plato's *Symposium*, 11
Contextuality, perceptual, 264
Continental Rationalism, 23
Continued existence of unobserved objects, 85–86
Coordination, 46
"Copernican revolution," 158–159, 191–192, 230, 261
Coping, xvii–xix, xxi, xxvi. *See also* Poise
  Merleau-Ponty on, xvii–xviii, xxxvii
  and practical knowledge of object, xx
  reidentification as, xxi
Correspondence theory of truth, 278
Critique of Pure Reason (Kant), 155, 261
Custom, reasonings as effects of, 84

Darwin, Charles, xliii, 209
Datum(a)
  interpretable, 269–270, 275
  theory-laden, 278
Davidson, Donald, xiii, xvi
Death, Stoic view of, 86
Deprivation, 222
Derrideans, 279, 280

Index

Descartes, René, 5, 13–22, 87–88
  and body, 5, 14, 26, 46
  and God, 15, 19, 20–21, 22, 25–26
  and idealism, xxix
  and Kant, 13, 89, 204–205
  and Leibniz, 30, 31, 32–33
  Leibniz-Hume split from, 5–6, 23, 28–29, 88–89
  and logical vs. real consequence, 246
  and mind-body separation, 27, 267, 268
  and motion, 30–32
  on perceivable object, 92
  and perceptual vs. conceptual knowledge, 91
  and representational view of experience, 15–16, 19–20, 21, 22, 27–28
  and self-evident principles, 270
  on spatial qualities, 31
  and unity of the world, 5, 15, 20, 22, 24, 25, 26–27
  as upward-looking, 287
Descent of Man, The (Darwin), xliii
Desire, 176–177
  and body, 37
  and Leibniz's analysis, 36–38, 39, 41
  and need, 86
  and perception, 290
Determination, 67–68
Dialectical philosophers, 284
Directed action, 65
Directed passage, 118–119
Direction, sense of, 106
Disappearance, 60–61, 301n.46
  local, 69
Disengagement, 271
Disillusionment, 272
Dissatisfaction, local, 69
Duration, and imagination, 144–145

Eckhart, Meister, 295n.13
Effective stance, 120–121, 127, 136
Embodiment, xi. *See also* Active body; Body
Empiricism
  British, 23, 96
  and conception, 283
  in Merleau-Ponty's critique, xxxv–xxxvi
Empiricist utilitarians, 287
Emptiness
  of impermanence, 57
  of inoccupancy, 57
  of placelessness, 57
Epistemology, traditional, 2
Evans, Gareth, xi
Events, 112–113
  irreversibility of occurrence of, 119
  perceivable, 103
  perceptual, 111
Evolution, and human body, xliii, 263
Existence. *See also* Reality
  in Kant's Antinomies, 253–254
  negative, 222
  and perception, 275
  of unobserved objects, 85–86
Existential order, vs. logical order, 246
Existential phenomenology, xii, xiii, xl
  modern, 8
  and nonconceptual intelligibility, xv
Expectation, and Hume on uniformity of nature, 77–78
Experience. *See also* Imaginative experience; Perceptual experience
  and body, xlii, xliii, 263
  active body, xix, 83–84
  as context-dependent, 264
  determinateness required in, xxxv
  and expectation, 78
  field of, 71, 81 (*see also* Circumstantial field; Horizontal field; Orientational field; Vertical field; World-field)
  intentional, 154
  and Kant, 163, 235
  on a priori conditions of possibility of, 167
  imaginizing of, 229, 235, 238, 259
  judgments of, 165, 191–193, 233
  object of, 29, 182, 195, 197
  unity of, 165

perceptual form of, 260 (*see also* Perceptual form)
as quest to meet needs, 178
regularity of, 51
representational character of
and Descartes, 15–16, 19–20, 21, 22, 27–28
and Hume, 28–29
and Leibniz, 28–29
subtentional, 154
unconditioned unity for (Kant), 236
as untotalizable, 232
Experiential significance, as contributed by human subject, 128

Facticity, 270–272
and sensuous abstraction, 272–276
Failure to exist, and nonexistence, 222
Feeling(s), 26. *See also* Body feelings
and Hume, 26
Kant on, 260
and subject body, 266
Felt unity of active body. *See under* Active body
Feyerabend, Paul, 278, 279
Fichte, Johann, 8, 200
Fictional stories, 148–149
Field of consciousness, xiii
Field of experience, 81. *See also* Circumstantial field; Horizontal field; Orientational field; Vertical field; World-field
appearance of things in, 52
as life-field, 71
Finding, 67–68
and object, 105
First cause, in Kant's Antinomy, 249–250, 252. *See also* Self-moved mover
Flow of passage, 111–113
Føllesdal, Dagfinn, xiii
"For itself and in itself," Merleau-Ponty on, xxxvii
Formal propositions, 203
Form of perceptual judgment, 8–9. *See also* Perceptual form(s)

Foucault, Michel, 279, 280, 284, 284–285
Freedom, 285
as act vs. as product of itself, 252
judgment as, 280–281
Kant on, 255
of movement, 282, 283
perceptual, 253
rational, 282, 283
and reason, 288
transformational freedom of understanding subject, 278, 280–292
as transformationally variant, 285

Gestalt psychology, xii
Goal, conceptual representation of, xix
God
and Descartes, 15, 19, 20–21, 22, 25–26
Kant on, 163
and Leibniz, 25
ontological argument for existence of, 15
Goodman, Nelson, xiii
Gravitation, xlv. *See also* Vertical field
Gurwitsch, Aron, xii

Habit, 63, 80, 82
Happening, 110. *See also* Events
Happiness, Kant on, 227
Hegel, G. W. F., 8, 200, 284
and "body politic," 3
and Reason, 220
Heidegger, Martin, xi, xxix, 8, 295n.2, 296–297n.19, 302n.53
and "alienness" of nature, xliii
and body, xliii
and Eckhart's views, 295–296n.13
on "existentials," 284
and *Geworfenheit*, xlv
and idealism, xxix–xxxv
on Kant and unity of ego, 200
and passivity-activity relation, xl-xli
and "standing back," 272
Henrich, Dieter, 200

Index

Hobbes, Thomas, and "body politic," 3
Horizontal field, xix, xlv, 104, 105, 122, 123, 125–126, 127, 264. *See also* World-field
　as ineliminable, 171
　and objects as minimally determinable, 160
　and object's sense, 176
Human body. *See* Active body; Body
Human Body as Material Subject of the World, The (Todes dissertation), xi, xii–xiii, xxviii–xxix, 277, 277n, 278
Human Body as Personal Subject of Society, The (Todes planned work), 277n, 278, 285, 286
Human Body as the Social Subject of the World (projected work), 2
Human individuals. *See* Individuals
Human necessity, 13–14
Human subject
　and body, 32
　classic view of, 10–12, 26, 87
　　Descartes's rejection of, 13–22, 32, 87–88
　and existential significance, 128
　as explicating unity of world, 23–27
　for Hume, 29, 40, 41, 87
　and Kant's Paralogisms, 242
　Leibniz on, 29, 30, 32, 33, 35, 36, 38, 40, 41, 87
　perceptual and imaginative selves of, 132
　subject body, 265–268, 277, 287
Hume, David, xi, xl, 71
　and active life, 86–87
　and atomic impressions, 74, 113
　on belief, 84–85
　and body, 6–7, 26, 40–44, 46, 71
　and conformity of perception to object, 160
　and continued existence of unobserved objects, 85
　and Descartes, 5–6, 23, 88–89
　on existence as unintelligible, 270
　on extension, 48

and heteronomy-from-below, 285
on human subject, 29, 40, 41, 87
and inference from constant union, 71–72
and Kant, 93, 94, 95, 97, 98–99, 160, 229
on "object," 55
and perceptual vs. conceptual knowledge, 91
on pleasure and pain, 72–73
on probability, 83–84
and representational character of experience, 28–29
on uniformity of nature, 73–83
and unity of world, 24, 26
Husserl, Edmund, xii, xxix, xxxix, 8, 266, 267, 272

Idealism, xli–xlii, 293n.7, 295n.2
　and Heidegger, xxix–xxxv
　and Merleau-Ponty, xxix, xxxv–xl
Ideal of pure reason (Kant), 238, 239
　antinomies, 256–259
Ideas of reason, Kant on, 231–232, 237, 238
Identical self, 282
Identity
　of active body, 109
　personal (Hume), 24
Illusory appearances, 56
　and imagination, 150
　vs. veridical, 53–56
Imagination, xxiv, xli, 130, 139
　and balance or poise, 140–143
　conceptual, 137–138, 155, 156, 161, 196, 226, 234
　and duration, 144–145
　as form of possibility, 290
　and Kant, 99–100
　and Knowledge, 229
　objective content of, 151–152
　and perception, xxv–xxvi, 130–137, 138, 142, 143–154, 201–202
　　and explication of determinate image vs. realization of determinable object, 147, 154

and factual vs. fictional stories, 148–149
Kant on, 156, 157, 159
and ordinary vs. technical language, 147–148
and origination vs. conveying of experience, 153–154
and significance of experience, 153, 154
and spectatorial attitude, 134, 135
and world as filled vs. open, 149–152, 154
practical, 135, 136, 137
and practical perception, 174
productive (Kant), 94–95, 97, 112, 155, 168, 235
reproductive (Kant), 235
as spontaneous production, 146–147
theoretical, 9, 180, 233, 243
transcendental, 194
as two-term relation, 159
unity of, 243
wholeness of image in, 145–146
Imaginative balance, 141, 143
Imaginative conception, 254
Imaginative experience, and Kant on transcendental object, 173
Imaginative field of experience, for Kant, 94, 95
Imaginative form, 244
Imaginative knowledge, 246
and Kant, 100, 204, 234
Imaginative poise, 143
Imaginative significance, 153
Imaginative thought, 228–229
Imaginative time, 150
Imaginative understanding, 290
Imaginative world, 259
Immortality, religious sense of, 86
Implication, perceptual, 308n.17
Impossible condition, 232
Individuals
  as products of socially constituted fields of meaning, xxviii
  and social regulation, 279

Inferences
  and nonconceptual readiness, xxvi
  perceptual, xx
  Hume on, 71–72, 80
Intention, vs. directed action, 65
Intentional arc, xvii
Intentional experience, 154
Interpretations
  theoretical, 269–270, 272
  world as composed of, xxviii, xlii–xliii, 279–280
Intersubjectivity, 2
"I perceive," 207, 209, 274
"I think," 179, 207
  and body's own spontaneity, xlvi

Judgment
  conceptual, xv, 225
  as exercise of freedom, 280–281
  Kant on, xx, 214
  and nonconceptual readiness, xxvi
  perceptual, xx, xxvii, 212–215, 217–218, 260, 261, 281–282
  rational, 281–282
  singular and universal (Kant), 190
Judgments of experience (Kant), xlvi, 165, 191–193
  systematization of, 233
Judgments of perception (Kant), xlvi, 191–193, 213. *See also* Perceptual judgment(s)

Kant, Immanuel, xi, xlvi, 7–8, 89, 130, 155–156
  and active body, 260
  and activity as formative, 173–174
  Anticipations of Perception of, 221
  Axioms of Intuition of, 221
  and body, xlii, xlvi
  categories of, 167, 179, 183, 188, 193, 198–199, 200–201, 215–217, 218, 220, 260
  deduction of, 160
  as imaginative idealizations of perceptual categories, 202–203

Kant, Immanuel (*continued*)
  metaphysical deduction of, 217
  subjective deduction of, 183, 192–194, 199, 202
  Table of, xv, 260
  and common unknown root of knowledge, 167, 171, 199–202
  and conceptual imagination, 137–138, 155, 156, 234
  and conceptual-nonconceptual dichotomy, xxv
  on continuity of experience, 225–226
  "Copernican revolution" of, 158–159, 191–192, 230, 261
  criticisms of, 261
  on degrees of reality, 220–221
  and Descartes, 13, 89, 204–205
  development of thought of, 90–95
  in *Dialectic*, xlvi, 229–235
    Antinomies, 187, 236–259
    Ideal of pure reason, 238, 239
    Paralogisms, 238, 239
    and transcendental illusions, 238, 239
  on ego (thinking self), 163–172, 178–180, 200–201
  on empirical ego, 165–166, 169–170, 171
  faculty psychology of, 140, 166
  and heteronomy-from-above, 285
  and Hume, 93, 94, 95, 97, 98–99, 160, 229
  and idealism, xxix
  as imaginizing categories of experience, 202
  as imaginizing ego, 165, 173, 174, 190, 202
  as imaginizing experience, 229, 235, 238, 259
  as imaginizing objects, 181, 183, 190, 199, 202, 243
  as imaginizing perception, 95–100, 140, 208
  as imaginizing world, 156–161, 190, 202, 259–260
  on intelligibility, xiv, xxvi
  and invariant form, 283–284
  on judgment, xx, 214
  on knowledge, 161–163, 165, 169, 171–172, 182, 213–214
    and Antinomies, 236
    a priori knowledge, 156–161, 259
    imaginative knowledge, 100, 204, 234
    knowledge of matters of fact, 235
    vs. predecessors, 91–92
    semi-objectivity of (spatiotemporal), 198
    threefold synthesis in, 183–185, 196
  on "limiting" predicates, 18
  on mind-body separation, 267
  on objective loss, 225
  and ontological argument, 15
  and perception, xxv, 231
    as anonymous process, xxxviii
    in *Dialectic*, 229
    imaginizing of, 95–100, 140, 208
    judgments of, xlvi, 191–193, 213
    perception as anonymous process, xxxviii
    and unconditioned unity, 236–237
  on perceptual variation, 221–222
  and percipient as bodily subject, 278
  on pleasure and pain, 226–228
  on practical principles and universality, 226
  on primary and secondary qualities, 311n.64
  on problems of philosophy, xiv
  and productive imagination, 94–95, 112, 155, 168, 235
  and question of objects of experience, 29
  and reason, 162, 189, 291, 309n.1
    in Antinomies, 254, 255
    Idea of, 237, 238
    and perception, 201
    practical principles of, 227–228
  regulative solutions of, 199, 202, 236, 247

Index

and scepticisms or dogmatisms, 70
on self-discovery, 179
on spatial objects, 181–189
  imaginizing of, 190
  locally determinable, 190–199
  and threefold synthesis, 183–185, 196
  spontaneous receptivity as problem for, xlvi, 172, 183, 194–195, 199
on synthetic a priori judgments, 156
and Table of concept of Nothing, 223–224
on "thing in itself," xxx
and transcendental attitude, 272
and "transcendental object = X," 165, 166, 167, 172–173, 182, 189–190, 197, 199
and uniformity of nature, 74, 75
as upward-looking, 287
Kierkegaard, Søren, 8
Knowledge
  Descartes on, 16–18, 19, 21
  and imagination, 229
  imaginative, 246
  as interplay between imaginative thought and perceptual practice, 203
  Kant on, 161–163, 165, 169, 171–172, 182, 213–214
    and Antinomies, 236
    a priori, 156–161, 259
    conceptual plus perceptual knowledge, 94
    imaginative, 100, 204, 234
    of matters of fact, 235
    vs. predecessors, 91–92
    semi-objectivity (spatiotemporal), 198
    threefold synthesis in, 183–185, 196
  necessary facts as basis of, 98
  and order of being as reverse of order of knowing, 245
  perceptual, xviii, xxvi, xxvi-xxvii, 100, 203–209 (*see also* Perceptual knowledge)
  as precarious, 228

Knutzen, Martin, 93
Köhler, Wolfgang, xii

Language, ordinary vs. technical, 147–148
Leibniz, Gottfried, xiii, xl, 5–6, 23, 88–89
  and actual world, 5
  and body, 6–7, 26, 30–39, 40
  and Descartes, 30, 31, 32–33
  and human subject, 30, 32, 33, 35, 36, 38, 40, 41, 87
  and Hume, 40
  and Kant, 90–91, 93–94, 95, 95–96, 97, 98–99, 229
  on knowledge, 8
  and Locke, 13
  and movement, 49
  and perceptual vs. conceptual knowledge, 91
  and principles of reason, 238
  and representations, 28
  and sufficient reason, 5, 270
  and unity of world, 25
  and universe as plenum, 51
Life-field
  field of experience as, 71
  practical spatiotemporal field as, 50–52
Limit, Kant on, 187
Limiting condition, 232
Lived body, xiii
Local connections, and categories, 260
Localization, 51, 67–68
Local (perceptual) object, 190
Local situation, 8, 275–276
Locke, John, 13
  and Kant, 95
  on material substance, 55
Logical forms, Kant on, 260
Logical negation, xvii
Logical order, vs. existential order, 246
Logical sequence, and causal sequence (Descartes), 20
Logifying of temporal appearances, 55–56

328
Index

Loss
  of desire, 177
  and need, 177
  objective, 225
  of self, 167
Lostness in the world, xvi

McDowell, John, xvi, xxi, xxv, xxvi, xxvi
Marcel, Gabriel, xxxviii
Marx, Karl, 284
Meaning, perceptual (Merleau-Ponty), xxxix, xlvi
Memory, 76–77, 274–275, 316–317n.2
  and Hume, 76
Merleau-Ponty, Maurice, xi–xii, xvi–xviii, xxii, xxix, 8, 264, 265–266, 295n.2, 296–297n.19
  and "alienness" of nature, xliii
  on body, xiii, xix, xxxviii–xl, xlii, xliii, 265–266
    anchorage of, xlv
  and colors, xxiv
  and freedom of movement, 283
  and idealism, xxxv–xl
  and Kant, xlvi
  and passivity-activity relation, xl–xli
Mersenne, Père, 24
Method, and appearance vs. appearing, 52
Mind-body relationship, 267–268
  Descartes on, 27, 267, 268
Mind and World (McDowell), xvi
Mirroring, compound, 121
Montaigne, Michel, 279
Morality
  and human experience, 286
  and social mind, 287–288
  and verticality, 286–287
Moral law, and Leibniz, 38–39
Motion, 302n.48
  and Leibniz, 30–32, 36–37
  and Descartes, 30–32
  and self-moved mover, 107–108 (*see also* Self-moved mover)
  translational, 111

Motor intentionality, xviii, xxi, xxv
Motion-mirroring, 121–122
Movement, 62, 64, 105, 302nn.48,49
  and awareness of extension, 48–49
  and illusion vs. veridical appearance, 53
  and self-moved mover, 107–108 (*see also* Self-moved mover)
  sense of, 118

Nature
  alienness of, xliii
  and Heidegger
    idealism of, xxxii
    nature as "unmeaning," xxxi–xxxii
    nature vs. world, xxx–xxxi, xxxii
  uniformity of (Hume), 73–83
Necessary being, and Kant's Antinomy, 253
Necessary facts, 98
Necessity, 291
  human, 13–14
  and human body, 64–65
  Kant on, 171–172
  in Ideal of reason, 258
  perceptual, 220
  rational, 220
  from rationalist vs. noumenological standpoint, 291–292
  social understanding as, 290–291
  in Table of Perceptual Categories, 219
Need(s), xvii, 86, 176–178, 180
  and finding, 67–68
  and Kant, 260
  and perception, xxvi, 290
  and response, 65–66
  satisfaction of, 51, 58–59
  and spatiotemporal emptiness, 57–58
  and unity of the world, 262
Negation
  in Kant's Antinomy, 248–249
  perceptual vs. logical, xvii
Negative existence, 222, 226
Negativity, of perception, 222

Index

Nietzsche, Friedrich, 8
Nonconceptual forms of judgment, xii
Nonconceptual intentional content, xxii
Nonconceptual perceptual beliefs, xx
Nonconceptual perceptual content, xi
Nonconceptual readiness to cope, xxvi
Nonconceptual skillful coping, xix, xxvii
Nonexistence, and failure to exist, 222
Norm, in perception (Merleau-Ponty), xxxvi
Nothing, 224–225
  concept vs. perceptual sense of, 220
  Kant on concept of, 223–224
Noumenology, 278, 288–289, 291–292
Nozick, Robert, xiii

Object(s). *See also* Perceptual objects
  abnormally undeterminable, 126, 153
  body as, 47, 54
  continued existence of, 85
  irreversible order of, 106
  and Kant's antinomies, 243, 248
  Kant's imaginizing of, 181, 183, 190, 199, 202, 243
  part(s) of, 109, 128, 305–306n.12
  passed-by, 63, 119–122, 306n.20
  perceived aspects of, xxii
  as perceived to be indirectly in the world, 115
  perceptual form of, 199
  and percipient activity, 127
  in percipient's world, 103
  and possible activity, 127
  as something-to-be-found, 105
  spatial (Kant), 181–189
    imaginizing of, 190
    locally determinable, 190–199
    threefold synthesis of, 183–185, 196
    and "transcendental object = X," 166, 167, 172–173, 189–190, 197, 199
Object of experience
  indefinite divisibility of, 186
  and Kant, 29, 182, 195, 197
  for spectator vs. active person, 53
Objective experience, perceptual and imaginative, xv, 100, 151
Objective imaginative experience, 151–152
Objective knowledge, practical, xxvi
Objective loss, 225

Objective satisfaction, 209–212, 261, 312–313n.90
  unity of, 213
Ontological argument for existence of God, 15
Ordinary language, 147–148
Orientational field, 103, 106, 112, 151

Pain, 59–60
  and disappearance, 60–61
  Hume on, 72–73
  Kant on, 226–228
Paralogisms of Kant, 238, 239, 241
  antinomies of, 239–247
  as Kant's product rather than discovery, 242
Part, 109, 128, 305–306n.12
  of perceptual whole, 145, 308n.10
Passage
  flow of, 111–113
  perceptual sense of, 113–114
  sense of, 115, 116
Passage of time, 110–114, 118
Passing of object, 63, 119–122, 306n.20
Passive synthesis, Merleau-Ponty on, xxxix
Passivity-activity relation, xl–xli
Perceivable event, 103
Perceivable object, Kant vs. Descartes and Plato on, 92–93
Perception, xii, 78–79, 264–265, 278, 312n.82. *See also* Practical perception
  as achievement, 264
  and active body, xxi
  categories of, 215–229

Perception (*continued*)
  vs. conception, 161, 197, 205, 217, 223–224, 226, 239
    for dialectical philosophers, 284
    and Kant, 93, 94
    and original determination, 250
  constancy phenomena in, 226, 275–276
  Davidson vs. McDowell on, xvi
  and deprivation, 227
  Descartes on, 21
  and determination of beginning of series, 254
  and existence of existing things, 275
  and existence of percipient (Kant), 204–205
  as form of actuality, 290
  as habit-forming, 80
  and imagination, xxv–xxvi, 130–137, 138, 142, 143–154, 201–202
    and conveying vs. origination of experience, 153–154
    and factual vs. fictional stories, 148–149
    Kant on, 156, 157, 159
    and ordinary vs. technical language, 147–148
    and realization of determinable object vs. explication of determinate image, 147, 154
    and significance of experience, 153, 154
    and spectatorial attitude, 134, 135, 307n.2
    and world as filled vs. open, 149–152, 154
  indeterminacy of, xvi, xx
  inhibited, 273–274
  and Kant, xxv, 231 (*see also* Kant, Immanuel)
    in Dialectic, 229
    imaginizing of, 95–100, 140, 208
    judgments of, xlvi, 191–193, 213
    perception as anonymous process, xxxviii
    and unconditioned unity, 236–237

  Leibniz on, 36, 41
  lived body in, xii
  McDowell on, xxv
  Merleau-Ponty on, xvi–xviii, xxxviii
  and order of existence vs. order of knowledge, 246
  and permanence of knower, 208
  as practical, xli
  and reason (Kant), 201
  as satisfaction, 209
    of our original unity of need for self-determination as percipient, 212–213
  as search for self, 104–105, 117 212
  situatedness of, xiii
  stages of, xxiii, 273
  and thought, xiv
  and world, 276
Perceptive body, self-actualization of, 292
Perceptual balance, 141
Perceptual categories, xxvi–xxvii, 219
  and assumption of perceptual forms, 203
  deduction of, 8–9
    from felt unity of active body, 202–203
  and Kant, 193, 196, 198, 202, 204
  local and provisional satisfaction from, 226
  Table of, xv, 218, 219, 222
Perceptual constants, in Merleau-Ponty's analysis of reality, xxxv
Perceptual contemplation, xli
Perceptual contextuality, 264
Perceptual events, as apparently reversible, 111
Perceptual experience, 140, 170
  determinacy and uniformity in, 76, 78–81, 82–83
  as figure-ground phenomenon, 264
  and habit formation, 82
  and Kant, 229
  and Leibniz, 33–35
  objective, xv, 100, 151
  as only momentarily filled, 149

Index

practical, 149
sense data analysis of, 113
Perceptual field, xiii
   as continuous, 112
   determinable contents of, 160
   for Kant, 94, 95
   in Antinomy, 248
Perceptual form(s), 203, 244, 259–260. *See also* Form of perceptual judgment
   of actuality vs. for possibility, 265
   and Kant, 199, 230, 237, 244, 254
Perceptual freedom, 253
Perceptual fulfillment, as practical self-composure, 128–129
Perceptual "I," 212. *See also* "I perceive"
Perceptual identification, xxi–xxii
Perceptual implications, xx, 196, 308n.17
Perceptual inferences, xx
   Hume on, 71–72, 80
Perceptual judgment(s), xx, 214–215, 217–218, 260. *See also* Judgments of perception
   as arguments, xxvii, 213, 217–218
   form of, 212–215
   and Kant, 260, 261
   and rational judgment, 281–282
Perceptual knowledge, xviii, xxvi, 100, 203–209
   and active body, 204
   dangers to, 228
   dimensions of loss of, 223
   and Kant, 94, 248
   objective satisfaction as conclusion of, 213
   objectivity of, xiii
   as reflexive, 208–209
   as retroactive, 218
   self-awareness of, 223
   and subjective vs. objective satisfaction, 211
   Twelve Categories of, xxvi–xxvii (*see also* Perceptual categories)
   unity of, 236–237

Perceptual meaning, xxxix, xlvi
Perceptual necessity, 220
Perceptual negation, xvii
Perceptual objects, xxii, 105, 265. *See also* Object(s)
   abnormally undeterminable, 153
   and body-sense, 264
   and circumstantiality, 206
   and Davidson or McDowell, xvi
   determination of, 143–144, 149
   and Kant, 195
   hidden aspects of, xx, 131
   Merleau-Ponty on, xxxvi, xxxix
   minimal or simple perceivable parts of, 249
   vs. perceptual fields, 128
   propositional beliefs about, xxii–xxiii
   sense of, 176, 178
   in variety of orientations, 146
   as whole, 145, 308n.10
   as wholly there, 131
Perceptual order, 198
   and Kant, 196, 197
Perceptual sense of "nothing" as loss of knowledge, table of, 223
Perceptual sense of passage, 113–114
Perceptual significance, 153
Perceptual space, 249
Perceptual time, xliv, 251, 301n.41
   irreversibility of, 106
   bodily basis of, 118–119
   passage of, 113
Perceptual understanding, 289–290
   traditional philosophers on, 283
Perceptual unity, and Kant, 255
Perceptual variation, Kant on, 221–222
Perceptual world, 142. *See also* World
   exploration and discovery of, 176
   as field of fields-within-fields, 103–104, 114–117
   as given, 147
   and Kant, 261
   as only locally filled, 149
   self-creation in, 180
Percipient, as self-moved mover, 102–103

Persons, knowledge of, 2
Phenomenological account, and causal approach, xliii–xliv
Phenomenology, xii
  existential, xii, xiii, xv, xl
  modern, 8
  transcendental, xiii
Phenomenology of Perception (Merleau-Ponty), xxxvii, xxxviii, xxxix. *See also* Merleau-Ponty, Maurice
Philosophical idealism. *See* Idealism
Philosophy
  accounts of reality and appearance in, 33
  and Hume's criticisms, 87
Plato
  and "body politic," 3
  on human subject, 10–12
  on mind-body separation, 267
  on perceivable object, 93
  and self-evident principles, 270
  as upward-looking, 287
  and world, 5, 25
Pleasure
  Hume on, 72–73
  Kant on, 226–228
Poise, xviii, xli, 65–66, 72, 79, 104, 124, 128, 138, 140–141, 142, 293n.4
  and balance, xlv
  and belief, 85
  and faculty of imagination, 139
  imaginative transformation of, 140–143
  of inactive experience, 70
  loss of, 70
Pose, 65
Possibility, 291
  in antinomies of Paralogisms, 240
  conceptual vs. perceptual, 215
  imagination as form of, 290
  from rationalist vs. noumenological standpoint, 291–292
Practical freedom, 255
  Kant on, 255
Practical imagination, 135, 136, 137

Practical interest, and Kant's Antinomy, 254
Practical objective knowledge, xxvi
Practical perception, 105, 312n.82. *See also* Perception
  and abstract thought, xxiii–xxv
  and conformity of knowledge to object, 159–160
  as creative discovery, 174–178, 180
  determining of object in, 170
  forms of, 161
  and factual content, 161
  and imagination, 174
  and self-movement, 168–169
  as subtentional, 154
  as three-term relation, 159
Practical perceptual experience, field of, 149
Practical perceptual judgment, systematization of, xv
Practical self-composure, 128, 151
  perceptual fulfillment as, 128–129
Practical space-time, 144
Practical spatiotemporal field
  and body-direction, 49–50
  as life-field, 50–52
Presence, 120
Presence-before, 135
Presence-to, 135
Presence-with, 135
Primary qualities, 31, 311n.64
Probability, Hume on, 83–84
Productive imagination, 97, 235. *See also* Imagination
  Kant on, 94–95, 112, 155, 168, 235
Propositional beliefs, about perceptual objects, xxii–xxiii
Purposive activity, 136–137. *See also* Goal; Intention; Will
Putnam, Hilary, xiii

Quality(ies), xxiii–xxiv
  in Ideal of pure reason, 257
  primary, 31, 311n.64
  secondary, 31, 311n.64

Index

Quine, Willard v. O., xiii

Rational freedom, 282, 283
Rationalism
  Continental, 23 (*see also* Leibniz, Gottfried)
  in Merleau-Ponty's critique, xxxv–xxxvi
Rationalist modal order, 291
Rationalist moralists, 287
Rationalist philosophy, 283, 291
Rationality, socialized, 280
Rational judgment, 281–282. *See also* Reason
Rational necessity, 220
Rational understanding, 291. *See also* Reason
Realism, xxix, 278
Realism/antirealism debate, xi
Reality. *See also* Existence
  in antinomies of Paralogisms, 240
  degrees of (Kant), 220–221
  disengaged questioning about, 271–272
  as intelligible (Kant), 222
  Merleau-Ponty on, xxxv, xxxvi–xxxvii
  problem of knowing, xiv
Reason. *See also at* Rational
  in contemporary social practice, 286
  in core of humanity, 285
  and freedom, 288
  and hope, 228
  and Kant, 162, 189, 291, 309n.1
    in Antinomies, 254, 255
    Idea of, 237, 238
    and perception, 201
    practical principles of, 227–228
  in traditional rationalist philosophy, 291
  unconditioned unity from (Kant), 230–233
Reciprocity, in Table of Perceptual Categories, 219
Regularity of experience, and satisfaction of needs, 51

Reidentification, xxi–xxii
  and imaginative representations, xxiv
  McDowell on, xxi
Representational character of experience
  and Descartes, 15–16, 19–20, 21, 22, 27–28
  and Hume, 28–29
  and Leibniz, 28–29
Reproductive imagination, 235
Response, 105, 117
  anticipatory, 141, 142–43
  failure of, 69–70
  and need, 66–67
  poised, 64–66
  in Table of Perceptual Categories, 219
Responsiveness, 62–70
Rooted person, 292
Rotation, 110
Rushing, 115–116
Russell, Bertrand, xi, 55

Sartre, Jean-Paul, xxxix, 265, 266
Satiation, 59
Satisfaction, 58–59, 81–82
  and coping, xviii
  and deprivation, 222, 223
  finding as, 67
  as global, 69
  in judgment, 214–215
  and Kant, 260
  vs. need, 177
  objective, 261, 312–313n.90
    vs. subjective, 209–212
  unity of, 213
  and perceptual knowledge, xxvi
  and regularity of experience, 51
  in Table of Perceptual Categories, 219
Schelling, Friedrich, 8, 200
Science, brute facticity of, 270–272
Scientific datum, 269–270
Search for self, perception as, 104–105, 117, 212

Searle, John, xvii
Secondary qualities, 31, 311n.64
"Seeming" language, 215
Self
  identical, 282
  Kant on
    and common root of knowledge, 199–201
    ego (thinking self), 163–172, 178–180, 200–201
    empirical ego, 169–170, 171
    unitary consciousness of, 185
    perception as search for, 104–105, 117, 212
Self-activity, 163, 165, 168, 169, 174, 175, 180
Self-actualization, of perceptive body, 292
Self-causing cause, first cause as, 250
Self-composure, practical, 128, 151
Self-consciousness, 95
Self-creation, 180
  practical perception as, 175–176
Self-discovery
  imagination as, 152
  Kant on, 174, 179
  in practical perception, 174–178
  and self-creation, 180
Self-moved mover. *See also* First cause
  Aristotle on impossibility of, 102–103, 107–110
  individual's sense of, 262
  percipient as, 102, 103, 168–169
  as pure activity, 110
Self-movement, 251
  and self-discovery, 174
Self-transformability, between perceptual and imaginative selves, 132
Sense data analysis of perceptual experience, 113, 131, 215
Sense of passage, 115, 116
Sensibility, in contemporary social practice, 286
Sensible action, and Kant, 96
Sensuous abstractions, 272–276

Sight, vs. feeling, 266
Significance, as human contribution, 128, 153
Singular judgments, and Kant, 190
Situatedness, of perceptual objects, xiii
Skill(s), 46, 126, 176, 212, 267
  exercise of, 180
  and perceptual judgment, 214
  percipient as characterized by, 79
Smith, Norman Kemp, 261
Social involvement, manner of (Heidegger), 284
Social issues, and natural issues, 1
Socialized rationality, 280
Social life, and stances of understanding, 289
Social mind, 287–288
Social normalization, 286
Social philosophy, 278
  and neglect of material subject, 277–278
Social subject, 277–278
Social understanding, 290
Society
  behavior regulated by, 278–279
  and neglect of material subject, 277–278
Solipsism, 2
Space
  as correlate of active subject's body, 48–52
  for Descartes, 31
  and Heidegger, 296–297n.19
  and Hume, 48
  Kant on, 96, 166, 169, 181, 186–187, 194, 234
  in Antinomies, 247–248
  for Leibniz, 31
  and Merleau-Ponty, 296–297n.19
  perceptual, 249
  and places, 112
  practical space-time, 144
Spatial objects. *See under* Object(s)
Spatiotemporal emptiness, 57
  and need, 57–58

Index

Spatiotemporal field, xi–xii, xxvii, xlii
  asymmetry of movements in, xliv
  as indivisible, 69
  mobility as generating, 60
  practical, 49–52
  produced by body, xix–xx
Spatiotemporal knowledge, semi-objectivity of, 198
Spectator, experience of, 53
Spectatorial attitude or view, xxiii–xxiv, xli, 55, 134, 135, 307n.2
Spencer, Herbert, and "body politic," 3
Spinoza, Baruch
  and Descartes, 20
  on order of ideas and of things, 245–246
Stance
  actual, 120
  effective, 120–121, 127, 136
Standing-back, 289
Standing-for, 289
Standing-up, 289
Startle-experience, 116
Stoics, 86
Stories, factual vs. fictional, 148–149
Subject body, 265–268, 277, 287
Subjective satisfaction, 209–212
Subtentional experience, 154
Syllogism
  and ideas of reason (Kant), 231–232, 237–238
  and Kant's categories, 216–217
  sophistic, 241
Synthetic a priori judgments, for Kant, 156–161
Synthetic a priori propositions, as formal, 203–204

Taylor, Charles, xi
Technical language, 147–148
Temporal field, and bodily asymmetry, xix
Theology of the human body, 1
Theoretical imagination, 9, 180, 233, 243
Theoretical interpretation, 269–270, 272
Thomas Aquinas, Saint, and "body politic," 3
Thought, and perception, xiv
Thrownness, xxxiii, xlv
Time
  and asymmetry of movements, xliv–xlv
  centrality of, xliv
  and change through motion, 301n.41
  as correlate of active subject's body, 48–52
  and front-back body distinction, 49
  and Hume, 48
  imaginative, 150
  Kant on, 96, 164, 166, 169, 181, 186–187, 194
    in Antinomies, 247–248
    temporality of perceptions, 197–198
  and Leibniz, 33–34, 36
  passage of, 110–114, 118
    ordered senses of, 15
    perceptual sense of, 103
  perceptual, xliv, 251, 301n.41
    irreversibility of, 106, 118–119
    passage of, 113
  practical space-time, 144
  and restriction on movement, 50
  and spatiotemporal field, xix–xx
Todes, Samuel, xi, xii–xiv, xv, xl
Transcendental attitude, 272
Transcendental ideas of reason. *See* Ideas of reason
Transcendental illusion, 231, 238, 239, 241
Transcendental imagination, 194
Transcendental logic, of Kant, 188, 190
Transcendental phenomenology, xiii
Transcendental unity of apperception, 167–168
Transformational freedom of understanding subject, 278, 280–292
Translational motion, 111
Truth, correspondence theory of, 278

Index

Trying, and coping, xviii–xix
Turning, 115

Unconditioned, Kant on, 237
Unconditioned series, two possible kinds of, 244
Understanding
 dichotomous view of, 285
 for Kant, 309n.1
 modalities of, 289–291
 rational, 291
 stances of, 289
 as transformationally variant, 285
Understanding subject, transformational freedom of, 278, 280–292
Uniformity of nature, Hume on, 73–83
Unity
 of actual experience (Kant), 234
 and Antinomies of Kant, 236, 247, 251, 252–253, 255
  in Ideal of reason, 258
 of Paralogisms, 240
 of bodily activity, 266
 in body, 46
 of consciousness and in object, 185
 felt unity of active body, 103, 109–110, 114 (*see also under* Active body)
 in imagination, 243
 of intuitions (Kant), 182–186
 of perceptual knowledge, 236–237
 and productive vs. reproductive imagination, 235
 in Table of Perceptual Categories, 219
 and theoretical understanding of experience, 233
 from understanding and from reason (Kant), 230–235
 of world, xli, 4–6, 262
  and classic view, 10
  and Descartes, 15, 20, 22, 24, 25, 26–27
  human subject as explicating, 23–27
  and Kant's project, 99

Universal judgments, 190
Unmoved mover. *See* First cause; Self-moved mover
Unobserved objects, continued existence of (Hume), 85

Veiled body, 29–30
 and Hume, 40–44
 and Leibniz, 30–39
Veridical appearances, vs. illusory, 53–56
Vertical field, xlv, 104, 122–128, 258–259. *See also* World-field
Verticality, 2887–288
 and morality, 286–287
Vertigo, 115
Visual point of view, 43, 300n.33

Weight, Merleau-Ponty on, xxxvi
Western thought, and socialized rationality, 280
Will
 vs. directed action, 65
 and poise, xviii
Williams, D. C., xiii
Wittgenstein, Ludwig, xi, xv
Wolff, Christian, 93
World. *See also* Perceptual world
 and body, xlii, 42
 as circumstantial, 39, 171
 and Descartes, 13
 and facticity, 276
 as field of all our fields of activity, 262
 and Ideal of pure reason, 256
 Kant's general antinomy of, 257–259
 and Kant's Ideal of pure reason, 243
 Kant's imaginizing of, 156–161, 190, 202, 259–260
 Merleau-Ponty on, xxxvii
 vs. nature (Heidegger), xxx–xxxi, xxxii
 as primary field, 114
 vs. something in world, 4
 as third term in practical perception, 159

Index

   unity of, xli, 4–6, 262
      and classic view, 10
      and Descartes, 5, 15, 20, 22, 24, 25,
         26–27
      human subject as explicating, 23–27
      and Kant's project, 99
World of experience
   appearance of things in, 52, 56
   as made habitable, 176
   and pleasure or pain, 72–73
   as world of custom, 84
World-field, 104, 105, 105–106
   and conformity of knowledge to
      object, 159–160
   and determination, 259

Body and World